COVETED

MELANIE
GRANT

COVETED

ART AND
INNOVATION
IN HIGH
JEWELRY

ONE

ABSTRACT DESIGN:
THE JOY OF REDUCTION

16

TWO

EAST MEETS WEST: CROSSING
THE CULTURAL DIVIDE

52

THREE

MAGNIFICENT DIAMONDS: ACHIEVING
BALANCE WHEN THE STONES RULE

92

FOUR

INSPIRED BY NATURE:
INDEPENDENCE AND CREATIVITY

128

FIVE

THE FEMALE AGE: REBELS,
GODDESSES, AND ALTER EGOS

162

INTRODUCTION 6
GLOSSARY 196
BIBLIOGRAPHY 200
INDEX 201

Hemmerle
Bangle, 2018
Ancient Egyptian faience and zircons
in bronze and white gold
Private collection

INTRODUCTION

The first piece of jewelry on earth wasn't made by human hands. It was created by Neanderthals 115,000 years ago in Spain and formed out of seashells. The art of the jewel is older than recorded history, older than human civilization, and older than the written word. Some forty thousand years ago, during the Upper Paleolithic age, our ancestors were fashioning elaborate ostrich-eggshell necklaces in Kenya, while in Russia they were wearing stone bracelets and marble rings. Jewelry was part of our earliest psychology, part of our deepest memory of what it was to be alive, and has documented the evolution of the human experience economically, socially, and creatively.

More than five thousand years ago jewelry was at the heart of the complex and flamboyant early civilization of ancient Egypt, where gold represented the flesh of the gods, and colored stones, such as emeralds, immortality. Egyptian hieroglyphs, such as the eye of Horus, were carved into amulets, offering the wearer spiritual protection. Jewelry built bridges between civilizations and formed an integral part of their trade with each other. The rich flaunted their jewels as a wearable currency that transcended language, religion, and culture so that a passerby in Egypt, Greece, or Mesopotamia could read another's status at a glance.

As trading routes opened up and the world became richer, jewelry became more powerful, communicating value across entire continents. High jewelry in ancient Egypt was devoid of diamonds but, after diamond mining and trading began in India in the fourth century BC, they became indispensable. Their cut, color, clarity, and rarity were tracked as an index of intrinsic value. There was only so much gold one could wear and big diamonds became a form of concentrated, amplified wealth. These glittering orbs of light eventually reached Europe, where they became popular in the fifteenth century when royal families favored them as a display of divine authority, sufficiently dazzling to keep dissent among their subjects at bay.

Art and jewelry were one. In Italy during the Renaissance, Leonardo da Vinci trained in metallurgy under the master Andrea del Verrocchio, himself a sculptor, painter, and goldsmith. The skill needed to create jewelry was taught as a matter of course to fledgling artists. By the sixteenth century, when a monarch commissioned an oil painting, the artist was often asked to make accompanying miniatures in watercolor-on-ivory or enamel-on-copper that could be worn or carried as a portable version of the art on the wall. These miniatures were framed in gold, encrusted with gems, and given as expressions of love or politics. Queen Elizabeth I encouraged her subjects to wear her portrait as a show of support when England was threatened by Spain in the 1580s. Sometimes, miniature portraits were added to the lids of precious boxes for holding snuff or sweets.

In the seventeenth century, King Louis XIV of France ensured the prominence of Paris as the epicenter of "supreme" luxury in Europe by prioritizing the creation of luxury goods over all other areas of the economy. Aided by his finance minister Jean-Baptiste Colbert, he created a network of guilds tasked with producing the most extravagant haute couture and jewelry imaginable, while working to the most rigorous of standards. Louis banned imports and imposed a strict dress code on his nobles at court, forcing them to buy French. At the time he came to power in 1643, Madrid was still the most influential of the royal courts of Europe; however Spain was at the tail end of its golden age and the obsession with black in that staunchly Catholic country gave Louis the opportunity to establish something different. The French monarchy may not have survived the revolution of 1789,

Reed Krakoff for Tiffany
Brooch, 2019
Blue and white diamonds in platinum
and gold
Private collection

(Following pages)
Harry Winston
Secret Combination Diamond Necklace
Diamonds in platinum

Bvlgari
Heritage Necklace (with convertible
sautoir-brooch), c.1970
Cornelian, diamonds, and turquoises
in gold

but the structures put in place by the guild system sired the Place Vendôme, a salubrious square at the heart of Paris, dominated to this day by the boutiques and ateliers of grand and celebrated jewelers.

In the wake of the French Revolution, the French crown jewels—potent symbols of historical power—were dismantled and sold off, with many of the most important stones finding their way to the New World and the United States. Here, the power of high jewelry emboldened a new type of industrial aristocracy that had become rich from steel, the American gold rush, and the railroads. Free from the rigid European rules of social etiquette, they wanted large diamonds in fancy settings, and Charles Lewis Tiffany was just the man to oblige. He acquired jewels smuggled out of France and reimagined them for collectors, such as the Rockefellers, Vanderbilts, and Astors, thereby perpetuating the age-old cycle of power flowing from the East to West and back again.

In Europe, an art movement known as the Vienna Secession had sprung up in Austria in 1897, its ranks filled with painters, sculptors, and architects. Its followers campaigned against boundaries between the fine, decorative, and graphic arts, spurred on by the growing heirarchies of prestige imposed by the establishment. The Secession's founder and president, Gustav Klimt, scandalized conservative Vienna with his most famous work, *The Kiss* (1907–8). Its sensual undertones and a surface smothered in gold paint marked the beginning of a fresh appreciation of the glamour of gold. Little did Klimt's detractors know that the world was on the brink of a cultural and aesthetic revolution that would alter the very nature and appreciation of art itself and that would engulf every single art form.

The revolution was modernism and it rejected suffocating traditions and embraced freedom of expression across all artistic disciplines. René Lalique, after a wildly successful career as a jeweler, decided in mid-life to become a master glassmaker, creating chandeliers, fragrance bottles, and vases in the Art Nouveau style. From the 1920s to the 1940s artists such as Salvador Dalí, Man Ray, and Pablo Picasso crossed over to jewelry design, using gold and precious stones as a fresh medium for their artistic vision. A new fluidity between art forms was discovered, and the labels "fine" or "decorative" were rejected in favor of simpler considerations of whether to stand, hang, or wear the creation in question.

Jewelry designers were, in turn, greatly influenced by art movements, with Cartier and Van Cleef & Arpels enthusiastically embracing Art Deco. Artists of all kinds collaborated. In 1941 jewelry designer Verdura (see pp. 26, 28–29) worked with Dalí to create five jewels dedicated to the ideas of love, loss, and faith, each one carrying a miniature painting by the artist. They were erotic, perverse, and intensely colorful, as if from a dream. In modern times that legacy is continued by British painter and sculptor Maggi Hambling, who similarly sees no separation between art and jewelry as she moves effortlessly between art forms. In 1997 she was commissioned by the Tate art gallery to make a bronze brooch of her own eye (see p. 12) that is startling in its sparseness. It maintains the tradition of Surrealist jewelry to reference a dismembered body part, usually an eye in homage to René Magritte or a pair of lips to Man Ray. The eyelashes curl seductively, the eyeball peers out delicately, inquisitively; and to create them she used the same lost-wax casting method she employs for her large-scale bronze sculptures.

In the 1950s, during the aftermath of World War II, the booming Western economy propelled a major shift in consumption, and branded jewelry, worn as a display of this new prosperity, flourished. Design houses, such as Bvlgari in Europe and Harry Winston in the United States, created jewelry for all levels of society. As monarchs became mere figureheads, wearing high jewelry became the preserve of the newly wealthy tech billionaires and steel magnates, while themasses wore fine and costume jewelry as decoration. The modern jewelry world now had three distinct layers.

The first, costume jewelry, was created as the finishing touch to clothing and often accompanied couture. This area was dominated by fashion houses Dior and Chanel, who produced finely crafted designs using plated base metals with crystal or glass gems. While many local designers chose to simply imitate much more expensive jewelry, some independents, including Kenneth Jay Lane, Léa Stein, and Gripoix, acquired cult followings with their bold signature styles. The low cost of production allowed for experimentation and whimsy.

The second layer was fine jewelry, made from precious materials, such as gold, silver, or platinum, with stones including emeralds, rubies, and diamonds. Fine jewelry was created in deceptively large quantities, yet it felt luxurious and was prized for its stylized design. It was the wedding ring and those everyday earrings that were small enough to be discreet but expensive enough to be a treat, receptacles of memory and identity held close to the body. The design of fine jewelry was usually symbolic or figurative—a flower, a bird, a star—because its primary function was to bring beauty to the wearer. It could be exquisite but was rarely considered art, because it was made to be sold instead of to be a pure expression of creative thought. The commercialization of the jewel reached new heights in the hands of global luxury brands, bringing it to more people than ever before, but in the process it weakened its perception as an art form.

The third and final layer of design was high jewelry. Rare, one-of-a-kind, bespoke, grand, and masterful in their creation, these pieces used innovative materials and radical design mixed with the most important stones. High jewelry was expensive, sometimes priceless, and it was big. It pushed jewelry into the sphere of art as wearable sculpture on the body. At the start of the twentieth century, the Maharajas of India were still bedecking themselves in colossal Golconda diamonds and natural pearls in designs that cascaded sometimes to the waist. They prized outrageous stones over avant-garde design. But after World War II, important private collectors began commissioning jewelry that would propel design beyond the stone.

The Duchess of Windsor was one such collector and in 1987, at a Sotheby's auction of her jewelry held the year after her death, ninety-five lots sold for more than $33 million. This marked the first time a major auction house had presented the jewel as art rather than as product. Here, too, a new breed of private collector was acknowledged, someone with the money, creativity, and style to inspire ever more innovation and risk taking in design. Until the 1970s most buyers at auction were from the jewelry trade, but the explosion of new money, especially from Russia and China but also from investment banking, compelled the auction houses to democratize access beyond a small coterie of insiders.

Gold and precious stones have always represented a safe haven for investors when economies stalled. Big diamonds, Burmese rubies, and Kashmiri sapphires have done particularly well in recent years alongside the purity of design found in the work of difficult-to-access living jewelers. One of the most notable of these who regularly smashes auction records and inspires devotion in his collectors, is JAR, or Joel Arthur Rosenthal, an American living in Paris. In 2014, JAR became the first living jeweler to have a solo show at the Metropolitan Museum of Art in New York. Four hundred of his creations were shown, many showcasing his unique pavé technique where tiny stones sit so closely together that they appear to be a continuous color like paint on a surface. JAR put the design back into high jewelry in the 1970s and paved the way for the experimentation that we now marvel at, from unorthodox settings to new materials.

JAR, like generations of jewelers before him, was entranced by the natural world, and infatuated by the penetrating beauty of flora and fauna as an all-encompassing creative inspiration. Throughout history, humanity's most important rituals have been accompanied by the wearing of seashells, feathers and flowers in reverence for nature and naturalistic jewelry design followed. As civilization developed and precious stones and metals were discovered, art paid

Maggi Hambling
Eye Brooch, 1997
Bronze

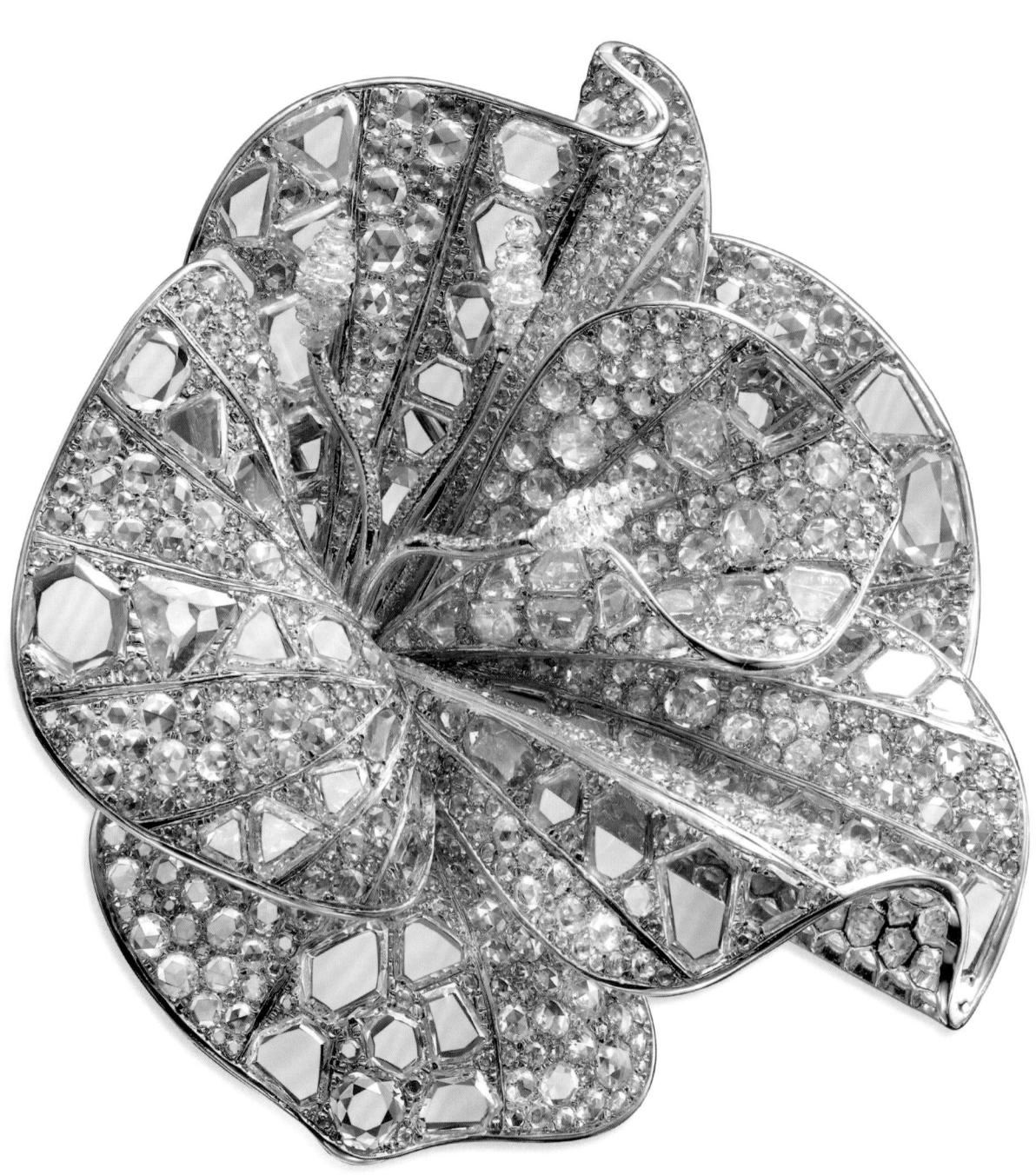

Michelle Ong
Mezmerizing Lily Brooch, 2014
White diamonds in platinum
and white gold

homage by capturing nature's likeness in the most elevated fashion. What once were laurel leaves wrapped around the crown or flowers pinned to a cloak are now immortalized in Chaumet's tiaras (see pp. 70–72) and Ole Lynggaard's Wild Rose brooch (see p. 138). Butterflies and blooms reimagined with such vivid artistry, connect their makers and owners to the land and even for high jewelry's expanding legions of digital devotees, nature remains an ever popular subject.

The development of smart phones since 1992, and the launch of Twitter in 2006, and Instagram in 2010, have precipitated a revolution in accessibility, where the continuous display of jewelry in glorious technicolor on social media amplifies its powers of seduction. Running parallel was an evolution in women's rights and a fight for equality that still rages on. With increasing disposable income, fewer children, and more freedom since World War II, women's taste for and ability to buy better jewelry has seen self-expression manifest itself in tough materials epitomizing the struggle for respect, equal pay, and access to opportunity. Titanium, aluminum, carbon fiber, rubber, wood, and steel are the new precious. While modernism may have run its course as a movement, its legacy—the dismantling of the old hierarchies—thankfully continues. If what happens at auction reflects desirability, then the escalating prices achieved by female designers, such as Cindy Chao (see pp. 86, 95, 116, and 119) and Michelle Ong (see pp. 104–6), signal that a female age is on the horizon.

High jewelry today occupies its rightful place, acknowledged as art by more museums, auction houses, galleries, and institutions than ever before. This book is a celebration of that truth. The intention of the artist is key: anything can be art and now, for jewelry, anything is possible.

ONE

ABSTRACT DESIGN: THE JOY OF REDUCTION

Yasuki Hiramatsu
Necklace, 1972
Gold
Schmuckmuseum, Pforzheim

Japanese metalsmith Yasuki Hiramatsu (1926–2012) emerged from his World War II military service profoundly changed and decided to create jewelry that would celebrate life, bringing happiness to everyday existence through its beauty. Hiramatsu was a pioneer of modern jewelry in Japan, where he contemplated the essence of his materials, experimenting with form and geometric shape. Traditionally, Japanese craftsmen used gold for hollowware, such as bowls and weapons. Although Hiramatsu was a third-generation metalsmith, he was fascinated by abstraction and used it to close the perceived divide between jewelry and art, in the process creating jewelry of exceptional beauty. His pieces were "living things" that he encouraged, worried about, struggled with, and played with. He hammered and folded thin sheets of metal as if they were paper so that they fluttered in the light and on the body. When, in 1972, he crafted a necklace of exquisite simplicity resembling a waterfall of pure golden silk hanging from a tapered loop, he was seeing gold as more than a cold, hard inanimate store of wealth. By combining an economy of design with precious metals, he was going against the highly ornate traditional Japanese style. Modernism had by then influenced every corner of the globe, turning innovative thinkers like Hiramatsu toward a vision of unembellished self-restraint regardless of their location. It had swept past borders and become a philosophical movement.

Modernism had its roots in the European Industrial Revolution, the growth of towns, and a burgeoning urban middle class; it surged through the worlds of art, literature, architecture, psychology, and music from the late nineteenth century onward with the aim of social progress through technology. It constructed a simple, coherent, analytical worldview around the idea of personal freedom, rejecting the power of the Church and breaking new ground within art by embracing paintings of ordinary life by such artists as Gustave Courbet and, later, stream-of-consciousness novels, such as James Joyce's *Ulysses* (1922). For Modernist jewelry, this meant that the unapologetic opulence that had come to symbolize wealth and power was stripped bare within this new style and as each new city developed its own social hierarchy, the metropolitan elite—those who acquired the best, most rare pieces—now competed with royalty for the attentions of the best designers. Their disposable income would push jewelry into the elaborate maisons and ateliers of Bond Street in London or Fifth Avenue in New York where it sits today, proof that a new world order had arrived.

This rapid transformation came to a shuddering halt in 1914 with the outbreak of World War I. "The war to end all wars" traumatized a generation and provoked a furious reaction from many, including those in the art world, who felt betrayed by world leaders. Ernest Hemingway was one of the writers who led the charge, describing World War I as "the most colossal, murderous, mismanaged butchery that has ever taken place on earth." Art rose up in all its many disciplines to give the world hope and to show there was a better way to live.

A revival of modernism was part of that reaction, a rebellion against social conformity, improving on and progressing from mistakes of the past and resulting in what French philosopher Henri Bergson aptly described as "the creative evolution of everything." In 1920s America, the Jazz Age introduced a completely different musical language and a completely different type of woman. The "flapper" drove fast cars, smoked, drank, took lovers, applied makeup liberally, wrapped layers of beaded gemstones around her naked throat, and cut her hair short, flouting social norms. At the same time Art Deco gave jewelry cleaner lines, geometric symmetry, and a graphic, mechanical boldness, cascading down the

Hemmerle
Earrings, 2016
Diamonds (5.47 and 5.02ct)
in blackened iron and white gold
Private collection

Ring, 2019
Emeralds (Main: 29.45ct)
in bronze and white gold
Private collection

now exposed backs of high-society women as they danced the Charleston. The structures and etiquette that had been holding society in place for centuries were cast aside and society embraced a previously unfathomable creative freedom as it hurtled toward the machine age.

The camera, that emblem of the new technological era, profoundly influenced how life was recorded and remembered. Photography took jewelry beyond the exhibition or museum, for the first time bringing it to the attention of the masses. Photographs in magazines and newspapers exposed jewelry to new audiences unaccustomed to such beauty. It was this combination of accessibility, innovation, and technology that saw the art of jewelry thrive. The starkness and simplicity of modernism was in complete contrast to traditional high jewelry. The idea of "reduction" in the jeweled universe, where more stones, more ornament, and more complexity had always added value, was shocking. Emphasis shifted from diamonds to design and sparseness equaled sophistication. Suddenly, self-expression took precedence and stones were just an element in a much larger vision, if they featured at all. Those looking to experiment even sacrificed gold and platinum. Modernism drove jewelry toward the industrial, with titanium, aluminum, and steel gaining importance as a type of blank canvas for modern design.

Among the pioneers in this field were two brothers, Joseph and Anton Hemmerle, who, in 1893 in Munich, Germany, had acquired a goldsmith's company that made medals. They renamed the fledgling business Hemmerle and by 1895 were official jewelers to the Bavarian royal court. After World War I, their sons joined them and several generations later, the family are still serving collectors from the original boutique on Maximilianstrasse, which first opened in 1904. Their style is resolutely Bauhaus, a school of thought that was established in Germany in 1919 and, as a reaction to World War I, attempted to merge art and craft. It advocated a return to functional, economical design and basic geometric form; although (as a school) it lasted for only fourteen years, it profoundly affected the modernist aesthetic in jewelry, championing metal as its preferred medium.

Hemmerle's exquisite talent, combined with an adventurous taste in materials that includes aluminum, copper, bronze, wood, and iron, has seen them go in just over a century from ornate court jeweler to one of the most prolific contemporary high jewelers in the world. Iron had had an emotional significance in Germany since its citizens elected to donate their gold to the government during the War of Liberation against Napoleon in 1813. Instead, they wore jewels made of iron and Hemmerle continue that custom today, setting big, round, icy-white diamonds into spiked iron earrings. Their current dedication to iron began in 1995, when an art-collector client asked for a Neoclassical, architectural jewel to fit into her collection of nineteenth-century iron jewelry. Hemmerle set a sizable diamond into textured iron and discovered a new strand of their work.

Alongside iron, the firm sometimes uses bronze in place of gold, its soft glow setting off glassy-green emeralds. The color, size, and boldness of their design underwent a subtle shift in 2006, when Christian Hemmerle, Joseph's great-grandson, and his Egyptian wife Yasmin joined the company. The injection of their influence pushed the house into a new era where Bauhaus restraint combined with the heat and density of African color. Egyptian-inspired pieces have since followed, but that coolness of form has never wavered.

That Egyptian spirit first influenced modernism in jewelry when archaeologists discovered Tutankhamun's tomb in 1922, igniting Egypt-mania across Europe. Hemmerle today pays homage to this original excitement, demonstrating the company's ability to acknowledge and transcend the past. Their bangle (see Introduction, p. 6) includes a faience Eye of Horus that peers out, unblinking from its textured green, patinated bronze exterior, contrasting a glossy white-gold interior with gleaming zircons at its blunt edges. Their design process is many layered, with Christian's parents Stefan and Sylveli codesigning and their twenty-two goldsmiths all venturing opinions. The result is a jewel of historic proportions that the collector will appreciate more with each passing year. A great jeweler will

Fabio Salini
Earrings
Diamonds and sapphires in
carbon fiber, white gold, and titanium

"Buckle" Cuff
Diamonds in carbon fiber and white gold

(Following pages)
Monique Péan
Ring, 2019
Diamond and pyritized dinosaur
bone in recycled gold

Ring, 2019
Diamonds and Sikhote-Alin
meteorite in recycled platinum

Necklace, 2019
Diamond and pyritized dinosaur
bone in recycled platinum

anticipate a customer's creative growth and feed into that, identifying a jewel that suits their vision of you rather than your own. This artistic sensibility is crucial and has elevated Hemmerle to role models within an industry where most jewelry is still sold on the high street and isn't art at all. "We try and nurture our collectors to introduce them to our way of thinking," Christian says softly. The Germans call it bedienen, or "serving," instead of selling. "Finding the perfect thing is what makes people come back."

Unorthodox materials have been moving jewelry toward a new future with increasing speed since the 1960s, when, among other things, carbon fiber was introduced. It is lightweight, strong, and durable, but it still took decades to filter down into jewelry as a credible alternative to gold. Fabio Salini, born in Rome and having worked at Cartier and Bulgari, launched his first collection in 1999 at Petochi boutique in his home city and then opened his own atelier in 2004. He began by playing with wood, leather, and even silk, but his true calling was more ambitious. "In my use of carbon fiber, I wanted to start a revolution," he smiles. He has taken the structural function of gold and exchanged it for a material used in the space industry and in high-performance racing cars. The flecks and tones of carbon fiber ape Impressionism's rapid brush marks, but Salini isn't painting a romantic landscape in his work. There are no flowers, ribbons, or bows for him. He makes double cuffs in carbon fiber edged with diamonds, abstract circular earrings stamped with blue sapphires, and fat circular disks of purply-blue titanium that reflect ripples of light. His message is about power, specifically the growing power that women have in society, and the audacious nature of his work celebrates that advancement. The boldness of his design has a defiant edge that pushes prettiness aside in favor of strength mirroring that of the woman who is buying to please herself.

Historically, jewelry was a way of trading in valuable materials; Salini believes that it has the potential to go beyond that to become more than the sum of its parts, but that the only force strong enough to accomplish that aim is design. The inevitable tension between jewelry as art and jewelry as commodity still hampers its progress. Designers such as Salini must take risks to make jewelry that is demanding and sometimes unruly and that unlocks the part of our collective psyche dealing with emotion to express the taste and style of an era. Jewelry of this quality charts the evolution of who we are. Each new material creates an emotional response but the market (collectors, the public, museums) can take time to accept it. Independents, including Salini, have more freedom than most, but they still have to push against the technical restraints of a new material or the ideological constraints of what has gone before.

Sourcing and using gems and minerals from the earth comes with a responsibility few take more seriously than New York designer Monique Péan. With a commitment that is rare at this level, she uses only recycled and ethical materials, such as fossilized walrus ivory or dinosaur bones, to fashion her delicate jewels. She has foraged for fossils in the Arctic Circle with the Inupiat and Yupik tribes, and for cosmic obsidian with the Rapa Nui people of Easter Island. Since 2003 she has traveled to sixty-seven countries to learn from local artisanal communities, building clean-water wells in Malawi, Haiti, and Nepal as she goes. Her jewels are magnificently simple but tell the complex story of life in space and on the earth. The white oval and pear diamonds of one ring (see p. 24) nestle into a roughly 4.6-billion-year-old Sikhote-Alin meteorite, a rock that predates the earth's formation and is around one-third of the age of the universe. An angular necklace (see p. 25) boasts pyritized dinosaur bone curved around a step-cut diamond, bringing the hard grays of recycled platinum to life. The bone is a fossil formed more than 145 million years ago and found near the Caspian Sea. The juxtaposition of brilliant gemstone and rocky archaeology is sublime, illustrating the deeper human journey from cave to boutique.

Péan's white diamonds may seem like the most obviously valuable elements of her work, but they are dwarfed by the history and importance of her ancient rocks.

Vhernier
Eclisse Ring, 2015
Diamonds in gray titanium

Serpente Brooch, c.2000
Diamonds and jet in white gold

The only thing separating these two minerals is our perception of value, and abstract design gives them equal weight. Péan challenges the assumption that all stones must sparkle if they are to be precious or that jewelry should be the reinterpretation of a classical flower. Beauty in her world is democratic.

Péan was an analyst at the financial services company Goldman Sachs before making the leap to full-time jewelry designer in 2006, and her dogged dedication to the sustainable cause underpins her entire design philosophy. Most jewelers want complete flexibility, but Péan avoids elements that harm the earth, and this adds a layer of cost and complication to everything she does. The abstract beauty of her work offsets the brutal truth of her message. A single wedding band produces more than 20 tons of waste, unleashing a chemical cocktail upon the environment. "Modernism for me is the idea of rethinking traditional methods of status quo," she says. The role of the designer goes beyond simply creating in order to sell. Artists have the ability to challenge and educate, however difficult the process and Péan's jewelry has a depth of soul and integrity of purpose that goes beyond luxury.

Italian design house Vhernier also makes a point of challenging the status quo by dispensing with stones altogether in many of its jewels. When stones are included, they are often carved slabs of crystal placed over mother-of-pearl, such as in their famous Toucan brooch. They appear as a light sprinkling of diamond pavé on a black titanium pebble bracelet or to accent the seductive slither of a snake in jet. They have a utilitarian beauty, but this dismantling of logical commercial thought takes them into new territory. As women buy for themselves in greater numbers, the jewels they want often dispense with the romantic depiction of subjects in so-called "figurative" jewelry; instead, they experiment with form, culminating in abstraction. Carlo Traglio, Vhernier's president and creative director, believes that his collectors neither seek approval nor entertain the judgment of others when wearing his designs. The Eclisse ring (also available in rose and white gold) is a sleek, streamlined heft of titanium crafted—in a production process that took two years to perfect—in the metal's original matte gray, with its two sliced ends turned inward. The volume is dense, the lines simple and understated, and as a jewel it redefines traditional beauty, bringing power to the wearer.

Traglio and his brother Maurizio bought the company in 2001 from Angela Camurati, who stayed on as head of design and production; together they have made three-dimensional sculpture wearable. Stone-free pieces, such as the Verso and Plissé collections, play with three-dimensional graphic lines and negative space so that light bounces off the metal as it would off a gemstone. Where diamonds run wild, they are applied in brown to diffuse their brilliance, such as in the Verso ear clips, or in white, set into the curled tail of the Chameleon brooch beneath a body of black jade and opal. Colors are either muted or intensely vivid, but simplicity unites all.

Color (or its absence) is of great importance within abstract jewelry, which typically works with fewer elements. Color can express the identity of the creator, send a message, demonstrate an emotion, or create an energy that increases both the wearer's and the viewer's sensitivity to the design. The ability to combine and contrast color or to apply a unique color theory is key to the overall aesthetic, and here the true pioneer was Fulco di Verdura.

Fulco Santostefano della Cerda, Duke of Verdura (1899–1978), was a Sicilian count who had intended to "marry well" and could have stayed safely in his pampered world in Palermo, but the irrational part of him longed for more excitement. Instead, he left for Paris to find himself and become a painter. He was an old-school dandy, charming and stylish with a taste for jewelry design that embraced both the modernist and Byzantine. He dazzled Parisian society by throwing extravagant masquerade balls, yet beneath the flamboyance and aristocratic title he was struggling financially. In the early 1930s the songwriter Cole Porter introduced him to Coco Chanel, who was at the peak of her fame working as a fashion designer for aristocrats and celebrities alike. She quickly

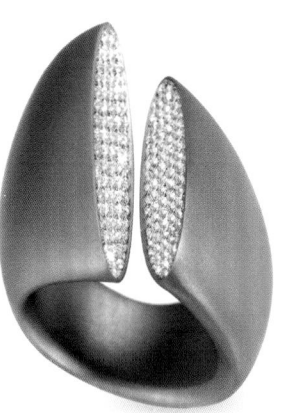

Duke Fulco di Verdura
Medusa Brooch, 1941
Gouache on vellum

Verdura
Theodora Byzantine Pendant
Brooch, 2009
Emeralds, rubies, sapphires, and
semiprecious gemstones in gold
(Shown with a gold Circle
Rope-Link Necklace)

Kaleidoscope Ring, 2017
Aquamarine, diamonds, and peridot
in gold and platinum

employed him as a jewelry designer, strategically using his nobility to access and sell to the top level of Parisian society.

Their partnership produced the iconic Maltese Cross cuff, mixing peridot and amethyst (considered semiprecious at the time) with the more fanciful yellow gold, pearls, and enamel. Verdura's Byzantine-style Peacock ear clips, mosaic earrings, and Ravenna cuff are a psychedelic mix of colored stones often contrasted with monochrome enamel. It was this method of stamping polished gold with a rainbow of haphazard gemstones in all different cuts that became his signature. As war approached, he opened an atelier in New York on September 1, 1939, the same day that Nazi Germany invaded Poland and triggered the start of World War II. Financed by Cole Porter and wealthy philanthropist Vincent Astor, he ingratiated himself into American high society just as Europe descended into chaos.

"He was a classicist in Renaissance and classical mythology," smiles Nico Landrigan, owner and guardian of the Verdura archives. Verdura took the elemental geometry of the Byzantine mosaics and radicalized them with blocks of color, intoxicating his collectors, who rarely turned down his ideas. He knew how to flatter a woman with his jewelry, putting his ego to one side even when he became successful. His jewelry embodied the way he lived his elegant, extravagant, and flamboyant life. The elegance of Verdura's personality and the originality of his design have proved hugely influential for subsequent generations of jewelers.

Like Verdura, James de Givenchy is a master jeweler and the torchbearer of color in contemporary design, infusing his simple lines with an intensity of tone that has elevated his work within American design from his base in New York. He combines stones with ceramic to create tension. In one seemingly simple ring (see p. 30), he has reverse-set yellow and brown diamonds into blackened oxidized silver with rings of pale blue, lime green, and yellow ceramic at its base. Yet the eye sees simple tones of white and yellow until, on further inspection, all the subtle shades and contrasting depths become apparent. It is like an optical illusion, with stones almost literally providing the icing on the cake, typical of a design that is simple but many layered.

Born in France as part of the fashion dynasty Givenchy, James considered going into fashion and interior design before jewelry claimed him. While he was working for Christie's in New York, his uncle, the fashion designer Hubert de Givenchy visited him in the jewelry department; determined to impress, James ushered him toward one of the headline diamonds. Hubert wasn't interested in the obvious and beckoned him over to a glass case, pointing out a simple leaf brooch made of glittering zircons of different colors. It was by Verdura. "I knew Fulco," Hubert said. "He was extremely talented and this is how you should look at jewels." That prompt to put design first, however tempted you are to prioritize the stones, and to study the work of the greats, such as di Verdura, Suzanne Belperron, and Jean Schlumberger, had a profound effect on James and, through him, on the world of jewelry. Gemstones may be potent carriers of symbolism and wealth, but they mean nothing without the harness of design. Di Verdura, Belperron, and Schlumberger all used a myriad of stones but within a design framework so compelling that the pieces themselves transcended into art.

After this epiphany Christie's sent James to run their Los Angeles office in the early 1990s and, having studied at the Gemological Institute of America, he accepted jewelry as his calling. He made several pieces by hand just to see if he could, with no intention of selling them. In Los Angeles he discovered a hunger to explore new ways of creation that went beyond figurative design. The leaf, the flower, the bird—all of which have been mercilessly reinterpreted throughout design history—held no allure for him. He wanted pure, unadulterated graphic form to express his artistic intentions, not a figure with limited ability to absorb meaning. After all, a bejeweled bird is just that, but an unusually shaped abstract brooch with a hypnotic stone in the center can metamorphose every time one contemplates it.

Setting up on his own in New York in 1996, de Givenchy rejected decoration in favor of abstraction and was at the forefront of shifting value from stones to design

James de Givenchy for Taffin
Brooch, 2018
Spessarite garnet (63.0ct) and Burmese sapphires in blackened white gold, oxidized silver, and rose gold

Ring, 2019
Light brown and yellow diamonds in blue, green, and yellow ceramic, oxidized silver, and platinum

Ring, 2017
Natural Blue Emerald (18.73ct), natural Ceylon sapphires, purple and pink sapphires, and rubies in beige ceramic, oxidized silver, and rose gold

ABSTRACT DESIGN

in the Western world, pioneering an era in which the simplicity of high jewelry has become part of his value. De Givenchy sometimes uses big stones where progressive abstract jewelry design shies away from them for fear of being labeled "commercial," but his style is too dominant for that. He sculpts in the simple curves of gold and he paints with stones held in place with the finest of settings. There is passion in every stroke. "Ceramic was a great way for me to add color," he says. "I'm continually asking myself, when do I move on? It is the moment I've exploited just about everything I think I can exploit in that direction."

Even his monochrome work in black ceramic and diamonds is unmistakably him, the stones diffused with intelligent, sophisticated design. A big rock isn't enough to rescue poor design—it is a distraction unless its purpose is to bring harmony to the piece. On the other hand, if a jewel has a strong voice and comes from a single artist, then it has the right to be called art. There is still a reluctance, however, to wear obviously expensive jewelry in the developed world. "It is much easier to buy a million-dollar painting to hang in your house where only your friends will see it than to walk outside with a $50,000 diamond ring," de Givenchy asserts. "People you don't know will think of you differently and call you names." The beauty of his work is that only those who know jewelry understand its importance. He has used minimalism to take his jewelry beyond intrinsic value, a feat that only a select few designers in the last century have achieved. There was perhaps only one woman in that elite club.

Suzanne Belperron (1900–83) was considered a goddess, worshipped within jewelry design as having created poetry. She wielded her talent expertly to become one of the greatest jewelry designers of all time, winning her first prize for jewelry design at just eighteen years old. She never signed her work, because she felt her design was enough. She confidently made the point that even though she managed a successful business, branding was beneath her. Instead, she created power in the market with pure forms and clean lines.

She was as exceptional in life as she was in jewelry. Her journey was a dangerous but exhilarating one, because she was a radical and a revolutionary at a time when women in every part of the workforce were considered less than equal. She grew up in Saint-Claude in the Jura region of eastern France, before moving to Paris in the "Roaring Twenties." It was there that she cut her teeth with the jewelry house of Boivin, then she moved to design exclusively for Bernard Herz, a Parisian stone dealer, in 1932. When World War II erupted in 1939 and Herz was harassed by the Gestapo for being Jewish, he passed the company into Belperron's hands to ensure its survival. He was deported to Auschwitz in 1942 and Belperron was arrested for running a Jewish business. When she was released, she decided to stay in Paris and join the Resistance. Herz's son Jean found his way back to the city after having been a prisoner of war, and together they started a new company that they ran for the next thirty years.

Belperron liked to spear emeralds, pearls, or blue sapphire pebbles onto cuffs of twenty-two-carat "virgin" gold, so called because of its raw texture. Her Couronne cuffs studded with rubies were typically worn two at a time on the same arm in a "tiara" style, with stones pointing up and down. The emerald versions were even immortalized by Matisse in pen and ink in 1936 on the arm of Dorothy Paley, an important jewelry collector. Operating more as a sculptor than as a jeweler, Belperron hammered great wedges of gold into submission, as can be seen in the design of her Toi et Moi ring (see p. 33). In one of her earring designs, sensuous spirals curling around diamonds at the ear illustrate the balance between volume and texture (see p. 32). Her shapes were plump, voluptuous, and feminine in an age where the hard lines of Art Deco still lingered.

In another break with tradition, Belperron also set precious and semiprecious stones in the same pieces. Transparent stones, such as rock crystal, or smoky quartz acted as a base material and were punctuated with big smooth emeralds, rubies, or diamonds. She created value with design and pioneered a daring sculptural nonfigurative style that at first glance didn't look expensive at all.

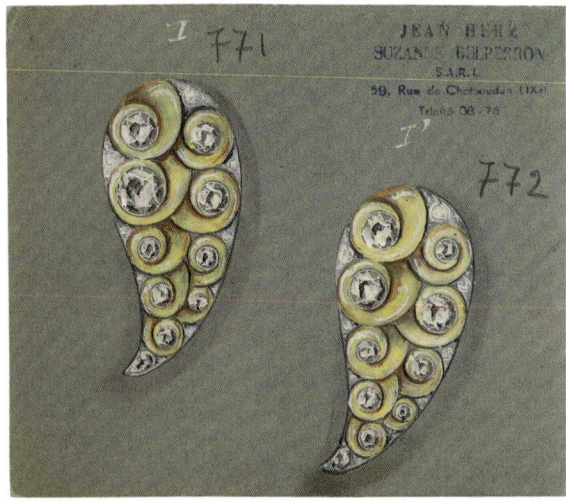

Belperron
Pair of Paisley Spiral Brooches, 1946–74
Painted rendering by Suzanne Belperron

Toi et Moi Ring, 2015
Virgin gold

Paisley "Serti Couteau" Ear Clips, 2017
Apatites and tsavorite garnets in gold

(Following pages)
Grima
Turquoise Brooch, 2019
Diamonds and turquoises in gold textured wire

Bird's Nest Ring, 1969
Diamonds and citrine in gold

Ring, 1968
Diamonds and tourmaline in gold textured wire

Lightening Earrings, 2014
Diamonds in white gold

Ring, 1985
Diamonds and South Sea pearl in gold

She played with silver both at Boivin, where she wrapped it in black lacquer as a foundation for turquoise, and at Herz-Belperron, where she applied moonstones. There was no hint of sparkle or glint of gold, just strong shape and harmonious color. Her pieces were comfortable yet grand, simple yet monumental, understated yet luxurious. She dispensed with the "parure"—a set of matching jewels worn on formal occasions, such as necklace, ring, brooch, or bracelet—and instead created "suites" or simpler groups of jewels that could be worn individually.

After Belperron's death in 1983, her legacy lay dormant until Ward Landrigan, a former manager of Sotheby's jewelry department, bought the name and trademark in 1999. His son Nico relaunched the brand in 2015 and from its base in New York has the enviable task of guarding the 9,300 gouache paintings and sketches in her archive. Belperron the brand is still alive today, producing pieces from that archive with a modernist aesthetic that feels current. Nico Landrigan acknowledges that Belperron was a rebel at heart. "I think she took an artist's approach to something that was essentially seen as an industry and a craft." Modernism was egalitarian in that anyone could create anything. Status quo could be superseded by talent, which is how a country girl from the Jura was able to create a style that rippled down throughout design history.

While Belperron's style changed the perception of jewelry from the 1930s to the 1950s, the birth of youth culture in the postwar period marked a radical shift in society. Aided by unparalleled wealth, the consumption of luxury rocketed with disposable income changing how the middle classes chose to entertain themselves. Consumer capitalism, promoted by Western governments as a means to advance social and economic reconstruction, fed a surge in appetite for novel design in the home and on the body. Personal style, the "me" generation, and a fascination with the future replaced a time in which teenagers had been mini versions of their parents. Design was used to encourage aspiration. London, set ablaze by music and fashion in the Swinging Sixties, became the global center of pop culture, ahead of Paris or New York. Independent, London-based jewelry designer Andrew Grima (1921–2007) played his part, with avant-garde, textured hunks of rugged gold combined with turquoise droplets and white diamonds. He took the pearl, then an antiquated, old-fashioned jewel connected to twin sets and helmet hair, and modernized it, sandwiching it in shards of gold or adding it to jagged brooches. "Andrew was the father of postwar modern jewelry," Jojo Grima, his wife of thirty years, says as she smiles ruefully.

They met in London in 1975 and she swiftly commissioned him to make a jewel out of shrapnel removed from her then boyfriend. Love blossomed, they married two years later, and had a daughter Francesca. She later joined the family firm and carried on his work after his death in 2007. Both mother and daughter have a deep love for the abstract ethos that came alive in Andrew. "Figurative jewelry in my opinion lacks imagination," says Francesca. "The wonderful thing about abstract design is that it can be reimagined every time you look at it." Andrew Grima used gold wire when solid gold was considered more appropriate for fine and high jewelry, thereby shifting the attention away from intrinsic value. Created in 1968, his textured wire ring gripping a green tourmaline (see p. 34) is a twisted sculpture, chiseled into a swirling tower on the finger. His intention was to celebrate form instead of symbolism. Another wire ring made a year earlier, this time with baguette diamonds and rubies, is graphic, futuristic, and jagged, and as far away from sweet, pretty design as possible. Much of his work can be read in different ways; even the 1969 "Bird's Nest" ring (see p. 34), with its wire twigs and orange citrine perched within, could be seen as a simple cocktail ring to the uninitiated. The possibilities are endless with pure design.

Francesca's contribution to the Grima style is smoother, flatter, but it is also equally uncompromising in its abstraction. Her Gherkin ring is playful. Close inspection reveals that a smoky quartz or lapis lazuli center stone is cut with the same facets as the gold ring holding it in place. Her white gold-and-diamond ear clips streak across the ear like lightning, and her twisted South Sea pearl ring

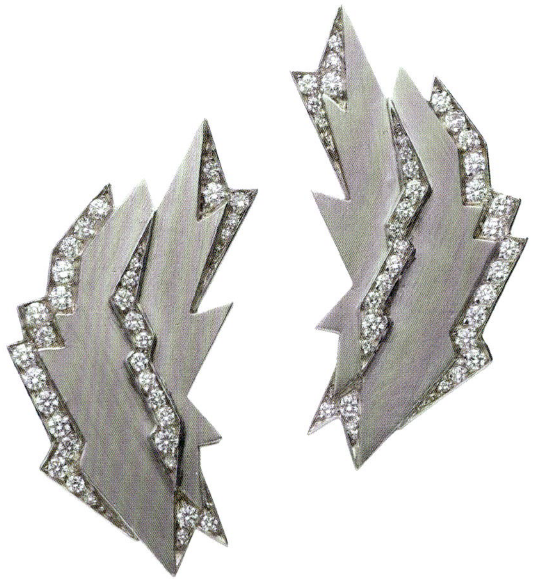

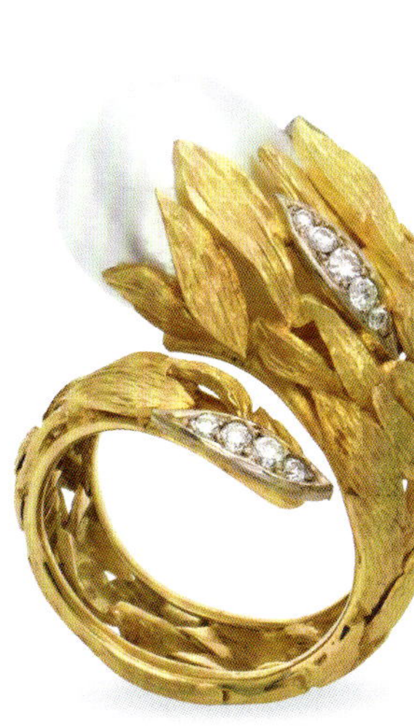

places shards of gold almost like laurel leaves around the finger. She has advanced and evolved her father's art, sometimes simplifying its codes of design but still retaining its abstract truth. The wearer is free to take what they want and need from each piece, every time.

The 1960s were all about rebellion and, while London was wearing graphic gold jewelry from the likes of Grima, American collectors were turning inward to homegrown talent. David Webb (1925–75), a country boy from North Carolina, had moved to New York City at the age of eighteen and by 1948, when twenty-three years old he was creating oversize sculptural floral jewels from his store on 46th Street. His design language was steeped in the flora and fauna of his rural upbringing, but it then evolved as he absorbed the sights and experiences of the city life around him. He sent one of his foremen to Austria to study the art of enameling and, between 1963 and 1967, made a series of oddly beautiful animal pieces. His focus on the natural world turned to ancient history with jade carvings and Greek themes using found objects. This continued into the early 1970s, by which time the women's liberation movement was in full swing and taste in jewelry had become more brazen with defiant statement pieces being worn to the office.

Rampant consumer spending in Western society during the Cold War inspired a whole new style of jewelry on an exaggerated scale. Webb was the poster child of this "spend now, save later" attitude, with his jewels celebrating the boldness of American prosperity. He created imposing Dragon brooches worn by trendsetters, such as the Duchess of Windsor and dancer Martha Graham. By 1975, Webb had died from pancreatic cancer at just fifty years old, but he left behind approximately 40,000 drawings from his final design phase, full of abstract creations: totems with color-saturated stones stacked in geometric patterns, the Bent Nail collection using everyday objects as inspiration, and woodworks combining ebony and deep rose-colored bloodwood with yellow gold in an ode to geometric modernist design. The responsibility of bringing these ideas to life now rests with Mark Emanuel, a jeweler and co-owner of the design house who rescued it from bankruptcy in 2010. As creative director, he oversees the twenty-five-strong workshop, creating new pieces from Webb's archive. "American style back then was ahead of the rest of the world," says Emanuel. "Everything was a little bit bigger because of the money and a little bit newer and embracing a sort of new world vision."

The wealth and freedom of that economic era encouraged designers to experiment, and this pushing at the boundaries of what jewelry could be propelled it beyond decoration, adornment, and even art into the realm of the sociopolitical. Evelyn Markasky, a Greek-American maker-designer living in California, feels jewelry should have a higher purpose. "Most jewelry is born to be sold rather than to be great," she sighs. "A lot of jewelry is dull enough to be offensive." In her world, jewelry can be risqué and difficult, challenging our vision of society. Growing up in Youngstown, Ohio, Markasky was attracted to the raw, edgy roughness of physical things. It was the 1960s and the Vietnam War was raging, giving her a taste for protest and rebellion. Youngstown was a steel town and metal was everywhere, turning the sky pink with heat from local blast furnaces. The smell and taste of it never left her. At school she enjoyed taking things apart and putting them back together again, welding and dismantling. Today she makes all her pieces by hand, and she feels that this process separates her from other designers, many of whom use workshops. The essence of who she is, her energy, is in each twist of metal.

Her "Dangerous Vagina" ring (see p. 39) is a folded and forged sheet of copper, colored with enamels and torch fired. Inspired by human form, she designed—and named—it to be slightly uncomfortable, because the word "vagina" is still socially unacceptable despite half the population having one. Her Primitive Organic necklace (see p. 39) of rough metal links fired green belongs to a series called "Scars Make Your Body More Interesting," where Markasky makes the point that our need for perfection, whether that be with makeup or plastic surgery, is banal. Difference and imperfection is to be celebrated in her world.

Archival Totem Pendant
Rendering, c.1970
Gouache on black presentation paper
David Webb Archives

David Webb
Chevron Ring, designed 1976
Black and white enamel and diamonds in gold and platinum

Mega Cubist Ring
Black enamel and diamonds in gold and platinum

Shoulder Cuff, designed 1972
Rosewood and polished gold

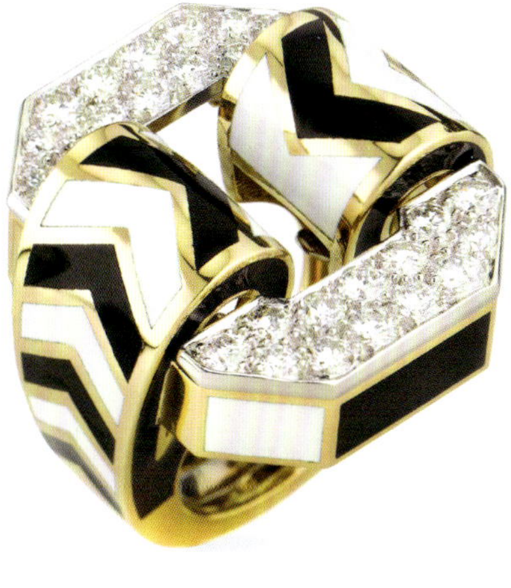

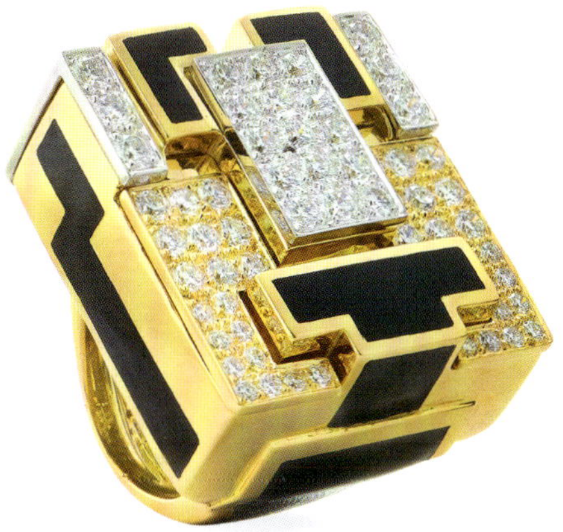

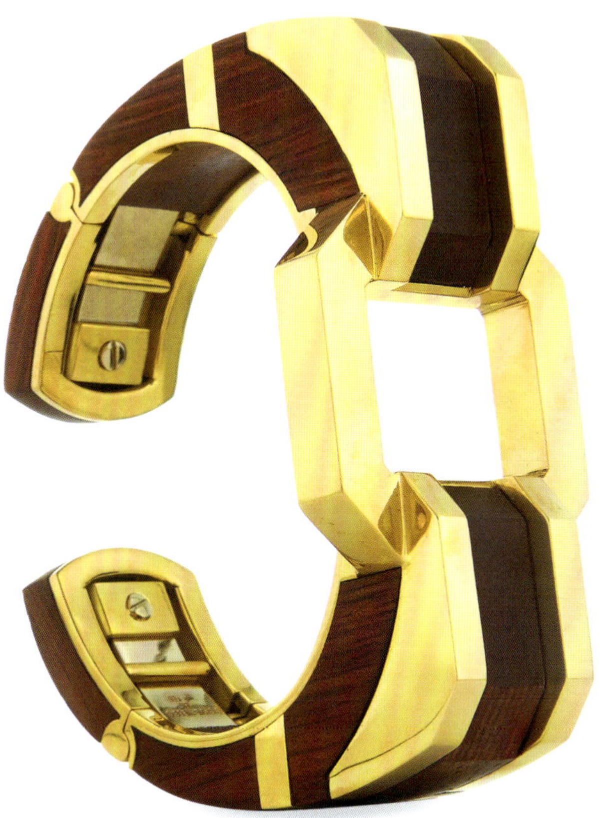

Evelyn Markasky
Primitive Organic Armor
Neckpiece, c.2017
Vitreous enamel on copper
Collection of the artist

Dangerous Vagina Ring, 2016
Swarovski crystal pearl in forged copper
Collection of the artist

(Following pages)
Elisabetta Cipriani—Wearable Art
Frank Stella
Ring, 2008
Gold

Elisabetta Cipriani—Wearable Art
Giorgio Vigna
Vento Ring, 2018
Diamonds in oxidized silver

She has a fearless soul with a penchant for realism, and this informs her design aesthetic. In addition to copper and enamel, she uses food, insects, concrete, melted-down credit cards, and dirt in her work. She even has a torched rice noodle ring, white with crispy brown edges. Putting a price on dirt must be difficult, but the price reflects what it would take for her to make it again. The concept behind the piece has more value to her than precious parts. "I feel these materials are just as valuable and valid as using gold and silver. Nobody uses gold and silver in a painting," she sniffs. The brilliant-cut diamond isn't the only path to the jewelry utopia of the future.

Someone else defying the diamond is gallery owner Elisabetta Cipriani, who partners with and commissions contemporary fine artists on one-of-a-kind jewels as an extension of their art. Before moving to London in 2003, Cipriani curated exhibitions at the Museum of Contemporary Art in Rome and in 2009 the birth of her daughter inspired her to open her own gallery. She approached painters and sculptors, including Ania Guillaume, Frank Stella, and Giorgio Vigna, challenging them to make a jewel in precious metals, often for the first time. The process begins with each artist using a series of sketches to express who they are in jewelry form. This evolves into a single prototype, which is brought to life either by goldsmiths or by the artist themselves. The making of each jewel can be an emotional and difficult process, but it's also rewarding and full of meaning. Italian sculptor Giorgio Vigna's Vento ring (see p. 40) represents the wind and nature's ability to engage our senses through sound and movement. Its oxidized silver tentacles are blunted by the soft gleam of white diamonds. The diamond is relegated to a supporting role while the progression of ideas is central, dominating materials and making the piece desirable.

The work of Frank Stella, the American artist based in New York City, has eliminated the boundaries between painting and sculpture. He adds protruding materials to some of his own paintings and also paints some of his sculptures. This experimentation with space finally led him to a piece simply called "Ring," (see p. 40) crafted in yellow gold. Interweaving tangles and spirals of polished metal, it has twenty-eight welded parts and is an illusion, inspired by Baroque artists who would paint subjects as if they were emerging from the canvas into reality. It is his first piece of wearable art.

Monaco-based painter and sculptor Ania Guillaume creates texture by plating gold onto silver; her Gingko Leaf ring references a tree native to China that is thought to be at least 270 million years old. Guillaume admires the spirituality of the natural universe, with the gingko leaf symbolizing well-being and longevity.

"Jewelry is art, I think, because it, like art, has a presence that reminds us of the importance of memory, of life, of our idols," Cipriani says. The market for fine artists creating jewelry has been growing for the last twenty years and is often an affordable entry point to their other work. The artist keeps the prototype and, once the edition or unique piece is sold, it will never be made again. Most artists' jewelry looks back to the simplicity of modernist design in feel or in mood. There is a wildness to it that more commercial design can sometimes lack. The artist or gallery is selling a single jewel, meaning that only one collector has to love it enough to buy. When thousands of people have to approve a design, it is inevitably compromised, because it will need to be easier to wear, prettier, and most often figurative. It must be understood and accepted far more quickly and be "value for money," containing precious stones in socially recognizable configurations, such as the solitaire in a claw setting or the channel-set eternity ring.

One way to produce commercial jewelry while keeping design credibility intact is to use silver, the so-called "denim of jewelry design." Gold is a finite resource, meaning there is a limited amount on earth that can be mined, so essentially, we recycle what we have in new and interesting ways. Silver is also found underground in what is called its "native" form, but it can be created artificially under controlled conditions, making it more plentiful than gold and less precious in terms of its perceived value. Traditionally, the warmth and intensity of gold have appealed to

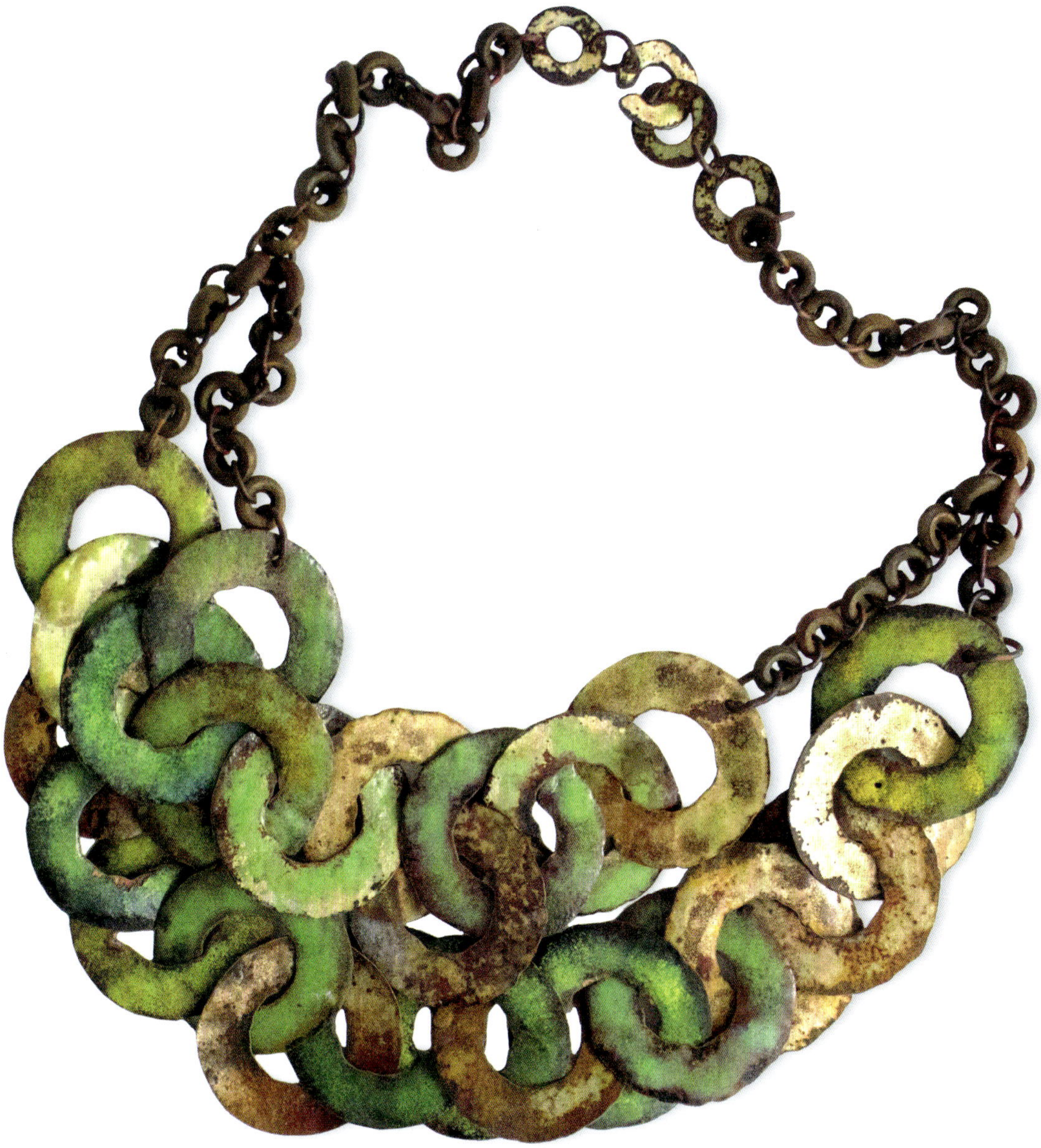

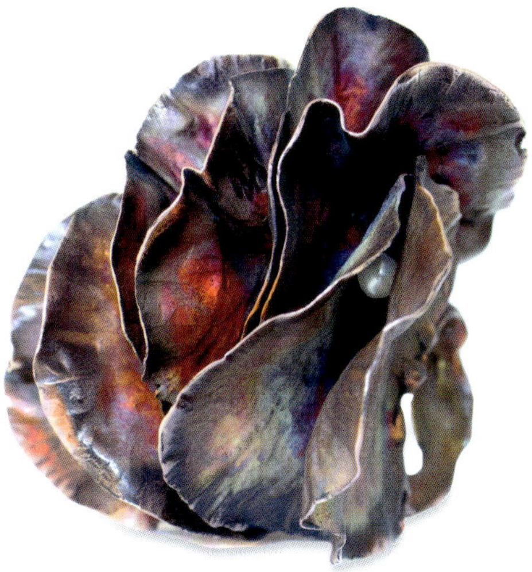

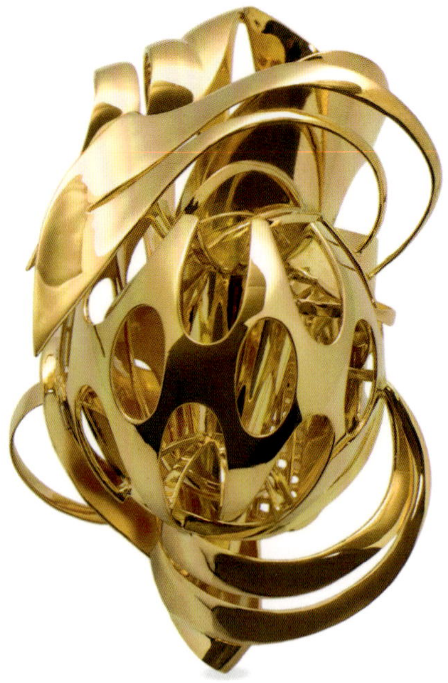

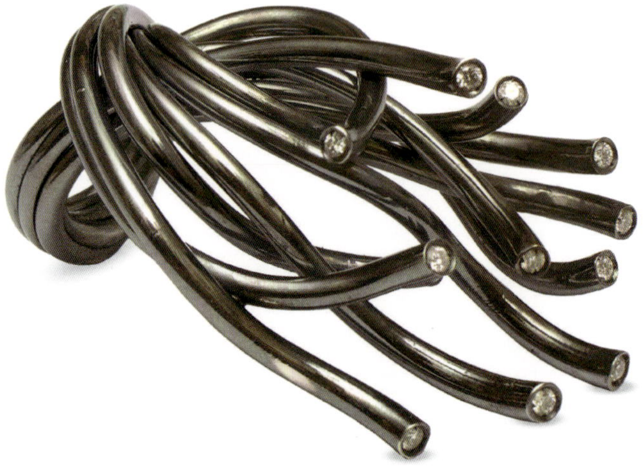

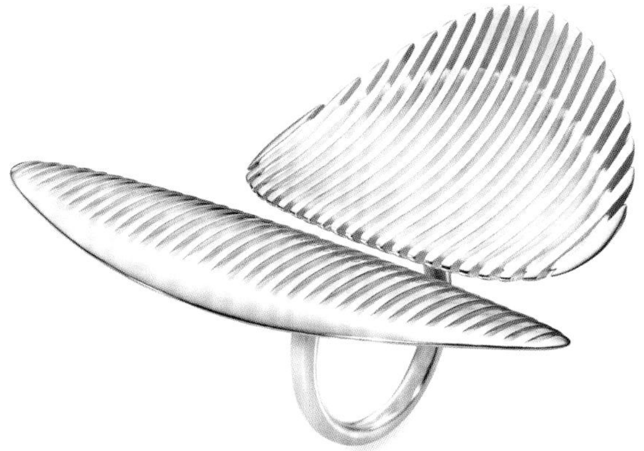

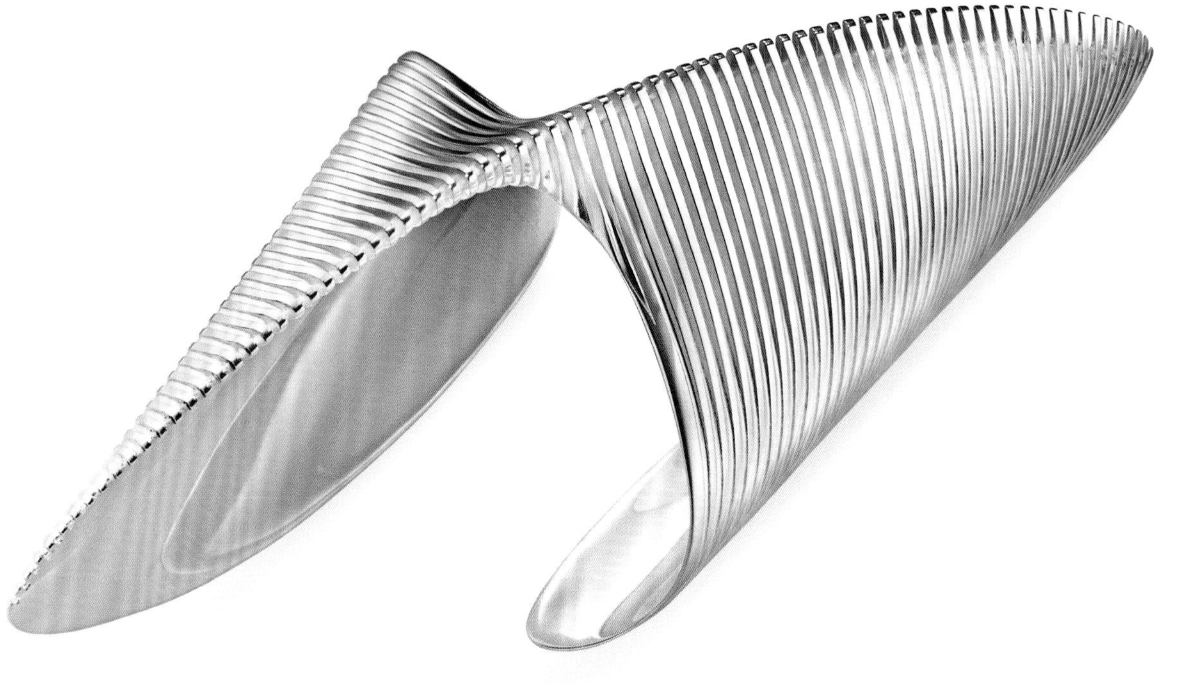

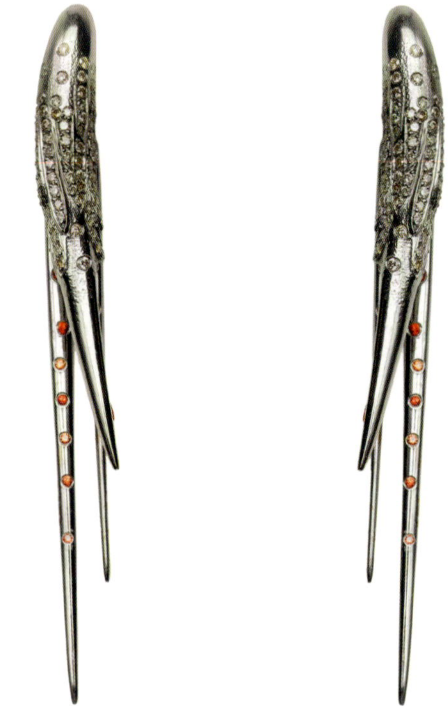

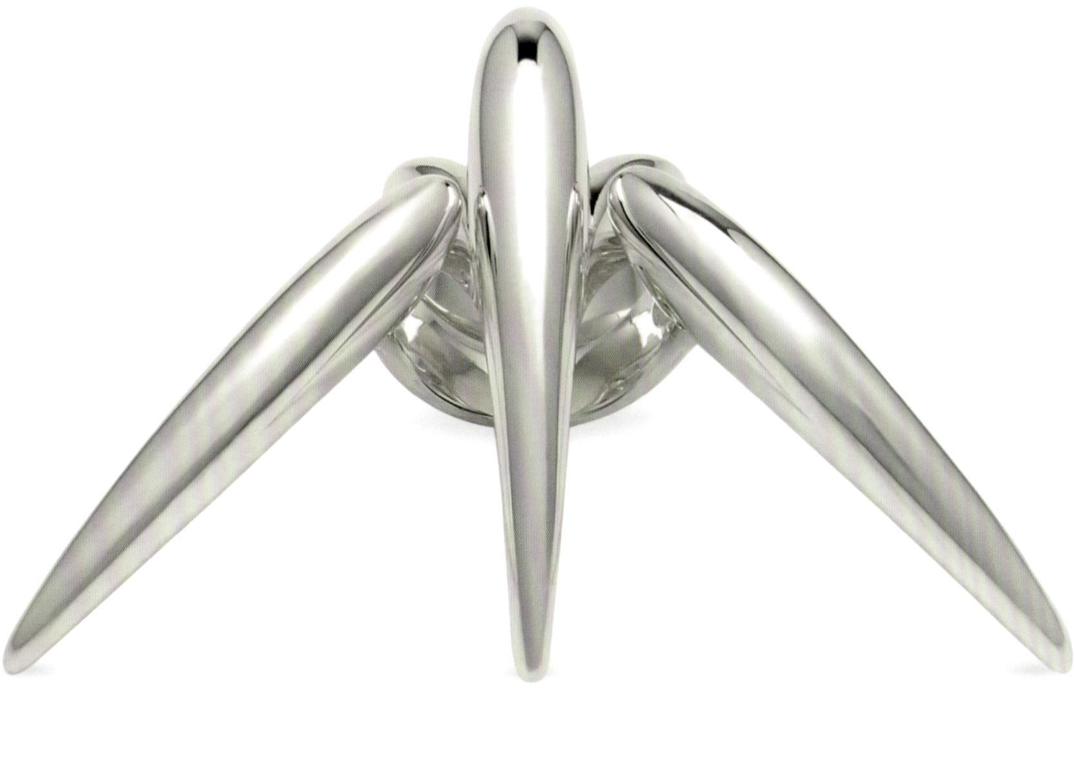

(Preceding pages)
Zaha Hadid for Georg Jensen
Twin Ring 623D, 2015
Sterling silver

Twin Cuff 623A, 2015
Sterling silver

(Opposite)
Arman Suciyan
Goddess Wing Drop Earrings, 2014
Brown diamonds and orange sapphires
in textured rhodium-plated silver

Gliding Goddess and Gliding Spirits United
Stacking Ring, 2014
Sterling silver with enamel detailing
on reverse

hot countries, while the cool white luster of silver has found a place within chillier climes, specifically in Nordic culture. The unpretentiousness of silver appeals to the Scandinavians, especially since Denmark was occupied by the Nazis in World War II and hardship and scarcity led to a design philosophy that embraced the bare essentials. Ornamentation was just too expensive. Georg Jensen (1866–1935) was the youngest of eight children born to a father who worked as a knife grinder in Raadvad, northern Copenhagen. He left school at thirteen to work in the local knife factory but hustled his way into a metalworking apprenticeship at fourteen and eventually going on to find fame and fortune as a sculptor and silversmith. He later was described (in his obituary in the New York Herald Tribune) as "the greatest silversmith of the last 300 years."

In 1904 he opened his first store in Copenhagen, where his flair for fluid lines in the Art Nouveau style secured him a place in the Danish Museum of Decorative Arts later that year. His designs were startlingly modern in turn-of-the-century Denmark and attracted other designers to his studio who were eager to collaborate. This mindset of combining talent to foster creativity continues today, with guest designers being invited in to create unique collections. The Danish sculptor Henning Koppel (1918–81), Iraqi-British architect Zaha Hadid (1950–2016), and now American jewelry designer Jacqueline Rabun have all enabled the brand to flourish well beyond Jensen's death in 1935. "We look for people who will challenge us and reflect our values back to us," says Nicholas Manville, chief creative director. Hadid's twisted Lamellae cuff in silver with accompanying ring (see p. 41) was part of an eight-piece collection for Georg Jensen. It aped the sweeping sculpture of her architecture in a form that could be worn, echoing the Wangjing Soho towers she created in Beijing the previous year and demonstrating her unique skill at scaling her designs up or down, depending on the project. These were pieces that expressed the architecture of jewelry through global eyes.

The perception of Scandinavian design is different from the outside and these designers add a twist to the Georg Jensen narrative with their own style and experiences, channeling its heritage through the prism of a different culture and leaving Danish design refreshed each time. The organic shapes of the Jensen style pull it away from any attempt at structured perfection and there is a geometric simplicity. The Möbius earrings in polished silver refer to a term in mathematics meaning a surface with only one side. The Dew Drop bangle wraps around the wrist while a rock-crystal cube perches serenely at its center. The pieces are gloriously, defiantly abstract, universal, and timeless.

Silver as a material offers respite from our unrelenting preoccupation with intrinsic value in jewelry. It is inexpensive, more of a speculative investment, and provokes less emotion, whereas gold is undeniably tied to power, passion, and sensuality. Contemporary abstract jewelry incorporates both; however, silver is the more accessible of the two and is often a place where collectors start, rifling around market stalls for a fistful of simple silver rings. During the Ottoman Empire, from the fourteenth to the early twentieth centuries, artisans called ehl-I hiref were employed to create elaborate jewels within a guild system in what is now Turkey. When Mehmed II stormed Constantinople (now Istanbul) in 1453, ending the Byzantine Empire and linking trade between East and West, he decided to build a Grand Bazaar, that would help to jump-start the economy. It was here that the culture of silver jewelry flourished in what was to become one of the biggest covered markets in history.

As a Turkish-Armenian kid growing up in Istanbul in the 1970s and 1980s, Arman Suciyan's main ambition was to learn a craft. He gravitated toward the Grand Bazaar and, when he was fifteen years old, he apprenticed under master Misak Toros in the old tradition. After a stint of military service, he felt the need to know more about jewelry. He learned to design well in Turkey, but he wanted creative freedom, so in 1994 he headed to Great Britain, where he discovered for himself the history of European modernism.

Roule & Co
Starburst Halo Bangle, c.2013
Emeralds in blackened gold and
yellow gold

It wasn't simply academic progression Suciyan yearned for, but innovation of thought. At the Kent Institute of Art & Design (now the University of Creative Arts), he found ways to unleash his imagination and cultivate his fantasies away from the "copy economy" of Istanbul. He crafted minimalist aerodynamic rings in silver (see p. 42), symbolizing a traveling space goddess with the power to give planets life. Swooping birds with textured gem-encrusted wings wrap around the ear and glide over the collarbone. Now based back in Istanbul, Suciyan makes twenty to thirty pieces a year, often drawing on time and space travel. "I think we are still trying to move forward from the old ways," he says thoughtfully. "My jewelry gives life to mythological creatures in futuristic forms." This is his nirvana. The bareness of his silver universe offers something unique for all who consider it. As the aforementioned Frank Stella once said about his own work, "What you see is what you see."

"Intrinsic value is the Achilles heel of jewelry," laments Christopher Roule. He and his wife Laurin Lucaire, owners of Roule & Co, are self-taught designers who play with ideas of structure, architecture, and geometry in their jewelry. Art can so easily be corrupted by commerce, and he and Lucaire want to be brave enough to reach beyond the acceptable idea of preciousness in jewelry. Like a pair of golden handcuffs, intrinsic value provides a fundamental income while stifling creativity. The horrific cost of materials to support the way jewelry is made and sold currently stops many talented designers from reaching their potential. Roule & Co are part of a movement from the independent sector to jump-start the next era in jewelry design by questioning the purpose and legitimacy of what creates value.

Perhaps the ultimate embodiment of modernism and the ideal of modern form and function is the skyscraper, and these towering glass-and-steel tombs of modern industry struck a twelve-year-old Christopher Roule like a streak of lightning when he first saw one in New York City. His young mind was intoxicated by the complexity of exposed beams running like a giant trellis of iron on that construction site, and he has been captivated by Modernist architecture ever since that first visit.

The mesh-wire structure of their signature black agate cabochon ring echoes the iron lattice of the Eiffel Tower, which Roule visited in the late 1990s. This graphic, industrial style evolved into "Pixel Dust" a cage of blackened white gold studded with white diamonds and curved into a bracelet on the wrist or crescent hoops at the ear. For color, the Starburst Halo bangle, a slice of wire mesh edged in yellow gold, is punctuated with emeralds flashing green. Teardrop earrings enclose a jangly selection of loose sky-blue aquamarines, and ripe orange sapphires tumble the length of golden yellow hoops. Tone may veer from darkness to light, but the components are often the same, a metal grid holding the treasure within. In many ways, the stones represent people encased in high-rise buildings of wire and glass, with the mirror cabochon ring providing a moment of literal reflection. From their base in New York, Roule and Lucaire create models using 3-D printing in wax, and then they cast them using the lost-wax technique, hand-finished and set with stones. The big-domed center stones or cabochons are carved from the rough by skilled gemstone carvers and then set by hand. Their aim is to make something wearable, light, strong, thin, and beautiful enough to inspire obsession. They work seven days a week to turn their design into objects that symbolize a break from the past. "As long as there are traditions, there will be modernism, which is a constant questioning of how things are done," says Lucaire. "It's a sort of struggle between what has come before and what will come in the future."

Creating darkly graphic jewels can be challenging in a market as commercial as that of the United States. Roule lives for the day when the public are able to dream much bigger dreams than the current marketing landscape and the diamond solitaire allow. They have "unicorn clients" who buy into their creative vision, but wholesale is difficult. The crowd-pleasing beauty so valuable in a department store is the absolute opposite of their design language.

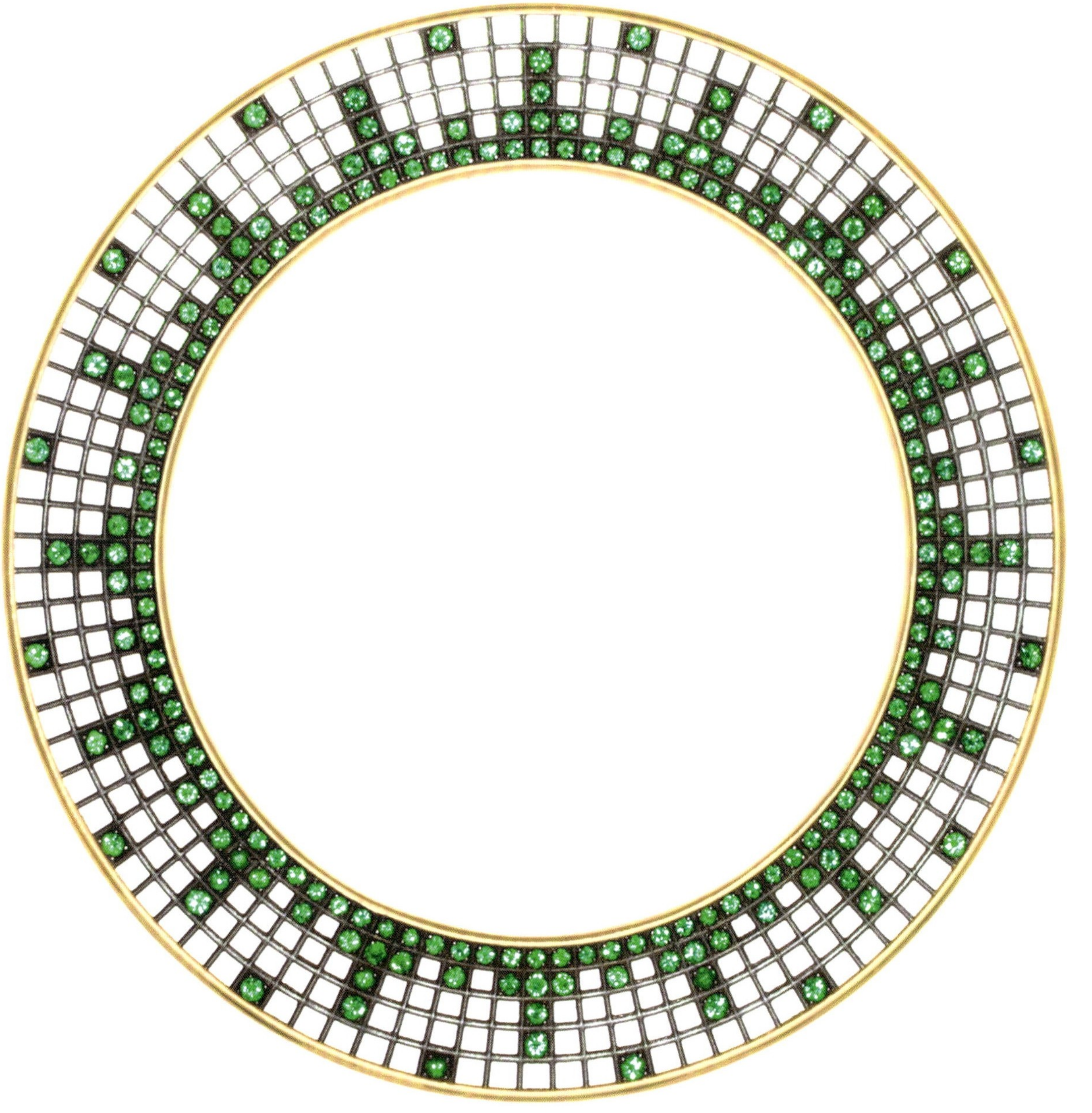

Brutal lines and geometric mathematics are everything to Roule & Co, but London-based jeweler Fernando Jorge takes his power from the soft sensual curves that dominate his native Brazilian culture. In Brazil, even minimalism is rounder. In 1500, when the Portuguese arrived, the indigenous Tupinamba people were unencumbered by European prudishness, or even clothes for that matter, and seemed to the visiting colonizers to be sexually free. This fluid sensuality is seen as completely natural within Brazilian culture and has influenced how the rest of the world perceives them, touching everything from jewelry and music to product design. Jorge's style plays with this notion of desire, and he relishes the fact that his "dripping shapes" embody a palpable sense of Brazilian passion. His forms are sensual and plump, like his tanzanite-and-boulder opal, rhodium-plated Arara earrings or his Stream labradorite-and-aquamarine pendant. His jewelry has become more graphic and abstract as he gets deeper into his career, with works such as his Stream cuff, an elegant gold loop that bends and curves around the joints of the wrist, embellished with graduated brown diamonds or etched grooves into the metal. The circular minimalism of his Satellite earrings feels cosmic, as if they were miniature planets orbiting a distant universe.

Jorge argues that around the beginning of the twenty-first century, jewelry experienced a shift, becoming more innovative, creative, and exciting and encouraging people like him to consider it as a career choice. One of the biggest hurdles to becoming a jewelry designer is being aware of it early enough to begin what is inevitably a lifetime spent studying first the craft and then the art. It often takes a minimum of ten years to know if you possess the talent to survive and twenty to know if that talent can evolve into greatness. Jorge studied product design in Brazil before coming to London at the age of twenty-nine to do a master's in jewelry design at Central Saint Martins school of art. He was always fascinated by small objects and the intimate connection design has with people's lives. In London he learned how to stop listening to the noise of other people's work so that his own could come out. Compared to Europe, the Brazilian market operates in a fairly young jewelry economy and is overwhelmingly commercial with elaborate ornamentation as its foundation. Success in Europe is measured by "critique" as well as sales, and that kind of intellectual power appealed to Jorge. Brazilian design favors colored stones, but to sell at a certain level in North America and in Europe, diamonds are the unspoken requirement. This presented a challenge, because Jorge has a love-hate relationship with diamonds. "A diamond on its own means nothing," he says. "They are like steroids. You take too many and you're strong but you don't do the necessary work." In 2017 he finally launched his first major diamond collection, Brilliant, and was taken aback by the amount of attention it received. The cost of diamonds often prohibits innovation, because the designer has to recoup the investment before committing to making more jewelry. Art can be the casualty, yet the longevity of the diamond industry depends on inventive designers, such as Jorge, reinventing and reigniting desire for the stone over and over again. The business of jewelry needs Jorge's art as much as he needs to keep experimenting with new ideas; achieving that balance is everything.

Another compelling stone that depends on innovative design for survival is the pearl. Natural pearls were once the most expensive jewels on earth, and at their height the Roman emperor Aulus Vitellius (AD 15–69) sold one of his mother's pearl earrings to fund an entire military campaign. Yet, as history wore on, pearl jewelry and design languished in the doldrums. Pearls were too expensive and too precious to be modernized and, thus, acquired a reputation as being old-fashioned and traditional.

Change came when, in 1893, a Japanese entrepreneur called Mikimoto Kōkichi (1858–1954) created the first cultured pearl—essentially a pearl born in captivity—and gave birth to an industry that mass-produced enough pearls for the world to wear them. He "seeded" an oyster shell by introducing a tiny particle of mother-of-pearl and the oyster wrapped it in nacre to protect itself. Pearls are different from other gemstones in that they are produced by a living organism, and they come

Fernando Jorge
Satellite Earrings, 2018
Diamonds and mother-of-pearl in gold

Stream Cuff, 2015
Gold

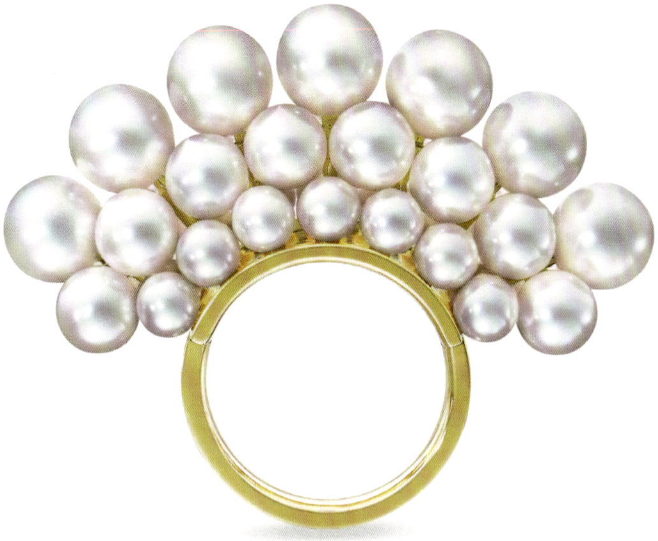

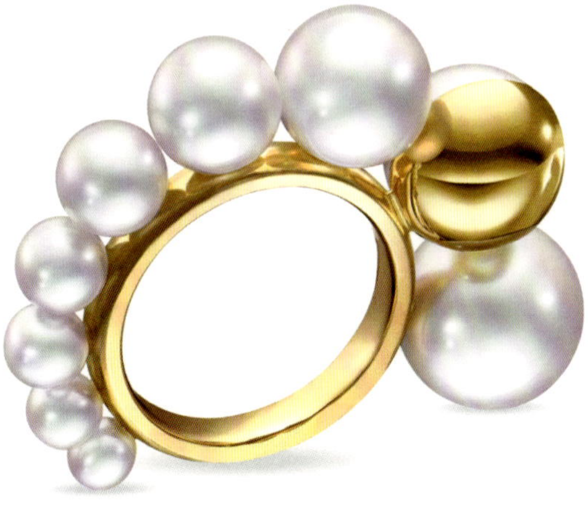

TASAKI
Pyramid Pearls Ring, 2016
Freshwater pearls in gold

SHELL Ring, 2013
Freshwater pearls in gold

from the sea, whereas gemstones come from the earth's crust. They also don't require any cutting or polishing. They inhabit their own universe with a separate hierarchy, which means they acquire value differently. They are mostly grouped into three tiers: costume pearls, which are found in fashion but are artificially made; cultured pearls, which are cultivated on pearl farms for fine jewelry; and natural pearls found in the wild and used almost exclusively in high jewelry, because of their rarity and cost. Abstract jewelry often thrives by using design to subdue the power of stones; however, pearls can work in tandem with design as a type of negative space, with their blank opaque sheen providing a pause, instead of sucking you in with a thousand facets.

The fashion industry propelled pearls back into the spotlight in the early twentieth century, particularly through the talents of Coco Chanel and Christian Dior, who included costume pearls into their collections from the 1920s onward. This trend for long pearl necklaces triggered demand in Europe and North America, compelling the Japanese pearl industry to crank up production. Pearls suddenly had a modern identity and, after World War II, when Japan was looking for ways to boost its economy, a multitude of pearl farms sprung into life for the export market.

One such company was Tasaki, which began farming pearls in 1954 and by the 1970s had decided to design modern abstract jewelry to differentiate itself from the competition. Opting to be different in Japan was a startling act of revolution. Today, Toshikazu Tajima, Tasaki's chief executive officer, compares traditional pearl design to the classical Japanese art of the sixteenth- and seventeenth-century painters Kano Motonobu and Kano Sanraku. What renegade artists, such as Tadanori Yokoo, have done to change perceptions of the fine arts in Japan, Tasaki aims to do for pearls. This involves radically different design using traditional akoya pearls, which have a soft pink sheen reminiscent of the sakura cherry blossom, a cherished symbol of beauty in Japan. The Abstract Star necklace, jagged and open with an invisible hinge at the back, is a worthy example of this new style. The SHELL ring brings abstract form to black freshwater pearls, and white gold in another example of streamlined simplicity.

Tasaki have pioneered their own mabe cultured pearl—bigger and bolder in color than akoya—with a rainbowlike sheen and grown against the wall of the oyster shell, so that it is flat on one side. Tasaki aspire to achieve "supreme beauty" and have turned a much loved but tired jewel into something that has become precious again. That in itself has its challenges. "I love and hate the same thing about jewelry," says Tajima thoughtfully. "The market needs more [pearls], which we cannot supply, but that creates value, which I love."

Jewelry often derives its value from big stones encased in ornate figurative design, but this perception of value has evolved to accommodate the elegance of simplicity. With contemporary jewelry, stones are part of a bigger design universe where the slices of carbon fiber in Fabio Salini's earrings are just as important, or the pure design of Vhernier's Eclisse ring doesn't require stones at all. Emotional value can mean more than monetary value, because in a thousand years from now all the materials we use today may be worthless. American jewelry designer and sculptor Robert Lee Morris says it best: "Good jewelry raises your frequency every time you look at it." You feel it first.

In a way abstract jewelry destroys expectation. It acts like a blank canvas on which individuality can blossom. The freedom from and reduction of ornamentation represents progress, because jewelry is worn in public and must be read at a distance; the meaning and gravitas of simple jewelry hides power in plain sight and can be taken in at a glance. Jewelry may have been, as Nico Landrigan so eloquently puts it, "relegated to the second shelf" in the hierarchy of art, but it has been as affected by the major art movements—Art Deco, Art Nouveau, Modernism, Surrealism—as any painting or sculpture. It must learn from fine art by prioritizing integrity over money and power if it is to rise above material value and attain the respect and attention it deserves from museums, schools, and the wider world.

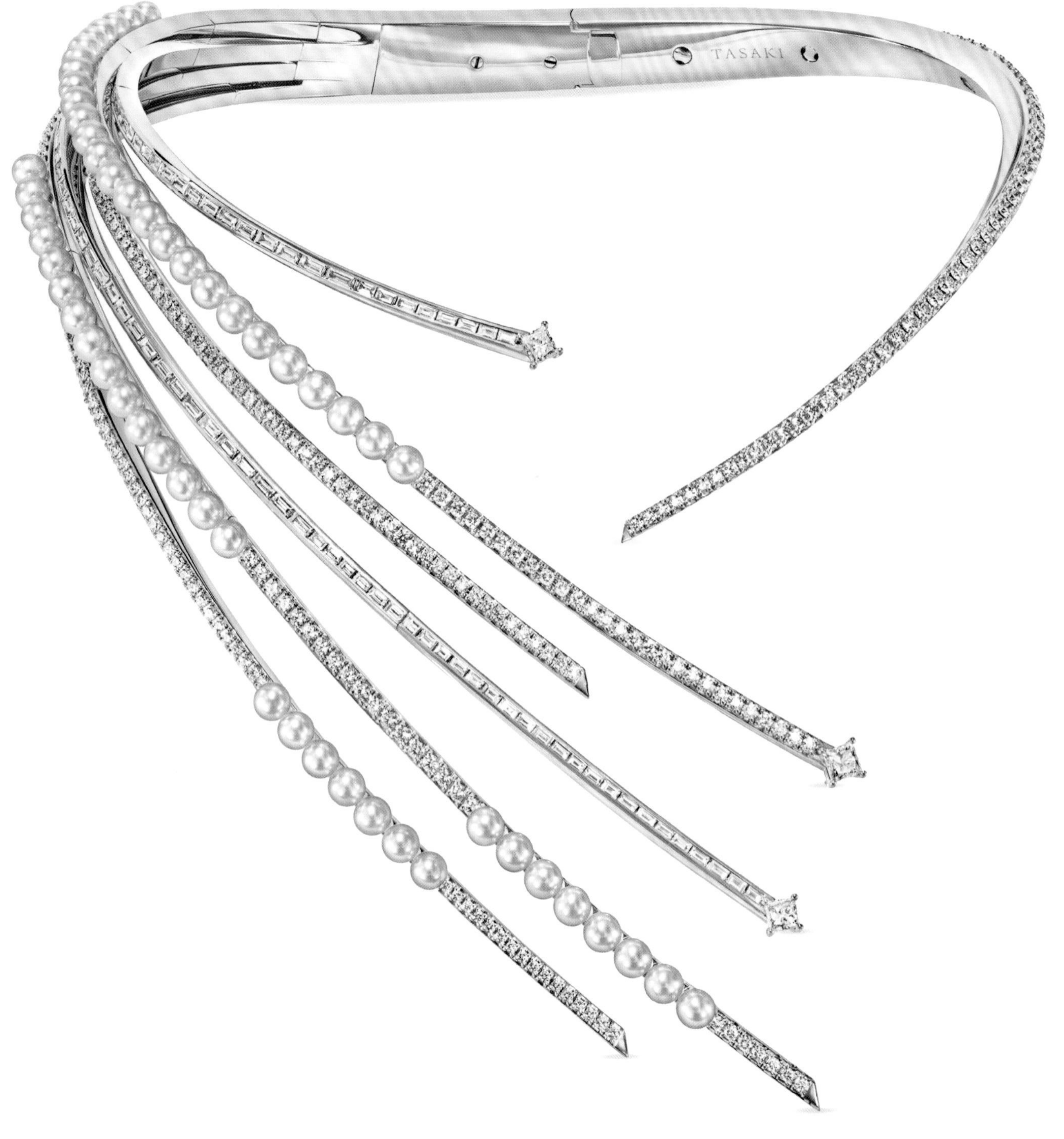
TASAKI

TASAKI
Surge Necklace, 2019
Akoya pearls and diamonds in white gold

Design is the tool and, while beauty is the inevitable outcome, abstraction helps to widen its parameters. In some more ornamental pieces, the beauty is so obvious that it can drown out the message, but, when the balance is right, a jewel can change the world.

War, politics, and economics have played crucial roles in the development of abstract jewelry throughout history. Hemmerle's iron jewels might never have been born if it weren't for the War of Liberation, and Georg Jensen's daring minimalism would surely have been more extravagant without the poverty and bare brutality of the Viking age searing itself into the national character of Scandinavia. From the beginning of the twentieth century, modernism encouraged the exploration of unusual materials, such as aluminum and titanium, often with an industrial bent. Materials are the bones of great jewelry design, stones are its flesh, and in jewelry today power has been transferred to the former, giving it the strength to grow in the future. Big stones can still play their part, as James de Givenchy attests, as long as they are used intelligently to achieve balance. The gratuitous use of gemstones can undermine the more intellectual appeal of well-crafted design. Intellectual currency is now a form of power, with influential collectors displaying their taste and knowledge in subtle ways to others who can read the signals; without this, we are transported back to an earlier age of pretty but pointless jewelry.

TWO

EAST MEETS WEST: CROSSING THE CULTURAL DIVIDE

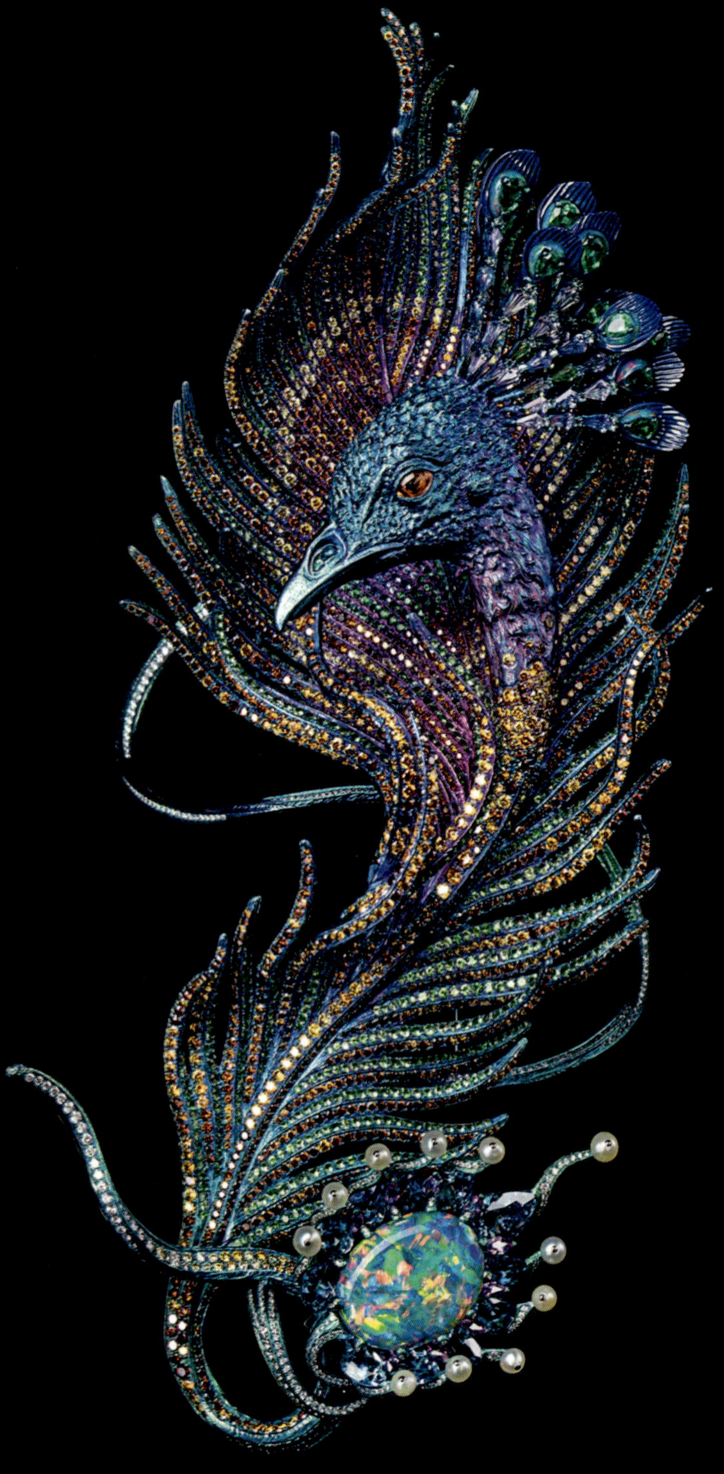

Wallace Chan
Hera Brooch and Ring, 2019
Aquamarines, black opal (14.64ct), crystal, emeralds, fancy-color diamonds, fancy sapphires, lapis lazuli, opals, padparadscha sapphires, and tsavorite garnets in titanium, and the Wallace Chan Porcelain

China's colossal buying power in modern times has seen taste in high jewelry around the world shift to accommodate jade, dragon motifs, and Chinese zodiac themes. Two new billionaires are created in China every week, and in the last twenty years Asian economies have enjoyed their biggest growth ever. Power in the West is dominated by the United States, which owns approximately one-third of the world's wealth. China and India combined have just over one-third and this affects how we consume jewelry. Aside from global taste-makers like Cartier or Tiffany, who have hundreds of stores around the world, many jewelers follow the money as they once did by travelling from royal court to royal court. Collectors from the East flock to Europe and North America from Taiwan, Singapore, Hong Kong, and Japan, expressing a voracious appetite for jewelry fueled by this new era of abundance. Asia's middle classes are rocketing in size, buying online and creating an entirely new digital powerbase that design houses are scrambling to accommodate. Out of this heady cocktail, a new generation of jewelry designer has emerged from the East, fusing Asian culture with Western art. This group is challenging the historic dominance of the French houses and in the process, for the first time in generations, inspiring students in their own countries to consider jewelry design as a serious career.

Europe's fascination with the East can be traced back to the time of the Venetian explorer Marco Polo, who in the late thirteenth century spent seventeen years in the service of the Chinese emperor Kublai Khan. Traveling on the emperor's business, he made arduous journeys along the famous Silk Road, the trading route linking East and West. Kublai had given him a golden tablet a foot (30 cm) in length, inscribed with the words "By the strength of the eternal heaven, holy be the Khan's name. Let him that pays him not reverence be killed." So, essentially, give him all the horses, food, lodgings, and help he needs or face the consequences. Armed with his golden passport, Polo went on many missions to places where no one had ever seen a Westerner. On his travels he acquired precious stones and gold—lapis lazuli and balas rubies from Badakhshan, Afghanistan; jasper and chalcedony from near the Taklamakan Desert in China. By the time Kublai eventually released him from service, he was a rich man.

When Polo's diaries documenting his travels and his time at Kublai Khan's court were published, they sparked a feverish curiosity in the West about the places he had seen. In the fifteenth century they even inspired Christopher Columbus to set out on his own epic journey to chart a maritime route to Asia. Columbus discovered the Americas by chance, but it was the outrageous wealth and extravagance of the East that had originally lured him onto the high seas.

In China, before the Cultural Revolution of the 1960s and 1970s banned the making and wearing jewelry, and in India before British rule introduced a taste for platinum and white diamonds, no other art form surpassed the scale and opulence of jewelry in those countries. Its decorative nature did not relegate it to a place below painting or sculpture, as eventually became the case in the West. On the contrary, its ornamentation was celebrated as another and equal expression of art. It was an essential part of everyday life whatever one's station, tied to everything from dowries to death rituals. Because of this connection to tradition, experimentation in terms of design was limited. From around the late twentieth century onward, Eastern jewelry designers tended to go West in order to take risks, because Western culture celebrated individuality. A unique vision was easier to get off the ground in the West and, in terms of creating art, that added a lot of value.

Cartier Paris
Tutti Frutti Strap Bracelet, 1925
Diamonds, emeralds, enamel, onyx,
rubies, and sapphires in platinum
Cartier Collection

Hindu Necklace, special order 1936,
altered in 1963
Diamonds, emeralds, rubies, and
sapphires in platinum and white gold
Cartier Collection

The French houses, however, are still fundamental to our understanding of high jewelry, and the most powerful of them all is Cartier. As one of the biggest jewelers in the world, it designs with impunity, seemingly unencumbered by market forces, so ingrained in luxury culture that its red leather box has become a rite of passage to discerning jewelry collectors. Cartier is itself described as a "living language" by Pierre Rainero, a jovial man fused to the house's monumental history by sixteen years spent as image, style, and heritage director. Cartier has a style and taste that resides in a dimension all its own, managing to combine the simplicity of universally lusted-after fine-jewelry collections, such as Trinity, Love, and Juste un Clou, with the drama of high jewelry commissioned by British queens and Indian maharajas. Yet Cartier was built from modest beginnings. Louis-François Cartier (1819–1904) took over Adolphe Picard's small workshop in Paris in 1847, but it was his three grandsons who sowed the seeds of a global brand: Louis (1875–1942), the creative force who from 1898 steered the overall vision from Paris; Pierre (1878–1964), an astute businessman based in New York; and Jacques (1884–1941), the affable charmer who built relationships within high society in London. The exquisitely detailed archive of images and sketches they built up still exists today for their workshop to reference.

In the late nineteenth century, the West was hungry for jewels with an exotic flavor. Just as Marco Polo's travels had done more than five centuries earlier, Japan opening its borders in 1853 sparked a huge interest in the East, creating opportunities previously unexplored. But it was India that ignited the magic of Cartier. In 1901, when the British court was in mourning for Queen Victoria, the new Queen, Alexandra, wife of King Edward VII and also now Empress of India, summoned Pierre Cartier to Buckingham Palace and asked him to make a necklace from existing Indian jewelry in the Royal Collection. It was Cartier's first commission from the palace and an early attempt at India-inspired design. The company, intoxicated by the spirit of creation, designed a necklace of seventy-one pearls, twelve rubies, and ninety-four emerald cabochons. In an age when most jewelers simply referenced the taste of the times, a "Cartier style" began to emerge, with an ornate Neoclassical gem-set design housing explosions of color within a sumptuous white-diamond landscape, sliding elegantly into Art Deco after the 1920s.

In 1909 Cartier moved its small London store into New Bond Street and opened a boutique on Fifth Avenue in New York City. At the same time, the Ballet Russes were captivating Paris with their combination of dance, music, set design, costume design, and performance that was often erotic, violent, and set in ancient worlds, such as Egypt and medieval Asia. The company's founder, Sergei Diaghilev, persuaded artists as diverse as Wassily Kandinsky and Pablo Picasso to contribute to his outlandish productions. Louis Cartier, inspired by the color and spectacle, began experimenting with color, mixing the blues of turquoise and lapis lazuli with the greens of jade, sapphires, and emeralds. Then in 1911 his brother Jacques traveled to India, where he attended the Delhi Durbar, a ceremony of accession for King George V as Emperor of India. During his visit, he sold jewels to a handful of maharajas and also bought stones, among them carved emeralds, rubies, and sapphires in a riot of color resembling boiled sweets; carved into the shapes of leaves, flowers, and fruits, they would form the basis of what was later dubbed Tutti Frutti designs that became one of Cartier's signature styles. These were both risky ventures: however fascinating the Eastern styles might have been, Europeans also considered them somewhat vulgar; no high-society lady would have worn them. Tutti Frutti was considered quite shocking by certain critics in the 1930s and even the color combinations were taboo. Mixing green and blue, originally a borrowing from Islamic culture, was seen as an affront to civilized society. The linking of red and black associated with the Chinese was also risqué, but Cartier persevered. Freeing Western society from the monochrome of platinum and white diamonds enabled the more adventurous in royal circles to wear new and exciting designs.

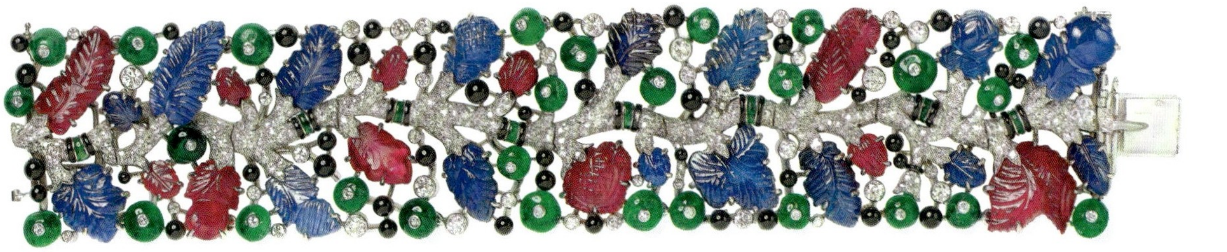

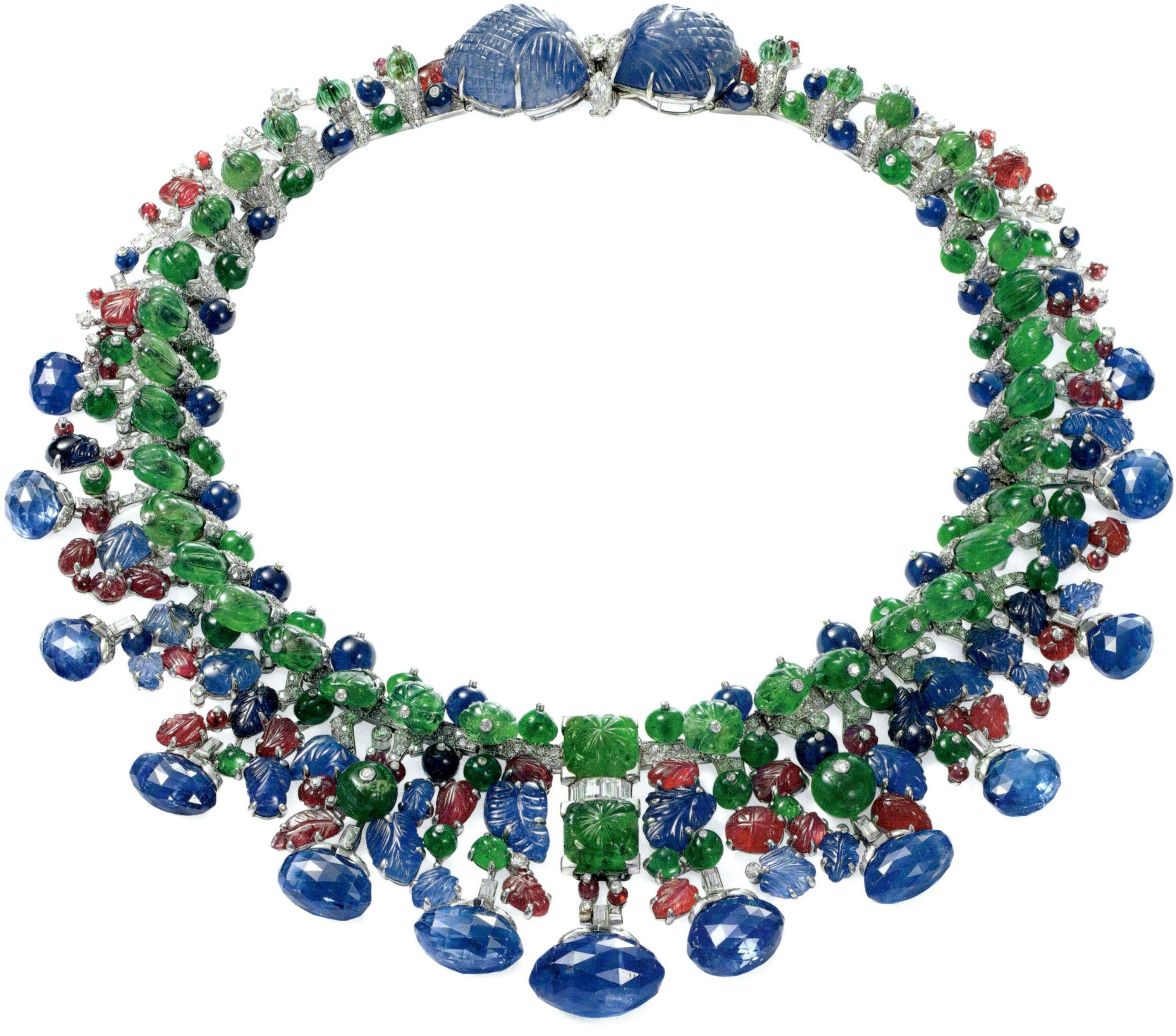

Cartier London
Design of a Ceremonial Necklace, 1934
Executed for the Maharaja Jam Sahib
of Nawanagar in platinum and diamonds.
In its center, the Ranjitsinhji diamond
(136.32ct) is combined with several
colored diamonds
Graphite, Indian ink, and gouache on
tracing paper
Archives Cartier, London

Necklace, special order 1932
Diamonds and emerald (143.23ct)
in platinum
Cartier Collection

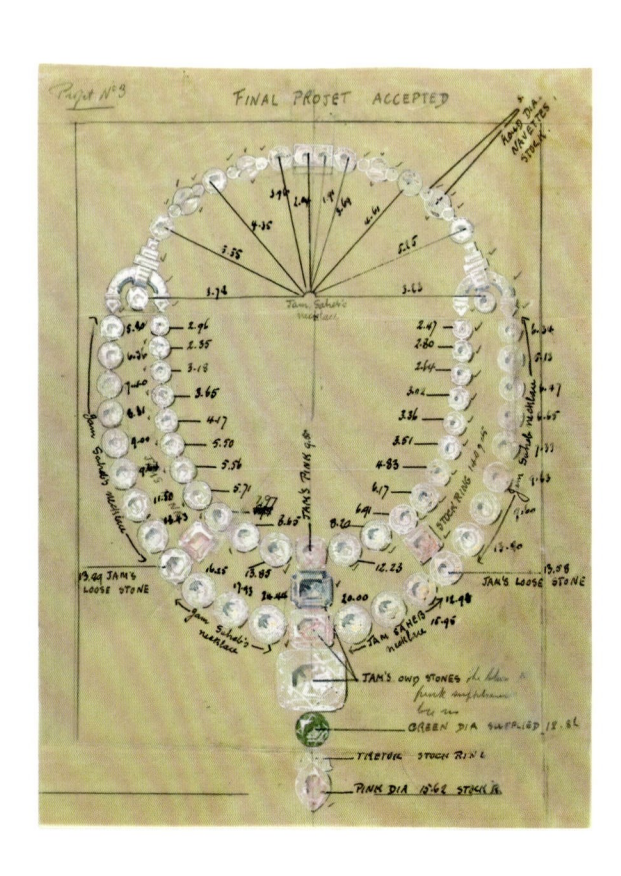

The Tutti Frutti tiara worn by the beautiful young English Countess of Mountbatten raised eyebrows in 1928, but by then a wave of Indian royalty had swept into Paris and London for their own taste of the brand. Maharajas would appear complete with large entourages carrying trunks of glittering stones to commission wildly ornate jewelry in the Cartier style. In 1928 the Maharaja of Patiala collected a necklace containing nearly three thousand diamonds, including a 234-carat yellow diamond center stone named the De Beers. It was Cartier's single biggest commission and had taken years of work. In 1930 the Maharaja of Nawanagar commissioned his own necklace, giving Jacques Cartier a 136-carat colorless diamond with bluish highlights to play with; it was named the Ranjitsinhji and to it were added pink, blue, and olive-green diamonds, creating a jewel the like of which the world had never seen. The brothers are thought to have made many of such necklaces in five years at the peak of Maharaja spending.

The Wall Street Crash of 1929 saw Cartier forced to create more affordable pieces and objets d'art, but by then the house had successfully seduced both sides of the globe, downsizing the color and extravagance of Indian style to suit Western taste and setting myriad white diamonds in white metal for Indian royalty, pushing style boundaries to new limits. "It's interesting to see that beauty is not an absolute term," says Rainero thoughtfully. "It is something that evolves with time."

Over in the United States, the other juggernaut of the history of jewelry, Tiffany & Co., had opened their first store in 1837, a decade before Cartier. American independence from Great Britain only sixty-one years earlier had meant severing the ties to European society, royalty, and design, so the new nation could craft its own identity. Tiffany's first day's takings were $4.98, but bigger things were to come. In 1862 President Abraham Lincoln bought a seed-pearl jewelry set for his wife for the princely sum of $530, giving the firm an important stamp of approval. Then, in a highly symbolic gesture, Charles Lewis Tiffany (1812–1902) bought nearly one-third of the French Crown Jewels at auction in 1887, outbidding former French royals who had been forced to give them up after the abdication of Napoleon III in 1870. Tiffany introduced the idea of high jewelry to North America during the Gilded Age (about 1870–1900) when rapid economic growth created a demand for extreme luxury. He sold jewels owned by Napoleon III's wife, the Empress Eugénie, to wealthy socialite Caroline Astor, and reset stones from other pieces into Tiffany designs for the new industrial billionaire class, rich from steel, oil, and railroad money. The Astors, Vanderbilts, and Rockefellers, with their vast fortunes and dazzling lifestyles, assumed an aspirational role at the pinnacle of American society.

A few years later Tiffany's head of jewelry design, an unassuming but brilliant designer, sculptor, and metallurgist called George Paulding Farnham (1859–1927), won a series of gold medals at some of the world fairs. He unveiled an exquisite collection of two-dozen hard matte enamel and bejeweled orchids in the "Orientalist" style—a Western interpretation of Eastern culture through art, literature, and design. His teacher and mentor Edward C. Moore, chief designer at Tiffany's studio, had an impressive Islamic and Asian art collection to which his apprentices had access and it was here that Paulding immersed himself. Although Tiffany became known for Art Nouveau-inspired design with subtle curves and lines—and for its trademark "robin's-egg blue" branding—Paulding's personal fascination with a more ornamental style influenced their early years.

By the 1920s the ornate and intricately decorative style of the Orient was giving way to modernism, which was cleaner and simpler, but Tiffany continued to bring elements of the exotic into their jewelry through stones such as morganite from Madagascar and tanzanite from the foothills of Kilimanjaro. Today these stones sit in a uniquely informal, laid-back style championed by Reed Krakoff, who was appointed in 2017 as Tiffany's first chief artistic officer. They are worn on leather instead of the stiff platinum of old. "One of the first pieces of jewelry I made was a circular pendant in diamonds and aquamarine hung on a leather cord knotted at the back," Krakoff says.

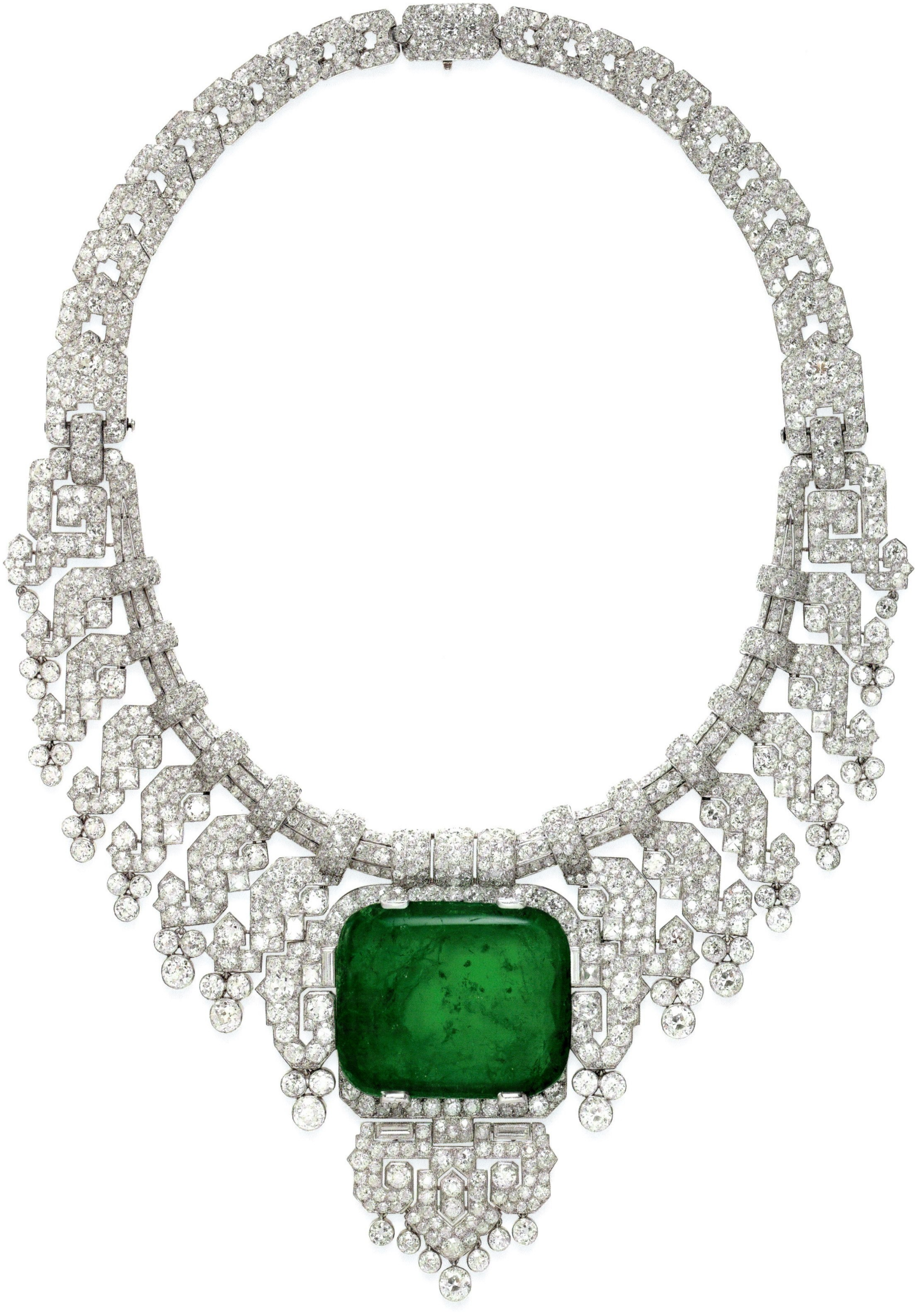

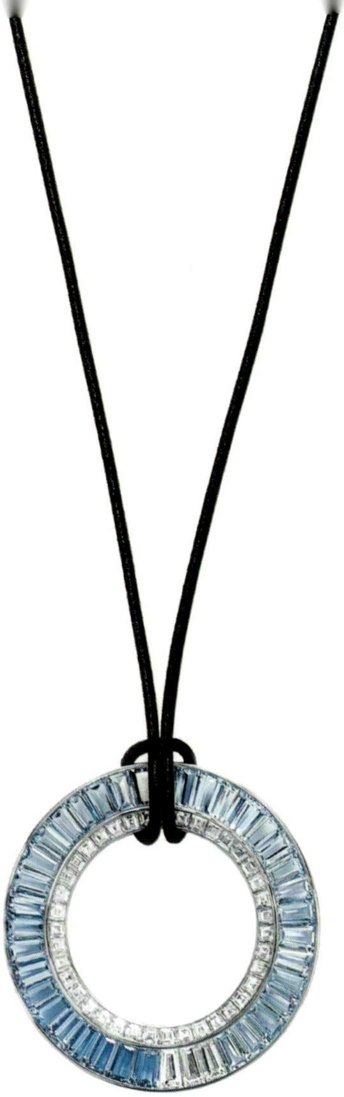

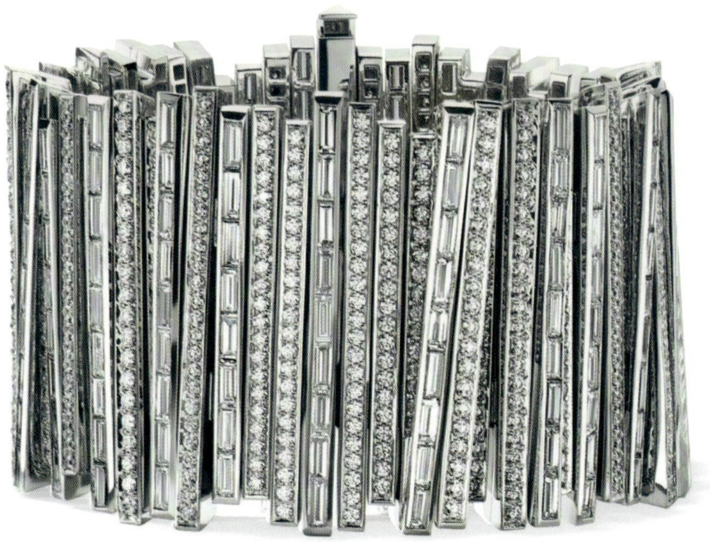

Reed Krakoff for Tiffany
Pendant, 2018
Aquamarines and diamonds in platinum
on leather cord
Private collection

Bracelet, 2018
Brilliant white, rare fancy blue-gray,
and gray diamonds in platinum
Private collection

(Following pages)
Bvlgari
Cinemagia High Jewellery Necklace
Diamonds, coral, emerald (11.14ct),
mother-of-pearl, and onyx in gold

Heritage Necklace, c.1970
Diamonds, emeralds (Main: 300.84ct),
and rubies in gold

EAST MEETS WEST

With such pieces selling for six-figure sums, some of his colleagues thought he had lost his mind, but Krakoff felt the world had changed, with the Astors of today wanting discreet luxury they can wear with a white T-shirt and jeans. Krakoff makes sensual and informal jewelry in a world where every possible style and taste is already catered to twenty-four hours a day. He can't be seen to be favoring one country over another, however powerful it may be; his vision must strive to express American culture to the world. China has eclipsed India in terms of international jewelry consumption since the days of the maharajas, but the economic might of both countries has been instrumental in bringing incredible jewels to the world at a scale previously unimagined outside royal circles. "The biggest challenge is to stay relevant," explains Krakoff, mindful of the difficulties that steering a business turning over $4 billion a year brings.

Another way to stay relevant is to find a niche and make it your own. The Chinese have a passionate connection to color based on a traditional system called the Theory of Five Elements, which encompasses everything from mythical animals to the seasons. According to this theory, every color has its own significance: black is associated with water, green and blue with wood, red with fire, yellow with earth, and white with metal. Yellow is traditionally the imperial color, representing the best of everything life has to offer. Red symbolizes good fortune and is deeply ingrained in Chinese identity. In order to communicate with Chinese collectors, Western jewelers have to see color theory from a Chinese perspective. For Italian house Bvlgari, China is the biggest market and color is key to understanding their needs, according to Mauro Di Roberto, managing director of Bvlgari's jewelry business. "We represent the spirit with color," he says. Bvlgari has a history of combining an array of odd, intensely colorful stones in its extravagant style to create a look that is purely Italian, purely Roman, yet exotically alluring to the East. Their red, black, and green collar from the 2019 Cinemagia collection (see p. 62) is classic retro Bvlgari, but with an Eastern color palette.

Rome, its history, and style are at the heart of Bvlgari. As "a museum under the sky" and a city saturated in beauty, it was forged from far-flung cultures when, during its heyday two thousand years ago, the Roman Empire ruled over most of Europe, the Middle East, and North Africa. Jewelry, adopting the styles of these conquered nations, was high octane, expressing the boldness of Roman power. It was this cultural melting pot that gave birth to the flamboyance of modern Italy. When Sotirio Voulgaris (1857–1932), the firm's founder, moved from his small Greek village in Epirus to Naples in 1879 and opened his first small store in Rome five years later, he was part of a much bigger history than he may have recognized at the time. He initially sold silverware, accessories, and the odd jewel, but his sons Costantino (1889–1973) and Giorgio (1890–1966) really developed the jewelry side of the business.

In the 1940s Bvlgari—a Latinized version of the founder's name—rejected the French style that was prevalent at the time and combined a Greek and Roman classicism to dramatic effect. In the 1970s the world fell in love with long, chunky gold necklaces studded with colored stones, and the Bvlgari style naturally reached its zenith, becoming internationally known. Bvlgari may not go in for innovative materials, such as titanium, but they do take risks with stones and have since the 1920s used semiprecious gems, such as turquoise and amethyst, in their high jewelry. Jade, a stone with a fanatical following in China, was barely given a glance in the West, but Bvlgari now adds it to its collections, earning the attention of an increasingly sophisticated Chinese audience.

The flamboyance of Bvlgari has had a profound affect on other important designers, such as Fawaz Gruosi, the Lebanese-Italian founder of jewelry house de Grisogono (see pp. 112–13, 116) who worked at Bvlgari before starting his eponymous brand, and Viren Bhagat, the Indian master jeweler who produced work in the Bvlgari style early on in his career. Bhagat was on vacation with his family in Rome in the 1980s when he stumbled across a large cabochon sapphire in the window of Bvlgari's flagship store. He was already a fourth-generation

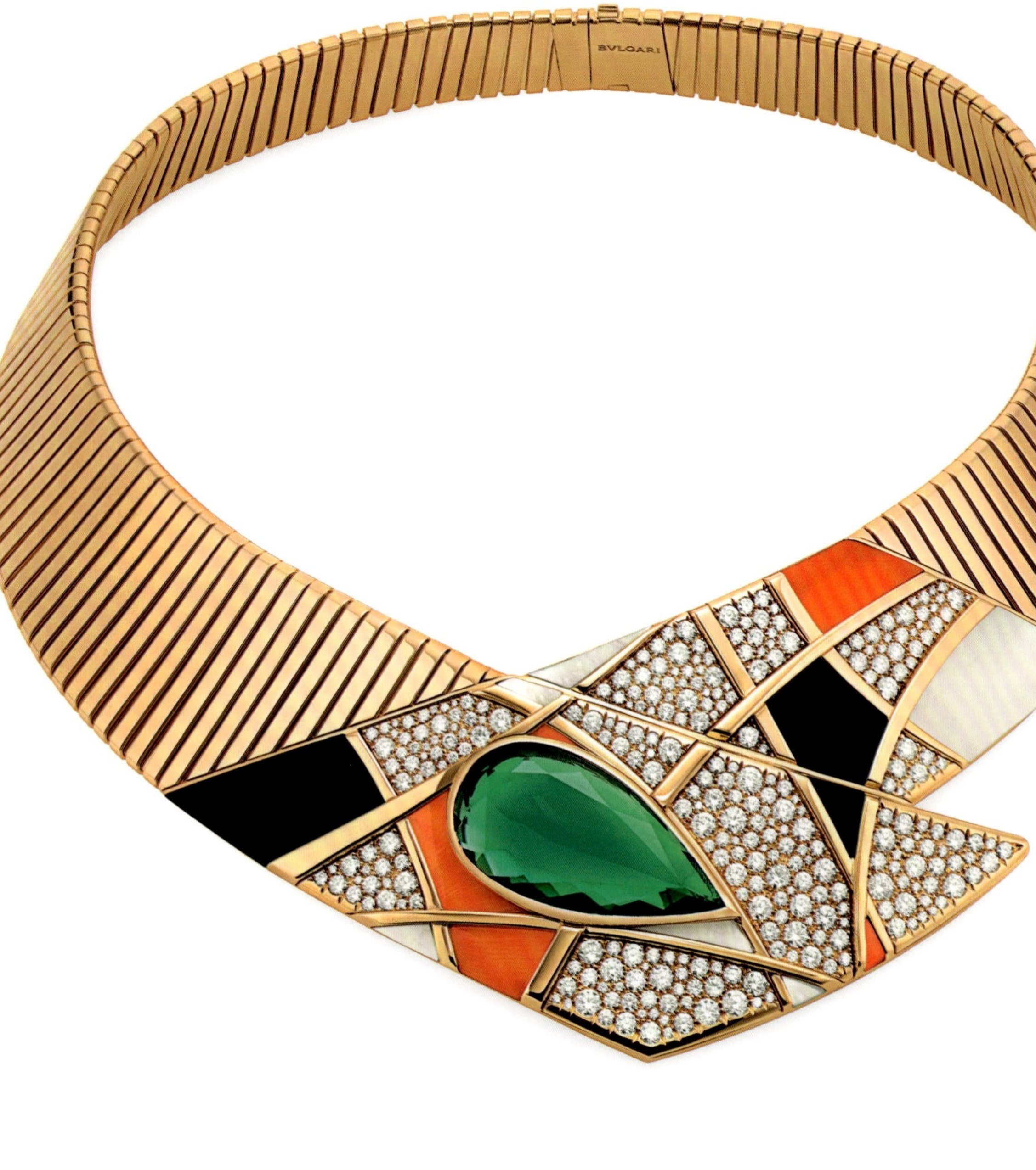
BVLGARI

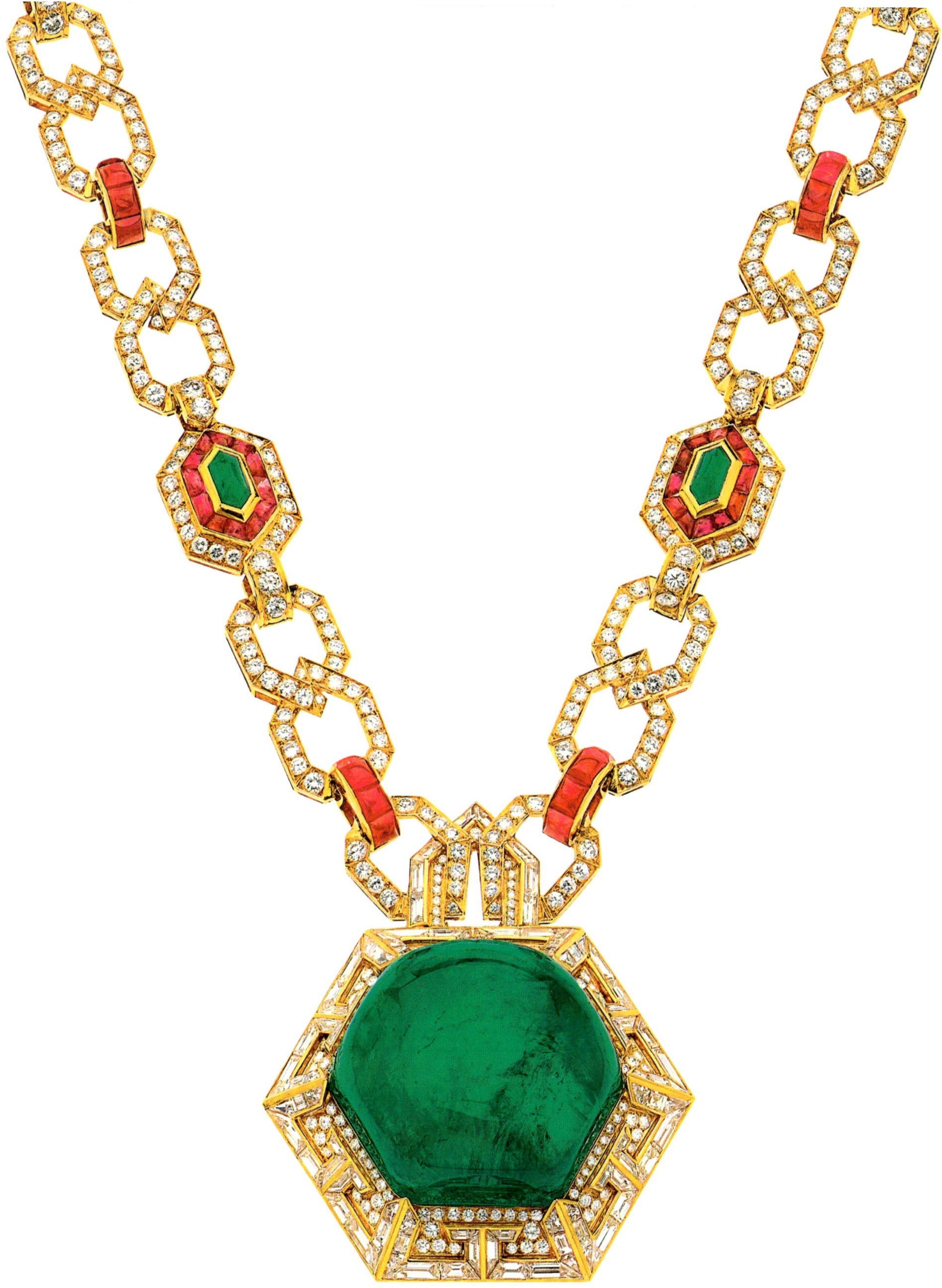

jewelry designer and what he lacked in formal training he made up for in a singular determination to evolve jewelry in India. He was so inspired by the beauty of Bvlgari that, when he got back to Mumbai, he began to draw jewels, sending the sketches to Gianni Bulgari—Giorgio's son and by this time head of the firm—who offered him a job. But Bhagat was consumed by the art rather than the business side of jewelry; he needed the freedom to create unencumbered by someone else's vision, so he declined the offer and instead decided to open his one and only store at Kemps Corner in Mumbai in 1991.

It was from there that he changed the course of Indian design history. Sidestepping the customary heavy yellow gold, he embraced white diamonds wrapped in the slimmest of platinum settings in a delicate combination of Art Deco and Mughal design. Art Deco was in his blood: it was in the mid-century furniture he had sat on as a child, the opulent buildings he had walked past on the way to school, and the house he had lived in. After Miami, Mumbai has the second largest collection of Art Deco buildings in the world and this seeped first into Bhagat's subconscious and then into his work. "The last Renaissance that one saw in jewelry design was during the Art Deco period," he says thoughtfully. "Almost a hundred years since then I see that same renaissance today."

Bhagat operates in a culture with a deep and complex love of jewelry that is connected to every element of daily life. On a spiritual level, Hinduism advises the wearing of jewelry as a tribute to the divine within and it is offered at the feet of the gods in temples. The gems Bhagat uses are old school—natural pearls, rubies, emeralds, diamonds, spinels, and even sapphires, which in India are considered so powerful, so full of spiritual energy, that they need to be diffused with other stones, and many jewelers won't work with them. Instead of using technology or odd materials to make his mark, he reinvented and refined the Indian aesthetic itself. He has now started to take tentative steps toward China, adding jade to his restricted palette and exhibiting his work alongside the spectacular Al Thani collection in the Forbidden City in Beijing. His sons have joined the business and are challenging him creatively, but at the heart of his genius he's still a ten-year-old boy soaking up the Art Deco splendor of downtown Mumbai. Bhagat's jewels often reference traditional Indian motifs, such as the champakali, a flower that blooms from the champa tree and is thought to ward off evil spirits. His natural saltwater pearl and old European-cut diamond necklace pays tribute to this in a modern but thoroughly Indian way. He has a tendency to swing between classical and modernist design with a grace that is both effortless and masterful, as in his sapphire-and-diamond ring with beads that open at the back. The Bhagat style, however, is unequivocal in all its forms.

The most magnificent jewelry in history often starts from humble beginnings. Leading the march toward art in jewelry from China is a deceptively modest yet unrelenting force of a man called Wallace Chan, who creates innovative materials and combines them with Chinese mythology. Born in 1956 to a family of modest means in Fuzhou, Chan relocated to Hong Kong at the age of five. He left school at thirteen to help out financially and by sixteen had become a sculptor's apprentice working on religious objects. After studying Western art he opened his own workshop in 1974, where he was free to experiment with materials, and after thirteen years his first invention, "The Wallace Cut," was born. This involved carving a single human face inside a gemstone using 360-degree intaglio to create multiple reflections, so that from the back, front, and sides four faces can be seen (see p. 66). To stop the stone from cracking under pressure, he does the carving underwater using a modified dentist drill. Chan believes that gemstones contain the wisdom and memories of the earth and the face he created is a ghost, his own spirit trying to escape into the stone. It is a concept that baffled many in the West not used to seeing Zen Buddhism explained through the prism of high jewelry.

Chan went from sculptor to jeweler when art collector Yih Shun Lin persuaded him to make a stupa or religious shrine containing Buddha's tooth for a temple

BHAGAT
An Important Natural Pearl
and Diamond Necklace, 2019
Diamonds (Main: 17.73ct) and natural
saltwater pearls in platinum

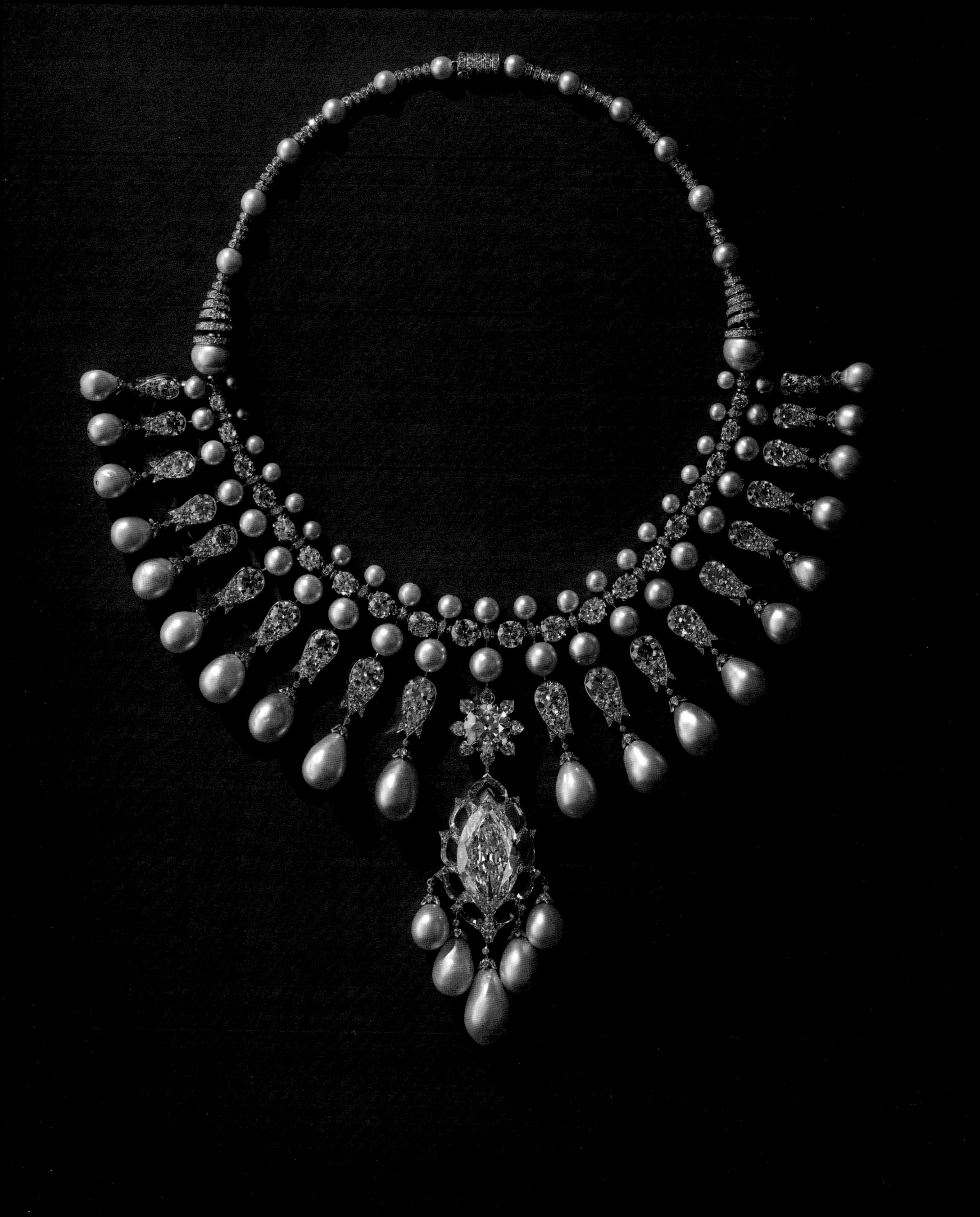

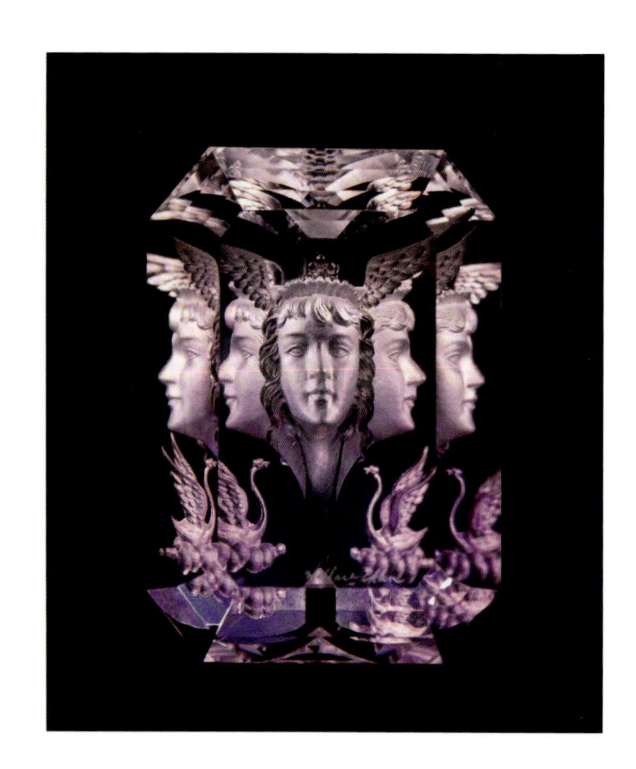

Wallace Chan
The Wallace Cut, invented 1987
Amethyst

The Unknown World Earrings, 2019
Diamonds and yellow diamonds,
pink and multicolored sapphires in
titanium, and the Wallace Chan Porcelain
Private collection, London

Butterfly Nebula Brooches, 2018
Amethysts, diamonds and yellow
diamonds, pink sapphires, rubies,
and tsavorite garnets in titanium
Private collection, Hong Kong

in Taiwan. He had to learn stone-setting techniques and his perception shifted to the miniature universe of the jewel. Combining this with Buddhism put him on the path to making jewels as a bridge to higher meaning within Chinese culture. In 2002 he patented a technique that allows him to refine jade to an almost translucent thinness, but his masterstroke was in replacing gold and platinum (as the base metal of his work) with titanium, which has one-fifth of the weight and enabled him to create large-scale sculpture to embrace the body. He played with the material for eight years, carving it using diamond drills, experimenting with color by sending an electric charge through electrolyte liquid, and setting titanium with stones. The results are spectacular in both tone and composition. His Water Lily Light ring is carved turquoise titanium within which nestles a square pink diamond. The petals of this flower unfold to reveal white diamonds edged in yellow with deep blue tips. In simple gold it might have been garish, but titanium is more understated and makes an entirely different visual statement.

Chan enjoyed challenging both the physical limits of titanium and our understanding of it as a material. Titanium in turn propelled him onto the world stage and into Europe, where he was the first Chinese jeweler to exhibit at art fairs, such as at the Biennale des Antiquaires in Paris in 2012 and TEFAF Maastricht in 2016. His most recent invention is porcelain five times stronger than steel, which he fires at between 2,800 and 3,000 degrees Fahrenheit (1,550–1,650°C) when the maximum temperature is usually 2,550 degrees Fahrenheit (1,400°C). "When traditional materials cannot fulfill my creative spirit, I start searching for new ones," he says. "When I cannot find the right material it is a form of depression, of pain." Two German manufacturers turned that misery to joy when they agreed to build him special ovens to create his new porcelain. He needed them custom built so that he could control and stabilize the heat in a process that requires absolute precision in both temperature and purity of ingredients. Porcelain also shrinks when it is being fired, so Chan places tiny porcelain beads under each piece as a cushion. He carves the results to his exacting specifications until a silky smooth, opaque finish provides the settings for stones of his choosing.

What makes Chan more than an inventor and alchemist is symbolism. He infuses his creations with meaning so layered that it takes patience and a willingness to see the world within an Eastern context to truly understand them. His porcelain, for example, is an attempt to connect the Chinese back to their roots. Two thousand years ago the first pieces of primitive porcelain came to life in China and 1,200 years of evolution saw it eventually replace jade for everyday use, because jade was considered the most precious and valuable of stones. White jade was loved for its translucence and seen as a vessel for spirituality: when light passed through it, some of that light remained in the object, symbolizing serenity. This reminded the owner that to be calm and courteous was a virtue to aspire to in everyday life. Attempting to imitate the tone and emotion associated with white jade, the Chinese developed porcelain into an art form, calling it "white gold." From the time of the Sun dynasty (third century AD) onward, they painted it with beautiful scenes, eventually inspiring admiration in the West, where myriad cheaper copies called "China" were produced.

Porcelain's value has been largely forgotten in modern life except for a few pricey antiques from the Qing dynasty (1636–1911/12). Chan wanted to give new life and value to a material buried deep in the Chinese consciousness and, as with the relationship the Chinese have with jewelry, he is trying to revive a lost art. The Theory of the Five Elements means that everything feeds into the Chinese understanding of beauty and balance. Chan ponders a considerable number of elements when making a piece of jewelry and often revisits pieces years later to make changes until he is satisfied. This makes finishing anything somewhat challenging, but the results have changed the perception of jewelry and his work sells privately for vast sums of money. His Great Wall necklace of imperial jade and diamonds went for $73.5 million in 2012 and his jewels regularly breach the

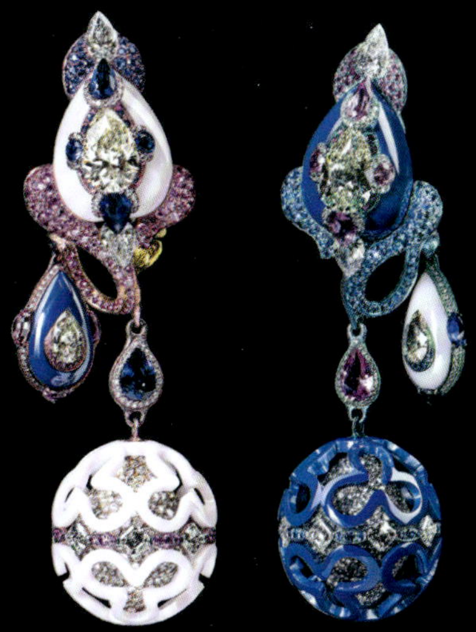

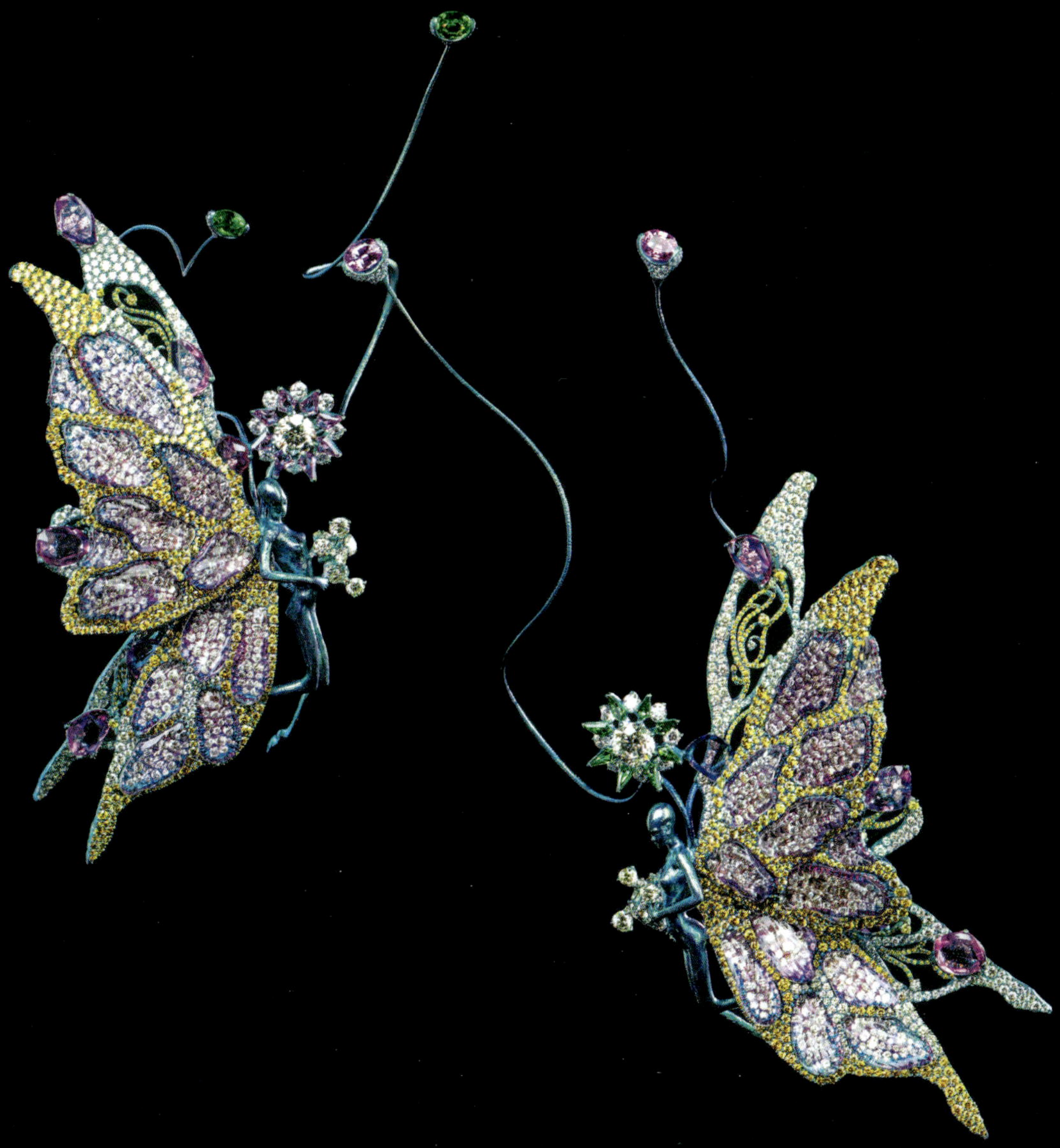

Moussaieff
High Jewelry Earrings, 2019
Colombian emeralds (6.04cts)
and diamonds in white gold

High Jewelry Flower Earrings, 2018
Diamonds and yellow diamonds
in white gold

million-dollar mark. The Legend of the Jade Dragon brooch at €4.5 million and Butterfly Nebula brooches at €1.6 million are recent examples. The Butterfly Nebula consists of twin titanium brooches and imagined cosmic entities from outer space that Chan envisages living four thousand light-years from the earth. Their wings are translucent slices of amethyst atop stone pavé edged in white and yellow diamonds, their antennae tipped with pink sapphires and green tsavorites. Their companionship and freedom celebrate the universe's infinite possibilities.

Chan makes fifteen to twenty jewels a year. "In the past two hundred years there has been a void in Chinese jewelry development. Nothing has really happened," he laments. Grinding poverty meant that for many jewelry was an unthinkable luxury. Then two decades ago, as wealth increased, the Chinese turned to the West for reassuringly expensive adornment as a means to express their newfound financial freedom. As their appetite grew, so did their knowledge and sophistication, but something was missing. Jewelry with auspicious meaning connecting to ancient tradition has a special place in the Chinese psychology. It must protect the soul and promote harmony as well as enhance the wearer physically. "Art can be anywhere and can be anything," Chan says. For him it can be a feeling, a chair, a sculpture, or a jewel, as long as it has meaning.

Before China became all-powerful in the market, the oil-rich nations of the Middle East were courted and lusted after for their extravagant tastes and deep pockets. As a region it has some of the richest and poorest nations on the planet. Qatar is a tiny country occupying less that 5,000 square miles (13,000 square km) but it has wealth beyond equal in gas and oil, making its population staggeringly rich. The similarly wealthy Kuwait, United Arab Emirates, Saudi Arabia, Bahrain, and Oman sit alongside Syria and Yemen, whose economies have been ravaged by war. Other small but wealthy nations, such as Brunei on the island of Borneo in the South China Sea, have also traditionally bought some of the biggest diamonds and most elaborate designs. The Sultan of Brunei was the world's richest man with an estimated fortune of $40 billion until Bill Gates of Microsoft outearned him in the 1990s. Gates, however, didn't shower his wife with pink diamonds: this penchant for multimillion-dollar shopping sprees is one of the things that sets the Eastern oligarchs apart from their Western counterparts. They have the money and they aren't afraid to spend it. This taste for the best stones and most audacious jewelry was cultivated hundreds of years ago in places such as Bukhara, an ancient city now in Uzbekistan. Known as the "shining pearl," it was a key destination along the Silk Road, where gem traders from Persia, India, China, and Russia would rest between journeys through the desert, enjoying the local culture while they traded. Moussaieff, a London-based design house famed for its enormous, high-quality diamonds, opened it's first London showroom in 1963, but the family have their roots in in Bukhara and had been trading stones for eight hundred years along the silk route. This deep history in the East connects present owner Alisa Moussaieff to her collectors in a cultural as well as an economic sense. Her father-in-law Rehavia Moussaieff, a stone dealer in Paris during the flamboyant 1920s, sold rare stones and pearls that he sourced in the Gulf to houses such as Cartier. Today giant Paraíba tourmalines, intensely purple sapphires, and natural Colombian emeralds as well as showstopping diamonds are the company's stock in trade.

Traditional wedding jewelry is of phenomenal importance in the Middle East, and for fifty years Moussaieff have created whole suites of jewels for dowries, merging dynasties together. Setting a fifty-carat sugarloaf Burmese sapphire as blue as the ocean into a ring with no distracting diamonds slapped on either side is a lesson in sublime restraint. The stone becomes everything, and leaving it alone takes as much experience and self-control as wearing it artfully. Taste, however, is changing. "People in the East would previously have gone for very discreet pieces and this has definitely shifted. They are going for larger, more conspicuous items, not necessarily of the same quality," Alisa Moussaieff observes. Younger spenders don't always want discretion and the vast wealth

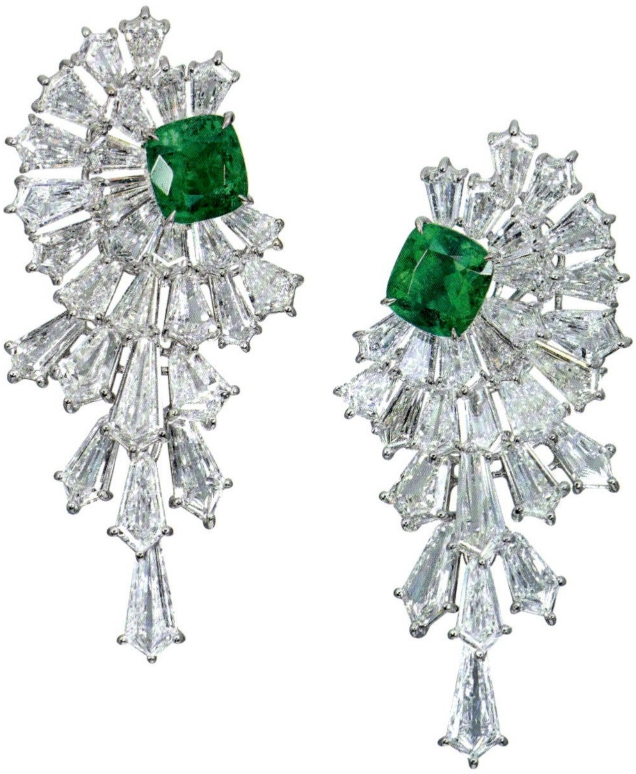

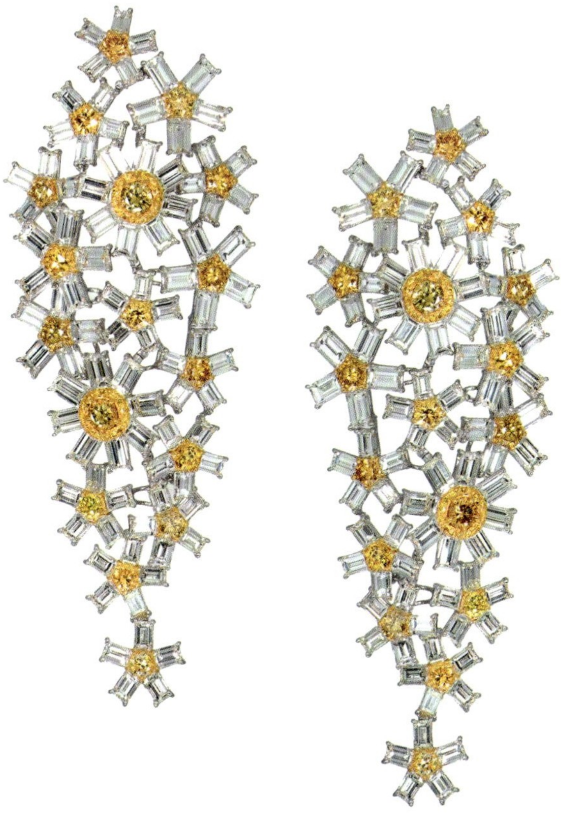

Joseph Chaumet
Study for a Leaf Tiara, c.1890–1900
Graphite pencil, ink wash, and
gouache highlights
Chaumet collections, Paris

François-Regnault Nitot
Wheat-ear Tiara, c.1811
Diamonds in gold and silver
Chaumet collections, Paris

Scott Armstrong for Chaumet
Vertiges Tiara, 2017
Citrines, diamonds, emeralds, green
beryls, green tourmalines, and yellow
garnets in rose and white gold
Chaumet collections, Paris

that courses through the East now means millennials don't have to wait until they are in their fifties to buy.

The Japanese, on the other hand, have always had deep reserves of elegance and self-control on which to draw and in jewelry lay great emphasis on the miniature and on high quality. Smaller gems housed within intricate, complicated design in materials such as coral, turquoise, agate, ivory, and pearls are mentioned throughout history. Although it is doubtful that Marco Polo ever made it to Japan, his diaries describe walls there gilded with gold and pearls everywhere the eye could see. Japan was an entirely closed society at that time, operating as a feudal system run by a military government. It wasn't until the Tokugawa shogunate opened its borders to the West in 1853 that the country experienced sweeping social, economic, and political modernization, enabling it to compete with and gain the respect of the Western world. This sparked a stampede for Japanese art and iconography in the West, with jewelers and couturiers creating collections in homage. Chaumet, the Parisian high-jewelry house, has a style that resonates with Japanese culture: a juxtaposition of lightness and strength, delicate design combined with intricate stonework.

Marie-Étienne Nitot (1750–1809), who founded Chaumet in 1780, had first been apprenticed within the court of Louis XVI and Marie Antoinette; later, after the French Revolution had abolished the monarchy and had the king and queen executed, he became official jeweler to Napoléon Bonaparte, reportedly earning his place at court by saving Napoleon from a renegade horse. Napoleon declared himself France's first emperor in 1804 and, with most of the former Crown Jewels having been broken up, destroyed, or sold, he adopted two new crowns. One was a more traditional affair in the medieval style, called the Crown of Charlemagne, and the other made of golden laurel leaves in reference to the Roman god Apollo. In Roman tradition the laurel wreath symbolizes triumph in battle, but in Nitot's hands this jeweled metaphor for monarchical power evolved into a tiara. A semicircle to be worn high up on the head or lower down on the forehead, often in gold and smothered in diamonds, the tiara became inextricably linked to Chaumet. In one example produced for Napoleon's empress Josephine in 1811, ears of wheat were depicted in windswept silver and diamonds to stunning effect. Wheat, a symbol of life and of both physical and spiritual nourishment, is a recurring theme in the sixty-six thousand sketches and paintings in Chaumet's archive. Leaves looped in classical circles painted in soft gouaches are also

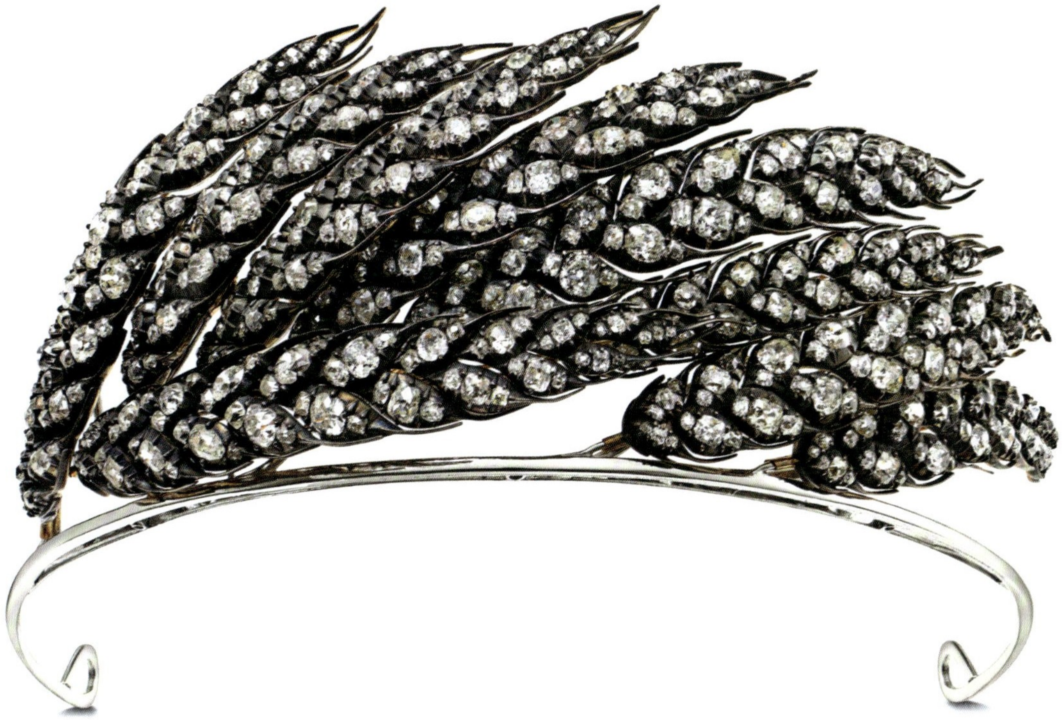

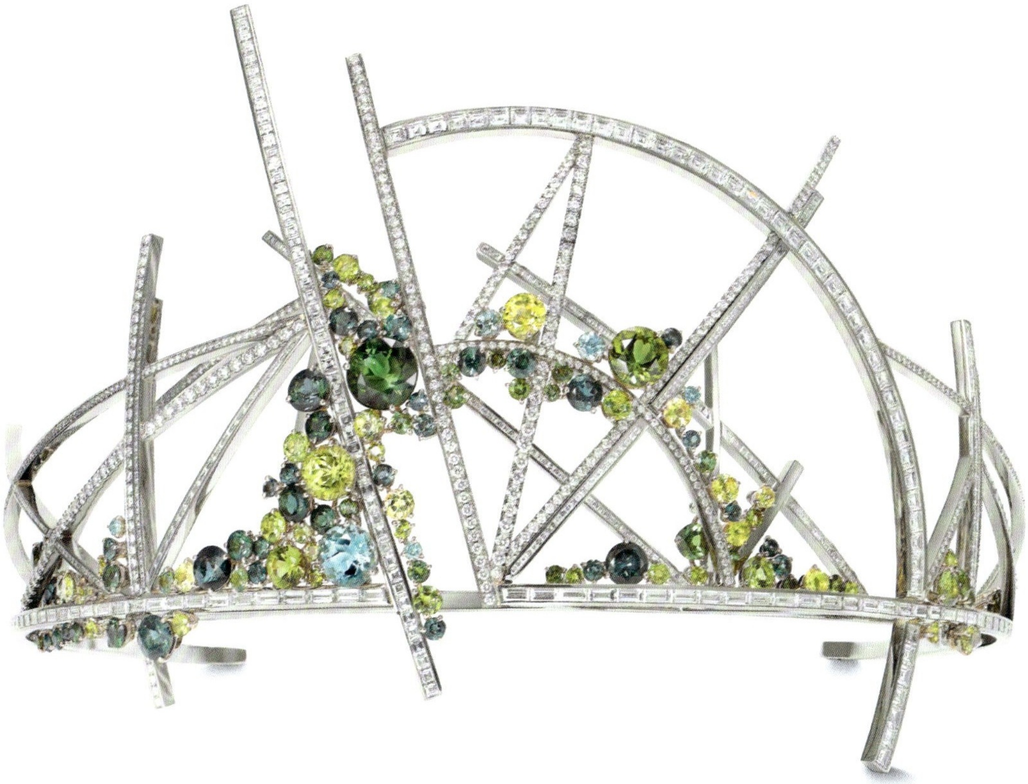

part of the 240 years of tiara history at the house, spanning 3,500 creations. For the modern age, strong geometric lines studded with gems appear as the Vertiges tiara (see p. 71) designed by Scott Armstrong, a student from Central Saint Martins in London who won a competition to create a twenty-first-century diadem for Chaumet, which they presented in 2017. Armstrong spent a year working on the piece, contemplating how it might fit into contemporary culture yet still represent the attributes of power, nobility, and beauty that have come to be associated with the Chaumet tiara. He took inspiration from formal French gardens and eventually beat eight other finalists with his graphic, structural diamond framework supporting free-flowing clusters of tourmalines and garnets.

Just as Paris went crazy for the tiara, relishing the democratized crown, so Asia, Chaumet's biggest market today, enjoys the romanticism of French history. For Japanese women who historically have worn jewelry in their hair and on the head instead of on the body, the tiara makes perfect sense. Or, as Jean-Marc Mansvelt, chief executive officer of Chaumet, puts it, "Napoleon encircled his head with a tiara. The implication was unmistakable as an object of social distinction." The combination of grace and glamour has ensured that Chaumet's modern-day crown can assert power beyond the confines of traditional royalty.

The newly powerful Asian jewelry collector now visits the Place Vendôme in Paris as a must-see destination to understand and connect with French heritage through its jewelry. Paris still has some of the best workshops in the world, clustered around stately high-jewelry houses, such as Chaumet, Boucheron, Mellerio, Cartier, and Piaget. Van Cleef & Arpels has been at 22 Place Vendôme since 1906 and, while it has always served an international clientele, with Indian, Russian, Middle Eastern, American, and, of course, French customers knocking politely at its door, the Chinese market has become increasingly important over the last fifteen years. There may be a temptation to add a Chinese tiger or a smattering of jade to new collections, to pander to the phenomenal wealth offered, but Nicolas Bos, president and chief executive officer, is made of sterner stuff. "We can pay tribute to their culture, but simply adding a red dragon isn't going to work," he says. Opportunism isn't enough.

Collectors from the East want Van Cleef & Arpels to provide artistry they cannot get at home, essentially heavy-duty French opulence. The Van Cleef & Arpels Mystery Set technique, patented in 1933, is a typical manifestation of what Louis XIV's finance minister Jean-Baptiste Colbert was trying to achieve back in the 1600s, when he created a network of guilds tasked with producing the most lavish and extravagant haute couture, of fabrics, furniture, and jewelry imaginable. Expertly cut rubies are slipped into gold rails one by one like a jigsaw puzzle, covering the entire surface of a design so that no metal is visible. The effect is sumptuous, almost velvety, and was inspired by Roman micromosaics where whole landscapes were constructed from tiny pieces of glass but from afar were sleek enough to look like paintings. The light and shadow of Van Cleef & Arpels's Chrysanthemum clip in rubies and diamonds gives it movement beyond the often rigid way in which nature is portrayed in jewelry. Flowers such as this were a favorite theme and were presented to an astonished audience at the 1937 Exposition Internationale des Arts et Techniques dans la Vie Moderne de Paris. Leaves in the shape of ivy, sycamore, and holly were then introduced during the 1940s and 1950s. The unusual technique caught the eye of the Duchess of Windsor, a high-profile collector of French design, and she suggested a new creation called the Zip necklace, which came to life in 1950 as one of Van Cleef & Arpels's most iconic productions: a real zipper cast in gold or platinum with beaded gemstone tassels, placed around the neck or on the wrist in a design that had taken years to perfect.

It is this blend of style, technique, and identity that creates desire over and over again for each new generation visiting Paris. Van Cleef & Arpels were one of the first French brands to settle in Japan in 1974, then opened in China in 2005 and, while their presence in Asia was crucial to sparking awareness of their work,

Van Cleef & Arpels
Zip Antique Transformable
Necklace, 2012
Coral, diamonds, emeralds, rubellites, and sapphires in gold

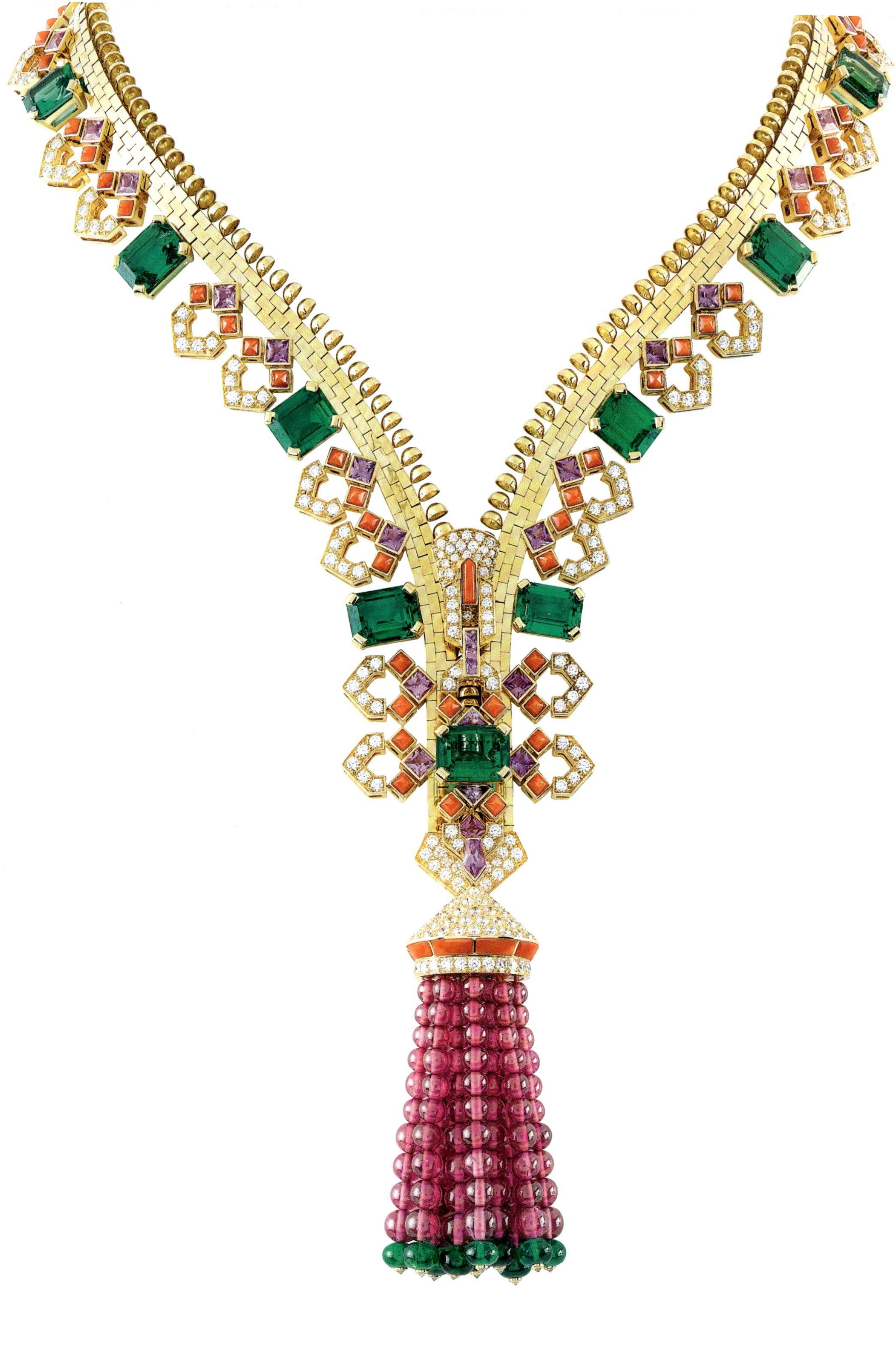

Van Cleef & Arpels
Pylones Clips, 1939
Sapphires in gold
Private collection

Vagues Mystérieuses Clip, 2015
Diamonds, Paraiba tourmalines, and
Mystery-Set™ sapphires in white gold

there are broader changes at play that have seen their prominence grow in the East. Museums, such as the Musée des Arts Décoratifs, have exhibited their work as art, the Internet has given them a much wider reach, in 2012 they opened a school that teaches hard-to-access elements of jewelry design, and major fashion houses, such as Chanel and Dior, have seriously entered the high-jewelry arena, bringing with them a whole new client base that goes on to buy from other houses. Better understanding of jewelry has resulted in more interest and higher prices at auction, not just for historic stones but also for design. "Collectors are now fighting over Cartier and Van Cleef like they would fight over an Impressionist painting," muses Bos. The Asian market is even buying estate or preowned jewelry when before it wanted only new.

The cycle of ever-increasing demand has Asia at its center but the size and stability of the American market as its foundation. Economically, high jewelers, such as Van Cleef & Arpels, need both to survive and to ensure long-term planning and investment. Asia is the rocket but North America is the launchpad. The respect Asia has for decorative art is something from which the West can learn. The sheer beauty of the Pylones ear clips in Mystery-Set sapphires or the Vagues Mystérieuses clip, is an undeniable force in the war for that respect and Van Cleef & Arpels are very much on the front lines.

As a result of jewelry's ever-growing allure, a sprinkling of Chinese designers are settling on hallowed ground in and around the Place Vendôme. Born only in 1985, Feng Ji shouldn't be selling high jewelry to collectors with a taste for fantastically rare and expensive gems, but she is. Her youth and shy charm hide the steely core needed to penetrate the inner sanctum of French high jewelry. The Place Vendôme is a brutal lesson in survival of the fittest, especially for outsiders, and her jewelry house was established only in 2016—without a dragon in sight. Feng J's great-grandfather was a painter for the royal court during the closing stages of the last imperial Chinese dynasty, the Qing (1644–1911). She herself was sent from China to Europe to learn about art and fell in love with modernism and Impressionism but also with the work of Chinese-French painters Zao Wou-Ki, a master of abstraction, and San Yu, a figurative specialist and calligraphy expert. Pointillism, the method of applying colored dots of paint to canvas to create scenes and abstract form, is reflected in her work alongside the romantic contours of Chinese watercolor. She avoids Chinese motifs, however, preferring the freedom of modernism and abstraction. Her Yellow Ginkgo Leaf brooch (see p. 76) is a combination of white diamond droplets splashed around yellow sapphires and set into eighteen-carat gold. The double rose-cut of the sapphires adds a soft glow that diffuses the harder glint of the diamonds. This is a bespoke technique created by slicing a stone into slithers about 1/32 inch by 1/16 inch (1 mm by 1.5 mm) and applying rose-cut facets on either side to catch the light. "Painting with stones to create jewelry as contemporary art is my motive," she explains—a statement that is borne out by her series of Dragonfly brooches, their haphazard wings a delicate testimony to the bizarre beauty of insects as they buzz about in nature. She is also fond of brooches inspired by the deep greens of lily of the valley, a poisonous but fragrant woodland plant, or, in the piece Cloud Atlas (see p. 76), the watery blues of the planet. The watercolor paintings she creates as the foundation of her work are as exquisite as the jewels themselves.

Feng J is one of a new generation of Asian designers challenging the stranglehold that Europe has over high jewelry and she is doing it from within, using the best of Parisian workshops to express her vision. When Western jewelers piled into China in the early 2000s, they reignited a passion for jewelry that Feng J's generation are now realizing by either buying, wearing, or creating their own. "Chinese jewelers need to understand the Western rules and codes in terms of taste and trends to get inside," she says. "Then we can turn our Oriental essence into form." The recognition that comes with an address on Place Vendôme opens doors, but sales are the real test. Feng J's clients are like her— young and selective with a truly global outlook. The Western media are only too

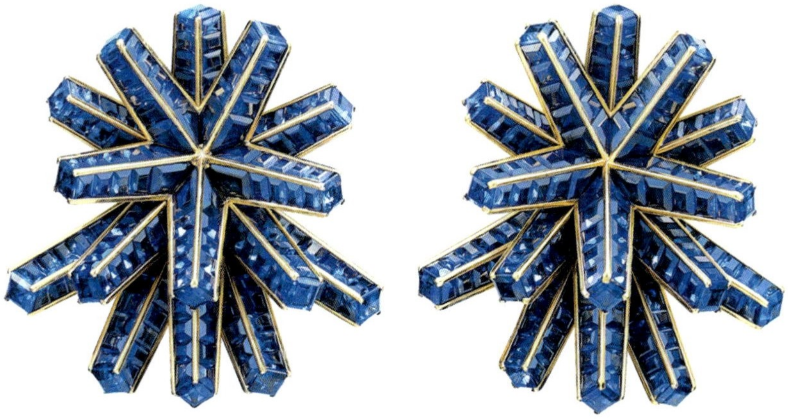

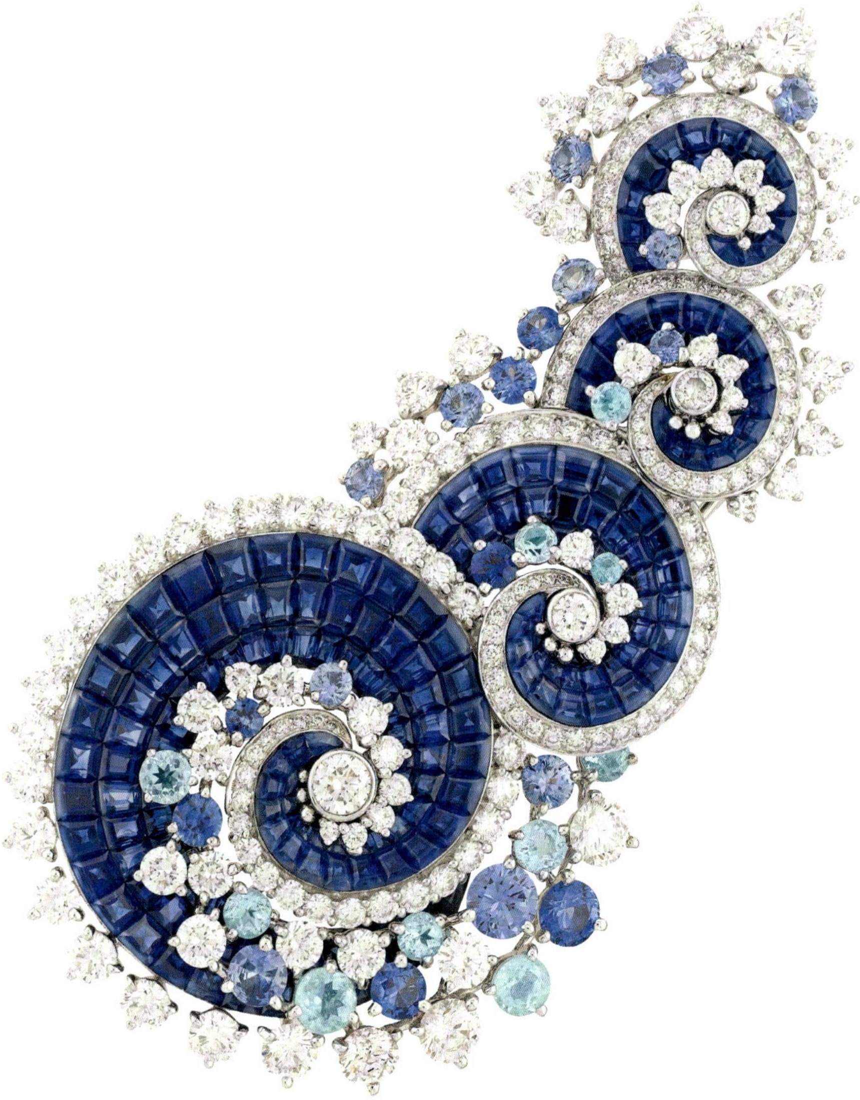

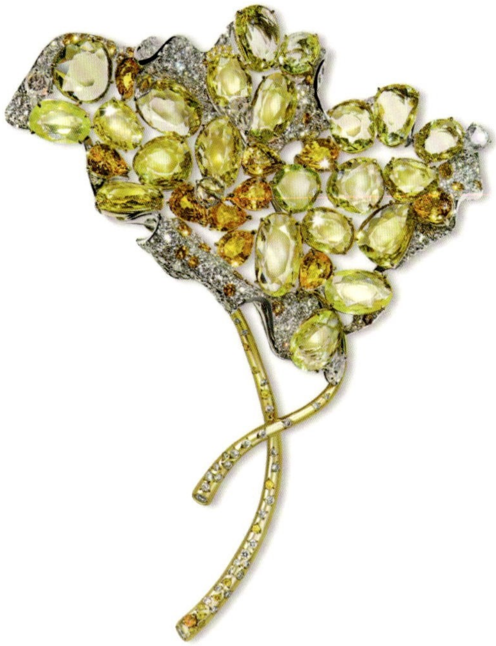

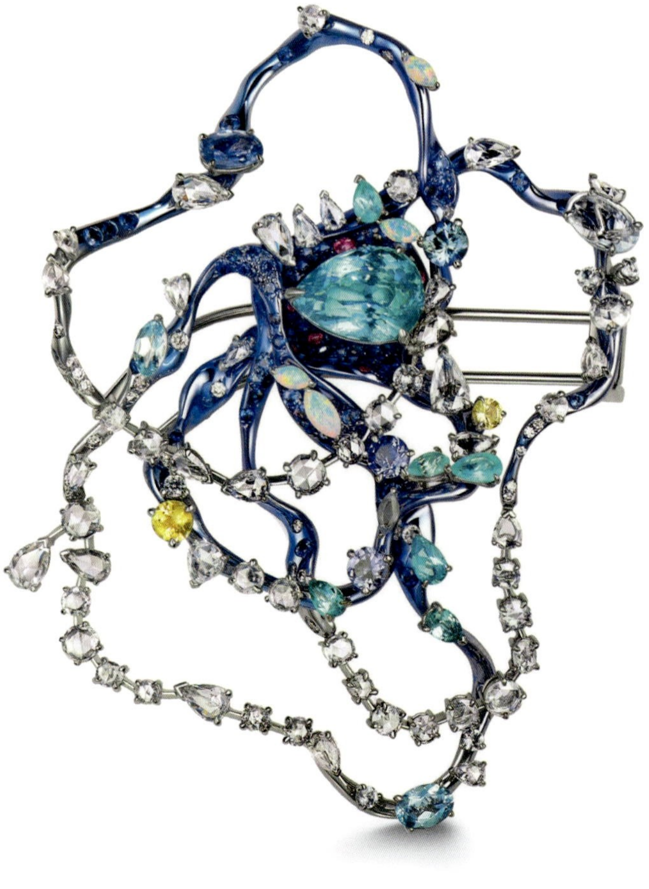

Feng J
Yellow Ginkgo Leaf Brooch, 2018
Diamonds and yellowish and orange sapphires in gold

Cloud Atlas Brooch, 2018
Diamonds and yellow diamonds, fancy-colored sapphires, Paraiba tourmalines (Main: 5.25ct) in electroplated gold

happy to rerun the "five best designers coming out of China" idea, and breaking out of that format to enable her work to stand on its own will be the challenge. She is right at the beginning, but her presence alone signals a crucial shift.

Jewelry can express power but it can also provide escape, either bringing peace from the harsh realities of World War II, as it did for Yasuki Hiramatsu in Japan (see pp. 18–19), or defying evil, as when Suzanne Belperron outmaneuvered the Nazis in wartime Paris (see pp. 31–33). In 1986 an eleven-year-old boy was plotting his own escape from a war-torn country. Born in Vietnam in 1975, Nghi Nguyen was one of the eighty thousand refugees to immigrate to Australia with his family after the nineteen-year Vietnam War. Life there was challenging. Until the 1970s Australia had banned any immigration from outside Europe, making integration tough for a brown kid with no English. Nguyen spent a lot of time drawing and taking solace in his own secret world, obsessed with Japanese manga and science fiction. After graduation he moved to Tokyo to create accessories for fashion designer Vaughan Alexander, then in 2003 to New York at the behest of eminent stylist Patricia Field. After night courses in metalsmithing and jewelry design he became head designer at Alexis Bittar, creating elaborate costume jewelry before finally taking the plunge with his own NN collection.

Nguyen's work, with its gothic, edgy, futuristic, and weathered architecture in blackened bronze, palladium, silver, and gold, is far from the sparkly glitter of Alexis Bittar. His Borg headdress with matching armor sleeve is futuristic in Ruthenian bronze and black onyx. His Wings of Desire mask and collar, also bronze, are jewels for modern-day warriors. He calls them artifacts from a different galaxy, excavated for the curious jewelry lover who is drawn to the unknown and the alien. Adhering to the Japanese concept of *wabi-sabi*, Nguyen embraces roughness, imperfection, and the idea of serene melancholy or, as he puts it, "a gentle darkness." His childhood in Vietnam was filled with temples, shrines, goddesses, and deities and there is something otherworldly about the twenty pieces of jewelry he produces each year. Having lived in both the East and the West, Nguyen is philosophical about life, viewing the surge of Asian wealth as part of a bigger cycle where East propels West and vice versa, infinitely. "I feel like the West is all about visual impact on the outside, which is very ostentatious. The East is more about discreet beauty and it's more about the self—the inside," he says. His ideas of East and West are not purely geographical: they also reflect opposing elements within us all. On some days he wants visual drama, on others discreet beauty. The trick is to find balance.

For Nguyen the value of jewelry lies in the art rather than the materials. He would like to see a "spiritual revolution" to pave the way for deeper meaning instead of increased consumption as the market's driving force. The rise in technology brings with it a society that is speeding up, which exhausts designers and manufacturers and affects quality. "We need to shift to a more conscious economy," he says passionately, to combat the waste of energy and resources that has sucked the joy out of creating for many designers who are constantly under pressure to produce more. The emphasis on profits is detrimental to peace of mind, so he consults on the side for design companies in New York, thereby removing any pressure he might feel to sell and avoiding the treacherous path of commercial jewelry. Again, it is all about balance and finding joy in creation through learning, which takes time. As an artifact, a jewel represents the very essence of humanity on earth at this moment, the achievement via technology of our creative spirit. Nguyen's cyborg-style pieces demonstrate that jewelry doesn't have to be elitist or impenetrable. His high jewelry is anything but.

Neha Dani, a designer based in New Delhi, is another whose childhood upheavals had a profound impact on her future. As a child she left her sleepy hometown of Coimbatore in southern India to go traveling with her parents, who believed that experiencing the world firsthand was the best education they could give her. Visiting top-class museums around the world in the 1980s and 1990s, Dani felt a sense of wonder during those formative years when her notions of art and design were developing. When she was eleven, her father built a community center in memory of his mother that won awards for its architecture; she knew then that whatever she did had to push past the ordinary and be bold and new.

Despite her parents' innovative approach to child rearing, Dani was still expected to finish her studies, find a nice boy, and settle down. She had other ideas, however, and instead went to the Gemological Institute of America in southern California to study. There she discovered titanium, using it to sculpt intricate stone-incrusted, one-of-a-kind pieces. This was a supremely odd choice for a designer operating from a culture where gold is still king, but she was entranced by its lightness and the freedom that gave her to express herself creatively. She still works with gold in pieces such as her Nerida ring, using more traditional white diamonds set in white gold, and the Vaneesha necklace, which is a cacophony of sapphires, opals, Paraíba tourmalines, and tsavorites in rhodium-plated gold. The weight of gold often imposes limits to the size of a piece—too heavy and it becomes uncomfortable to wear for long periods of time—so working in both gold and titanium gives Dani flexibility. Her pieces play with exquisite detail as designs develop organically. She likes to have fun with color, which injects energy into her work. In terms of production, she makes everything by hand and works with a team of wax carvers in India before bringing her jewels to life in Hong Kong, Bangkok, and Italy, finally selling mostly from the Macklowe Gallery on Park Avenue, New York. "As a culture we can't think without jewelry," she says, although India isn't quite ready for high jewelry in titanium, even if it is slowly accepting the fact that design can rival intrinsic value. The auction house Sotheby's included her work in a recent selling exhibition and that is indicative of how the market is changing. Especially for independent designers who have neither the means nor the inclination to create a global chain of stores, art galleries and auction houses are becoming the new storefronts for high jewelry, selling across continents and styles to established art collectors. Dani moves effortlessly between East and West with an Indian sensibility wrapped in a Western-flavored design. As India and China become more accepting of new forms of jewelry, designers such as Dani are able to benefit, bringing more variety to the landscape of design.

Apart from bringing to our attention artist jewelers who otherwise might remain unknown to the wider world, the auction houses provide a benchmark for value through high-profile sales. In the arms race for larger and more outrageous hammer prices, Asian designers are selling incredibly well. A platinum, diamond, and thirteen-carat ruby ring by Viren Bhagat went for $10.5 million in 2017 at Christie's Hong Kong, where Edmond Chin's 120-carat Burmese ruby necklace had sold for $13 million two years earlier. With Christie's in Geneva in 2013 the Taiwanese designer Anna Hu fetched $4.5 million for a fifty-eight-carat Burmese sapphire brooch called the Cote d'Azur. While jade is still popular and large, rare Burmese rubies are part of a growing hunger in the East for colored stones that reflect a time-honored love for intensely colorful design.

Sales above the $3-million mark are still relatively rare for contemporary female designers and Hu reached this pinnacle after only six years in the business. But then again, by her own admission, she is building an empire. In the process she has taken inspiration from two very different mentors. The first was the composer Ludwig van Beethoven, whose "Ode to Joy," the fourth and final movement of his *Ninth Symphony*, forged while he was ill, in great physical pain, and also deaf, was arguably his most magnificent gift to the world. Hu aims to bring to jewelry what Beethoven gave to music. She was a child prodigy and an accomplished cellist, and music still infuses every element of her design.
"I see gemstones like a melody, they come from the same root," she explains. Her parents are both gemstone specialists, so in between practice sessions she would play with diamonds on the "bling bling table" in their sorting office next door. Jewelry was, therefore, a natural progression when she stepped away from music as a career.

Vaneesha "Queen of the Universe"
Necklace, 2019
Blue and purple sapphires, diamonds, Paraíba tourmalines, tsavorites, and water opals in anodized titanium and gold

Neha Dani
Nuray "Bright Moon" Ring, 2019
Blue and purple sapphires, diamonds, and Paraíba tourmalines (Main: 9.33ct) in anodized titanium and gold

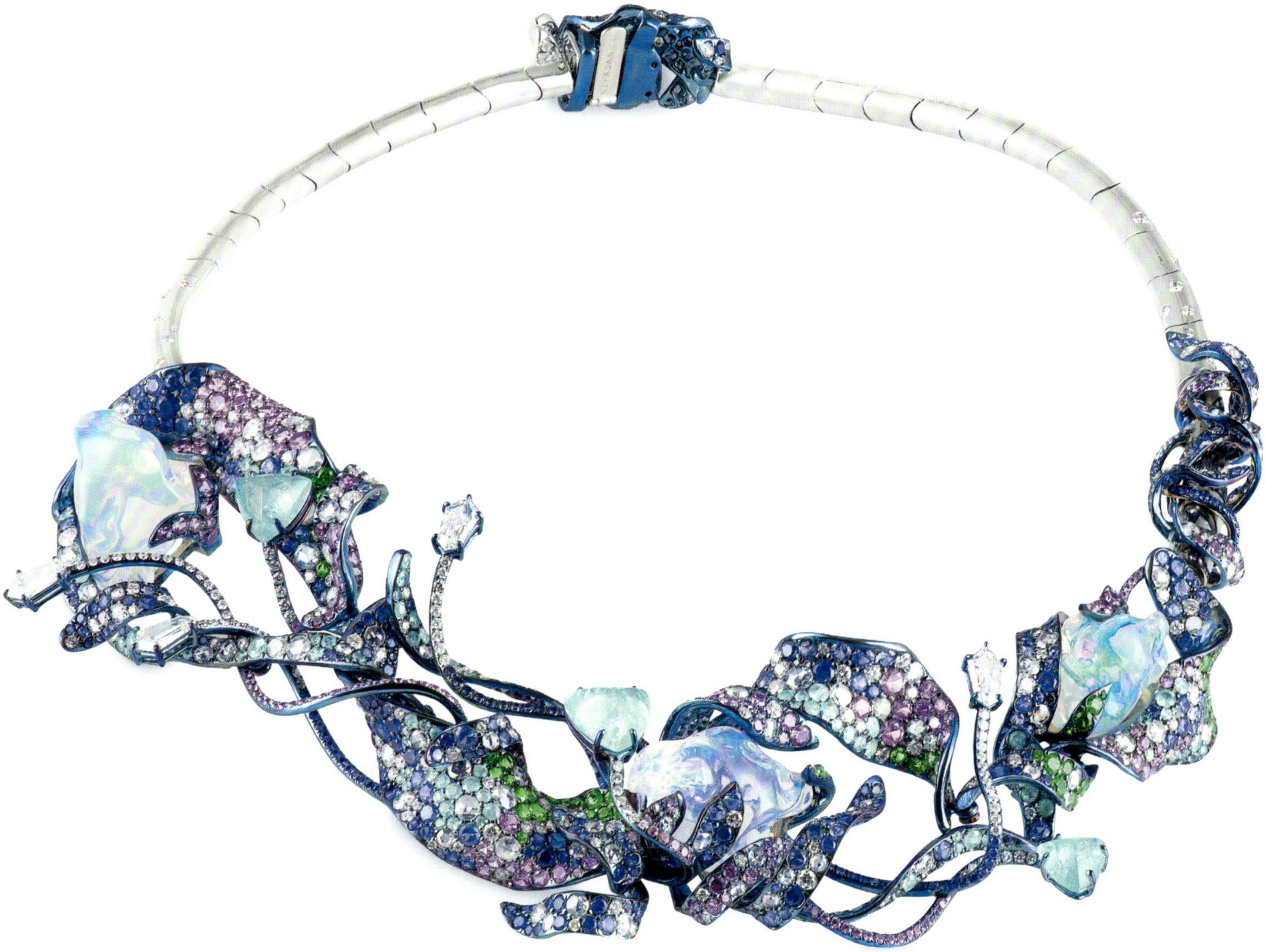

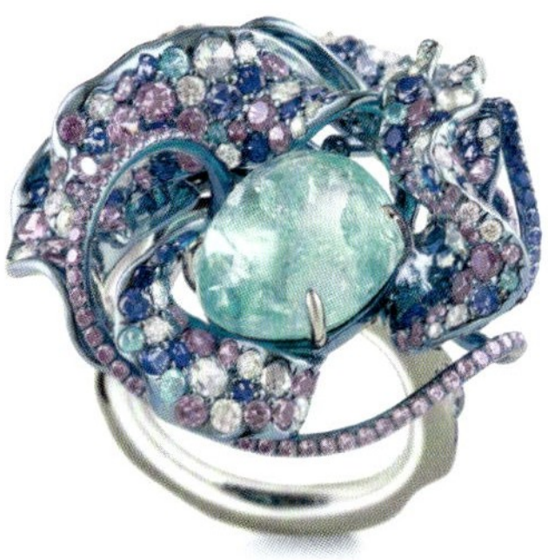

Anna Hu
Rainbow Chrysocolla Butterfly Brooch/
Pendant, 2017
Diamonds and rainbow chrysocollas
(90.04cts) in titanium and white gold

(Following pages)
Anna Hu
Enchanted Orchid Bangle, 2016
Demantoid garnets, diamonds and yellow
diamonds, and green, pink, and purple
sapphires in titanium and white gold

Red Magpie Brooch II, 2017
Colored, pink, and purple sapphires,
diamonds, natural conch pearl with
distinct flame structure (5.145ct), onyx,
and rubies in rose, white, and yellow gold

Her second mentor was a man called Maurice Galli, who ran Harry Winston's design department when she was working there and who urged her to leave her comfortable job in the merchandising department to create her own jewelry house when she was thirty years old. By this time she had studied art history at the Gemological Institute of America, interned at Christie's, and worked for Van Cleef & Arpels before settling at Harry Winston, which represented long-term security. She was listening to Wagner and drinking a little too much red wine with Galli when he asked her why she was working for someone else. He wanted her to take the chances he never had. "He always had to express someone else's creative ideas instead of his own," she reminisces. "He told me not to be a caged bird, to fly if I could." That was a seminal moment in her life; a year later she opened her first boutique at the Plaza Hotel in New York. She now sells from Paris, New York, Hong Kong, and Taipei.

Hu's jewels are romantic, classical, curvaceous, oversize, and intricate. She has created a magical fantasyland of stylized flowers carpeted in diamonds, butterflies, and birds that feels entirely Eastern. She believes that being Chinese in the sometimes stuffy world of high jewelry is actually an advantage in the West, as collectors seek her out for a taste of the exotic. Her clients are a complete mix, hailing from countries as diverse as Lebanon, Mexico, South Africa, Russia, and Morocco. "I don't really design pieces just for the Chinese culture," she says. In a sense she herself is the Chinese element in her work; as Chinese culture becomes more powerful in the world, there is more desire to own a piece of it, either consciously through the cicadas of Wallace Chan or more subconsciously via the oriental flavor of one of Hu's dancing butterflies.

While Paris has been the epicenter of high jewelry for centuries, the Jura mountains in Switzerland have been the equivalent in the watchmaking world: a place where long nights and deep winters have encouraged farmers to make high-precision watch movements. Piaget, a Swiss high-jewelry and watchmaking company, began life in 1874 when nineteen-year-old founder Georges-Édouard Piaget (1855–1931) was already assembling complicated watch mechanics for other brands; in 1945 the family set up their own local manufacture as part of a mission to create the thinnest watch of all time. The now legendary 9P Calibre was exquisitely slender at about $\frac{1}{16}$ inch (just 2 mm) and this freed up enough space on some of their watches to add elegant stone slices in place of the dial, in lapis lazuli, tiger's eye, malachite, opal, jade, turquoise, coral, ruby, and onyx. These in time became elaborate cuff watches in twisted, textured gold, or pendant watches set with diamonds, which eventually morphed into high jewelry. "Piaget created watches that became jewelry and jewelry that became watches," says Chabi Nouri, today's chief executive officer. They merged the two before the 1960s made it common practice to do so, unveiling their first jewels in Geneva in 1959.

Delving into the art of jewelry came next—in 1967, when Piaget collaborated with Salvador Dalí on a collection of beaten gold jewels featuring gold coins minted by the artist, who inscribed them with his and his wife's portraits (see p. 84). Some were used to disguise watch dials or suspended from bracelet watches on chains, but a handful became double-sided pendants decorated with eggs and laurel leaves in what grew into an extension of Dalí's Surrealist art. Three hundred years earlier King Louis XIV had created similar coins called *louis d'or*; in homage Dalí called his *Dalí d'or*.

In the last twenty years Piaget's interest in the boundary between art and design has won them a strong following in China, where they have 257 points of sale. The dense color of their stones juxtaposes the grainy texture of warm yellow gold in a calling card the Chinese find hard to resist, even if it is Swiss instead of French. The Chinese market is fast moving and tech savvy and Piaget communicates its modern codes of design in innovative ways, unusual in an industry still clinging onto bricks and mortar. It went live on a WeChat store in 2018 by creating a boutique within China's most popular messaging app to

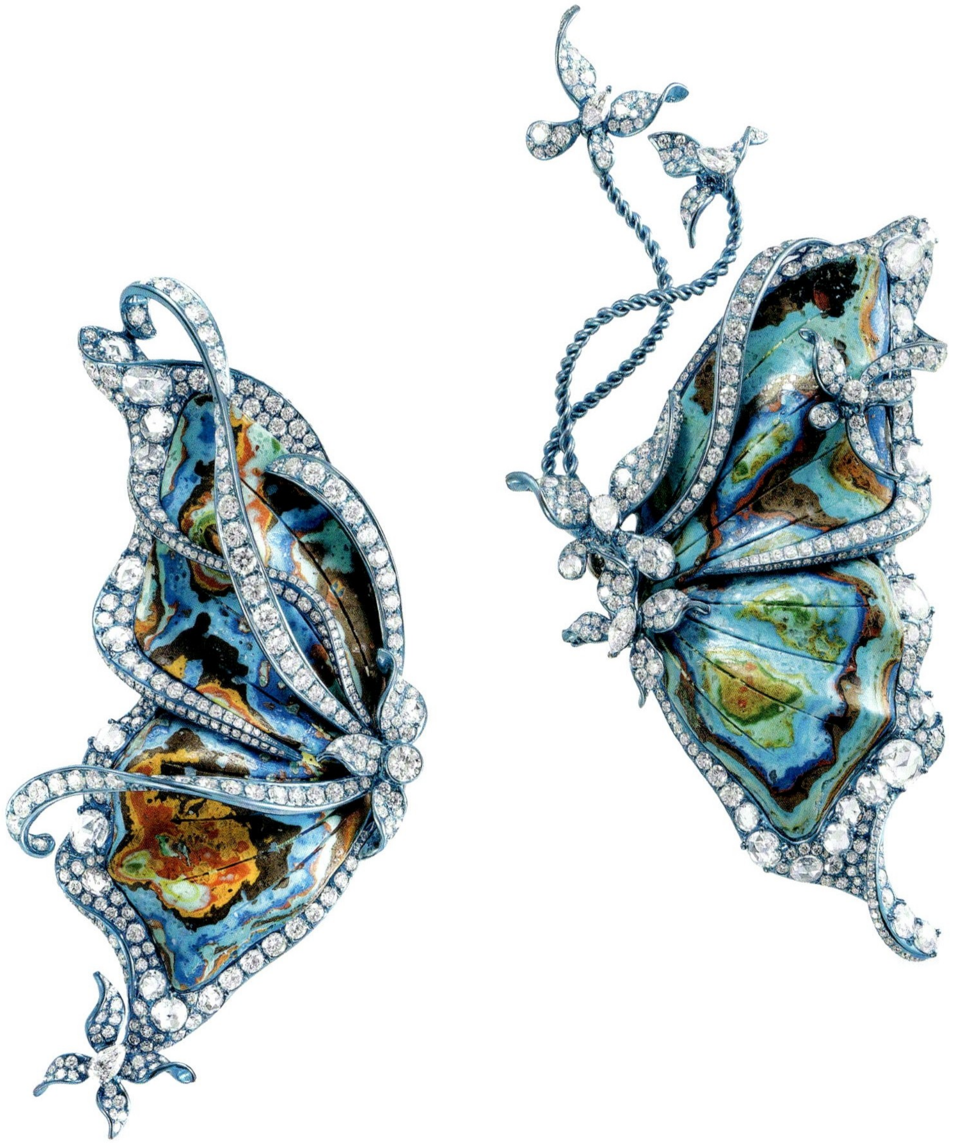

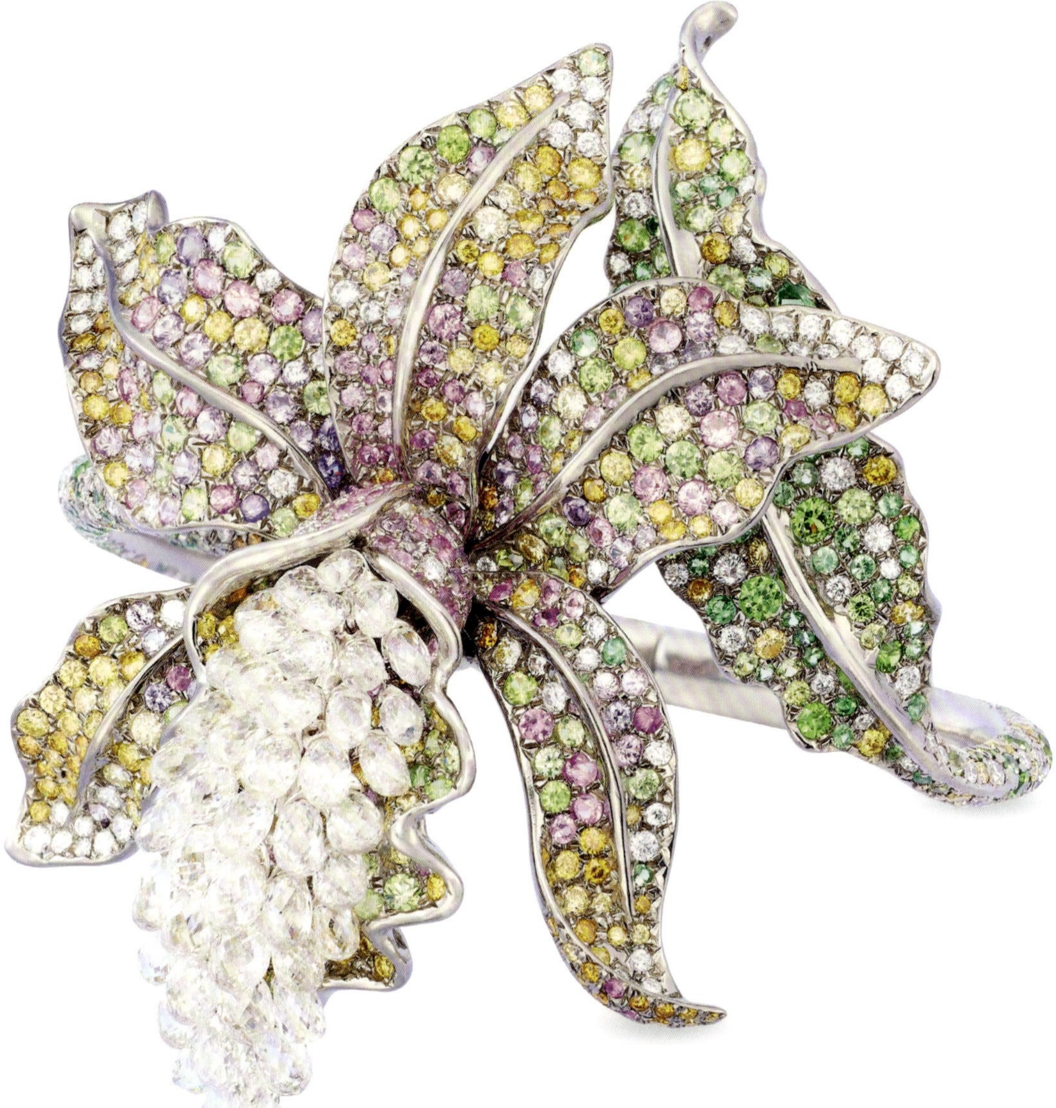

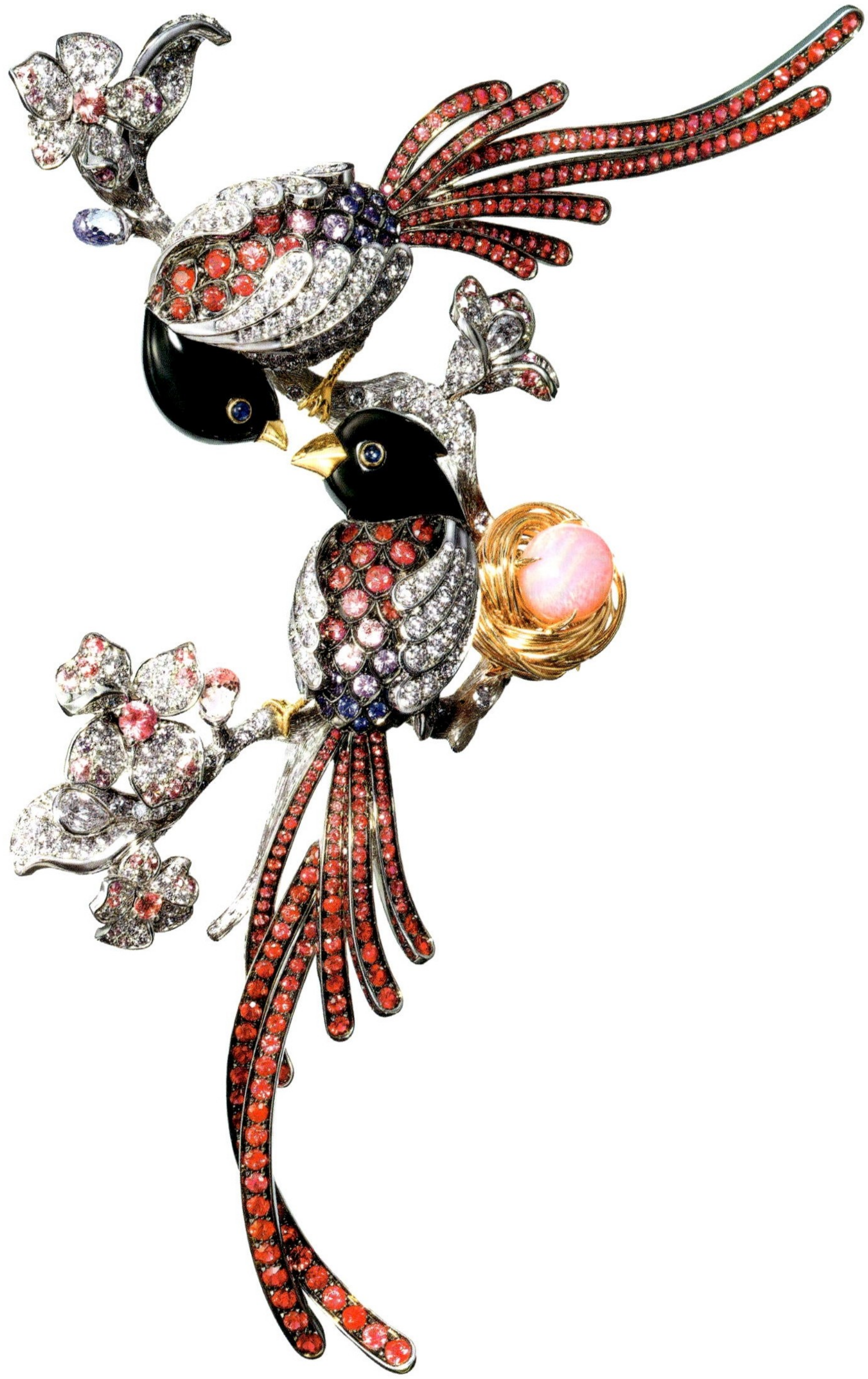

Piaget
Golden Dali Pendant, 1967
Gold

Limelight Manchette Story Cuff, 2017
Blue tourmalines (Main: 3.54ct), pink and red spinels (Main: 7.18ct), and white diamonds in rose gold

Limelight Mediterranean Garden Cuff, 2015
Blue tourmalines, emeralds, gray opal (14.82ct), and white diamond in rose gold

encourage new generations of consumers to experience jewelry differently. The irony is that its super-thin, understated watches gave birth to gloriously full-bodied jewelry bustling with stones and yet the success endures, because of their unconventional way of doing things: making everything entirely in house, so they have complete control within a relentlessly chic style. It is this steadfast DNA on which the Chinese can rely, and that cannot be underestimated in the ever-changing digital landscape.

The archives of a jewelry house are often where its history, style, heritage, creative heart, and soul reside, making sure that the original pillars or icons of design are imprinted on the memory banks of each creative team even if an entirely new line is created. Claire Choisne, appointed in 2011 as creative director of French jeweler Boucheron, does not always feel obliged to reference the archives, but acknowledges that they act as a backdrop to the jewels she puts into production. As one of the oldest jewelry houses on the Place Vendôme, Boucheron even preceded the Ritz by five years, helping to establish the famous square what would come to dominate French jewelry design.

The firm's founder, Frédéric Boucheron (1830–1902), left his family textile business in 1858 for a life that promised a little more glamour, creating jewels for the haute bourgeoisie. He draped gold like cloth, pleating it, throwing it around the curves of the body, rolling and twisting it in new and unexpected ways. His "Point d'Interrogation" or Question Mark necklace won a gold medal at the Exposition Universelle in 1889 for its ability to flex around the neck like elasticated gold, with no awkward clasps to impede its momentum. In 1893 Boucheron moved to 26 Place Vendôme where, on the corner of Rue de la Paix, his new atelier was prized for the way sunlight drenched the windows so that diamond rainbows dazzled passersby. One such pedestrian was the Maharaja of Patiala, who in 1928 entered the green marble entrance escorted by servants bearing six caskets of precious stones, including 7,571 diamonds and 1,432 emeralds and proceeded to place the largest and most important order in Boucheron's history for 149 pieces of jewelry.

Choisne is still feeling the effects of that moment today, with collections such as Bleu de Jodhpur in 2015, on which she collaborated with the modern-day Maharaja of Jodhpur Gaj Singh II to keep that link alive. Her 2017 Cape de Lumière (Cape of Light, see p. 87) pays homage to the train of a peacock, its feathers fanning out in arches of twisted chain like a plume of gold quivering around the shoulders. Frédéric Boucheron's penchant for fabric resurrected in metal is reimagined in one of Choisne's most astonishing designs; it took her workshop 925 hours to complete, weighing in at 2 pounds (almost 1 kg).

Important as the East is to Boucheron's heritage, Choisne won't compromise for the sake of sales. "I won't do a collection full of red because I want to catch a Chinese client," she says evenly. "It is not my way to work." She stays true to her vision of modernity viewed through a prism of the archives, striving for fun and pleasure instead of obvious displays of wealth. For her the emotional value of her work is unlocked with inexpensive materials, such as sand, marble, and rock crystal, and detail is paramount. She uses her own taste as a guide, hoping the art she creates will appeal to those who understand her creativity, wherever they are. After all, the maharajas came to Paris to experience the height of French culture in all its unrepentant glory.

Italian design, from the gold swirl of Baroque to the ornamental romanticism of Rococo art, draws unapologetically on its country's history, and the family-run Milanese jewelers Buccellati have remained untouched by the modern world since Mario Buccellati (1891–1965), nicknamed "the Prince of Goldsmiths," first opened his doors a century ago in 1919. Asia loves them for it. They are the present-day manifestation of the Italian Renaissance and through the art of engraving are keeping artisanal craft alive, swimming very much against the tide in this new age of technology. "The jewels made by machine may look similar, but the beauty of the piece lies in its imperfection," sighs Andrea Buccellati, honorary president and creative director, and one of four of Mario's sons to go into the business.

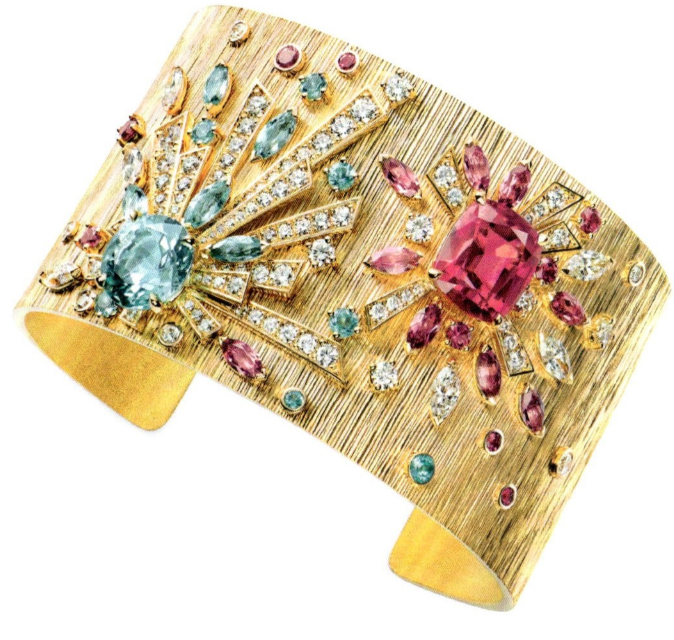

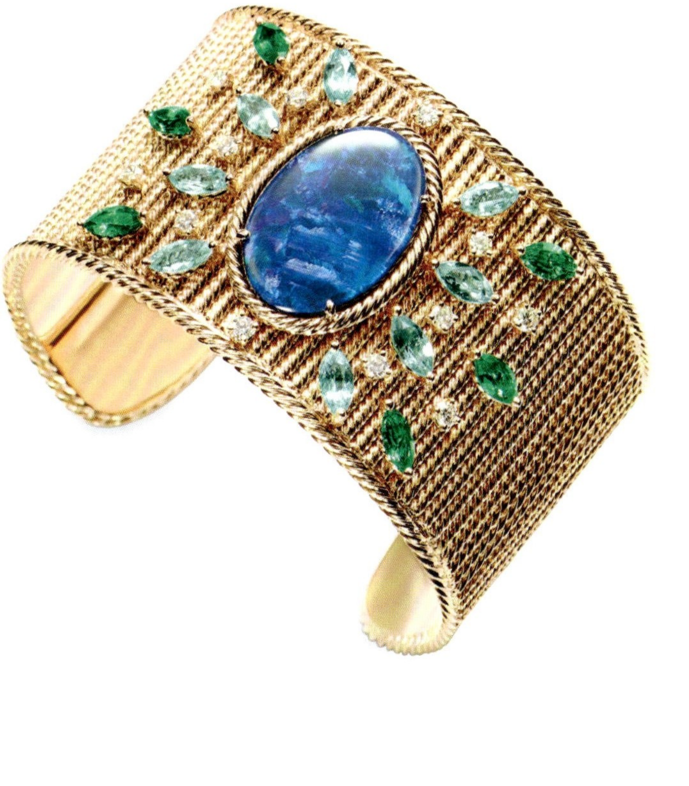

Boucheron
Drawing of Necklace for the
Maharajah of Patiala, 1928
Pen and wash on paper
Boucheron Archive

Cape de Lumière (Cape of Light)
Citrine (81.62ct) and diamonds in gold

(Following pages)
Boucheron
Feuilles D'Acanthe Necklace
Diamonds in white gold

Grosgrain Necklace
Diamonds, malachites, and onyx in white gold

"If technology takes over we will lose the humanity of the jewel." Buccellati's engravers take a burin (a metal shaft with a diamond-shaped tip) and apply pressure by hand to the surface of a metal. The angle and force affect the width and depth of the line. Peer at their jewels through a magnifying glass and you will notice a texture almost like silk staring back at you. This is the result of thousands of lines carved into gold by artisans at the bench leaning on cushions stuffed with sand in a tradition that stretches back to the fifteenth century.

Buccellati use five main techniques to express their creativity: *rigato,* where parallel lines culminate in a silklike sheen; *telato,* crisscross lines used to create a texture like linen; *segrinato,* tiny overlapping lines in all directions, providing a lustrous finish; *ornato,* the detail work around a leaf or flower to emphasize its boldness, as in the Morgana bracelet; and *modellato,* three-dimensional design chiseled on a minuscule scale to decorate the borders of a piece like a sculpture.

They also produce a delicate, intricate honeycomb metalwork technique where every available surface is inscribed. Texture and detail rule everything Buccellati do. Their Anemone necklace was dreamed up by Gianmaria Buccellati when a salesman offered him fifty-three uncut diamonds weighing 333.9 carats. Eager to avoid jewelry akin to a "mineralogical collection," he at first refused. Faceted stones were much more the Buccellati style, but in the end he agreed to handle them and their rocky, off-color beauty compelled him to create an almost medieval-looking necklace of golden flowers (see p. 91). Greek myth has it that Adonis, the lover of Aphrodite, was slain during a boar hunt; where droplets of his blood fell to the earth, anemones sprang up as a symbol of the goddess's passion for him. Gianmaria created the petals for his necklace individually from thin sheets of gold, each intricately engraved in this dedication to that love.

Buccellati made its first international venture—to the United States, a key market— in 1951 on 51st Street and in 1952 on 5th Avenue, both in New York, then in the 1970s they opened in Hong Kong, then Tokyo, Osaka, and Nagoya in Japan. This enabled them to connect with the Asian market long before most other Western jewelers apart from Van Cleef & Arpels. Paris and London followed, but now one-third of their new clients are from Asia, mainly Singapore, Hong Kong, Taiwan, and China. In 2017, in order to fund ambitious expansion, Buccellati sold a controlling stake to Chinese corporation Gansu Gangtai Holdings, who in September 2019 sold its shares to Richemont, the luxury owners of Cartier; Buccellati's connection to the East was surely part of the allure. As the business evolves, the delicate balance between continuity of style and appealing to the Asian market must be found. A Buccellati family member has been in charge of design since the beginning and this is the secret of its success.

Royalty today are the self-made tech billionaires from Silicon Valley and Beijing or the hedge-fund "masters of the universe," pop stars, movie stars, and property magnates. They buy new collections while traditional royalty are forced to recycle family heirlooms and play down their inherited wealth. Consequently, the newly rich are the lifeblood of the jewelry world. Much of that money is pouring out of Asia, where the style rule leans toward "more is more." This is skewing taste toward big, often colorful, ornate jewelry, and design has evolved accordingly. Much lighter materials, such as titanium, are being adopted by independents coming out of the East, such as Wallace Chan, Anna Hu, Cindy Chao, and Neha Dani, giving rise to larger, sculptured body art. Those who still choose gold, such as Viren Bhagat, are whittling away the metal to the most minimal of settings in which stones are paramount. The value of the jewel used to reside in its weight and beauty, but as jewelry moves into the art sphere its meaning deepens and, with the Eastern influence, becomes more spiritual.

Design must come before commerce if jewelry is to progress along its rightful path to art. In their eagerness to snag the Eastern collector, Western jewelers have to be careful not to fall into the trap of motif stealing, using the dragon or lotus for short-term gain. As jewelry still battles to be accepted by the art world, that tension between art and commerce often detracts from the purity of the

EAST MEETS WEST

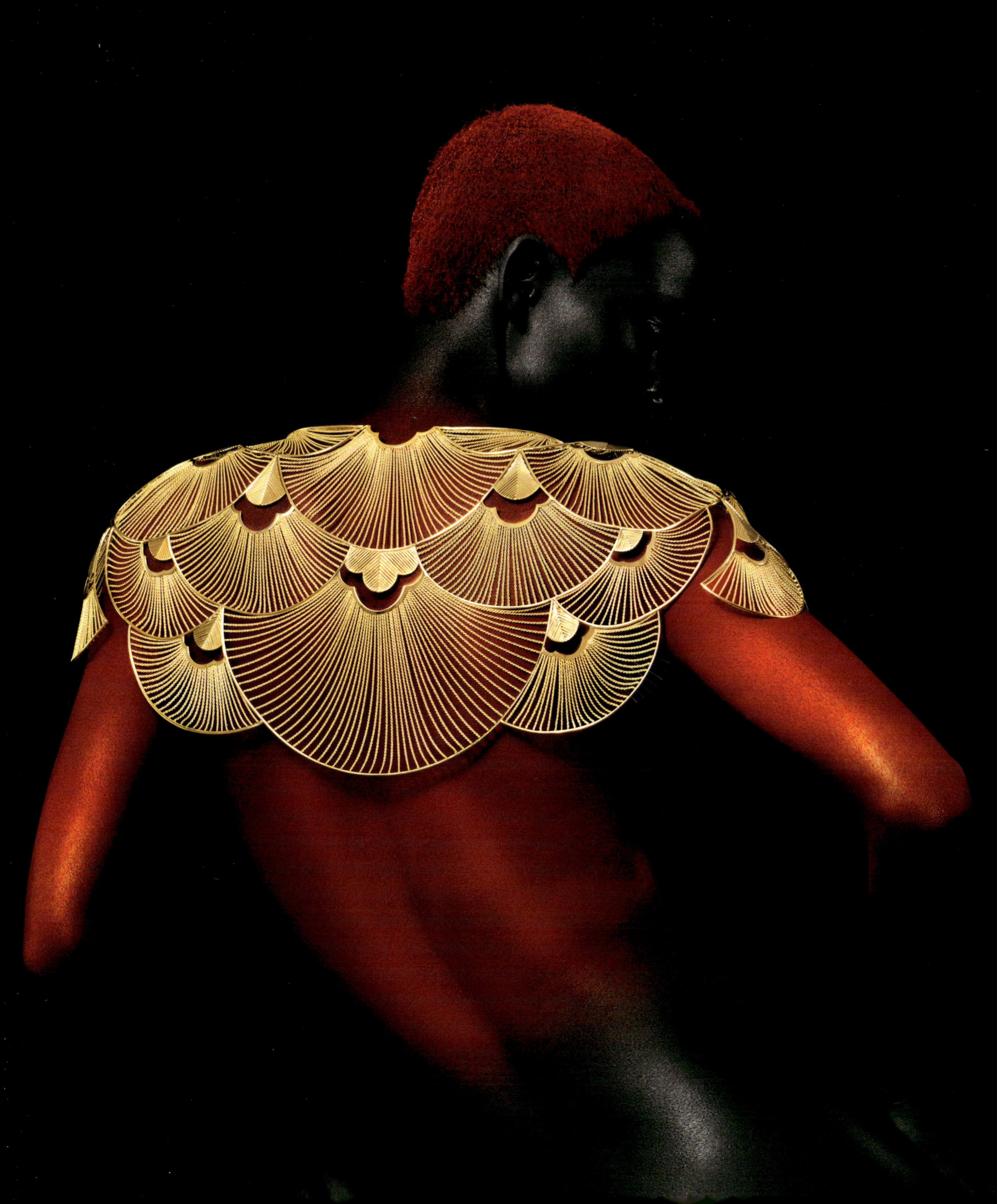

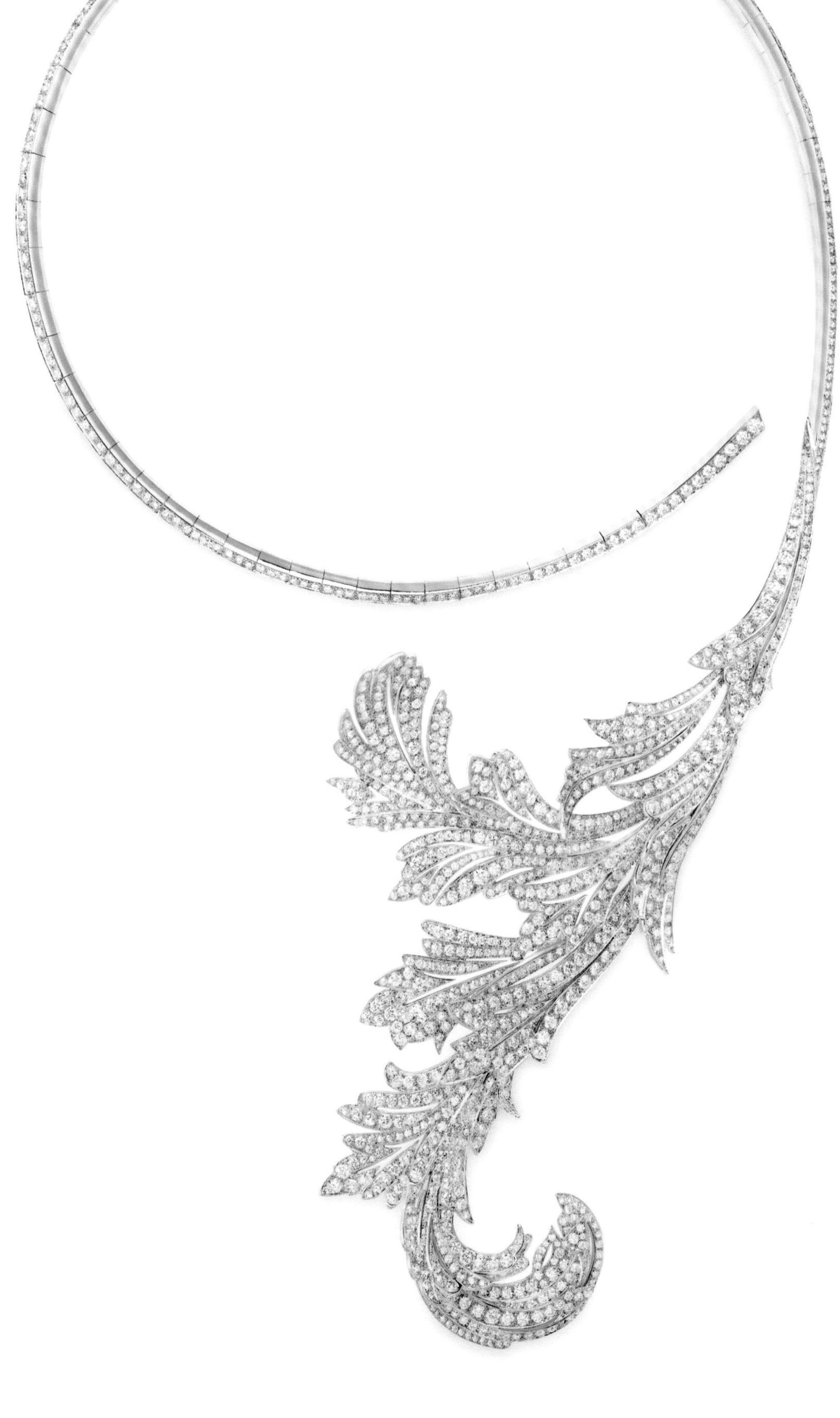

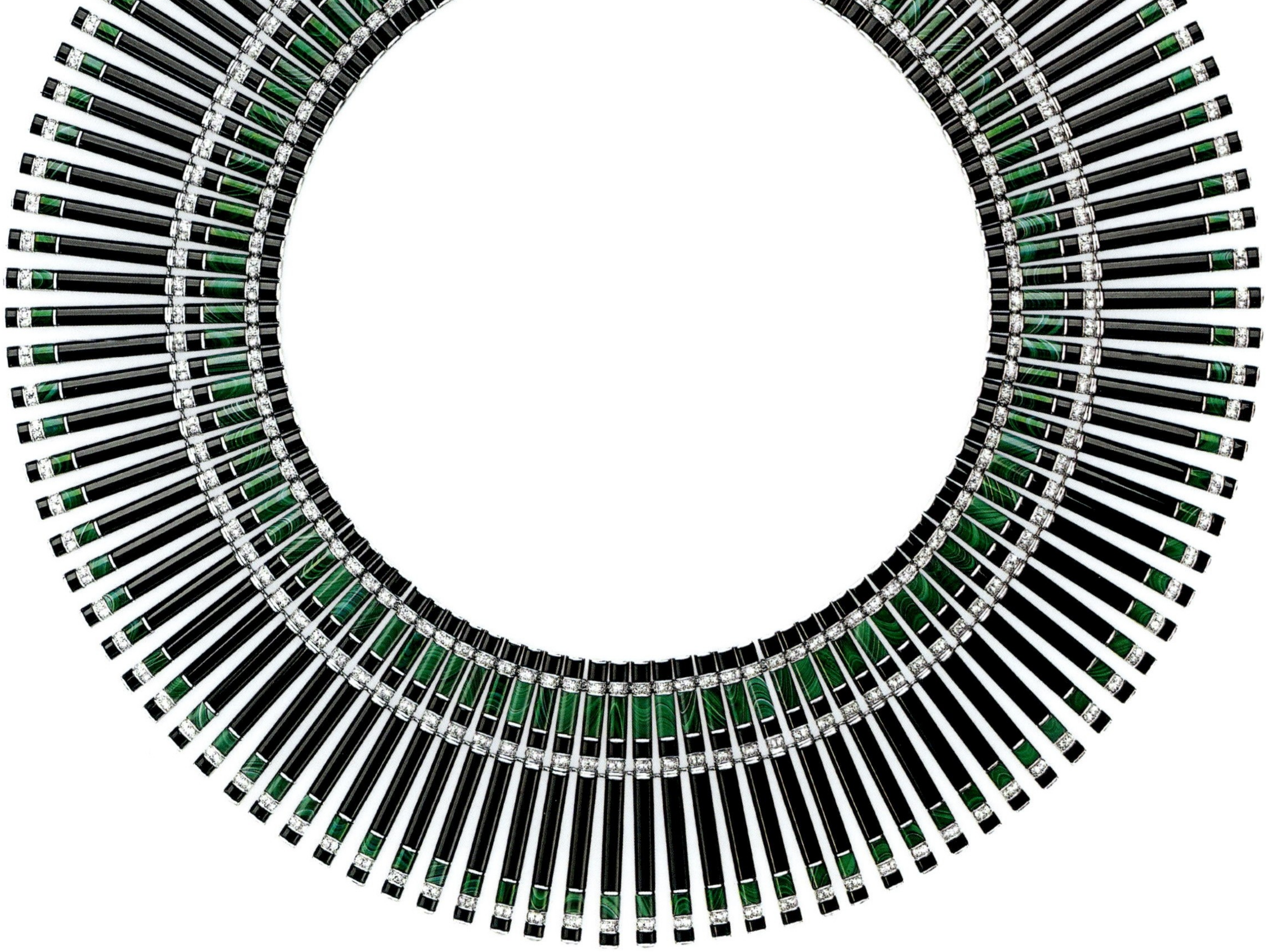

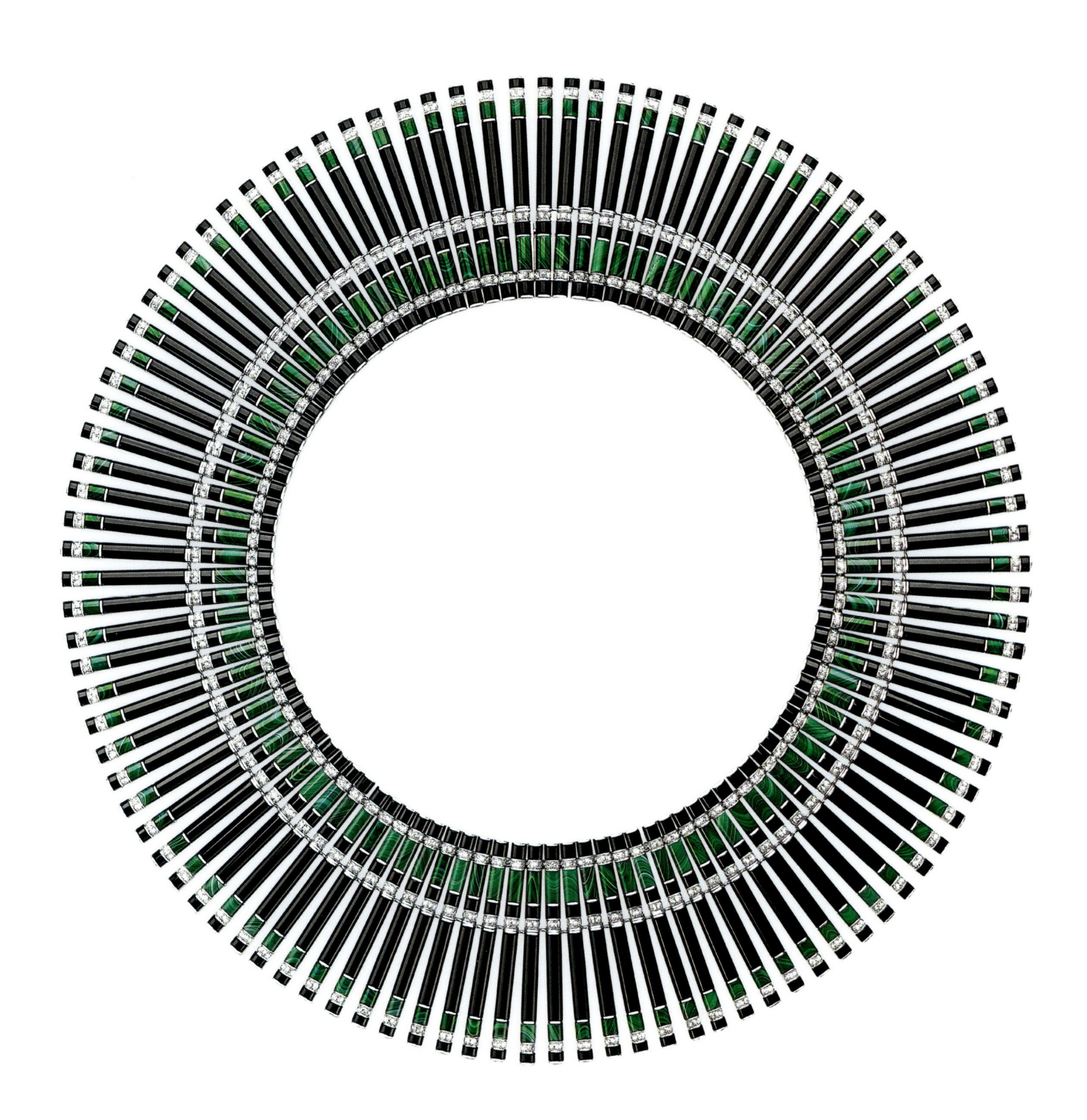

Buccellati
Anemone Necklace, 1988
Cut and uncut diamonds in gold

designer's intention. Ultimately the collector decides. Jo Stella-Sawicka, former artistic director of Frieze, a global art fair, makes a good point. "Our decision to expand to America was made several years ago in response to the demands of our clients," she says. She yearns for the gem-incrusted gothic skulls of Venetian designer Attilio Codognato, who is worn by several art dealers she knows. Desire is a tangible thing and art lovers have the bug. The collector base for fine art is changing, just as it is for jewelry. Art is becoming more accessible, less intimidating, more democratic. The collector as connoisseur is now only a small part of what was once a closed circle. As art opens up globally and becomes more competitive, the discussion about what it can be provides an opportunity for jewelry at the pinnacle to transcend. Art collectors need meaning if they are to be willing to invest their time, energy, and resources in jewelry, and it is this desire that leads to change.

It is too simplistic to say the East is more powerful now because it is on a roll economically. Its growth in jewelry is underpinned by the size and stability of the American market and by European production, which is still in a class of its own. India has the stones, history, culture, and obsession with jewelry that could well see a future surge in design; Mexico, Taiwan, and Japan are all harboring great potential in terms of spending power. As a broad rule, independent designers innovate while global brands lure that unsuspecting buyer into their first purchase, thereby opening the door to a lifetime of desire. The interplay between East and West provides the drama to what is otherwise a glacial pace of change in an industry that counts its evolution in centuries instead of years, within a wider world that values newness. The West still has the most radical design schools, museums, workshops, galleries, and infrastructure for high jewelry to flourish so, while money certainly talks, design ultimately wins.

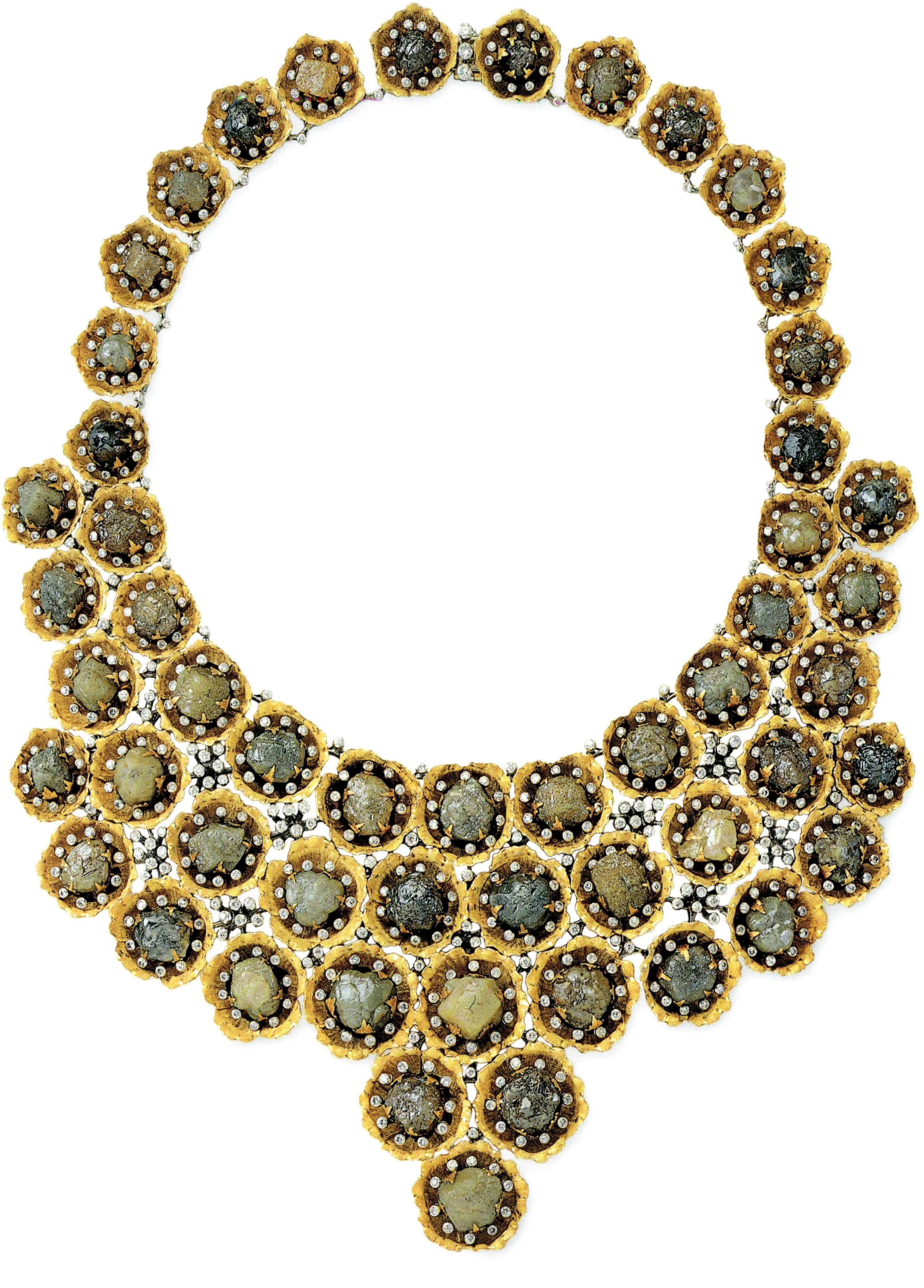

THREE

MAGNIFICENT DIAMONDS: ACHIEVING BALANCE WHEN THE STONES RULE

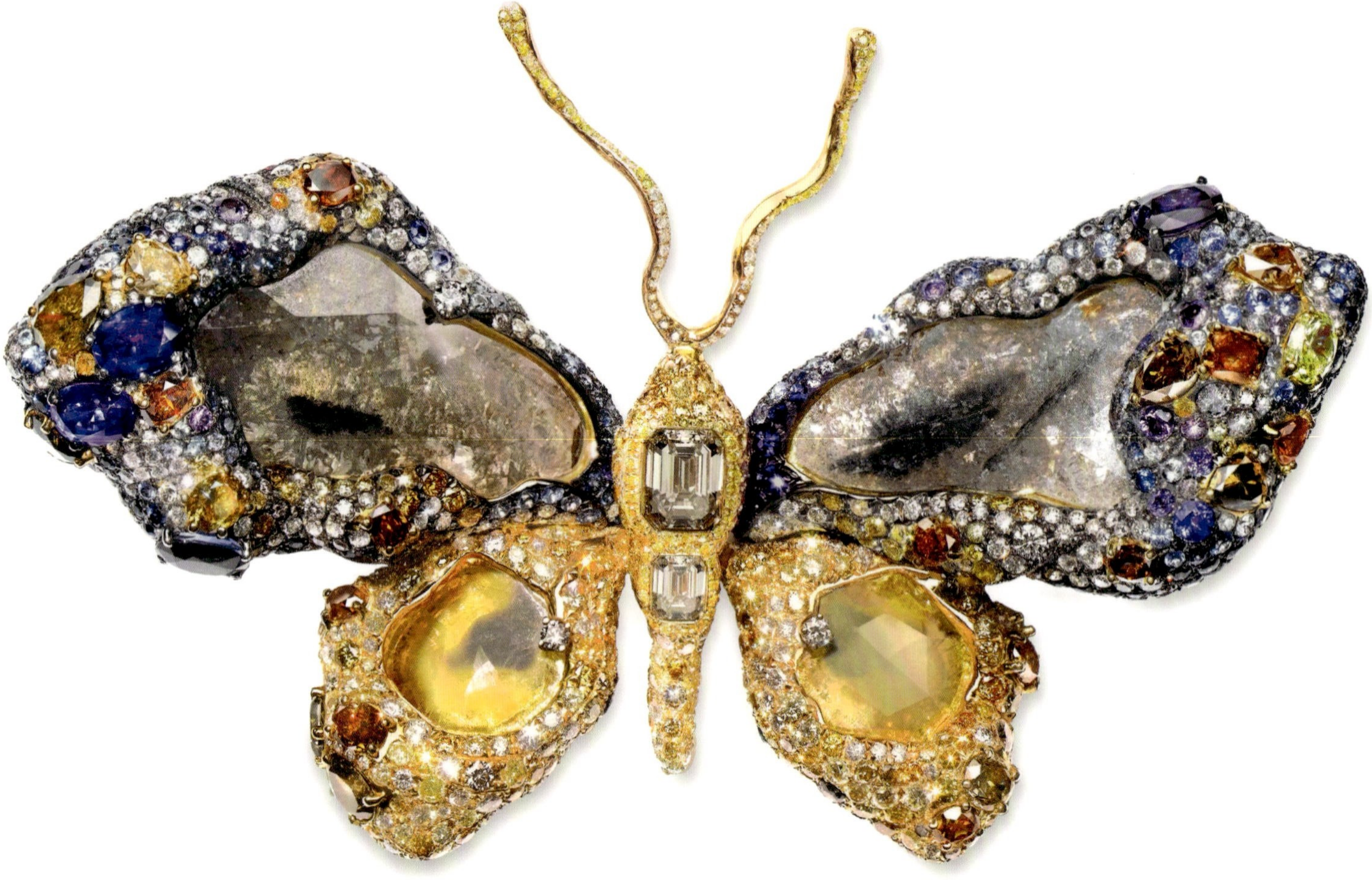

Cindy Chao
Royal Butterfly (Black Label Masterpiece) Brooch, 2009
Diamonds and fancy-color diamonds, gray (14.64ct) and yellow diamond slices, rubies, sapphires and color-changing sapphires, and tsavorites in gold
National Museum of Natural History at the Smithsonian Institution, Washington, D.C.

Diamonds are one of nature's greatest achievements: pure carbon frozen in time and eased out of the earth's deepest reaches by volcanic pressure. The most important of them change the world and forge their own identities; nations wage wars to own them. India is the earliest known source of diamonds and its most famous treasure, the Koh-i-Noor (Mountain of Light), symbolized a power struggle between Great Britain and India that changed history.

The Maharaja of Punjab, Duleep Singh, was ten years old when he was compelled to sign over the Koh-i-Noor to the British via the East India Company in 1849. His father, the previous Maharaja, was dead, his mother was locked away in prison, his royal court had betrayed him, and his armies were defeated. He had no choice but to relinquish his kingdom and surrendering this priceless gemstone epitomized the transfer of power. It was recut by London jewelers Garrard on the order of Prince Albert, consort to Queen Victoria, who paid £8,000 (more than £1 million, or $1.3 million, in today's money) to reshape it, in the process reducing its 190.3 carats to 93—an extraordinary thing to do to another country's national treasure.

A rumored curse has ensured that only female members of the British royal family have since worn the stone, although Elizabeth II has never done so: it sits within the front cross of the crown her mother wore at her coronation in 1937 and is displayed, with the rest of the British Crown Jewels, in the Jewel House in the Tower of London. India wants it back.

Diamonds like this, drenched in the blood, pain, and emotion of history, eclipse the jewelry they are set into. Duleep Singh wore the Koh-i-Noor strapped to his bicep as an amulet and the British royal family have amalgamated it into the Crown Jewels, but the stone is so potent that its casing is all but irrelevant. It goes beyond luxury, marketing, ownership, design, and money to take on a power all its own. It is said that whoever owns the Koh-i-Noor rules the world. Purity of design, usually so crucial to the art of jewelry, is pushed into second place by the cultural significance of an organic material one step away from coal. In order for the art of jewelry to prevail, big stones must be wrestled into daring design and balance achieved, but stones with identities such as this will always defy any attempt at subjugation.

Our relationship with diamonds may have begun in India, but Africa has since blossomed, with its mines yielding rocks of epic proportions. In the heart of Botswana sits a hard-rock open-pit mine, more than 1,000 feet (324 m) deep, called the Lucara Karowe. In 2015, unexpectedly, a magnificent rough diamond weighing 1,109 carats rumbled upward from the heat, dust, and dirt underground. It was heralded as the biggest gem-quality diamond discovered in more than a century and named the Lesedi La Rona (see p. 96), meaning "our light" in the local Tswana language. London jeweler Laurence Graff (otherwise known as the "King of Diamonds") bought it with the hope of producing a huge polished "hero" stone—the term given to the biggest and best—from its mysterious inner depths. The stone was too big for his existing equipment, so he had a new scanner custom-made to accommodate its girth. Imaging software scanned the diamond's core for imperfections and an intricate plan was hatched for cutting and polishing that would eventually take eighteen months.

Because diamonds of this size and scale are considered to have an energy of their own, what experts call "the will of the diamond," dictating how it should be cut, this was taken into consideration. But, in truth, once the lasers got to work, anything could have happened. Mammoth previously hidden imperfections could

MAGNIFICENT DIAMONDS

Graff
The Graff Lesedi La Rona, 2019
Diamond (302.37ct)

Graff inspired by Twombly
Necklace, 2018
Diamonds in white gold

(Following pages)
Graff
Threads Necklace, 2019
Fancy yellow and white diamonds in
white gold

De Beers Jewellers
Portraits of Nature, Knysna Chameleon
Necklace, 2019
Rough and polished colored diamonds in
white and yellow gold

Portraits of Nature, Knysna Chameleon
Earrings, 2019
Rough and polished colored diamonds in
white and yellow gold

have surfaced, or it could have shattered or splintered. Slicing into the highest clarity diamond ever graded by the Gemological Institute of America (GIA) was akin to open-heart surgery and few have the resources or the courage to take such risks. The GIA categorized it as "super deep," meaning it was formed three times deeper than most other diamonds, and Graff donated fragments of it to the Smithsonian Institution in Washington, D.C. for research. A 302.37-carat emerald square-cut diamond (the biggest in history) finally appeared and sixty-six baby satellite stones ranging from under a carat to more than twenty-six carats were born. Because of their value, rarity, and perfection these stones automatically became investment vehicles for an elite and rarefied circle of collectors. But they had to then be cut and polished, ready to create their own stories. "Cutting a diamond of this size is an art form," says Graff. "The ultimate art of sculpture." He has spent sixty years perfecting the techniques needed to master such operations from his London workshop and fine art continues to play an ever-growing role in that journey.

In the early 1970s Graff started collecting Impressionism before progressing to modern and contemporary works by such artists as Francis Bacon, Andy Warhol, Pablo Picasso, and Jean-Michel Basquiat. More recently he has become interested in African art and he shares part of his vast collection with his customers, for example, displaying a Jean Arp sculpture called *Torse Gerbe* in the flagship store opened in Paris in 2019. This infusion of fine art has affected his jewelry collections, with the once classical and somewhat traditional Graff style becoming braver and more abstract. In the 2018 collection inspired by the American painter and sculptor Cy Twombly, a spiral necklace referencing the artist's passion for continuity of movement translates the raw spiral into body sculpture. Imperfect loops are given volume, balance, and three dimensions in a clever departure from Graff's more commercial figurative design. Graff's emerging geometric style has taken bold steps toward jewelry art, past the butterflies and flowers of previous collections.

The Eternal Twins, earrings launched in 2017, are the pinnacle of this new style. The metal settings are almost imperceptible, with a simple abstract cascade of smaller stones flowing into huge fifty-carat emerald-cut diamonds. The pause or breath between stones is vital, according to Anne-Eva Geffroy, Graff's design director of ten years. "Space between stones creates a pattern or vibration and another way to read the jewel," she says thoughtfully. "The design is almost invisible, the stone will always be the star."

As the world gets richer, diamond consumption grows and our lust for bigger stones along with it. De Beers Jewellers is a company that deals only in natural diamonds. From the frozen wastes of Canada to the parched earth of sub-Saharan Africa, they explore some of the most inhospitable corners of the globe to find and extract diamonds in the rough to satisfy our craving. Once the stones are sorted according to size, shape, color, and quality, De Beers invite the dealers, cutters, and polishers in to buy and then sell on to designers in the final stage of a process that began in 1888.

In 1947 De Beers changed the jewelry universe with a simple slogan, "A Diamond is Forever." That marketing campaign democratized the diamond, publicizing it as a physical manifestation of love, desire, and commitment for the masses, where previously it had been the preserve of the aristocracy. A few years earlier, De Beers had also decided to promote the concept of the 4Cs, a grading system invented by the GIA detailing carat weight, cut, color, and clarity so that each stone could be judged against an index of value. They were attempting to involve the collector in the selection process to demystify a complex and at one time closed value system, but there was a problem. "The 4Cs were silent on the subject of beauty," says François Delage, chief executive officer of De Beers Jewellers. They could tell you how much your diamond was worth but not how to judge its beauty. Using these criteria to choose a diamond was like buying a masterpiece because of the brand of paint or the type of canvas. De Beers wanted beauty to come first and

MAGNIFICENT DIAMONDS

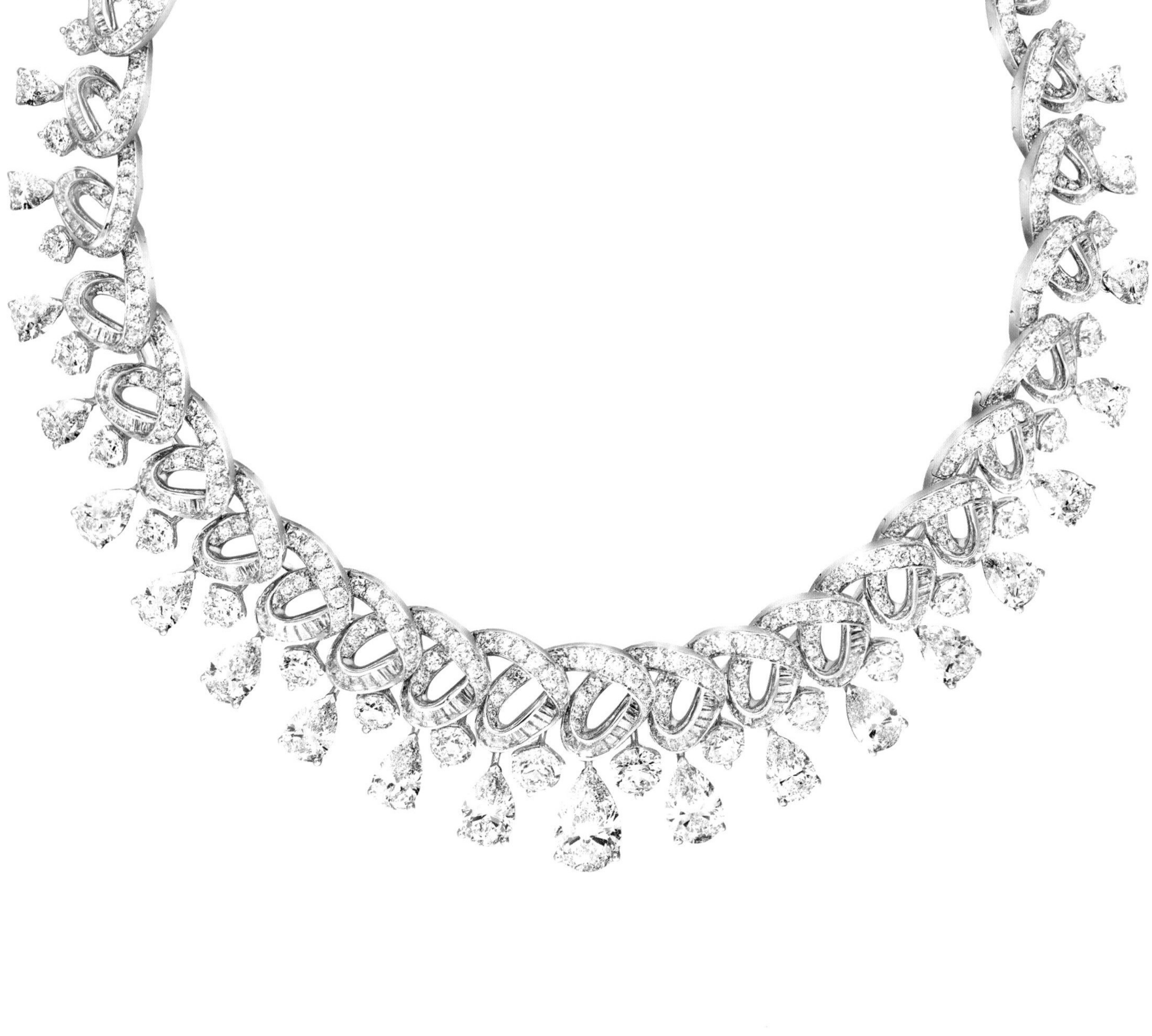

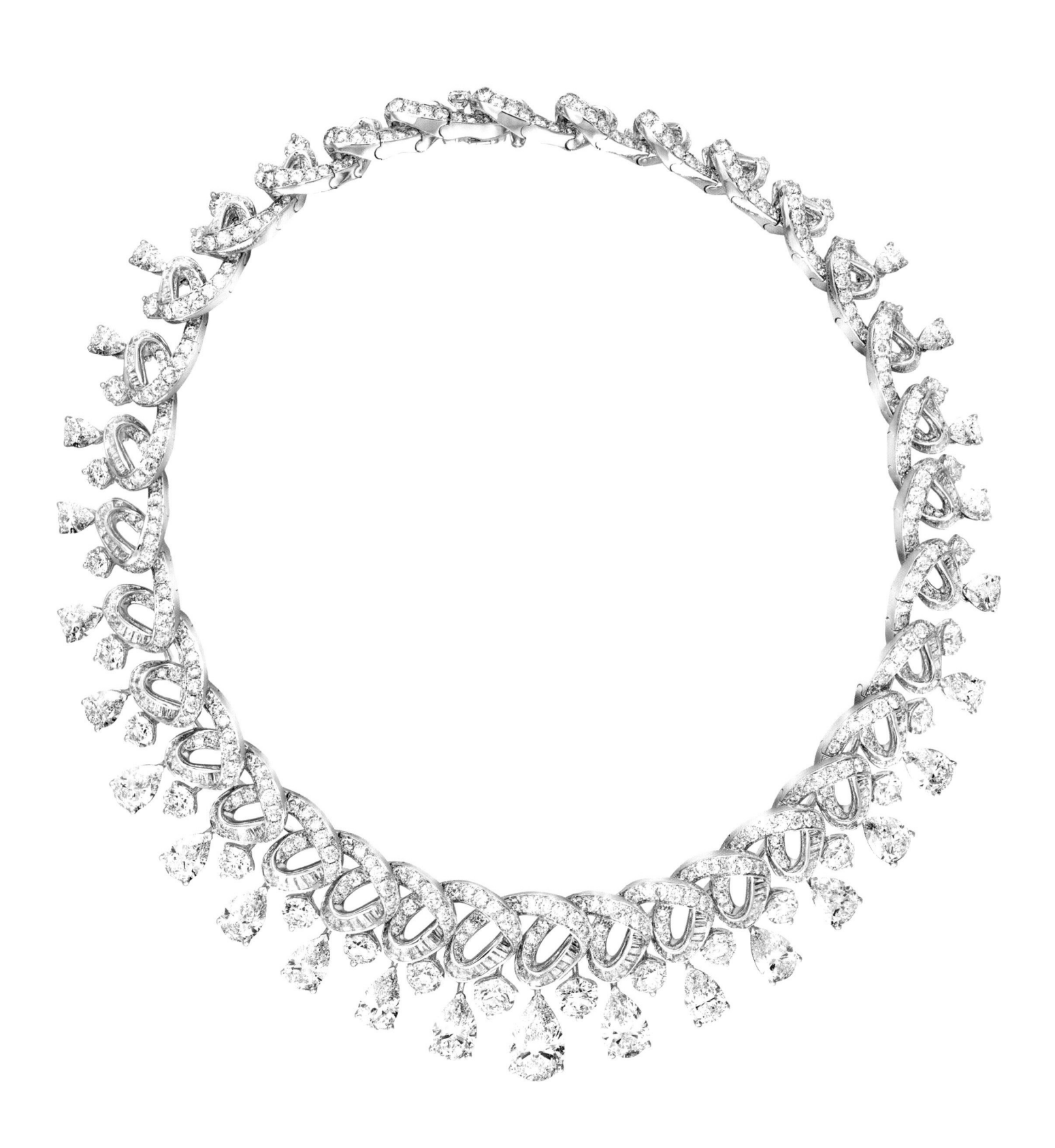

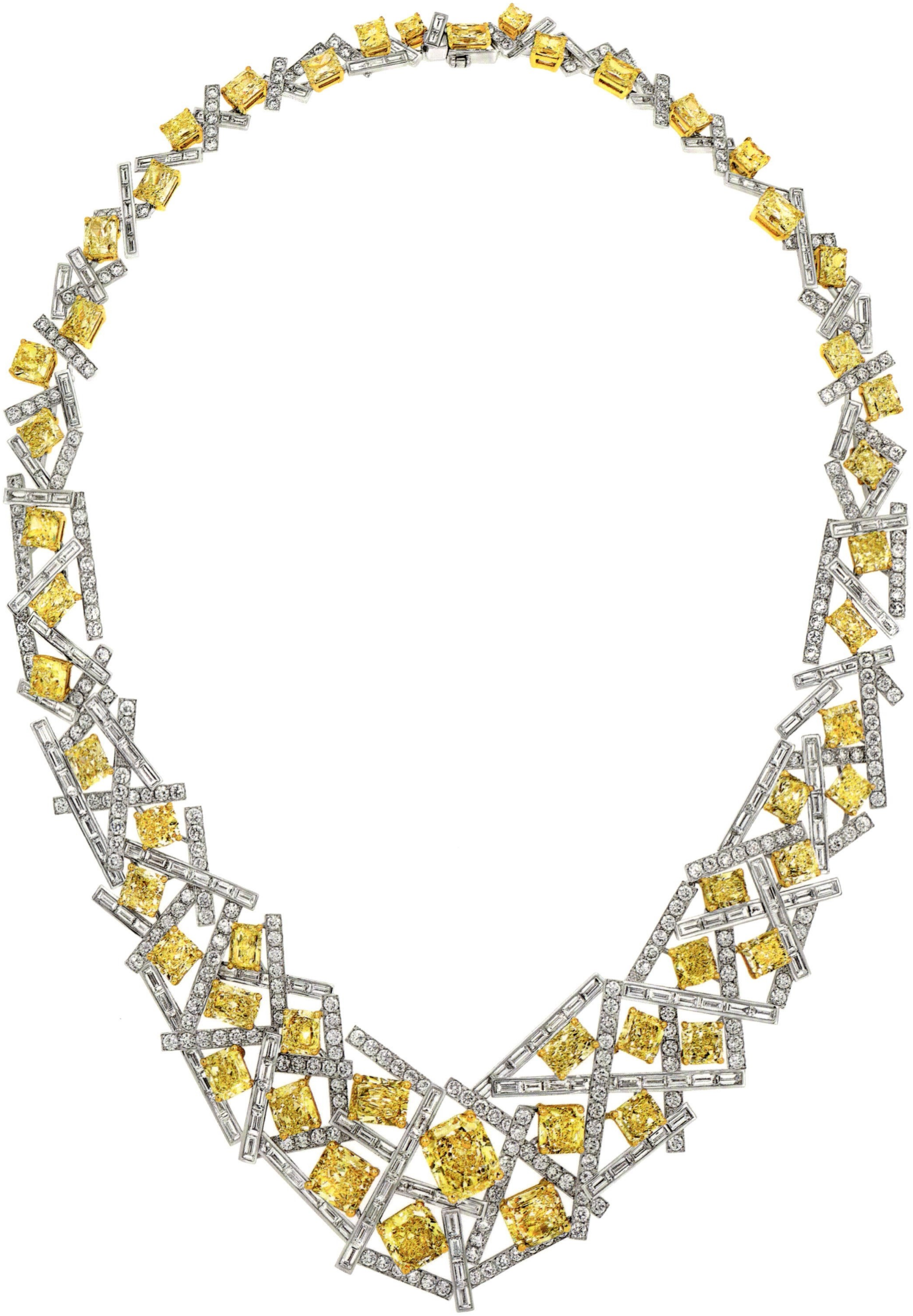

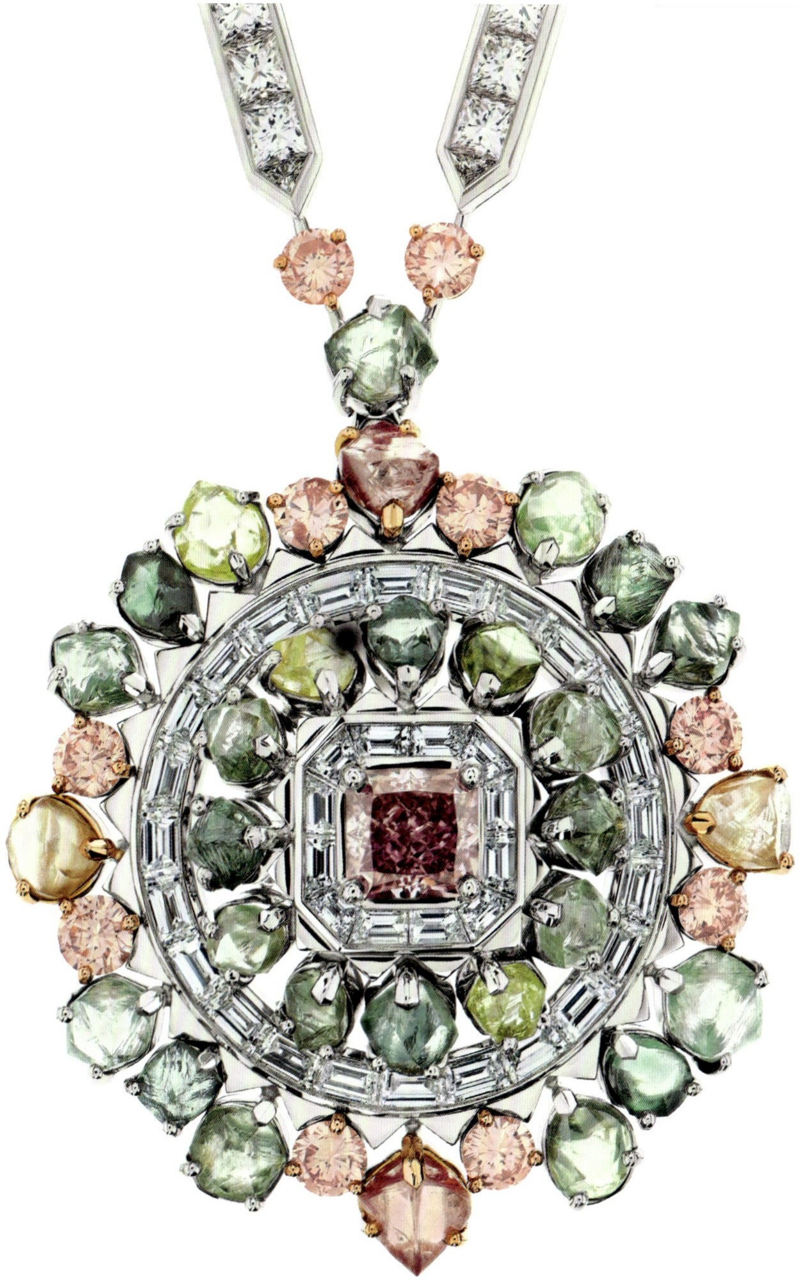

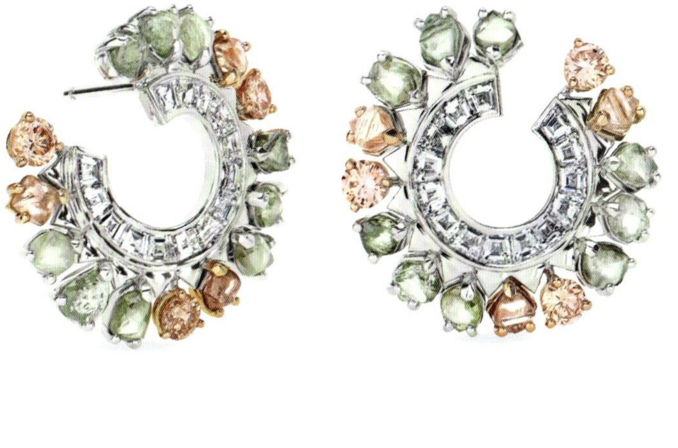

Glenn Spiro
Necklace, 2018
Natural Colombian emeralds (212.56cts)
in green titanium

wearing the stone made all the difference to that perception of beauty and the way it called to you as an emotional and visual experience.

In the 1990s De Beers acquired a 203-carat, pear-shaped, colorless, flawless diamond with fifty-four facets—the second largest of its kind in the world. Called the Millennium Star, it was cut for beauty rather than value or maximum carat weight, and it represented a shift in De Beers' philosophy, shaping a stone to be wearable instead of to languish in an underground vault. Then in 2001 the company decided to design and sell their own jewelry.

As the world entered a new millennium, luxury brands were also becoming more powerful and De Beers seized its moment. It offered big, high-quality stones in simple designs alongside expert advice on how to understand and view a diamond. Talisman, one of their first design-led collections, was born in 2005 and marked the first time the company had mixed polished stones (which were hard and brilliant) with the soft glow of rough diamonds in hammered gold, using a technique called *serti poinçon* to add texture. Rough stones had been thought to be worthless without their polished fire and light, so in many ways De Beers humbled the diamond, taking it back to its roots in India two thousand years ago, when carved and rough stones were used as talismans. For the first time in the company's history, the intrinsic worth of the stones were not the jewel's most important feature.

Design is becoming more important than value, and beauty is winning where investment once ruled. If that can happen for a company like De Beers, which employs twenty thousand people, then independent designers, unfettered by shareholders and sales targets, have an opportunity to push the treatment of big stones one step further. Away from the notion of large stones being an investment, designers face another constraint: taste. The boundaries and extremities of taste ebb and flow constantly, and while today it seems entirely reasonable to set a thirty-carat Burmese ruby into bronze or aluminum, twenty years ago it would have been inconceivable. London designer Glenn Spiro is taking the classic diamond Rivière—a simple string of stones worn tight to the throat—and turning it into something special. It happened by accident. He began by cutting a collection of exceptional emeralds but decided to ignore the traditional method of setting them with white diamonds in white gold or platinum to solidify their value. Instead, he pressed the emeralds into wax to hold them in position while he considered how he might design around them, not in contrast but in tonal harmony. He was so enamored of their deep green luminosity that he wanted an uninterrupted slash of color. His workshop protested at this break with tradition, so he turned the setting green as well, using titanium to intensify the effect. The result is weighty emeralds suspended in weightless metal in what feels like a new paradigm for the physicality of big stones.

It is not unusual for designers to push the boundaries beyond what workshops think is feasible or even desirable. Established industry rules for big stones are there to ensure an acceptable return on investment, making sure that jewelry is seen as precious. Green on green was a daring move at this end of the market, but this is one of Spiro's most confidently artistic pieces. "The stones have to be happy," he says—he listens to them above all other things. The interesting thing about Spiro is that he had no intention of becoming a designer. When he was fifteen years old, he had a roommate who one day decided not to go back to his job at English Art Works, a Cartier workshop in London. Spiro happened to bear a passing resemblance to his friend, so he went in his place, pocketing the £3.50-a-week (approximately $6.50) wages. It took the company three and a half months to realize he was an impostor, by which time, he says, his enthusiastic cleaning and tea-making skills were so highly appreciated that they offered him a full apprenticeship. He worked there until he was twenty-one and then opened his own workshop, creating designs for established high jewelers before decamping to Christie's and Los Angeles twenty years later.

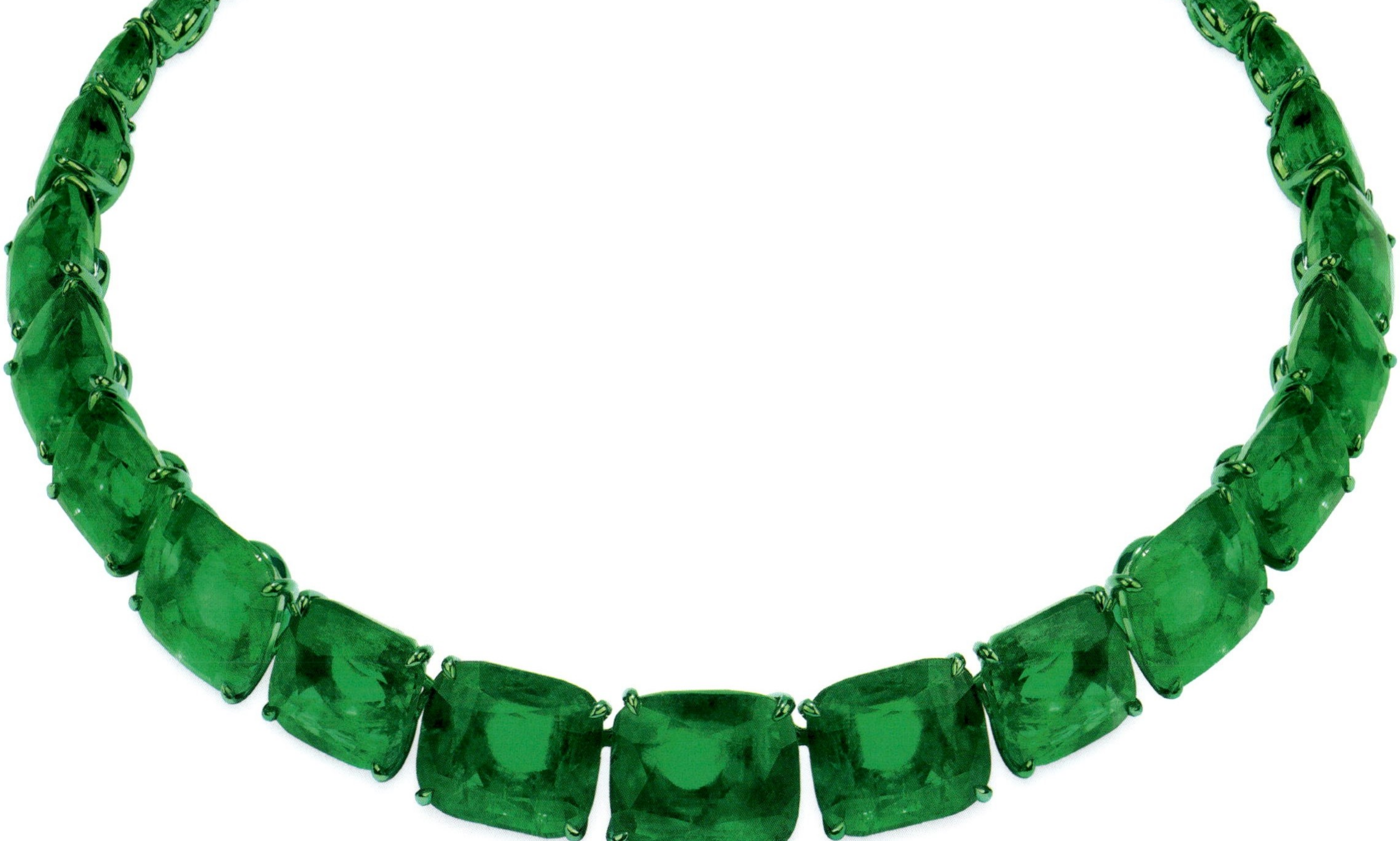

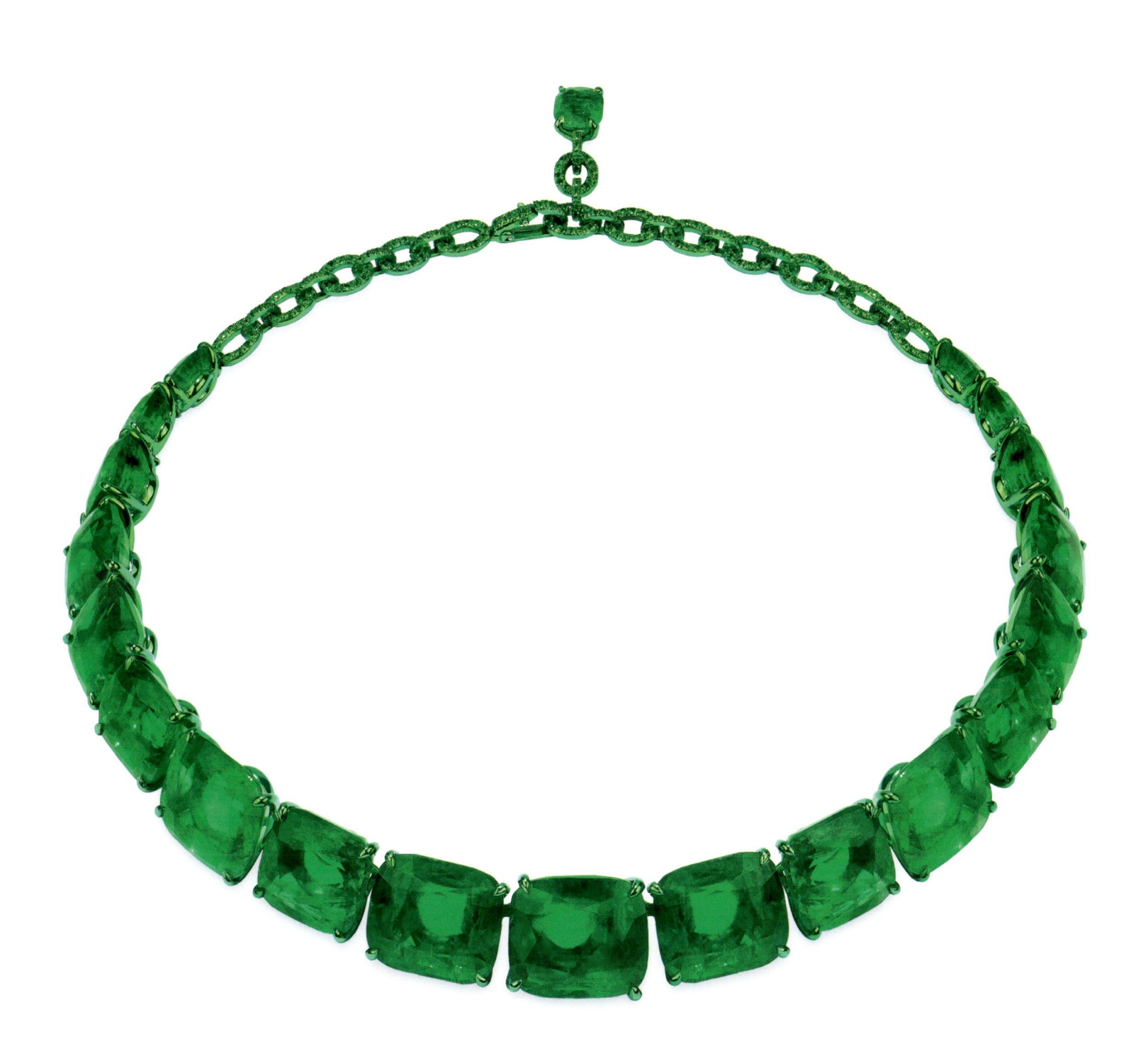

Harry Winston
The Hope Diamond, First sold 1668
Fancy dark grayish-blue diamond
(45.52ct) in platinum
National Museum of Natural History at
the Smithsonian Institution,
Washington, D.C.

Winston Cluster Diamond
Earrings, designed 1940s
Diamonds in platinum

Winston Cluster Diamond
Wreath Necklace, designed 1940s
Diamonds in platinum

His crowning achievement at Christie's was in bringing dealers and the auction house together so that important stones from private dealers came on to the market more frequently, instead of the auction house having to wait for a collector to die before it was asked to handle their estate. But Christie's and more specifically François Curiel, the company's current chairman of Europe and Asia, had a profound effect on him, teaching him how to deal with people in the world of jewelry and how to push himself. "You have to tread where you're uncomfortable," Spiro says. Creating desirable pieces from big stones takes a network of connoisseurs who can find and explain the gems, as well as designers who push the limits of their own creativity. The desire for jewelry is continually evolving as the industry opens up to accommodate novel materials, which in turn inspire new types of design. Big stones have a unique ability to slow that evolution down, because their rarity makes them harder to find and harder to buy. They are often sold privately and only the favored few are invited to join the inner circle of potential bidders. The collector needs challenge and aspiration to stay engaged over the long term and uninhibited designers such as Spiro are providing an element of surprise within even the most apparently classic of designs.

Some stones, however, defy competition, the market, desire, and even value, because in jewelry, there are diamonds—and there are diamonds. The Hope Diamond is a deep velvety violet-blue forty-five-carat marvel from the Kollur mines in Golconda, India, which are the source of some of the most magnificent diamonds the world has ever seen. Sold to Louis XIV of France in the seventeenth century, the diamond was recut and set into the French Crown Jewels as "the French Blue." A century later it was stolen from Louis XVI during the French Revolution and disappeared for forty years. Like all great diamonds, it eventually resurfaced, this time in England, and in 1830 it is likely it was the blue diamond included in the sale of the possessions of George IV on his death. It then found its way into the hands of collector Henry Philip Hope, where it acquired its current name. It remained in the Hope family until 1902, before being sold to Pierre Cartier, among others, and becoming a modern-day phenomenon in North America.

The United States were enjoying a vast new wealth at that time, with the emergence of billionaires who were hungry for noble stones to become part of their "jewelry wardrobe." In 1911 American mining heiress and socialite Evalyn Walsh McLean bought and wore the Hope Diamond as a conversation starter when she entertained in her home in Washington, D.C. When, after her death, her estate was sold at auction in 1949, Harry Winston (1896–1978) procured the stone and toured the country with it in a four-year traveling exhibition named "The Court of Jewels." This awe-inspiring spectacle must have been a sight to behold in the wilds of rural America. It was the pinnacle of Winston's diamond-buying career, which also included the Lesotho, a 601-carat rough that he cut live on television in 1968 before selling a 40.4-carat marquise-cut gem from it to the shipping magnate Aristotle Onassis as an engagement ring for Jacqueline Kennedy, the former First Lady.

This new royalty needed their own equivalent of the Crown Jewels, and for several decades in the mid-twentieth century, Winston was the man to provide them. Having spent twelve years in New York buying estate jewelry from auctions and resetting stones into his contemporary designs, he opened his namesake jewelry house in 1932, turning rough stones into legendary objects of desire, entrancing Hollywood actresses, and persuading movie directors, such as Alfred Hitchcock and Woody Allen, to feature them in their films. He eventually donated the Hope Diamond to the Smithsonian, posting it by registered mail; today it receives seven million visitors a year. In terms of design, his familiarity with perfection on this scale gave him a taste for simple, elegant shapes and minimalist settings to really showcase gemstones. While he was at home for Christmas in 1940, a holly wreath covered in snow hanging from his doorway caught his eye. Its interlocking leaves transfixed him: he decided that jewels

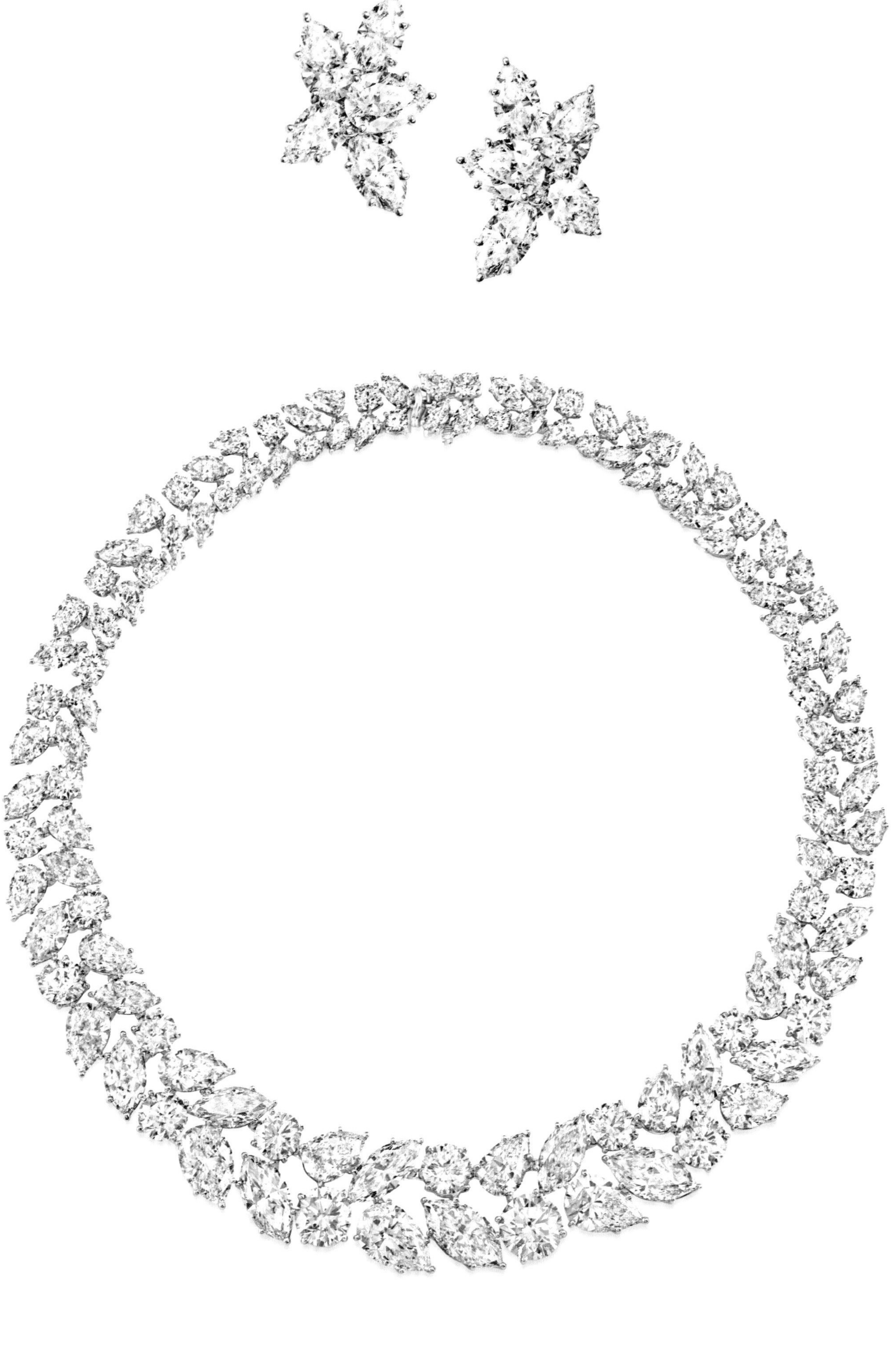

Michelle Ong
Sapphire Swim Brooch, 2017
Blue and pink sapphires, emeralds
(Main: 5.92ct), Paraíba tourmalines,
pink sapphires, and white diamonds in
platinum, titanium, and white gold

were his leaves, while the settings represented branches. From then on he would always place stones at the core of his design and keep the branches subtle and in the background. He devised a "clustering" technique that became his signature, grouping different cuts of mostly white diamonds together in the finest of platinum settings that were almost invisible to the eye. They were three-dimensional sculptures in pear, marquise, and round brilliant-cut diamonds, sometimes angled in opposite directions as earrings clustered around the earlobe or as necklaces in a garland of sparkling diamond leaves.

Winston died in 1978, but his work still represents an innate American glamour and sophistication that combines restrained but icy white diamonds with classical design. Today, Nayla Hayek, chief executive officer of Harry Winston, Inc., is seeing power jewels find a new home as an upcoming generation of wealthy Asians seek out their own diamond regalia. "A fine piece of jewelry is the perfect marriage between an exquisite stone and an exquisite setting," she says. "A setting that will not only enhance the fire and brilliance of its center stones, but also one that allows for extreme fluidity, durability, and wearability." High jewelry is worn a lot more informally than it used to be: in the past a queen might have selected a particular jewel once every few years for a state occasion, but today anyone who can afford it might wear a similar piece to dinner or to the opera every other week.

Jewelry tracks the taste and lifestyle of every era it serves and, while big stones often record the story of humanity, smaller ones deliver a surprisingly powerful impact in terms of design. A microlevel of intricate pavé work carpeting the petals of a flower or scales of a fish can achieve a "big look" through texture and movement, and this is where independent designers thrive. Away from the hefty, mortgage-crushing stones Harry Winston so enjoyed carving, there is a world of figurative allure in miniature. Hong Kong-based Michelle Ong is well aware of the power of stones. When she started out as a designer more than twenty years ago, she apprenticed under Siu Man Cheuk, an old-school gem dealer and one of the first to import diamonds into Hong Kong. He taught her about the nature, character, and properties of the stones that would one day propel her work to global prominence. At that time there were few women designing high jewelry in Asia, but the continent was beginning to gather pace both economically and culturally with a bold, color-saturated style of design.

Married to a heart surgeon, Ong had an intense social calendar that frequently compelled her to wear elaborate evening gowns, but she found that the jewelry to accompany them was lacking. So she made her own. A pair of floral earrings marked the start of her journey and also her homage to female power in a culture where intricate design is highly prized. "It is important to me that a big stone doesn't overpower the design, or become too much of a focal point," she says. "I look at each design as a whole." For men buying jewelry for their partners, especially in the 1980s and 1990s, the big center stone was often a trophy designed to be worn by a trophy, but as women started buying their own jewels, they opted for more adventurous design; in Ong's case this meant an oriental twist connected to nature.

When she uses important stones, they must contribute artistically to the piece. In the brooch called Sapphire Swim, a pear-shaped 5.92-carat emerald shimmers on the crown of a fish as it swims languidly in an imaginary sea, its scales a multitude of pink and blue sapphires, Paraíba tourmalines, and emeralds. In contrast, the all-white glassy beauty of transparent flat, single, and rose-cut diamonds in a cacophony of sizes embeds itself into the petals of her Lily brooch (see Introduction, p. 14) constructed in a curve of platinum. Ong's phenomenal stonework resembles a type of metal fabric that somehow manages to flow over the body in soft light ripples. Her use of titanium also allows for a lightweight, stone-focused design, because it "melts" into the color of each stone, allowing for more delicate, complex movement. In some pieces this metalwork is so minimal that her diamonds appear to be floating. While her jewels are substantial, they are

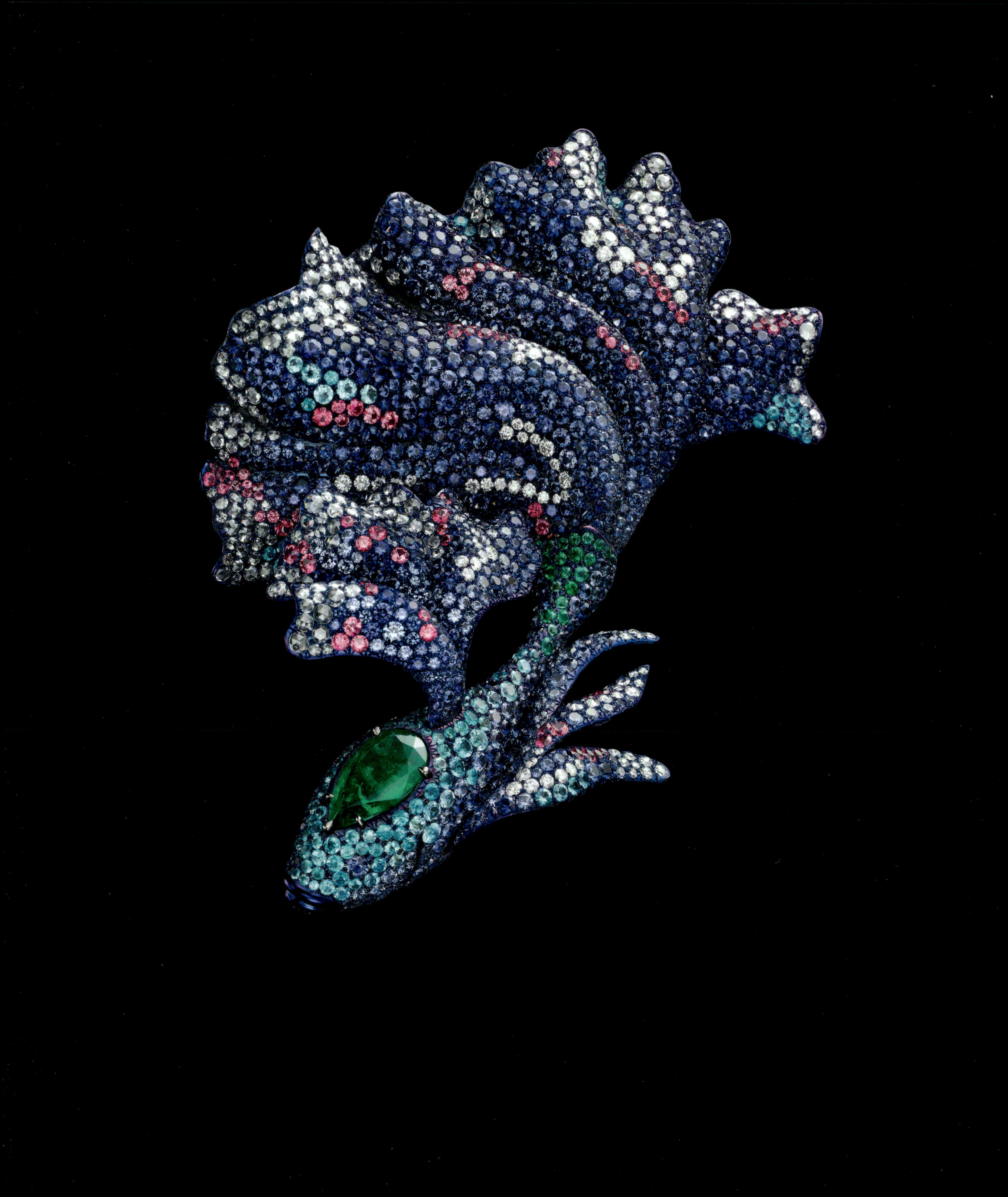

also softly, deftly sculpted; creating that harmony is a skill in and of itself. Ong manages to stay on the right side of extreme design, but not everyone is capable of getting that balance right.

"I've found that sometimes big creations in Italy are slightly vulgar," says Giampiero Bodino, creative art director of Richemont (the luxury goliath that owns Cartier and Van Cleef & Arpels, among many others) and chief executive officer of his own eponymous high-jewelry house. He makes an exception for Bvlgari, whose opulence he finds admirable. Gianni Bulgari (see pp. 61–63), with whom he worked in Rome for most of the 1980s, instilled in him the desire to design for the long haul, to ignore trends, and to place his faith in beauty, which means making a jewel that can be worn easily, however large or flamboyant it may be. Bodino is a man consumed by his passion for design, art, and precious stones, fascinated by their ability to seduce and by the way the body wears that seduction. Even if a diamond is hidden within the jewel so that only the wearer knows it is there, he feels its presence affects the energy of the design.

After leaving Bvlgari, Bodino decamped to Milan, where he has directed and edited Richemont's creative vision since 2002. In 2013 Johann Rupert the chairman, gave him the opportunity to showcase his own design and he now creates one-of-a-kind jewels in a 1930s Art Deco studio called Villa Mozart. This is the first jewelry house Richemont has ever created from scratch, so now Bodino juggles both jobs as well as a private penchant for painting and photography. Italy was deep in recession when he set up the atelier, so its very existence is a sign of how valuable his creative contribution is. He repaid Rupert by unleashing a force of romantic and Neoclassical splendor, referencing Italian history and heritage and lavishly applying gemstones both big and small. "The combination of style and stone interests me," he says. "A single stone is not enough." He doesn't set out to use big stones and advises collectors of hefty diamonds to go elsewhere, but large colored stones creep in now and again. His Primavera ring with its mandarin garnet nestling at the center of a bejeweled flower is a fine example. He considers the character of the collector, the story of the design, and his overall vision before turning a piece with a big stone into a jewel. It is an instinctive process that results in elemental harmony.

Formal jewelry worn informally is Bodino's raison d'être, a kind of casual luxury that lies at the creative core of the Italian soul. The obvious power of a humungous center stone doesn't need a designer of Bodino's dexterity to bring it to life. It already is. Where he is most useful and most at ease is in combining opposites, such as clashing colors, rough and smooth stones, the abstract and the classical, with effortless style. His Teodora cuff is an intricate mosaic of sumptuous volume. Chrysoprase, a type of green chalcedony with a deep hue due to its nickel content, is slipped into rails so that no metal is exposed. Purple sapphires provide the contrast and two other cuffs complete a trio, one in pink opal and pink sapphire in pink gold, the other in white chalcedony and white diamonds in white gold. This is design for the modern age and, while Bodino is used to anticipating the tastes and creative codes for the jewelry world in general or following "the temperature of the moment," his own jewelry taps into a deeper need for style over stone. A jewel with no great intrinsic value won't be broken up a century from now and ransacked for its stones, so it must be timeless. It must survive on its artistic merits and that is fairly new territory for high jewelry.

Although sizable gemstones add multiple zeros to the price of a jewel on the open market, private dealers make surprisingly little markup within the trade, and inventory can be agonizingly slow to move. Fourth-generation jeweler Pierandrea Sabbadini admits that while his great-great-grandfather started the family business as a gem dealer, first in Madrid and then in Milan, designing its own jewelry has let the company move into much more lucrative terrain. This is perhaps why so many stone dealers become designers but few succeed at the top level: that magic is either in you or it isn't and no amount of schooling can bring it forth. Sabbadini began his training at eight years old, going to

Giampiero Bodino
Teodora Cuff, 2012
Chrysoprase, diamonds, and purple sapphires in white gold

Teodora Cuff, 2012
Pink opals and pink sapphires in pink gold

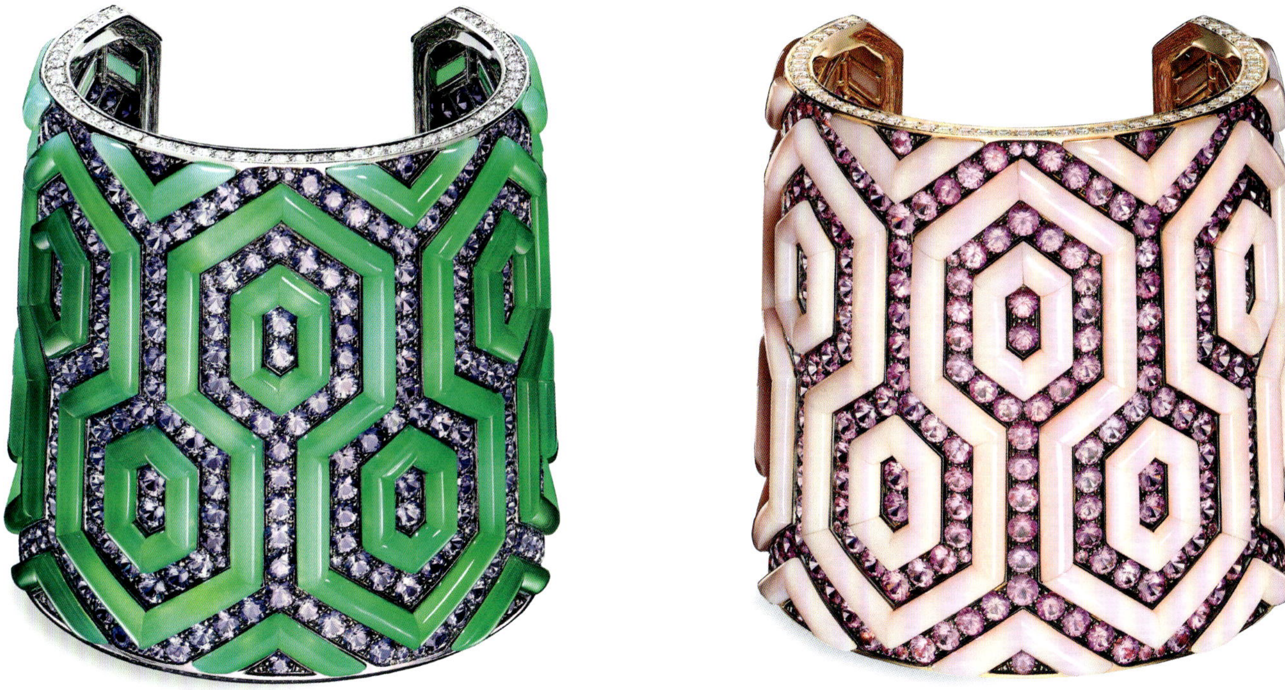

Fabergé
Potato, c.1890
Agate and gold with mounted hinged cover and a fleur-de-lis clasp

Clover Ring, 2013
Rare grass-green demantoid garnets and white diamonds in gold

Hibiscus Gold and Silver Flower Cuff Bracelet, 2014
Pink, white, and yellow diamonds and rubies in sterling silver and white and yellow gold

trade shows and watching his father and grandfather work while he played with stones. He didn't officially join the firm until the end of the 1990s, when he was twenty-five, but three years spent at Sotheby's in New York prior to that gave him the confidence and also the insight into the art of jewelry that enabled him to challenge his preconceived notions of design once he returned to Italy. At Sotheby's he regularly handled significant jewels worth hundreds of millions of dollars, but he felt torn. Clients would come in looking for important pieces and, as the employee of an auction house, he would be forced to tell them to wait for the next sale, yet the family jeweler in him wanted to make a call that afternoon and get them whatever they wanted. He knew then that it was time to go home.

Back in Italy he started to work alongside his father, morphing the family's style, a mix of renaissance classical and modern contemporary, into a tougher, edgier vision. Abstract guilloche-stamped blue titanium flowers edged in diamonds with a flurry of petals flicking outward in pink gold pushed the firm into a new age. Since about 2010 industrial materials have dominated their work. They use aluminum, ceramics, steel, matte chrome, and wood as well as titanium bent into geometric shapes to stand out in what is now a crowded market. Invisibly set bees, where the body of each insect is a jigsaw puzzle of interconnecting colored stones, are the trademark of the house, inspired by Napoleon I's coat of arms. They are designed to be worn as a swarm, as a cluster on the shoulder, or down the front of a dress like buttons.

Sabbadini is another designer who feels that the way jewelry is worn has changed. The ornamental necklace carrying elaborate stones, so typical in the 1950s, has given way to the firm's most popular jewel, the earring that can cross over from day to night or, as his clients put it, "from 10 a.m. to 10 p.m." "Earrings are the most feminine piece of jewelry in today's world," he asserts. "They are the only jewels a man cannot wear with any size and like clothing they transform one's physicality." Titanium lets him create earrings of considerable size that can be worn comfortably with anything; psychologically, his collectors consider them better value for money. He feels that industrial materials must be mixed with precious stones if they are to become artistic; the next material on his radar is rubber, but its failure to grip stones is still an issue. Finding new ways to preserve heritage, to offer design that is accessible both financially and aesthetically without cannibalizing your existing portfolio, and still managing to bring in new customers are the holy grails of the jewelry world. Innovative materials might be the passport to this new world, but stones remain its bedrock.

Long before the industrial materials favored by contemporary designers were born, the connection between art and jewelry began in the goldsmith's studio as artisans worked across fine art and jeweled objects. They set precious stones into golden snuffboxes and used enamels to paint detailed portraits onto ivory lids. They restored old masterpieces in grand museums, such as the Hermitage in St. Petersburg, Russia, where a fledgling apprentice called Peter Carl Fabergé (1846–1920) became inspired. When he took over his father's modest jewelry business in 1882, Peter Carl had ambitious plans to transform its ordinary offering into bejeweled objets d'art, and his unorthodox ideas caught the attention of Czar Alexander III at the Pan-Russian Exhibition in Moscow that year.

His first commission was an egg for an Easter present in 1885, its outer shell exquisite white enamel, which split in two to reveal a golden yolk. Inside the yolk was a hen and inside the hen a miniature crown and ruby pendant. It was a breathtaking display of humor, craftsmanship, and subtle extravagance. A delighted Maria Feodorovna, wife of Alexander III, was so enamored that she placed a new order every Easter, the holiest day in the Russian calendar, and sparked a series of fifty-one eggs, all with surprises hidden inside. By the 1890s Fabergé was a favorite of the Russian court, with the extreme opulence of his creations changing the concept of how jewelry could be presented. The traditional jewelry box became part of the jewel itself, an elaborate shell, encouraging discovery. "Fabergé opened a window on a particular segment

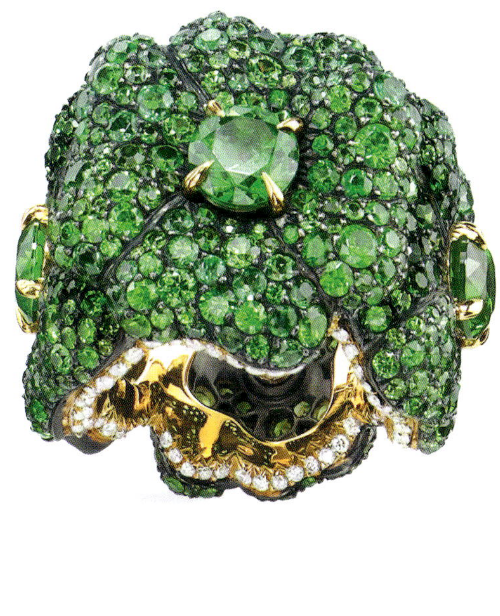

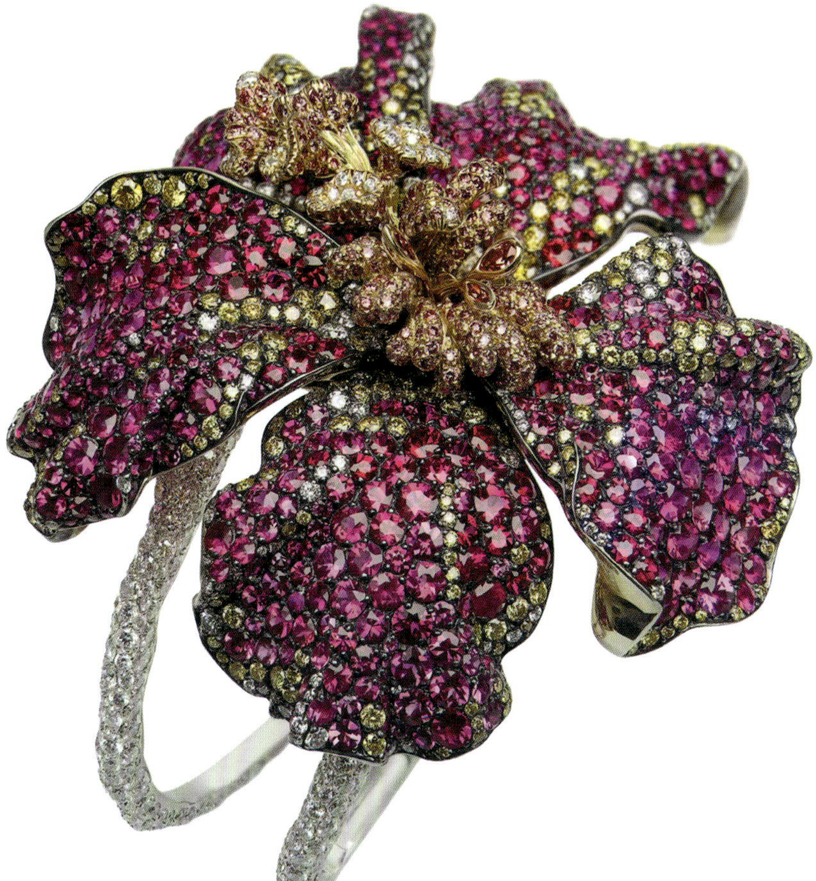

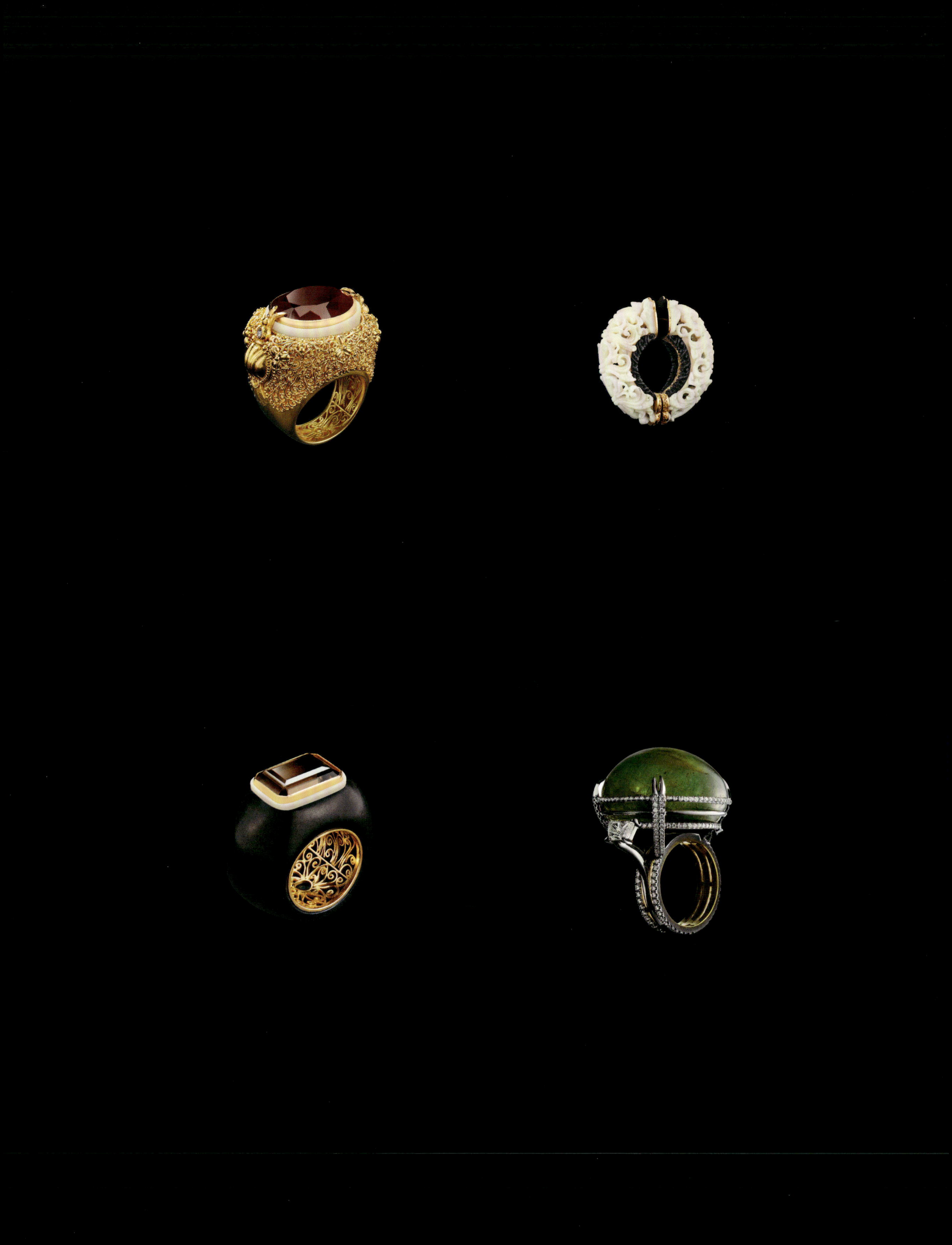

Alexandra Mor
Ring, 2017
Rich orange garnet (22.40ct) in gold
and tagua seed

Subang Hoop Earrings, 2017
Areng ebony, gold and tagua seed

Ring, 2017
Diamond and smoky topaz (10.55ct)
in Areng ebony, gold and tagua seed

Ring, 2010
Diamonds and emerald (83.30ct)
in white and yellow gold

of Russian history that continues to fascinate and inspire," says Sarah Fabergé, his great-granddaughter and one of the founding members of the Fabergé Heritage Council. One of Sarah's favorite Fabergé jewels is a life-size crab with chalcedony shell and finely engraved segmented silver body. The legs and claws move and the protruding eyes look out inquisitively, set with cabochon moonstones.

Seeking a periodic pause from the excessive luxury of the Russian court, Peter Carl Fabergé also carved stone into jeweled vessels, transforming spotted agate, nephrite, and serpentine into apples, pears, tomatoes, and potatoes (see p. 108) whose plainness provided relief from the intricacy of his better known work. Golden worms occasionally wriggled free from the stonework as these polished, hollow carvings with golden linings and sometimes a sprinkling of precious stones trickled forth from the firm's workshops.

The house of Fabergé was nationalized in 1918 after the Russian Revolution, and the family fled the country, fearing for their lives. "Peter died a broken man in Switzerland in 1920," says Sarah forlornly. "He had always hoped to return to Russia." Other members of the family scattered around the globe and the jewels were confiscated, many smuggled out of the country. A handful are still missing in what was a tragic end to a groundbreaking era in the goldsmith's art. Now the Fabergé name is owned and managed by Gemfields, a mining company specializing in colored stones. It continues to create designs in his style, such as the Hibiscus cuff, an ode to Fabergé's love of flowers, encrusted with rubies and pink, yellow, and white diamonds that conjure up thoughts of imperial hothouses at the Russian court. Similarly, the Clover ring (see p. 109) from the Les Fleurs de Fabergé collection was created in honor of the 1902 Clover egg, part of the legendary series. The ring, a circle of four-leaf clovers studded with demantoid garnets edged in white diamonds, references the original egg's smooth green enamel covering. These new jewels are ways to wear the history of the house.

In Imperial Russia, Fabergé paid no attention to ethical values or sustainable sources, because art was his only consideration. How the world has changed. Today, the way we mine, treat, and use stones has become a conversation in itself, a part of the designer's journey. To Alexandra Mor, a jewelry designer based in New York, sustainability is about transparency and striving to do better, as well as preserving ancient techniques and culture, which encompass human values, humanity, and spirituality. "I used to call myself the nuts lady," she says jovially, referring to her tagua-seed jewelry collection of 2017, formed around a milky-white seed found in Bali (where she moved to in 2016) and sometimes known as vegetable ivory, because it is the same color, density, weight, and hardness of elephant ivory. Despite being small, tagua is ideal for carving into lavish shapes. Mor has created hoop earrings edged in gold, a garnet ring embedded in a pillow of golden filigree, and also punchy rings crafted from Balinese wood with ornate and complex gold carvings—all using the seed as a receptacle for the stone. She demolishes the myth that sustainable jewelry is worthy, dull, and traditional. In her view it is not enough for the West simply to crusade against all forms of traditional mining, because local communities need support in finding alternative income. In her use of tagua she aims to help elephants, local carvers, and the environment, but her more daunting challenge lies in persuading collectors of the value of completely new materials such as this.

Mor was raised in Israel, where she says the culture of the diamond as precious and aspirational was largely absent. She became accustomed to their magic only when she settled in New York and married the son of a 47th Street diamond cutter. Marrying into a family diamond business was a fascinating and educational experience for her and the timing was excellent. It was the early 2000s and the industry was going through a monumental shift, with mines beginning to produce their own jewelry to sell directly to customers, and dealers, such as Mor's husband, deciding to try their hand at design. She was invited along to learn at the bench while four months pregnant with her first child. She loved it and felt immediately at home.

De Grisogono
Melody of Colours Earrings
Emeralds and turquoises in platinum

Melody of Colours Earrings
Amethysts and turquoises in pink gold

Melody of Colours Ring
Peridot, tsavorites, and turquoises in white gold

Melody of Colours Ring
Amethysts and turquoises in pink gold

Mor's style emerged as stone heavy, combined with a graphic modernist approach within an ethical framework. She celebrated both simplicity and symmetry, crossing the Buddhist notions of emptiness and the absence of self with the Cabala concept of nothingness. She was drawn to empty space, an element of design that lets the object exist in a balance between the positive (what we see) and the negative (the pause between). This led her to create jewels in which an emerald orb or stone was suspended by what appeared to be diamond-encrusted scaffolding that leaned if viewed from the side but was entirely centered when seen from above (see p. 110). Her stones are often soft and round in briolette or cabochon form, and they command our attention, from the milky opaque dome of her Andean blue opal double ring to the hanging pearls, aquamarines, tourmalines, opals, and white topaz of her curved chandelier earrings. Yet despite their scale, her style dominates, as do her sustainable ethics.

She pulled out of retail in the 2010s, because the constant need to follow trends was crushing her creative spirit. "There is a theory in nature that everything which comes to full capacity basically overflows or explodes," she says. Increasing accessibility and the subsequent speed of jewelry production has changed high jewelry and our understanding of its value. This may enable designers to sell more, but sustainability teaches us the benefits of waiting for that seed to fall to the ground, for an artisan to pass down skills, for a diamond to come to the surface. Much of successful jewelry design is about a lifetime of teaching and being taught, and those teachings must be passed on to the collector. Mor is schooling us in the idea that ethical design can be sumptuous and flamboyant as well as honorable, but that we cannot rush the process. The upside to high jewelry being more openly available, however, is that the price tends to be lower. Traditionally, the mere mention of a red carpet-quality jewel would elicit an eye roll from anyone with a budget of less than $1 million. Half a million may get a toe in the door, but big stones required big budgets and, historically, that often ruled out women buying for themselves.

Fawaz Gruosi, founder of Swiss luxury jeweler de Grisogono, decided to disrupt that particular business model when he started the company in 1993. He took a handful of what were then secondary or semiprecious stones, such as turquoise, amethyst, topaz, aquamarines, garnets, and spinels, and mixed them with huge emeralds and white diamonds. His Melody of Colors collection ranged in price from €50,000 to €250,000 ($60,000 to $300,000) and today 90 percent of de Grisogono clients are buying for themselves—a staggering figure, even if a husband or two is lurking in the background. The drama of Gruosi's palette was heightened by his outstanding color combinations and restricted use of pavé, which involves a lot of small stones set closely together. Small stones are cheaper and often lower quality, but they can achieve an intense sparkle, keeping production costs down.

Gruosi also championed the black diamond, long ignored and underappreciated because of its lack of light and stubborn resistance to cutting. In 1995, after taking full control of the company, he became obsessed with the story of the Black Orlov, a 195-carat rough black diamond that surfaced in India. Legend has it that the stone was cursed, having been stolen by a French Jesuit cleric from a sacred Hindu statue in the eighteenth century. Several subsequent owners, from diamond dealers to Russian princesses, committed suicide while it was in their possession and, because it is a cushion-shaped 67.5-carat stone, it has been auctioned a number of times, most recently by Christie's in 2006, where it disappeared from public view.

In 1996 Gruosi decided to launch his own black diamond collection in homage to the Orlov's mysterious power. Although he left the company at the end of 2018, black stones still pepper the collections. His true genius, however, lay in the way he clustered stones together in unorthodox ways. "We like density," says Céline Assimon, de Grisogno's chief executive officer.

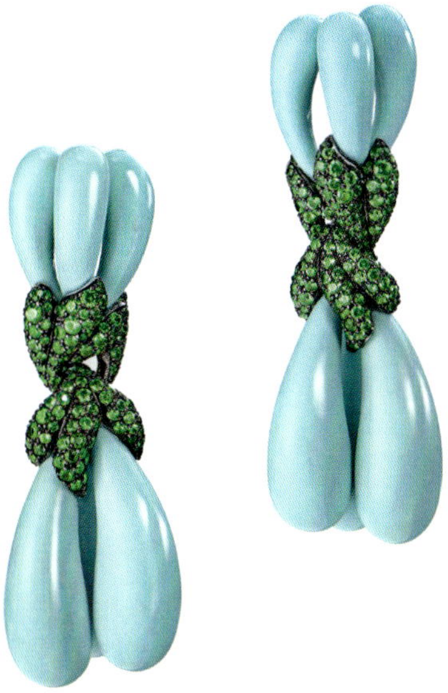

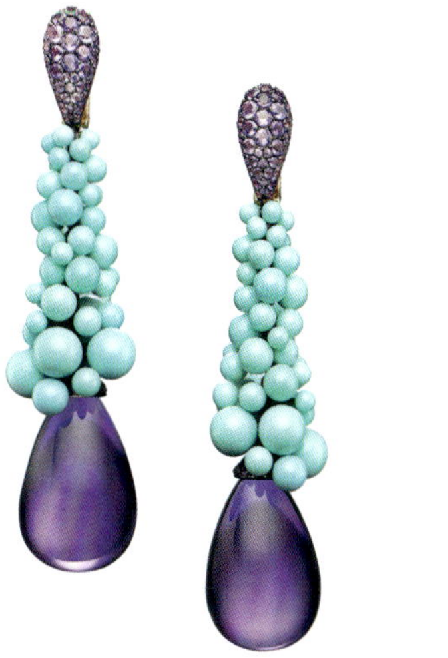

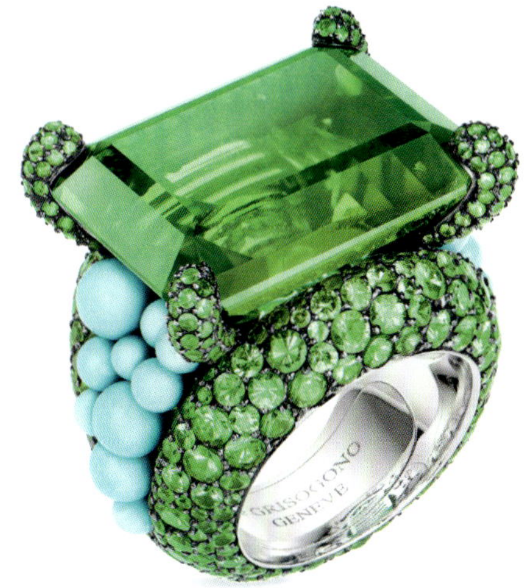
GRISOGONO
GENEVE

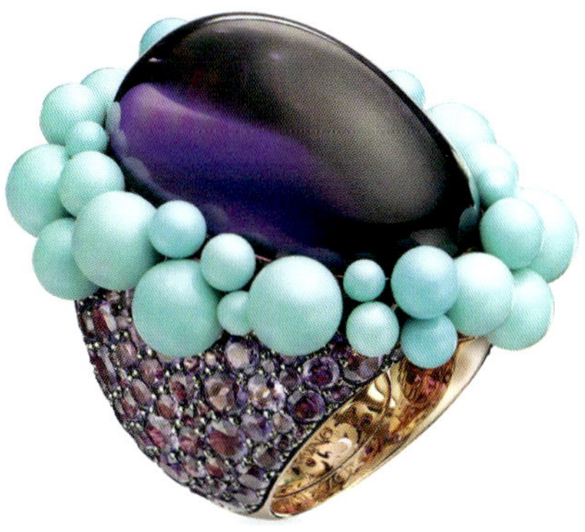

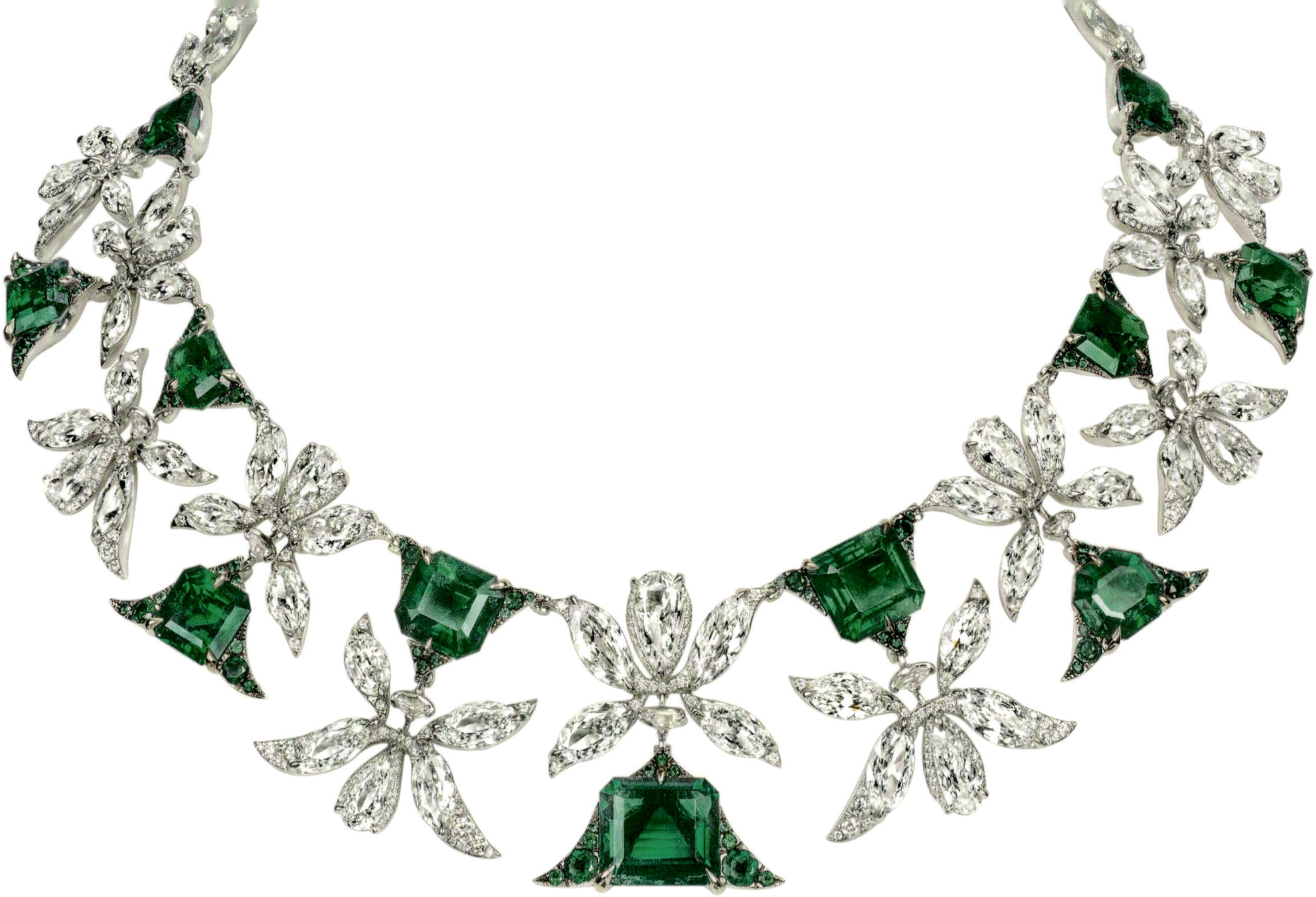

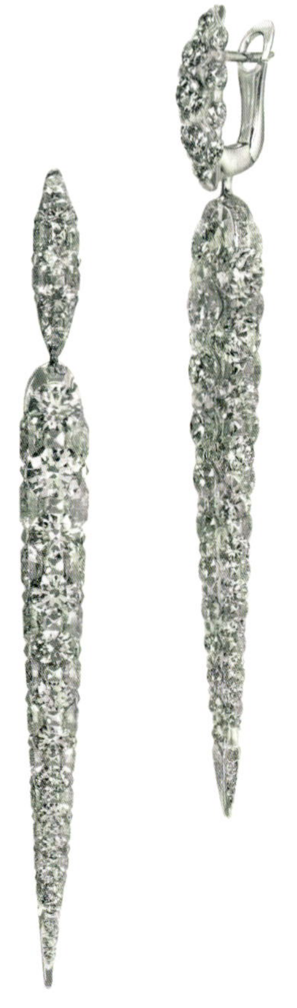

(Preceding pages)
Boghossian
Palmette Necklace, 2017
Diamonds and emeralds in
white gold

Merveilles Icicle Diamond
Long Earrings
Diamonds in white gold

Flawless No Oil Emerald
and Diamonds Necklace
Diamonds and emerald (10.23ct)
in white gold

(Opposite)
Cindy Chao
Peony (Black Label Masterpiece XVIII)
Brooch, 2018
Diamonds, lacquer, and rubies in
titanium and white and yellow gold

"The language between the stones and the materials is a key element in how we communicate our creations, our spirit." Smooth opaque droplets of turquoise cling to the side of a ring or hang provocatively from a pair of ear pendants. Rubies bunch together like cushions around a white diamond center stone. De Grisogno's design codes embrace color, cut, and finish; there is very little metal on show, the stones are packed together to stimulate energy and tension, and the emerald, their favored "noble" stone, is supported by gold or platinum electroplated with black rhodium for a darker, more intense richness. De Grisogno often celebrate such a stone by staging it with a contrasting metal or a cluster of supporting lesser gems to give it prominence. Contrast is the key.

This is not discreet, nondescript jewelry. Gruosi's first client was the Begum Salimah Aga Khan, who commissioned a pair of pearl-and-diamond earrings. His world was high energy and glamorous, representing an international jet-set lifestyle. Gruosi liked to mix a handful of trusted clients with royalty and celebrities at glittering parties in exotic places, so that opening stores in resort locations, such as Porto Cervo in Sardinia, St. Moritz in Switzerland, and the Caribbean island of Saint-Barthélemy, made perfect sense. Assimon's challenge now is to export this particular blend of European allure to Southeast Asia, mainland China, and Hong Kong. She is sanguine about the task ahead, acknowledging that high jewelry is evolving alongside the lives of her clients. De Grisogono jewels are now more likely to be worn to lunch, on the school run, or in the boardroom than to a grandiose formal event. Assimon is pushing titanium and giving her design studio in Geneva free rein. The staging of a hero stone is still integral to the philosophy of the house, however, as is demonstrated by the smooth dome of its cabochon-cut amethyst cocktail ring ensconced in a froth of turquoise beads, supported by pink gold and carpeted with 148 amethysts.

Whereas de Grisogono represents a type of maximalist hedonism that Europeans have enjoyed for decades and in which China is now enthusiastically participating, parts of the Islamic East are still wrestling with tougher times. The civil war that has raged in Syria since 2011 has seen the savage sacking of cultural and artistic monuments. The destruction of archaeological treasures was so shocking that, in protest in 2015, one design house decided to create a necklace using a palmette motif found on the walls of the ruined city of Palmyra (see p. 114). Boghossian, a Geneva-based family jewelers with roots in the Middle East, incorporated eleven rare emeralds separated by matching diamonds to express their profound connection to Syria.

The Boghossians originated in Mardin, "the small Jerusalem," a medieval town perched on the slope of a mountain in what is now southeastern Turkey. Generations of the family traded pearls and diamonds along the Silk Road to Aleppo, Beirut, and Cairo. They were travelers buying colored stones from as far afield as Burma, Thailand, and Colombia, as well as dealing in pearls from China. Albert Boghossian, the current chief executive officer and five generations deep, recalls how each twist of fate and each new location shaped their signature style. At eighteen years old he arrived in India to complete an apprenticeship. "My experience in India gave me a better sense of what beauty could be," he says. "The expansion of colored stones came from the Orient." That influence now shines through in the Islamic curve of the firm's earrings the symmetry of their stonework and the profusion of their color. Boghossian also pioneered the "art of inlay," a technique practiced in ancient Egypt and in the Moghul Empire, where large stones were abundant. With inlay, one stone is set within another with hardly any metal present. Usually, a colored stone, such as an emerald, paraiba, or morganite, is cut so that a smaller diamond can slot securely into its center like a gemstone puzzle, with the light and color of each merged. In one particular necklace, deep blue sapphires are expertly carved to slip into a flat, fiery, 240-carat opal, edged in diamonds.

Another example of how inventive Boghossian are with stones can be found in a collection called Merveilles, where the designer set diamonds on four sides

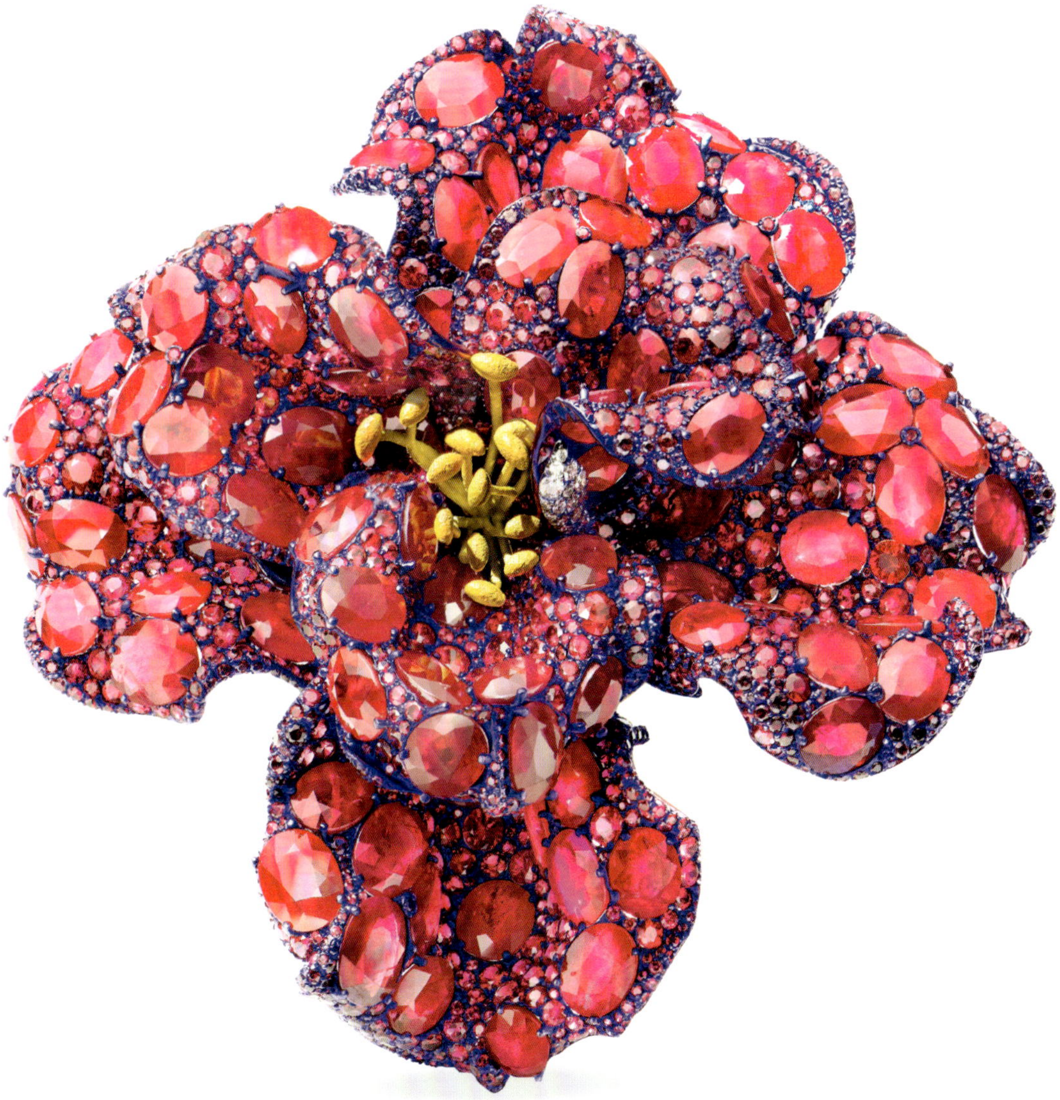

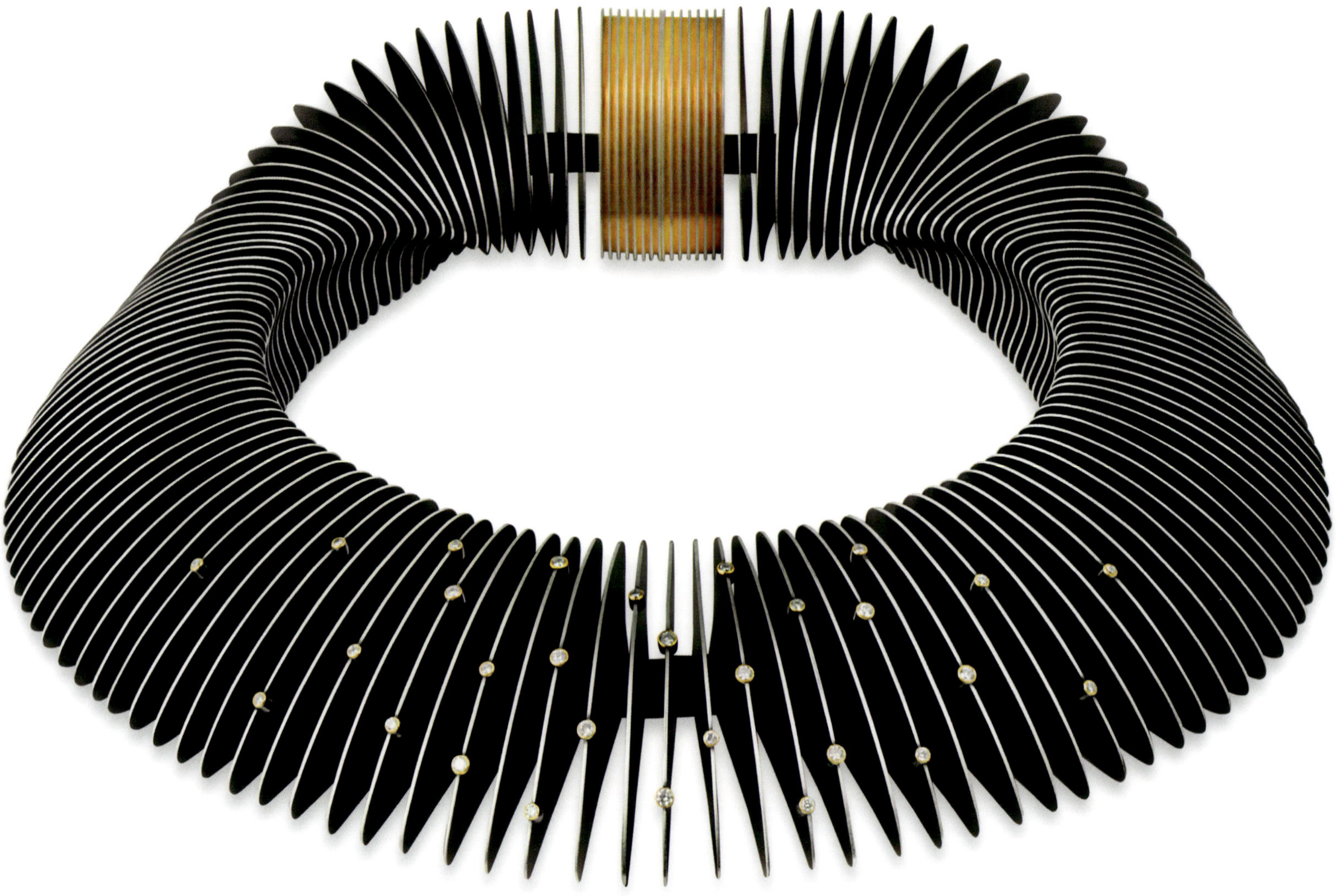

John Moore
Verto Necklace, 2015
Diamonds in extruded silicone, gold, and oxidized silver with magnetic clasp

of a slender metal frame so that the flow of light and reflections remains uninterrupted by metal. The Morvoilles earrings (see p. 114) resemble miniature daggers, sending spears of light from one gemstone to the next; the bracelet is punctuated by emeralds—important stones in the Middle East, where green symbolizes paradise. All colored stones are considered vessels of meaning across Asia: it is a region ablaze with color, from the brilliant blue mosques of Isfahan and Samarkand to the deep red of the Forbidden City in Beijing. While a jewel can have meaning without stones, in this part of the world color is an essential part of its seduction, giving it another dimension.

In East Asia at least, big stones are often combined with highly intricate figurative design. The tradition for complex and delicate craftsmanship remains undisturbed in Taipei, where Cindy Chao spent her childhood learning the merits of art and design. First from her grandfather, who was an architect who built temples across Taiwan; he taught her how to contemplate materials with a detail-orientated patience and passion. Then from her father, a sculptor who showed her how to think with her hands. "Architecture can be a concept in addition to being an academic practice," she says. "Architecture is a mindset to me; it is about the art of arranging color, light, and shade in space governed by its structure." Chao applies that ethos to the extraordinary jewels she creates, with her organic forms of twisted, sculpted metal embracing a density of stonework that dazzles the eye. No surface is spared, no line straight. She quotes the Modernist architect Antoni Gaudí, whose sensual curves influence her work: "The straight line belongs to men; the curved line belongs to God and nature"—and nature is her most potent inspiration.

When she began in 2004, alongside her black and white label collections (black being unique masterpieces limited in number and white her more accessible but core collections), she decided to make one butterfly a year to symbolize her continual metamorphosis as an artist. Her first fluttered to life in 2008, and in 2009 her Royal Butterfly brooch (see p. 94), with its haphazard antennae and stone-studded body, found its way into the permanent collection of the Smithsonian. The wings were a feat of engineering comprising a bottom layer of diamond pavé amplified by four flat rough diamond slices placed on top in a technique she developed specifically for the piece. Some 2,328 stones weighing a total of seventy-seven carats were used in a palette ranging from brown to purple, yellow to gray from the front and green to red from the back, giving us two distinct jewels in one. Her big diamonds are not gratuitous or attention-seeking in terms of design, but they do require confidence on the part of the wearer, because her jewels are very, very large. This scale, combined with intricacy of execution, emphasizes a purity of design that is both silky smooth to the touch and mesmerizing to the eye.

The Peony brooch (see p. 117) is a case in point and is literally a handful: perhaps her most ambitious project of stone engineering yet, it required 87,000 hours of work. Around 2010 one of her earliest collectors approached her with an old family necklace containing 105 rubies that he wanted reimagined. Chao meditated on it for some time before a flower consisting of 2,485 rubies totaling 228.6 carats emerged in her mind. Her workshop created a honeycomb titanium base and anodized it purple to contrast with the blood red of the stones. She resisted the temptation to add a big center stone, instead opting for an array of acid-yellow pistils. It was a phenomenal construction of undulating metal; each stone was set at a particular angle using a wax-modeling technique called *la cire perdue* (literally "lost wax") that goes back to the eighteenth century. Chao's design may be modern but the way she works—her sketching, casting, and stone setting—are centuries old. Philosophically, she admires the greats of European history and has embraced the thinking of Michelangelo, who during his creative process, described the experience of seeing an angel in a block of marble and carving until he set it free. Chao does this in her own way, using a network of stones to summon her natural wonders.

Nikos Koulis
Oui Earrings, 2018
Black enamel and white diamonds in white gold

Feelings Earrings, 2019
White diamonds in white and yellow gold

Many designers acknowledge that stones have a soul, an inexplicable allure that at the very least warrants introspection, but relatively few are willing to limit the impact or inclusion of stones within high jewelry for the sake of the art. When he began in the late 1990s, British designer John Moore was entirely consumed by metal, especially sheet metal, because of the way light glides across its surface. He felt that stones, with their jaunty cuts, interrupted that effortless sheen, and that diamond-encrusted gold would lose its poetry. He discovered anodized aluminum while at university, and was attracted by its lightweight, tough, and most importantly affordable nature. It was "student-loan friendly" at a time when he was playing with the idea of creating large-scale winged tiaras on a budget. But still the absence of stones was deliberate.

Moore's 2008 Elytra collection was formed from drilled flat strips of aluminum threaded together. This morphed into his next collection, Vane, but the global recession hit him hard and his bigger bespoke pieces stalled. He attempted to water down his work and for a time churned out smaller, prettier earrings in pastel shades, but he soon realized it was creative suicide. So, when in 2010 an art collector from Singapore called Tuan Lee commissioned a necklace that pushed him creatively to the next level, he went the other way, into bigger, darker, and bolder territory. The brief was open and he made a model from old cereal boxes, getting the green light to produce what eventually became the Verto necklace. He threaded ninety disks of colored aluminum, a metal softer and more brittle than gold, with extruded silicone rubber in an invention of his own making. The rubber allowed for the piece to flex into different shapes on the body. It was a triumph, a towering sculpture of metal rising up like a fortress around the ears, but the scale and uniqueness of his work made it difficult to price. It stood squarely outside the normal parameters of jewelry, just as his talent had produced a jewel beyond the realms of the ordinary. "In Victorian times aluminum was more expensive than gold, because it was harder to extract from the earth's crust," he says thoughtfully. Our value system has always prized scarcity as the ultimate luxury, so the proliferation of industrial materials is disrupting centuries of accepted preciousness.

Moore eventually succumbed to the lure of precious stones in 2015, when he included diamonds in the smallest version of his Verto necklace (see p. 118), on the edges of each disk at the front of the piece. Its weight and suppleness meant it clung to the collarbone with a satisfyingly cold yet firm grip. Then came a much larger version of Verto, which creatively dwarfed all previous incarnations. It was called the Lacewing, and the perforations running through each blackened oxidized silver disk became a symbolic reference to the veins of an insect's wing. This monster of extremity also had diamonds sprinkled across the curves at the front, its disks shaped like blackened blades fanning out around the shoulders.

Moore's stones were still small, but their very existence got him the attention he had yearned for from galleries, carrying him to a much wider audience and winning him numerous awards. However, the balance was key: too many stones and his futuristic edginess would be muted; too few and they would be lost within the dark foliage of metal. He is dabbling with the idea of a larger center stone but worries about a big gem stealing the limelight. Although his ambition is to go bigger and wilder, his priorities will always be sculptural form, movement, and texture. He will make sure design comes first—his survival as an artist is at stake.

While some designers turn to bigger stones (especially diamonds) in a bid to foster collectability in their pieces, the idea can quickly backfire if the design is too commercial. The niche and unique may attract only a handful of collectors, but quantity is not the aim for smaller independent jewelers such as Moore. They are entrepreneurs by default, building a business as a means to facilitate their art and to attain financial freedom so they can design without limits. Greek designer Nikos Koulis appreciates the investment component of his jewelry, because he wants to create jewels his clients can rely on in times of economic need. He required all the "instinct and persistence" he could muster when he opened

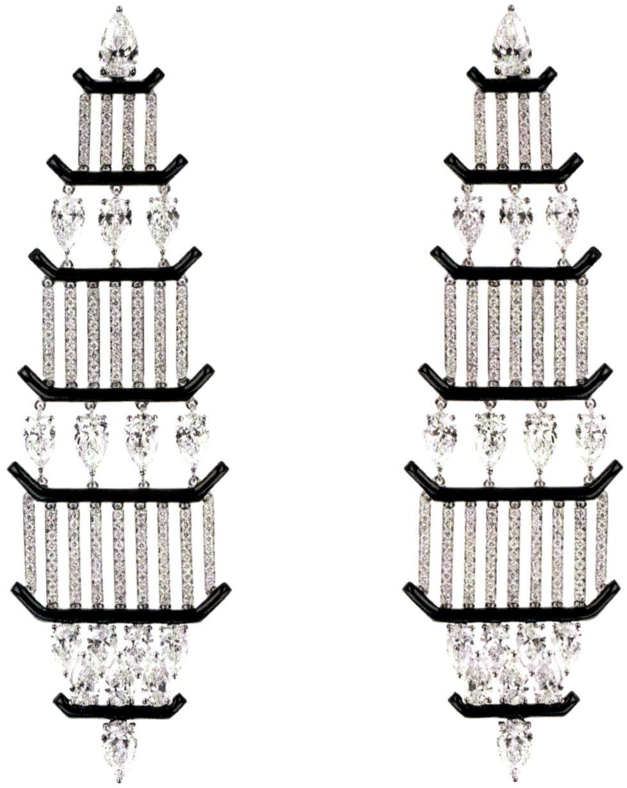

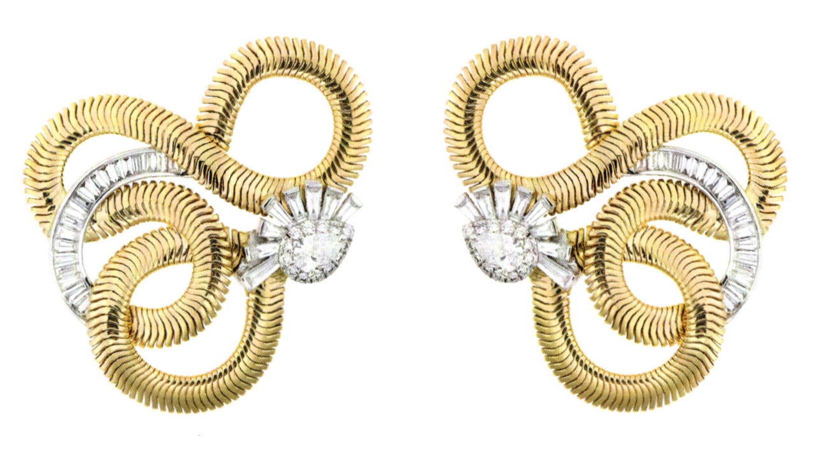

Lorenz Bäumer
Scarabée d'Automne Brooch, 2015
Citrine, enamel, and white and yellow diamonds in white gold

Scarabée d'Eté Brooch, 2015
Blue and yellow sapphires, chocolate and white diamonds, enamel, and fire opal in white gold

his flagship boutique in Athens in 2014, because Greece was experiencing its toughest economic crisis in living memory. Koulis stayed, despite the predictions of doom and negativity. His work was selling well in the rest of Europe, the United States, and Russia and that gave him the confidence to brave the downturn and to further develop his creative Greek identity.

Koulis's jewelry is a mix of stylized architectural influences instead of the more obvious Greek symbolism. He employs twenty artisans to bring his visions to life from workshops in the center of Athens; as traditional goldsmithing techniques, such as hot enamel, are passed down through the generations, they are adapted, modernized, and given new life. All his pieces are handmade, using a plethora of stones and an ornate simplicity. "I never desired to be modern," he says. "I cherish classics. I wish my pieces to convey a timeless, light, eclectic energy, and a liberating spirit that won't fade away."

Although modernism may not have been his intention, his design is highly geometric, featuring clean lines with a variety of tapered stone cuts. Art Deco infuses his work and he references the classic pillar, deconstructing it in a pair of chandelier earrings (see p. 121) using pear-shaped white diamonds and black enamel, a signature added to many of his collections. His monochrome jewels are delicate and airy with an occasional burst of color in red, green, or blue. He avoids the usual round, brilliant, solitaire diamond, preferring oval, cushion, crescent, bullet, pear, marquise, baguette, and trillion-cut gemstones, designed with a captivating poetry of movement. The Feelings collection is his most esoteric to date, paying homage to Greek maritime knots, using flat flexible gold chain as the framework and lacing it with tapered diamonds (see p. 121). This is a deceptively light-hearted vision of high jewelry. The stones are big but jump around between springy gold loops, the curves and spirals of which beg to be played with. There may be stark lines, but the collection is overwhelmingly focused on sensual curves; the challenge for Koulis has been to create a new kind of fluidity capable of housing an eight-carat cushion-cut diamond without interrupting his flow.

The idea comes first for Koulis: it "can be based on a beautiful stone I found that I will torture myself to turn into an exquisite piece." He is magnetically drawn to emeralds for their color and the imperfections to be found in the "garden" of the stone—the inclusions that are usually considered flaws in other gems but are valued in emeralds—and he believes that jewelry is more than vanity and luxury. It is an ingenious, beautiful, fearless expression of our most compelling inner selves, an emotion in precious metal that is meant to last forever.

So much of jewelry is caught up with emotion, but rarely does it expand beyond three of the five basic senses: sight, touch, hearing, taste, and smell. Sight is first, attracting the magpie in each of us to touch, reinforcing our notion of beauty in the smooth contours of a jewel. Occasionally, the sound of an armful of bangles chiming together or the clack of a pair of free-flowing earrings adds another dimension to wearing jewelry, but it is not often that smell enters the equation. Paris-based designer Lorenz Bäumer, however, has given the stone a function beyond beauty. Using science to inject another dimension into his work, he has introduced perfume to the experience of wearing his jewelry in a strangely beautiful series of insect brooches. In his hands, the humble beetle has been reborn as a palm-size brooch, each a unique example of one of a handful of Scarabée (stylized scarab) designs with a secret mechanized compartment. Press down on a gemstone near the creature's head and the wings part to release a waft of fragrance held within in a material similar to a metallic sponge. Bäumer made the body of the Automne (Fall) beetle with aluminum and did extensive research into the use of titanium in prosthetics, finding that the metal's porousness lets it hold and then release matter, in this case scented matter. He then adapted that technology to increase the sensory perception of his jewelry.

Having first studied engineering, Bäumer opened a salon in Paris in 1989 selling his own costume jewelry, and by 1992 he decided to devote all his time to making jewelry, just as the Internet had become publicly available. It was

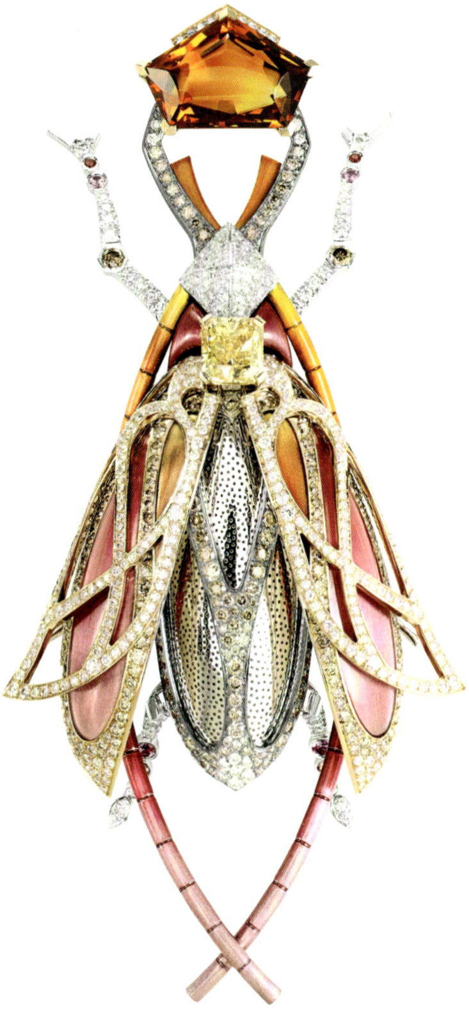
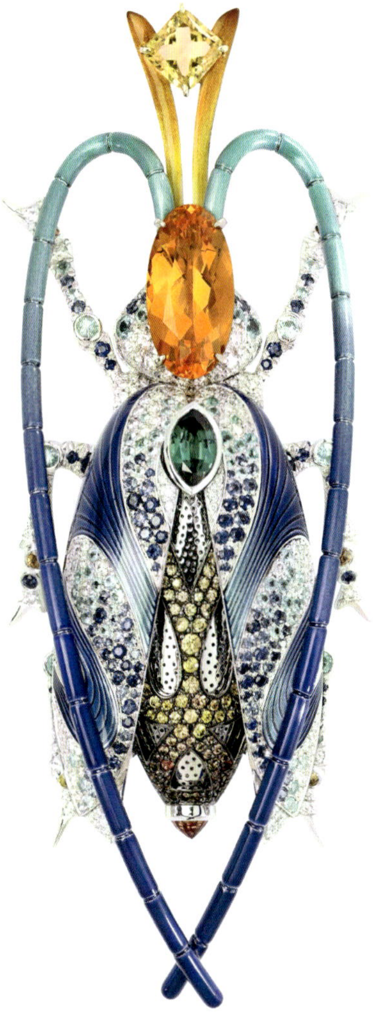

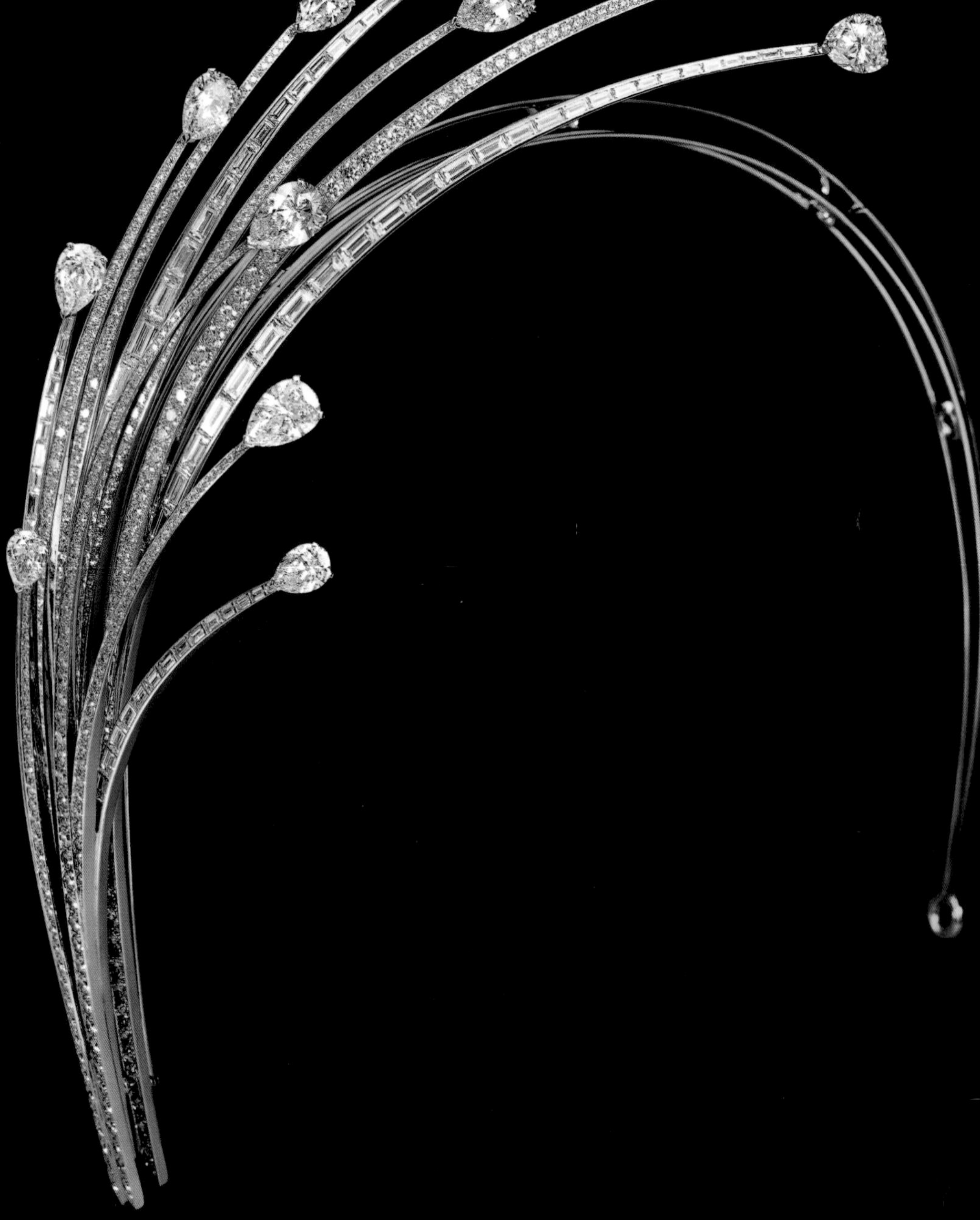

Lorenz Bäumer
Diamond Tiara "Ecume de mer", 2011
Diamonds in white gold

a fortuitous piece of timing; as the world's understanding of communication, consumption, and accessibility changed, he began developing and selling fine jewelry to a wider audience. "I'm an artist, a shrink, and a craftsman," he says ruefully. When he is not conducting scientific research, he makes geometric jewelry for royalty, among others; in 2010, prior to the wedding of Prince Albert II of Monaco and former Olympic swimmer Charlene Wittstock, he entered and won an anonymous competition to design the bride's wedding tiara. His creation, called *Ecume de mer* (Sea Foam), celebrated the diamond as frosted water with an arc of pear-shaped stones symbolizing the unfolding crest of a wave. It is asymmetrical modernism, typical of his shapely architectural style.

If there were ever a poster child for value in jewelry, it would be the pear-shaped white diamond. Gold on its own is only worth so much, but stones increase the value of design exponentially and diamonds, in particular, are loved and loathed for their index of value. Obscure gems, such as grandidierite or andalusite, are harder to pin down and price, which gives designers more freedom to assign their own value and encourages collectors to think for themselves. Diamonds still reign supreme, however, and jewelers leave them out at their peril. Nak Armstrong, a designer based in Texas, knows this to his cost. "Include them if you want to sell," he says pointedly. Stones are his passion in their every conceivable size, shape, and color, but, despite his acknowledgment of the power of diamonds, he relegates them to a supporting role in his own work.

When he created his first eponymous collection in 2011, his inspiration was fabric, so he focused on smaller stones that he ruffled, pleated, and folded into metal in a haphazard ruched configuration he called "stone plissé." The gems he chose were sharp, triangular, and flowed tonally into each other so that the yellows, pinks, greens, and browns had a rainbowlike quality. With his travels influencing his creativity, Roman architecture and Japanese origami have seeped into his work, and using tiny stones, he builds patterns with blocks of pixelated color. Armstrong starts with an idea, a design, and then he cuts the stones to fit, using specially selected cutters from all over the world to realize his ambitions. He is fond of labradorites, but few cutters are willing or able to carve labradorites $\frac{1}{12}$–$\frac{1}{8}$ inch (2–3 mm) across into tapered cuts. Even $\frac{1}{8}$–$\frac{1}{4}$ inch (3–6 mm) presents a challenge, and although he sometimes goes large, to the forty-five carats of his Parrot earrings (see p. 126) in opals, tourmaline, golden brown sapphire, tanzanite, tourmaline, and diamonds, the majority of his design is miniature and intricately assembled.

In the late 1990s, when he switched from scarves to jewels, gold prices were low enough to let him experiment. The dot-com revolution was in full swing and the luxury economy was booming. Then came 9/11 and Armstrong assumed his fledgling jewelry career was over. Strangely enough, the opposite happened. "We saw this dramatic increase in growth right after 9/11 and it continued for many years," he says. It resembled a postwar spending surge and a joyous sense of being alive. Americans rallied together, supporting the economy and, before the global recession of 2008 hit, jewelry in the United States became more elaborate and experimental. Armstrong's three-dimensional mosaics with their splinters of color became surprisingly popular in upmarket department stores Barney's and Bergdorf Goodman in New York, given that in the country, bigger is usually better. His Encrusted Ruched Roman Helmet ring (see p. 126) is a rare departure from his delicate earrings: it has a colossal spessartite center stone looming out like an eyeball from a patchwork of jagged diamonds, aquamarines, sapphires, labradorites, andalusites, and topaz. But then he enjoys challenging the relationship between the gold and the stones in different ways. He creates sharp, structured silhouettes within a style that feels decidedly graceful for something this gem heavy, and although his work is dedicated to gemstones, its genius lies in a touch so light, so delicate that the stones melt into each other with just a flickering rainbow of color remaining.

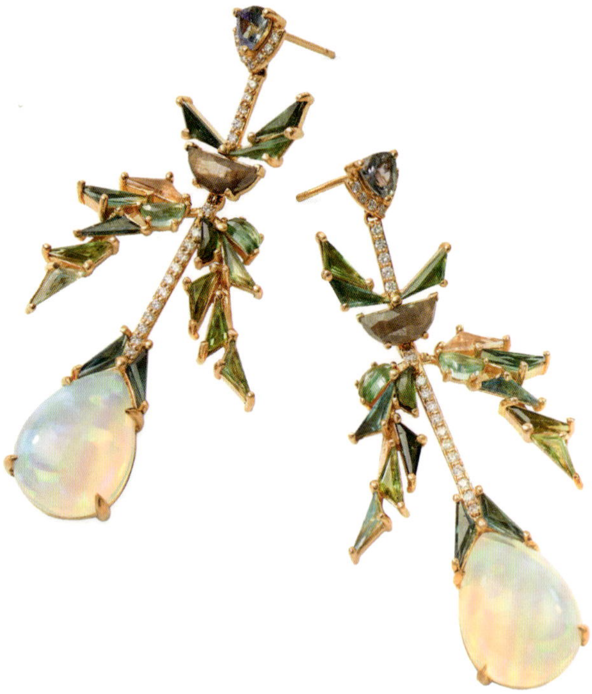

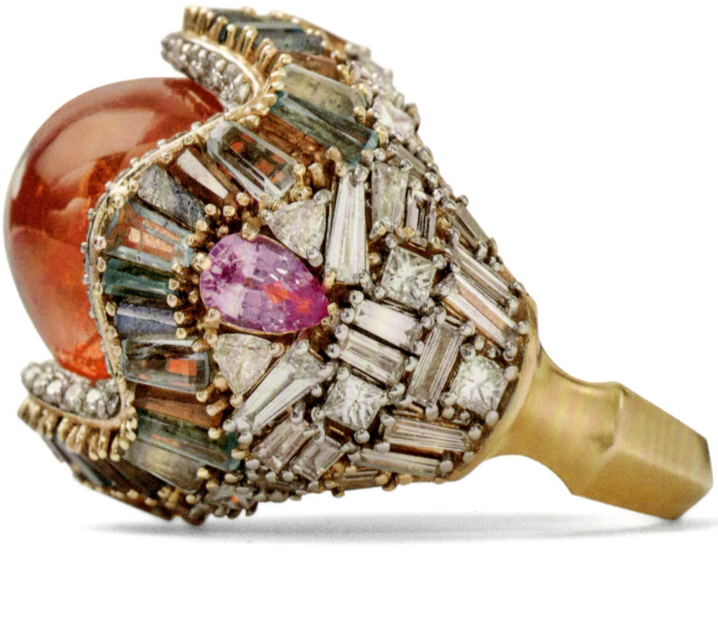

Nak Armstrong
Parrot Earrings, 2018
Ethiopian opals (14.94cts), golden brown sapphires, green and peach tourmalines, tanzanites, and white diamonds in recycled rose gold
Private collection

Encrusted Ruched Roman Helmet Ring, 2018
Andalusites, aquamarines, imperial topaz, labradorites, pink sapphire, reclaimed pink and white diamonds, and spessartite (32.64ct) in recycled white gold
Private collection

Stones represent the purest form of investment in high jewelry and have done since the Renaissance, when painters and sculptors learned their craft in goldsmiths' workshops, turning rocks into art. They were a beautiful store of portable wealth when war was ever-present and before named or branded design added value. The simple brooch of the Middle Ages gave way to pendants, rings, earrings, gems clipped onto bodices or sown into fabric, even tucked into the hair with elaborate features and clips. From the late 1600s great matching sets of jewels called parures, which include as many as sixteen pieces, from a tiara to a single button, gave the upper classes new ways to wear stones.

It wasn't until the nineteenth century that contemporary jewelry ushered in a rebirth of design. Stones were humbled, the design powerfully simple by comparison as Art Nouveau, Art Deco, and modernism took hold. The value of gemstones remained sacrosanct, but they were now at the service of design, so now they could be playful and irreverent.

Auctions provide a global platform for artists to showcase their work and to track fluctuations in stone prices. Trends in taste often emerge through high-profile auctions that change the course and perception of jewelry design. In 1987 the recently deceased Duchess of Windsor's jewels were auctioned at Sotheby's in Geneva and, having had an original estimate of $7 million, fetched $33,507,131, making it then the most expensive jewelry sale of all time. Nicknamed "the alternative Crown Jewels," the sale featured an embarrassment of rubies and diamonds with ninety-five lots and three hundred jewels in total. Bidders included Elizabeth Taylor, who phoned in from beside the pool in her Los Angeles home to buy a diamond clip for $632,327. Apart from a 206-carat sapphire pendant, the attraction of many of the jewels was their design. "This was a turning point which propelled jewelry into the media," says David Bennett, the worldwide chairman of Sotheby's jewelry department.

The Duchess of Windsor represented the transition from the old world to the new. After Edward VIII had abdicated in order to marry her, this American divorcée and serious jewelry collector flaunted cutting-edge design, wearing pieces traditional royalty could not. She would often involve herself in the design process at her favorite houses Van Cleef & Arpels, Cartier, and Belperron. Her rebellious, rule-breaking, contemporary style eclipsed the stones entirely, paving the way for a new era in design-led jewels. Her style *was* the event at that 1987 sale, compelling Sotheby's to exhibit and auction her collection as if it were art. Gemstones, whatever their size, could not diminish the art itself. After all, as jewelry historian Vanessa Cron points out, "The relationship you have with the jewel is not based on the stones."

FOUR

INSPIRED BY NATURE: INDEPENDENCE AND CREATIVITY

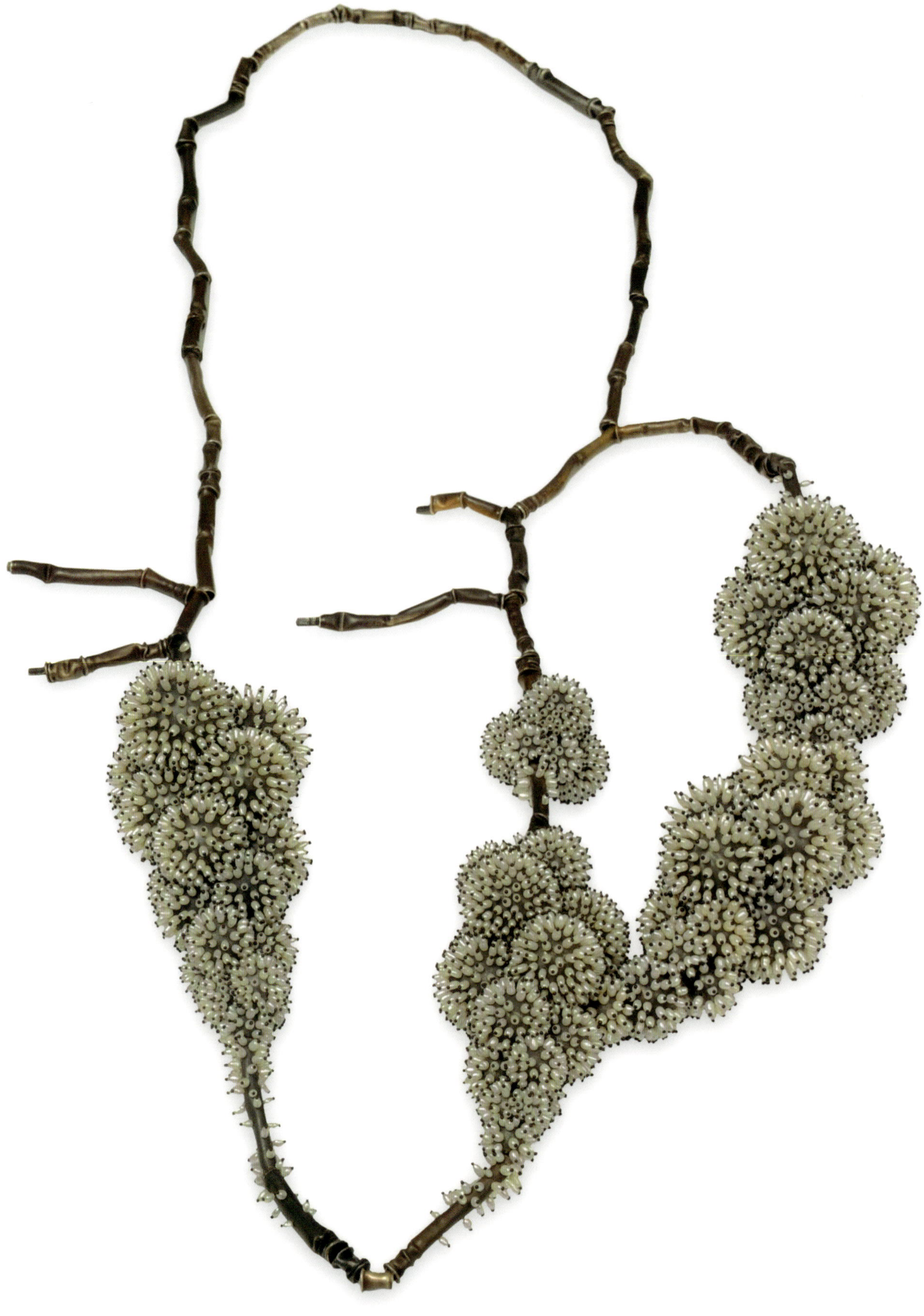

Sam Tho Duong
Frozen Necklace, 2013
Freshwater pearls, nylon,
and oxidized silver
Private collection

Independent thought rejects convention and uses personal experience to create a new way of seeing. The natural world is one of the first and most basic connections we have to a power greater than ourselves and design acts as a channel for this energy, materializing objects of great ingenuity and beauty. In jewelry, Naturalistic design has inspired figurative depictions of flowers crafted in glass by the likes of René Lalique (1860–1945) and abstract sea creatures etched into gold pendants by the Surrealist artist Max Ernst (1891–1976). Each creator adds a part of themselves to this reinterpretation of nature and independent designers, in particular, have taken Naturalistic design to new heights. A luscious garden, a dense forest, or a secluded mountain provides not only the depth of quiet from which creation is born, but also a chance to connect to the ultimate source of beauty and add meaning of a spiritual and physical kind.

French jeweler René Boivin (1864–1917) became fascinated by botany in the late nineteenth to early twentieth century. After his premature death, his wife Jeanne took over the business, unleashing the full force of her own Naturalistic leanings and creating some of the most iconic jewels of the 1930s. One of these was an enormous articulated ruby and amethyst Starfish brooch made in collaboration with in-house designer Juliette Moutard in 1937. It was so realistic that it seemed to come to life in the palm of the hand, as if it were struggling to crawl back into the sea. The brooch was bought by Oscar-winning Hollywood actress Claudette Colbert, who pinned its glittering body to her oversized lapel. Another Boivin piece was acquired by the heiress Millicent Rogers and another by São Schlumberger, a stylish and well-connected patron of the arts. These were all powerful women, ready to buy the kind of design that propelled Boivin to preeminence among designers whose work was characterized by a combination of staggeringly intricate detail and delicate, realistic depictions of nature. Then in 1948 Jeanne Toussaint, working at Cartier, unleashed a lithe, three-dimensional Panther brooch in yellow gold, emeralds, and black enamel onto an unsuspecting Duchess of Windsor, who would have had little idea of how iconic her big cat would become. While it was by no means an exclusively European phenomenon, the exquisite craftsmanship required to achieve this degree of realism was often carried out in the workshops of Paris. It attracted the grandest patrons with the deepest appreciation for magnificent jewels in a society where extravagance still reigned.

One of the most prominent of these patrons was the Spanish-born Silvia Rodriguez de Rivas, Countess of Castilleja de Guzmán, who married into the French aristocracy. She lived a lavish existence in Paris, which included changing her classic, gem-studded jewels three times a day to match a succession of glamorous outfits. Her young granddaughter Victoire watched intently at her knee, transfixed by the movement of her jewels and dazzled by their beauty. At just five years old Victoire de Castellane realized that jewelry would be her passion, because she was fascinated with the way it danced on the bodies of the women around her.

Silvia's glamorous social circle included the fashion designer Christian Dior (1905–57), who scandalized Paris after World War II with his "New Look" of curved shoulders, tightly cinched waists, and full skirts. That silhouette would become synonymous with 1950s style and its postwar appetite for an exaggerated femininity. In 1947 Dior's first collection featured jewelry, his Corolla—a "river of diamonds" twisted around the body and peppered with black pearls—creating a stir despite being fake or "costume" and crafted from glass and paste. Floral design ran through his entire life's work, a love affair with flowers having started in childhood in Normandy, where his mother created a rose garden housing

Victoire de Castellane for Dior Joaillerie
Diorissimo Necklace, 1999
Cultured pearls, diamonds, and emeralds
in white gold

Victoire de Castellane
Acidae Lili Pervertus Bracelet, 2010
Colored sapphires, diamonds, emeralds,
lemon chrysoprase, tsavorites, and rubies
in lacquered silver, white and yellow gold

Cana Bisextem Now Bracelet, 2010
Diamonds, emeralds, and garnets in
lacquered silver, white and yellow gold

twenty different varieties, as well as jasmine, lily of the valley, honeysuckle, and passionflowers. The young Christian would pore over seed catalogues, bewitched by their beauty.

When Dior died suddenly in 1957, the company was left in chaos. A twenty-one-year-old Yves Saint Laurent was appointed artistic director but departed three years later to to do his military service. Marc Bohan took over, introducing a slimmer, more conservative vision, and the house's jewelry entered a deeply conventional phase. Male customers were buying showy but staid jewelry for the women in their lives as an investment and sticking to the safety of traditional stones.

In 1978 the Boussac Group, then owners of Dior, filed for bankruptcy. Bernard Arnault, head of multinational luxury goods conglomerate LVMH, acquired and resurrected the company in the mid-1980s. In 1988 he asked Victoire de Castellane to head a new fine jewelry department, and twenty years on her vision for a playful, colorful, offbeat design is maturing nicely. "I arrived in Place Vendôme, which was very classical, conformist, and in a way bourgeois," says de Castellane, now artistic director at Dior Jewelry. "They weren't having fun. They were very strict with no risk of creativity." The lily of the valley necklace called Diorissimo was one of ten designs in de Castellane's first high jewelry collection, inspired by Christian Dior's infatuation with flowers. Its organic, delicate spray of buds and leaves wrapped around the throat in a cluster of pearls and diamonds.

The collection that changed de Castellane the most came in 2007 with the flower-inspired Belladone Island. Dissatisfied with the simple shades of white, yellow, and rose gold, she used lacquer to amplify her color palette and pushed herself and her workshop to the limit with her exacting requirements. This eyebrow-raising collection included a Gothic floral fantasy of fat blooms hanging from a branch that clung to the neck, edged in pink lacquer with spiky, unruly leaves. In 2014 these multicolor triffids spilled over into a personal collection called Animalvegetablemineral in which she created "cyborg blooms"—best experienced, according to de Castellane, by the light of the moon. The Amanita Santana Diabolus necklace and Cana Bisextem Now bracelet are both masterly blends of menacing petals in electrified hues, with the glossy lacquer-on-silver of the futuristic blooms interrupted by a sprinkling of colored stones. The dense red of the Opiom Velourosa Purpra necklace and glittering blue of the Lunae Lumen Holly Colorum bracelet are more conventional and subdued, but still intense. Each jewel is mesmerizing in texture and tone and each dominates with a curvaceous sensuality.

De Castellane's 2019 collection Gem Dior is her biggest yet, at ninety-nine pieces, and is a colorful jumble of geometric stone cuts: baguette, square, pear, marquise, cushion, and oval. She describes it as a pixelated close-up of the past twenty years. "I'm not working for the market, I'm working for women," she asserts. She is part of a chain of creativity spanning thousands of years in which jewelry has been fundamental to identity. It is a witness to the female experience: as women progress, so do their jewels. These days her male clients are also more sensitive to the "decor" of the jewel, feeling the pull of desire rather than first approaching her work as an investment. Thanks to de Castellane, Dior has evolved from showy, commercial design to a more experimental, avant-garde look.

If color is the lifeblood of jewelry and precious stones its beating heart, lacquer and enamel add dimensions of texture and tone to both metal and mineral and traditionally bring drama to design. Sometimes nature's hues are best illustrated in an exaggerated palette and, when applied by de Castellane, lacquer becomes an intense, gleaming backdrop to accent and contrast stones in acidic colors. For some makers, painting with enamel becomes the primary element of the design itself like paint on a canvas. Russian artist Ilgiz Fazulzyanov re-creates astonishingly accurate scenes from nature in the Art Nouveau style by using enamel glazes of different thicknesses on top of engravings to play with light and shadow. He is so ensconced in this world that he has even developed an invisible gem-setting technique, where pavéed stones appear to be an extension of the enamel.

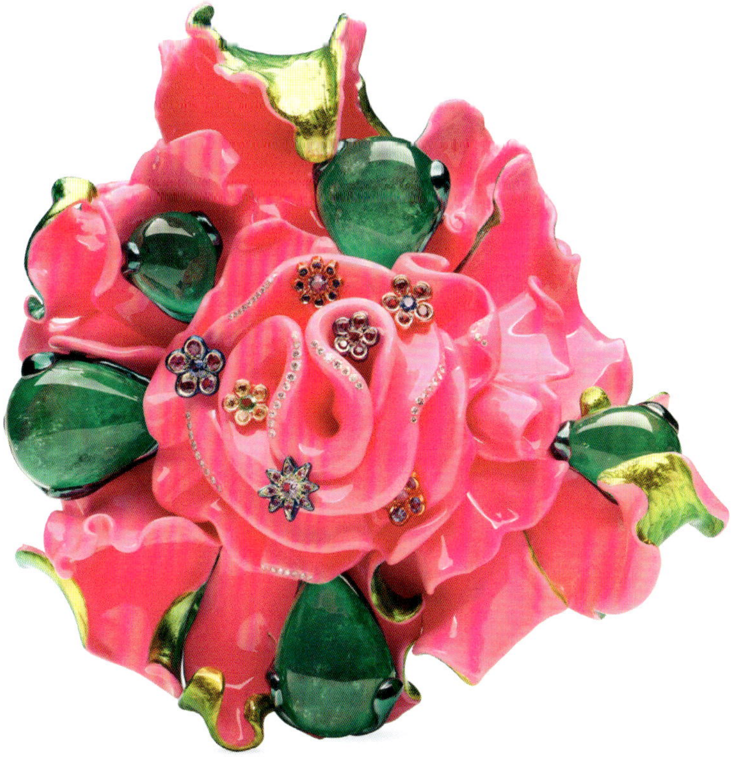

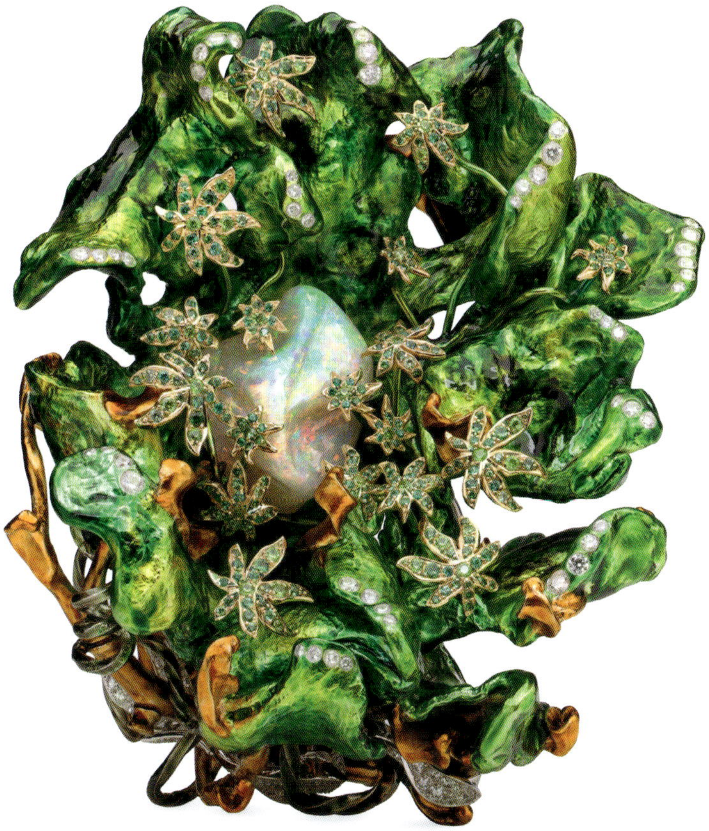

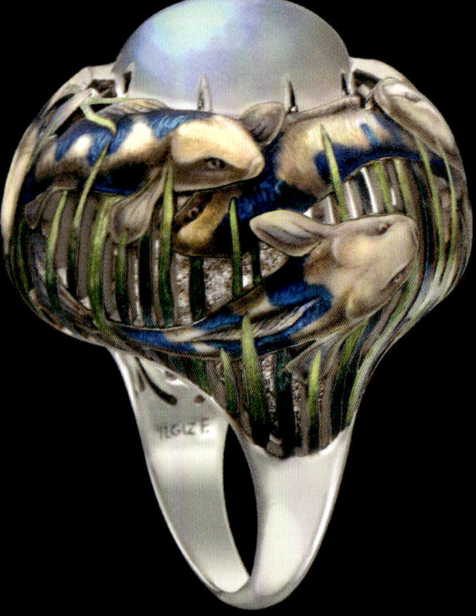

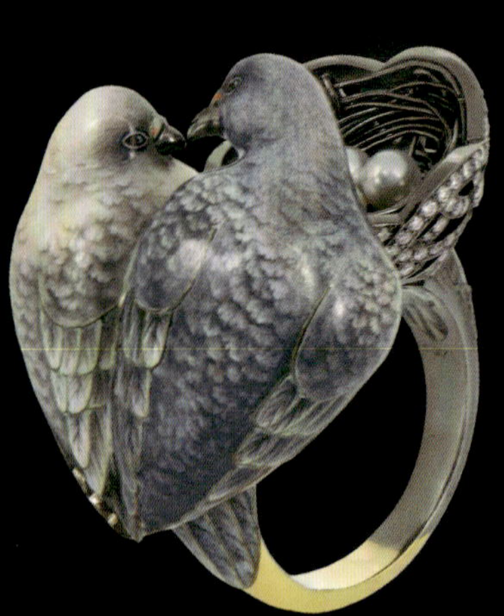

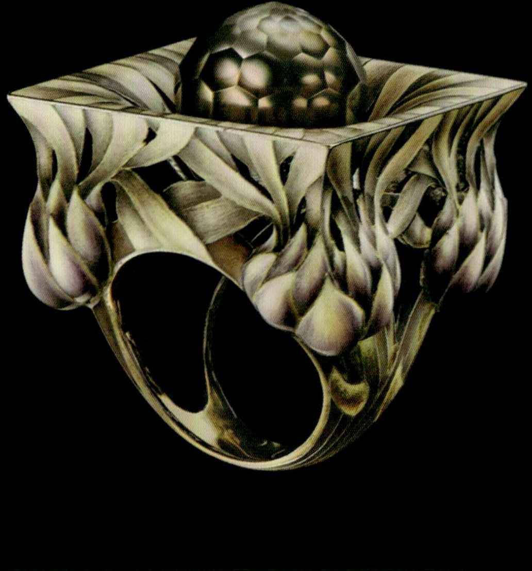

Ilgiz Fazulzyanov
Carp Ring, 2014
Champlevé, hot and painted enamel, diamonds, and moonstone in rhodium-plated gold
Private collection

Doves Ring, 2017
Akoya pearls, *basse-taille* and painted enamel, and diamonds in rhodium-plated gold
Private collection

Artichoke Ring, 2012
Basse-taille and painted enamel and faceted pearl in rhodium-plated gold
Private collection

None of this seemed like an obvious career choice in the far reaches of Tatarstan 450 miles (700 km) from Moscow—where Fazulzyanov was born in 1968, near the republic's capital, Kazan. In the late Middle Ages, Kazan was a key political and trading outpost for the Golden Horde, part of the Mongol Empire, and today it boasts one of Russia's oldest art schools, at which Fazulzyanov became a student. The first commissions he accepted were crafted using dentist's instruments, but he soon found his way to the heat and texture of high-quality enamel, discovering a preference for mixing French and Russian enamels to achieve his own unique finish, smelting at 1,800°F (970°C). He was at home creatively, later expanding his repertoire to include the filigree and engraving that appear in much of his work.

Fazulzyanov opened a workshop in the Kazan Kremlin and won a series of competitions in the 1990s, then in 2003 traveled to Moscow, where he achieved international acclaim. Here, he created an array of intricately complex jewels and entered a higher level of artistry. His fascination with nature expressed itself in vivid color and through the complexity of his creations. His Carp ring features champlevé and painted enamel so detailed that light appears to catch the silky blue scales of each fish as they flick in and out of reeds swirling around a center moonstone. His doves in *basse-taille* enamel, kissing tail to tail as they stand guard over a nest of akoya pearl eggs, or his scramble of dragonflies, the vein of each quivering wing echoing the red rubies beneath, express a monumental talent. He has come to symbolize a Russian style and, while the execution of his work takes into consideration Japanese, Chinese, Georgian, Armenian, Russian, and French enamel techniques, his unique voice is enhanced by his Kazan identity. This is his ode to nature, a type of poetry he feels for the world around him.

He has always made one-of-a-kind pieces; his 2018 Mountain rings were his first foray into an actual collection. They feature handmade guilloche engraving under enamel. This masterful display of technique pays homage to the flawless execution of Fabergé (see pp. 108–11), the master craftsman who 150 years earlier had elevated enamel to the level of national treasure. When Fabergé tired of creating elaborate eggs and sumptuous jewels for the Russian court, he turned to the humble vegetable for inspiration, creating a potato out of pink-brown agate and gold. Fazulzyanov has followed suit with an Artichoke ring of sublime beauty. Square and almost stone-free save for a magnificent black-faceted pearl at its center, it is a lesson in tone, with soft purples blending into browns and greens and culminating in a shelf of leaves. Inspired by visits to New York, he dedicates it to that city, specifically the geometric shapes of its architecture as he remembers the warmth of color shining from the lower levels of each building.

In 2016 Moscow's Kremlin selected Fazulzyanov as the first independent designer to have a solo show and he presented 250 pieces, his life's work, at the Assumption Cathedral. This and much of what he has achieved symbolize an important shift in Russia since the 1990s, with art and design now challenging material value. "At the beginning of my career, jewelry as a culture did not exist at all, especially attributed to a single author," he says. Production was state owned, stuck in the dark ages of primitive metal processing, and the only thing of value was the gold. With the new millennium a new mentality began to emerge and enamel has given Fazulzyanov a multitude of ways to create jewels of importance. "I finally chose this profession when I found a way to fulfill myself as an artist, not only through form but also color." The simplicity of nature appeals to him, yet his work is complex like Russia itself and it is these contrasting elements that make him so compelling as an artist.

Another who took inspiration from Russia's history is British designer Elizabeth Gage, who enjoys delving into the past for creative inspiration. Her mother and grandmother were painters and the expectation was that she would follow them, but it was the eighteenth-century Russian Empress Catherine the Great, known for wearing jewels sown into the folds of her robes, who compelled her to make her own jewelry. Gage wanted the power to preside over the exact design of her choosing and the freedom to create anything. She studied goldsmithing, enameling, and diamond mounting in London in the 1960s, then spent a year in Crete learning ancient jewelry-making techniques. In 1968 she achieved her first high-level commission for Cartier and her bold, classical style incorporating ancient bronzes, carvings, and baroque pearls enabled her to open a studio-cum-store in London in 1979. Combining ancient relics with jewelry to create unique pieces has been a fruitful exercise for her over the last forty years.

In the beginning Gage rarely used diamonds, because they were too expensive, but when she did they became accents to figurative design inspired by the animal kingdom. Her love of animals is evident in everything from a giraffe munching on golden leaves to a kingfisher in flight. Her Caribou brooch features a Roman bronze from the second or third century AD with tiny gold beads and brilliant round-cut diamonds. It illustrates the annual migration of the caribou, a type of reindeer that makes a hazardous trek between its summer and winter habitats. The blue stone of the brooch is aquamarine and symbolizes the crossing of a river carved with fish; the gray mabe pearl is the riverbed. It is a magnificent example of Gage's ability to bring the ancient world back to life through jewelry.

While gems and gold are part of the age-old jewelry lexicon however they are applied, yogurt containers are certainly not and it is this interplay between the unloved and discarded on the one hand and stones and metal on the other that fascinates Sam Tho Duong, a Vietnamese-born designer living in Germany. He experiments with radical design, creating hugely elaborate necklaces from plastic yogurt containers cut up and pieced together like a lace ruffle that hangs to the waist with onyx at the edges. He has also made floral garlands from toilet paper threaded together by steel wire, a tribute to the restroom as a modern-day sanctuary. Recycled plastic bottles, cherry pits, and ginger find their uses, too—materials we take for granted challenging our acceptance of what precious means.

Tho Duong's greatest work, however, came out of a series called Frozen (see p. 130), in which his observations of nature, particularly ice crystals on branches, have become a focal point, combining pearls with silver to create necklaces, rings, and brooches of supremely delicate beauty. He drilled small holes into minute freshwater rice pearls and threaded black nylon through each one to tie them together in knobbly clusters resembling ice and frost on the blackened branches of a mythical silver tree. He then melted the thread to form black tips on each pearl, creating bunches of tiny spikes much like a family of sea urchins clinging to each other for support. It is a stunning reimagination of a winter landscape, crystal cold and also a metaphor for his jewelry. "Inside the pit lies the origin of growth and just as the seed develops, so my jewelry grows. Steady, branching, rich in variety." These elements of nature that we rarely take the time to notice, captivated Tho Duong, who in his masterpieces has amplified their importance.

London's Victoria and Albert Museum bought a Frozen necklace in 2013, but despite the beauty of Tho Duong's garlands, such major institutions still need an element of preciousness in the mix for their permanent collections. The art establishment prioritizes objects that can physically endure as historical artefacts. The "craft" of toilet paper is yet to rival gold and diamonds in the hierarchy of applied arts, although silver is now better recognized as an artistic material.

Silver has always provided a robust, solid, and economical way to express beauty in jewelry design. It was the metal of choice in Denmark, until the postwar boom fueled an optimism and curiosity about the wider world aided by tourism. For one young designer itching to find his inner voice, the lure of exotic adventures proved too much. Danish-born Ole Lynggaard set off on a voyage of discovery across Africa, Asia, Europe, and North America, returning five years later with a sketchbook stuffed full of ideas. He settled in Copenhagen, where in 1963 he began to create large sculptural jewels of yellow gold, crammed with opals and diamonds—a significant departure from the brutally minimalist Danish style. As he became more established, the domestic design landscape shifted to embrace bright, colorful stones that many Scandinavians expected to see only in design

Elizabeth Gage
Caribou Brooch, 2018
Aquamarine (32.80ct), diamonds, mabe pearl, and Roman bronze Caribou (AD 2–3 century) in gold

INSPIRED BY NATURE

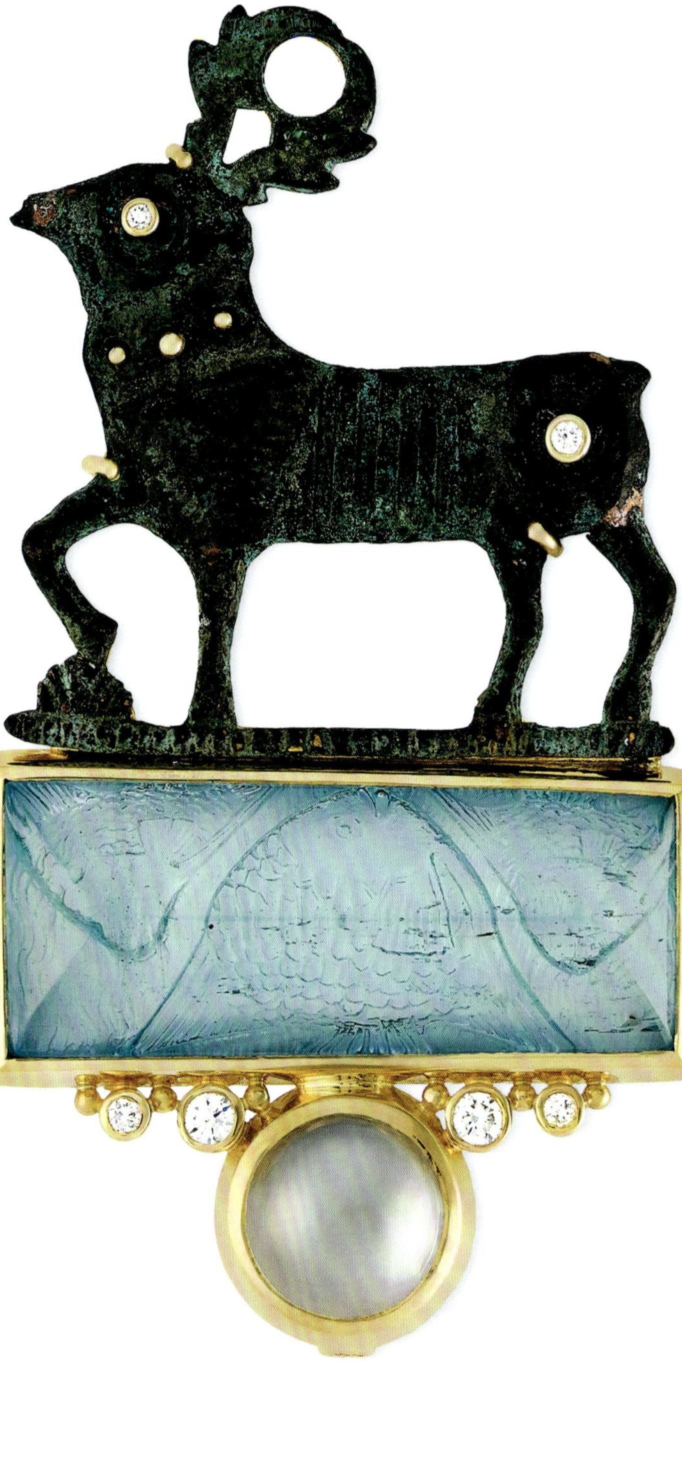

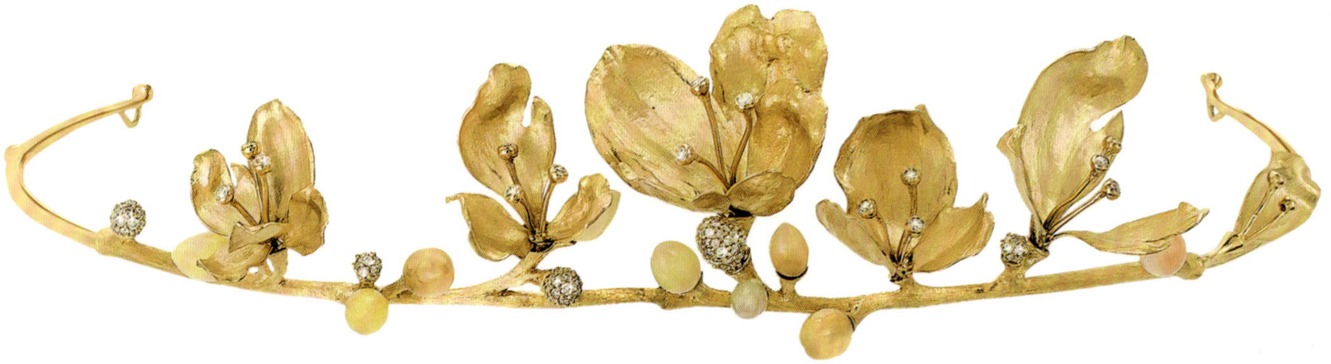

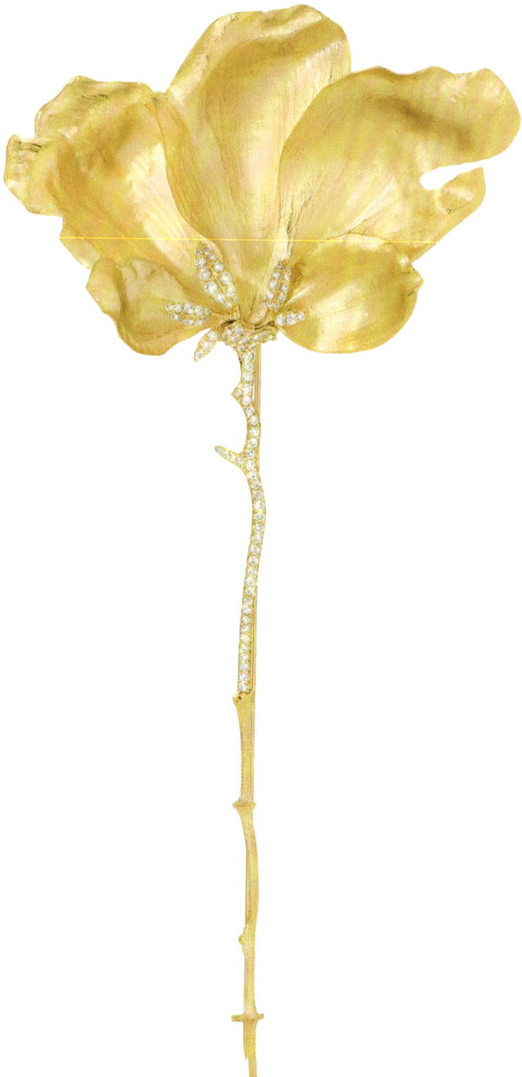

Charlotte Lynggaard
for OLE LYNGGAARD COPENHAGEN
Wild Rose Tiara, 2017
Blush, coral, and gray moonstone,
diamonds, and yellow amber in gold

Wild Rose Brooch, 2017
Diamonds in rose and yellow gold

(Following pages)
Lydia Courteille
Monkey Earrings, 2018
Aquamarines, diamonds, and
sapphires in white gold

Chicken Ring, 2019
Blue and yellow sapphires and brown
diamonds in blue titanium and gold

Dragon Cuff, 2019
Aquamarine (295.7ct), brown and
white diamonds, and sapphires in blue
titanium, silver, and gold

Pendant Skull, 2019
Aquamarines, blue and yellow
sapphires in gold and titanium

Spiderweb Tiara, 2019
Aquamarines, fancy sapphires, and
rubies in gold and silver

from Southern Europe. During the oil crisis of the late 1970s, when gold prices became agonizingly high, Lynggaard briefly considered introducing a style that used less metal, but he held his ground at the behest of his clients, rejecting the easier silver option. A generation later his daughter Charlotte joined the business as creative director, sharing her father's vision of the natural world in hot yellow. But while Ole has the soul of an adventurer, Charlotte is the poet. Her style is lyrical, classical, and romantic, and in her own way she rebelled against her father, who focused on animals, such as the snake, influenced by ornaments he had seen in the Museum of Cairo in the 1960s. "That was the pressure I had in the beginning to do something which was not my father," Charlotte says energetically. "I knew my father would never do a flower and for me flowers were such a big part of my life."

The 2017 Wild Rose collection embodies Charlotte's rebellion. Her roses are large and powerful yet organic, with silky satinized golden petals and diamond stamens. She struggled with weight during the design process, because she wanted a style that was delicate and modern but also sculptural. The petals of the Wild Rose brooch are paper thin, supported by a slender diamond-encrusted stem and miniature winter frost leaves; the single earrings have a fat silky pearl suspended from a gold chain or a lozenge of rutilated quartz. What started out as two pieces expanded into a much fuller collection, culminating in a tiara sprouting yellow amber buds with coral and moonstone. It ranks as some of her finest work.

While the rose symbolizes desire, passion, hope, and purity, it has throughout history also been combined with the skull as a symbol of the eternal cycle of life and death, good and evil. Western culture tends to shun the visual representation of death in nature in its jewelry, but there is one Parisian designer who embraces the idea of beauty in death with a dark humor matched only by the ambitious scale of her design. Lydia Courteille, a jewelry designer and antiques dealer of more than thirty years' experience, expresses her taste in Gothic Surrealism with diamond-encrusted skeletons embracing on an Australian opal, skull-and-crossbone cameos, and a crown complete with a dangling skull wearing a fetching blue bonnet (see p. 141). Her provocative messages of memento mori—the darker side of nature—are poignant reminders that life is short, death is inevitable, and jewelry is perhaps a pleasure one should literally grasp with both hands. She includes a skull in every collection. "It is a reminder of humility, a philosophical lesson whatever your fortune, beauty, or intelligence. Everyone comes again."

Courteille's style is bold, baroque, and very, very large. Small, superfine, fussy jewels baffle her. She makes and wears magnificently voluminous creations drenched in color set off by blackened gold and often sporting important center stones that are part of her "treasure," or jewels worthy of enthralling future generations. She discovered the artist Salvador Dalí (1904–89) when she was fifteen and became fascinated with the surreal and the inexplicable, letting her imagination and dreams cross over into real life when she started to make her own work in 1998. She had already trained as a gemmologist and was working as an antiques dealer with specialty knowledge of Suzanne Belperron (see pp. 31–33) at a time when collectors had all but forgotten Belperron's genius. Selling rare antique and vintage pieces enabled her to bring long-forgotten jewelry art back to life, and this attracted the attention of collectors in the fashion world, such as Yves Saint Laurent and Karl Lagerfeld.

Her own designs combine tribal folklore, archaeology, art, and nature. The skull adds a touch of tongue-in-cheek humor in keeping with the work of her heroes Dalí, Max Ernst, and René Magritte (1898–1967), whose design rarely took itself too seriously. For Courteille this approach manifests as a handsome chicken laying the ring it sits on (see p. 140), its feathers dusted with sapphires and diamonds. From the same Marie Antoinette Dark Side collection, a dragon peeps over a 296-carat aquamarine pear, sticking out its tongue at passersby, and cheeky monkeys dangle from the ears, waving bunches of briolette diamonds, aquamarines, and sapphires (see p. 140). High jewelry tends to be earnest but in Courteille's hands the comical aspect of nature shines through.

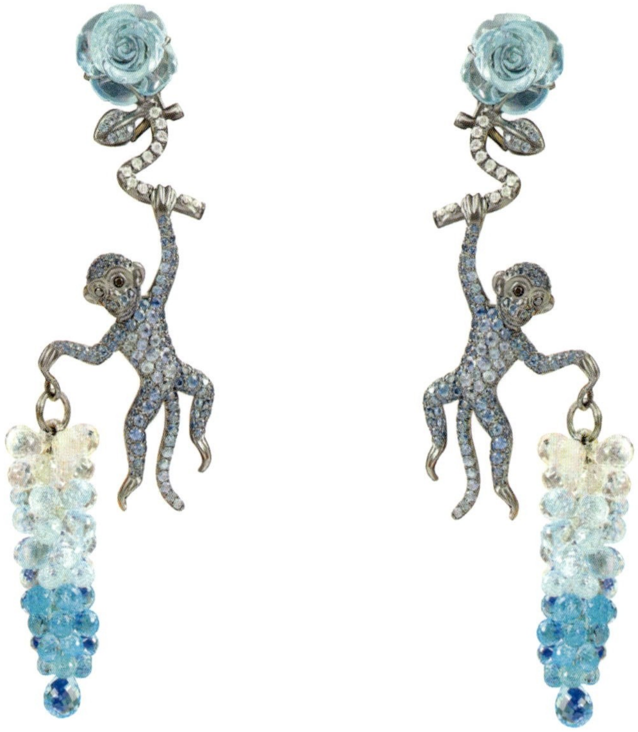

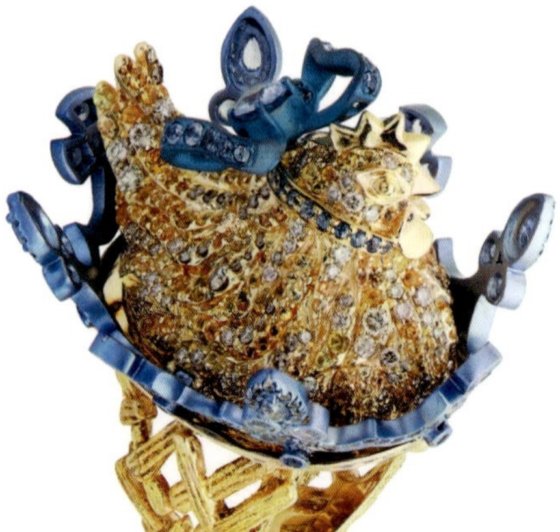

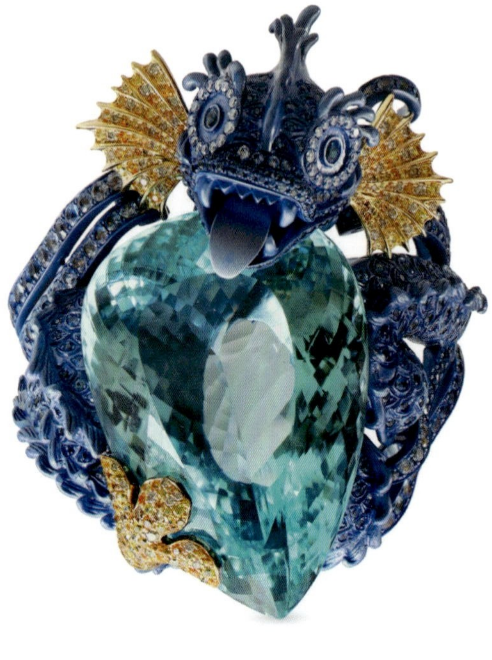

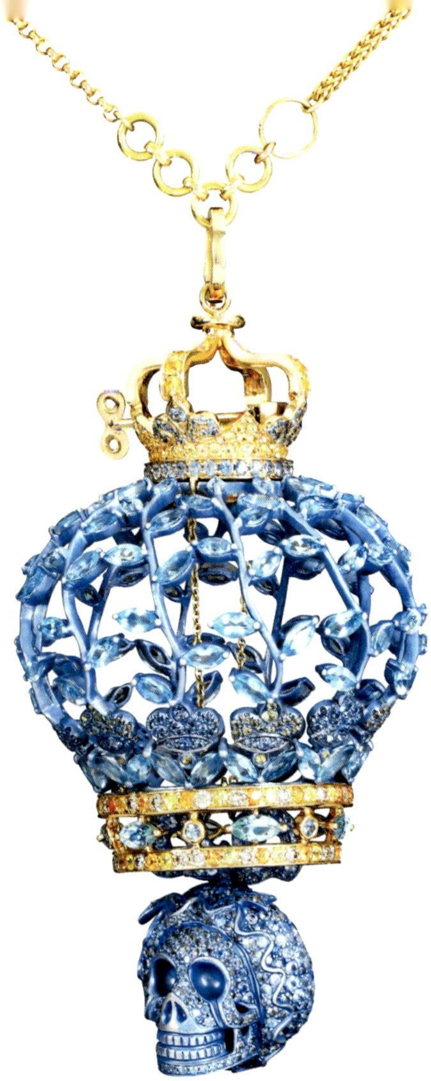

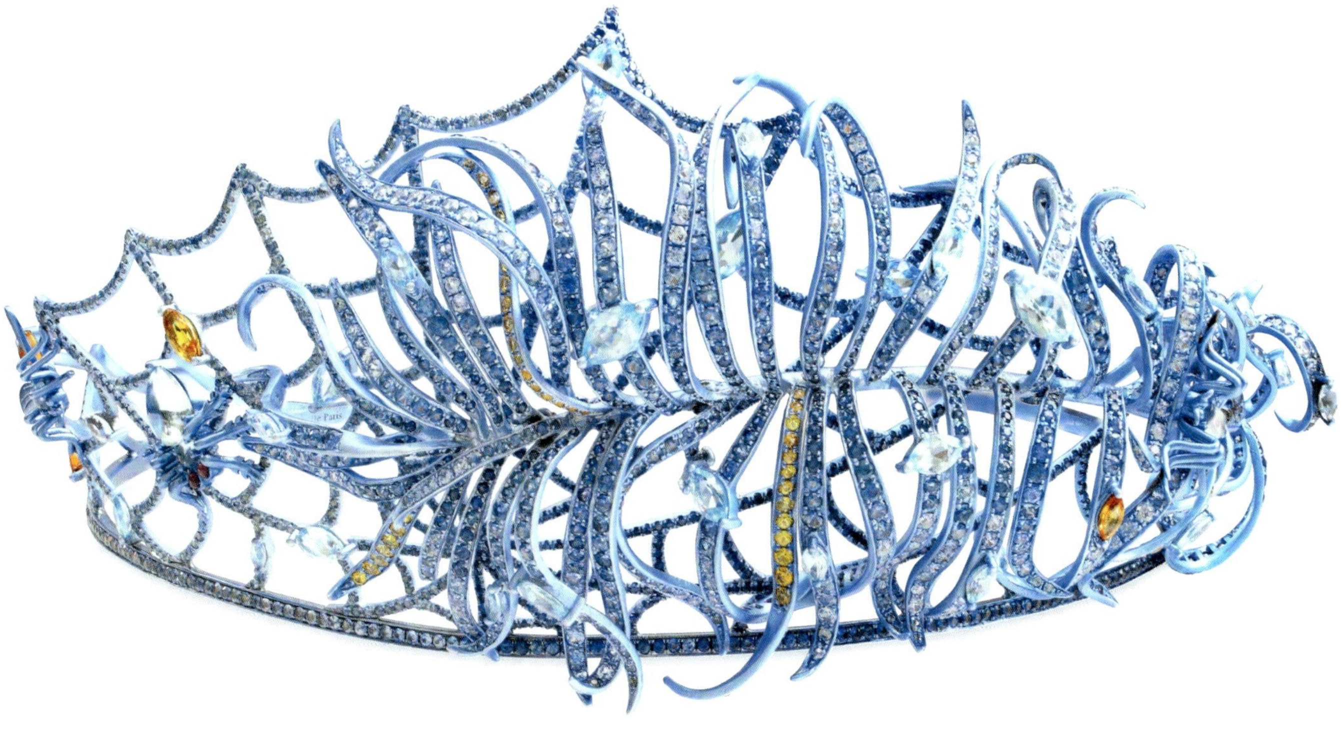

Dashi Namdakov
Arsalan Pendant, 2004
Citrines in gold

Beetle Deer, 2006
Bronze and gold

Lemur Ring, 2007
Diamonds and pearls in gold

Death is thought to be a transformative experience instead of a loss in some nomadic cultures. Buddhism, unlike Christianity, encourages the contemplation of death using prayer and meditation throughout one's life. For sculptor and jewelry designer Dashi Namdakov, the everlasting laws of transformation and revival were part of his childhood in Transbaikalia, Siberia. His father, Balzhin, crafted wooden statues and painted Buddhist icons for local monasteries. When he was fifteen years old, he became seriously ill and was cured by a shaman doctor who explained that the spirits wanted him to become a shaman too. He, however, wanted to be an artist and used his newly found robust health to pursue his dream of becoming a sculptor. "My concept of beauty took shape during my childhood, when as children we used to sit around the bonfire in the steppes and look at the bottomless black skies with shimmering stars above our heads . . . It is the harmony, the single law of the universe." He studied under the sculptor Gennady Vasiliev and then at the Krasnoyarsk State Fine Art Institute, where he was expected to apply that beauty to a range of art forms simultaneously, using metal, fur, wood, leather, and bone, so that by the time he graduated he was proficient in many skills. Jewelry was a single expression in a vast array of creative endeavors.

Namdakov's first solo show in Siberia in 2000 included bronze sculptures, pencil drawings, and bone carvings. His second unveiled horsehair tapestries and jewelry of a strangely ethereal type, echoing an oriental mysticism mixed with Mongolian art that has featured in his work ever since. He had found his style and "inner gaze." He uses mammoth tusk, leather, horsehair, gemstones, copper, wood, silver, and gold. His Arsalan pendant is a mischievous beast and keeper of its master, shaped in gold, chained to its owner as a warning and for protection. "In Buddhism the Arsalans are considered to be defenders of the Doctrine," he says thoughtfully. "People call them Buddha's dogs." The use of ancient materials demonstrates the wildness of his experience of nature and a raw spirituality from his childhood that has fueled his transformation from nomad to artist. His diamond-encrusted lemur with black pearl eyes is soft and alluring, while his beetle with silvery horns is determined and purposeful. Each jewel feels otherworldly.

Beetles and lemurs have rarely been common themes in high jewelry design, but in recent years—as our way of wearing jewelry has become less formal—more unconventional, less romanticized creatures have begun to make their mark. Insects are the unsung heroes of the animal kingdom—they exist in vast quantities and without them our planet would die—but we tend to take them for granted, because of their diminutive size. High jewelry often neglects to pay heed to these much-reviled creatures, but for Mexican-born Daniela Villegas, bugs are like "living jewels." She studies them, collects them, admires the role they play in the balance of the natural world, and dedicates her jewelry to them, believing that they infuse the serious monetary value of her pieces with fun. She grew up in Mexico City, where her great-grandmother advised her that jewelry should not just be worn for special occasions, that the emotion it inspires is the most important aspect of it, even if that means sitting alone in your bathrobe and sweat pants with all your best jewels on. Villegas has taken that advice to heart.

She moved to Los Angeles in 2008 and, with her life savings, created seven jewels in a first collection called Freedom, featuring flamingos with bejeweled bodies and abstract earrings inspired by feathers. It was with her second collection, however, called Backyard and full of crickets, beetles, and scorpions, that insects came to be seen as her trademark; even the wedding band she designed for herself is shaped like a worm. As her confidence grew, her creatures became bigger, resulting in fish, eels, crabs, shrimp, lobsters, and sea urchins. Visits to Peru inspired alpaca designs, then in the Chromatic Paradise collection Mexican coyotes and snakes materialized. In 2018, for the twenty-fifth anniversary of the movie *Jurassic Park*, she collaborated with NBC Universal on a series of dinosaur pieces that included a pair of earrings with *T. rexes* astride chunks of Montana agate (see p. 144) and another with a triceratops balancing precariously atop a couple

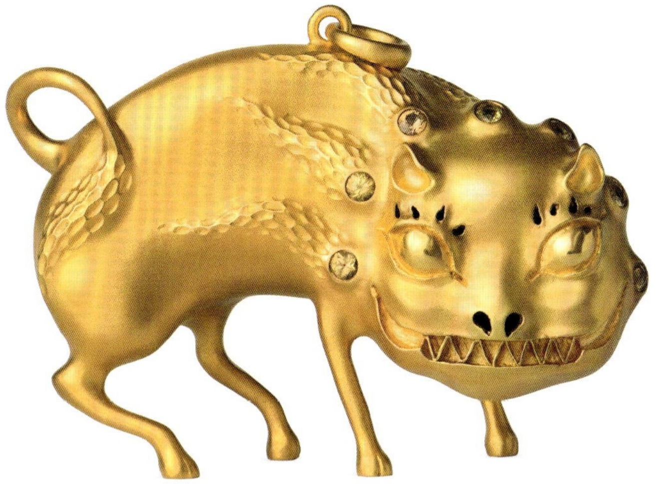

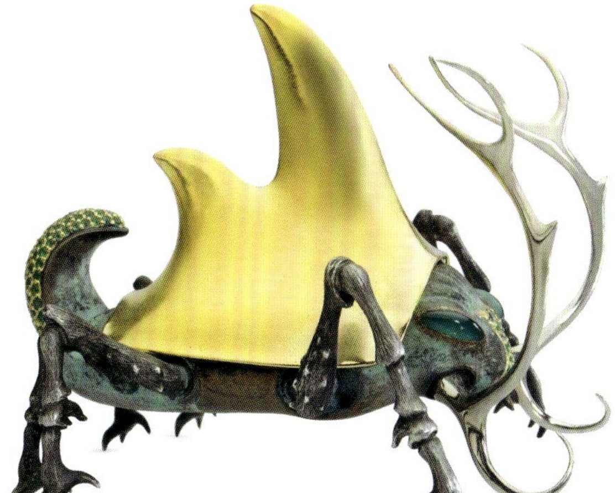

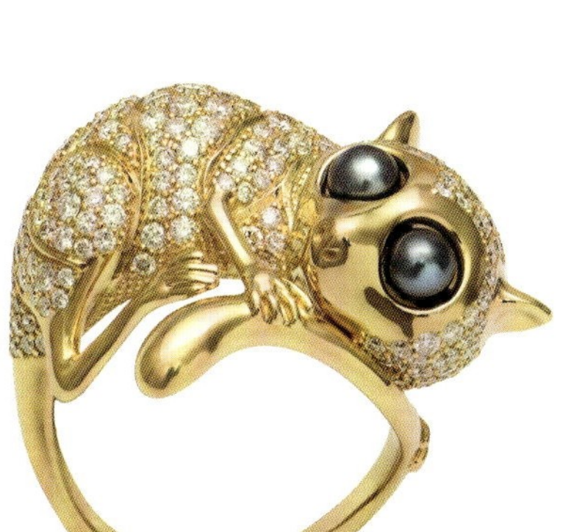

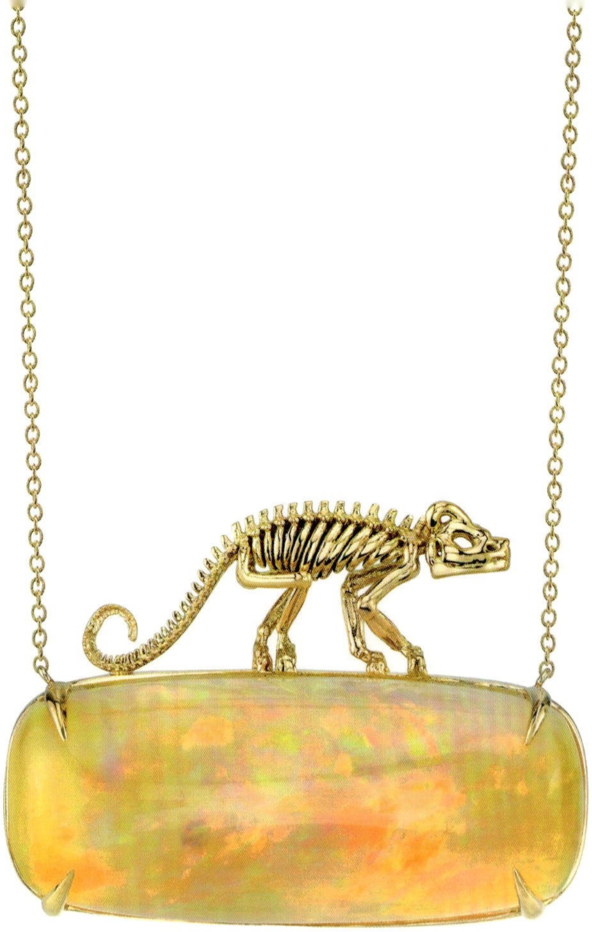

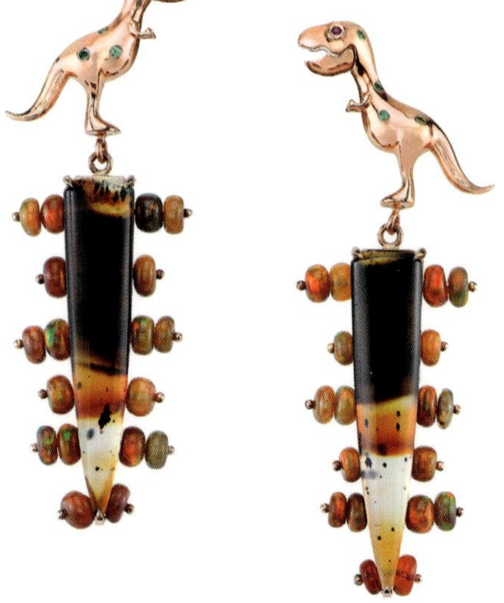

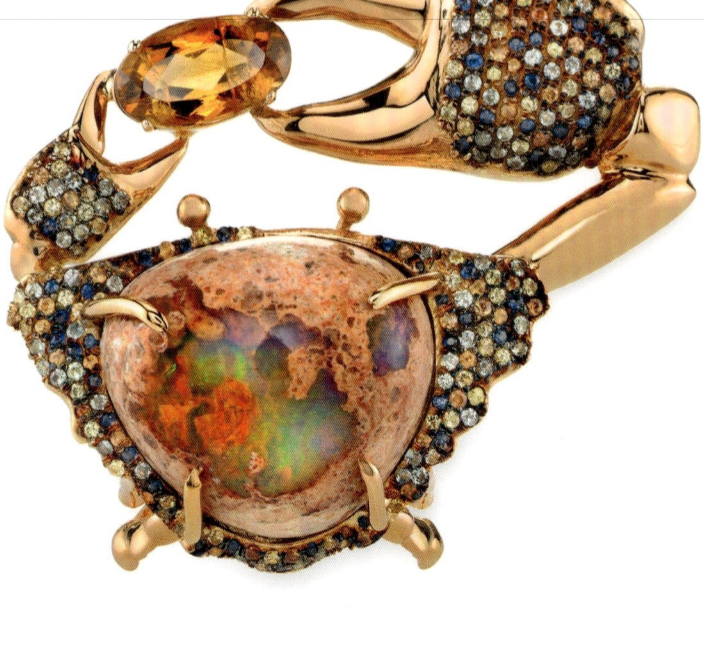

Daniela Villegas
Sunset Chameleon Necklace, 2018
Ethiopian opal (46.23ct) in gold

Victoria Earrings, 2017
Agates (49.3cts), opals, and tsavorites in pink gold

Grannus Ring, 2017
Mexican opal (24.5cts), orange tourmalines, and sapphires in pink gold

of South Sea pearls. There was also a series of brachiosaurus rings in red and yellow gold with spiky spines of pearl, black diamond, and tanzanite beads. Villegas's creatures are playful and figurative with a touch of fantasy. Her Grannus crab ring with its oversize claw has a watery Mexican opal clinging to its back as it scuttles up the arm looking for a home; the Victoria earrings have an almost ancient Mayan vibration, combining bullets of striped agate and knobbly opal beads. The Sunset Chameleon necklace with a grinning golden skeleton balanced on an opal lozenge is genius and illustrates the childlike delight that Villegas captures in a world of serious grown-up jewelry design.

She dreams them first, her wild world of animals. They come to her naturally, without judgment, at night, then she sketches, sometimes adding watercolors before casting her designs in wax. Her workshop of fifteen years makes them real, and her colleagues there are a crucial part of her creative family. Villegas may dream the ideas up, but it takes a different kind of creativity to construct their physical form with the right balance, beauty, and scale. Nearly every piece is unique, which presents a huge challenge in terms of production, especially because she makes four hundred jewels a year with no outside investment. But value comes from the art and the emotion they encompass. "Not everything needs to be hard or complicated," she says. "Think about it too much and the piece becomes robotic and manipulated." When she's not making, she is adding to the four thousand-strong collection of insect specimens that forms the basis of her design universe. The stag beetle is still one of her favorites, because of its strength and fortitude. In many ways it reflects her mantra in life: be patient, follow your own path, work hard, trust in the process, and believe.

The world of jewelry abounds with people who came to it by chance, knowing they were destined to be creative but feeling unfulfilled by other disciplines. Like Daniela Villegas, Wendy Yue followed her instincts and found her place in the jewelry landscape after deciding to leave Hong Kong at seventeen to study in Vienna and Japan. The experience transformed her, opening her eyes to the beauty and richness of other cultures, so that when she returned home and a family friend introduced her to Japanese wholesaler Yoko, she jumped at the chance to be an apprentice.

She worked behind the scenes for years, opening her first atelier in 1998 and then her own design house ten years later. With no formal training, she relies on experience and intuition. "Being self-taught gives me the flexibility to create from my own imagination," she says. And she designs with impunity, connecting art and emotion in her eclectic, playful dreamworld of animals and insects. Fish wink at each other in an odd pairing of golden and champagne diamonds. Snails hang lazily from diamond twigs, antennae extended in curiosity. Bats, wrapped in their wings, sway upside down; dragonflies dangle from flowers; and golden coral hangs from yellow jade shaped like a bejeweled ear.

Snakes are a recurring theme in her natural universe, and a single client from Geneva bought an entire collection of them at a pivotal moment in her development, cementing the animal kingdom as her go-to playground. She usually combs through her vast collection of stones with the germ of an idea in mind, waiting for it to take shape and solidify. The obvious value of a more commercial design, such as the bloom of a rose in pink pavé, is at odds with her off-center aesthetic, so that her work does better in less obvious points of sale. Smaller stores in globetrotter outposts, such as Capri and Bellagio in Italy or Mykonos and Athens in Greece, where wealthy travelers can appreciate an octopus ear cuff peppered with black pearls and opals, are her natural home. Color makes her happy, as do the simple natural textures found in petals, grass, and feathers. A recent design features a Brazilian plant called *Syngonanthus nitens*, otherwise known as *capim dourado,* or "golden grass." It is rare, light, tough, and eco-friendly, most commonly woven by the indigenous Xerente people to make bowls. Yue has twisted and curled the grass to hang from bejeweled orchids, and this foray into renewable materials is perhaps a new area for her in the future. Remote, indigenous tribes using local materials and ancient skills offer an added dimension of creativity

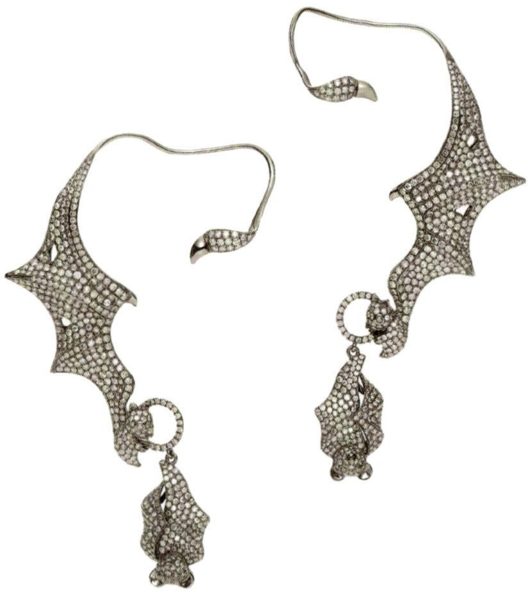

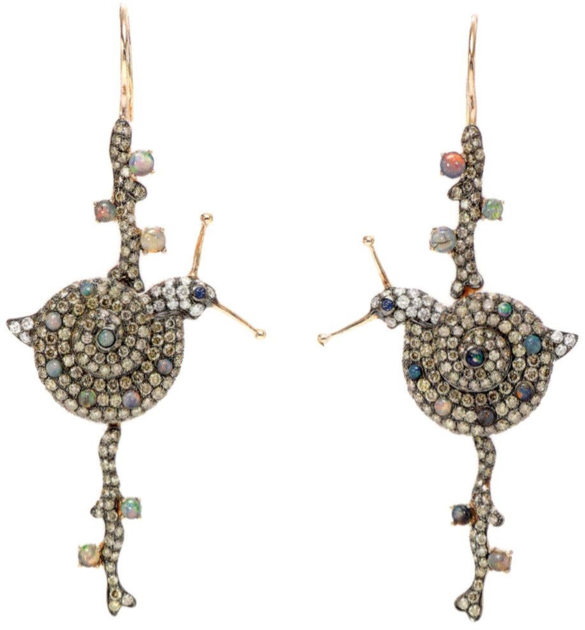

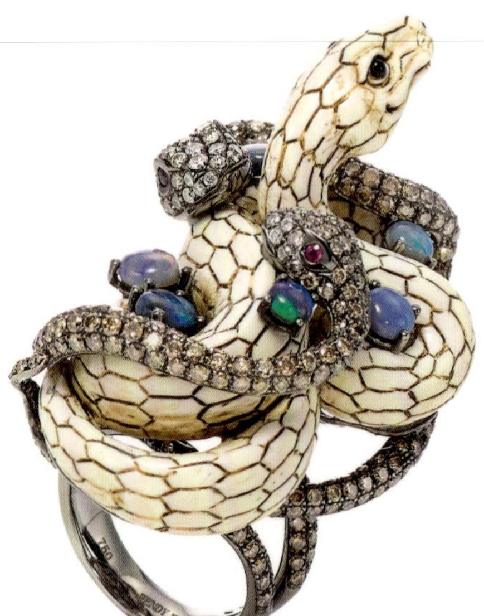

Wendy Yue
Dangling Bats Ear Cuffs, 2013
Champagne, gray, and fancy diamonds
in white gold

Opalized Snail Earrings, 2014
Blue Sapphires, champagne and white
diamonds, and opals in rose gold

Serpent Wrap Ring, 2013
Champagne and white diamonds, opals,
rubies, and white agate (48.05ct)
in white gold

(Following pages)
Silvia Furmanovich
Bamboo Earrings, 2011
Diamonds, emeralds, and knotted
bamboo in gold

Geometric Trompe L'Oeil Marquetry
Earrings, 2017
Diamonds, emeralds, and wood marquetry
in gold

India Earrings, 2017
Diamonds, emeralds, hand-painted
miniatures on camel bone, and pearls
in gold

Mushroom Earrings, 2018
Diamonds and wood marquetry in gold

to designers who take the time to visit and learn from them. The jewelry techniques we use today are often older than we imagine and, while some reference nature artistically, others incorporate its physicality from grass to wood.

Deep in the Amazon rain forest in Brazil, the tangle of vines, leaves, and fungi on the forest floor is home to an abundance of multicolor insects all scurrying around. Occasionally a branch peels itself from a tree, falling to the ground and becoming part of the dense undergrowth. The wood salvaged here by local artisans is warm, soft, light, and ripe for carving into strips to create some of the most unusual jewelry Brazil has ever produced. In 2016 Brazilian designer Silvia Furmanovich traveled to Acre, in the west of the country, where it borders Peru, to meet a local craftsman who had mastered the art of marquetry, the technique of creating intricate patterns by pressing thin veneers of wood into a wooden surface. In sixteenth-century Antwerp, cabinetmakers had used wood in place of stone for its luster and richness, but in modern times this strain of decorative art had largely been forgotten. Furmanovich's contact, born in the forest, had a talent so startling that local Jesuit priests sent him to Germany as a child to train under European masters. He returned many years later to school others and, on the condition of anonymity, he revealed to Furmanovich the secrets of his art. This knowledge changed her life, and wood became a crucial material in her work as a designer. With the guidance of her forest collaborators, she scaled down the technique to ape the patterns and reflections found in gemstones, so that what appear to be thirty-carat square-cut emeralds are in fact wooden reinterpretations edged in the real thing (see p. 148), while her pear-shaped brown diamond drops are thick, multicolor wooden shards swinging from the earlobe. Mimicking the geometric patterns found in mineral gemstones, her Marquetry collection was wildly successful and wood became her signature.

It took Furmanovich a while to find her calling. She started an appointment-only jewelry business in 1998 but it wasn't until she did a goldsmithing workshop in 2000 that the full force of jewelry hit her. She was watching gold bubble under the heat of fire and she had a flashback to her childhood. Her father, an imposing man with huge hands, had made the most beautifully delicate jewelry in São Paulo before his untimely death when she was seventeen. During that workshop experience, Furmanovich made a bracelet of porcelain beads inspired by Native American medicine pouches and began a creative journey she is still on twenty years later. "I travel the world in search of the guardians of extraordinary skills which may be forgotten or disappear," she says in her singsong Brazilian voice. By incorporating these skills into her jewelry, she is ensuring their survival, but she is also creating value for the natural materials she loves so much—not only Amazonian wood but ebony, shells, bamboo, oxidized copper, even real orchid petals dipped in lacquer.

In 2016 she was at the Metropolitan Museum of Art in New York and saw someone peering through a magnifying glass at a series of exquisite Rajasthani miniature paintings on the wall. She was intrigued and went on a forty-day pilgrimage to the art school of Udaipur to investigate. In arguably her finest work, she commissioned students there to paint luscious scenes of Indian life on thin slices of camel bone, using fine brushes made of squirrel hair. Under her creative guidance, they conjured military generals leaping on horses, swans sailing effortlessly past dense greenery, lovers caressing under moonlight (see p. 149). These paintings are placed at the heart of a series of mismatched eighteen-carat gold earrings, with each pair offering two snapshots of the same scene, and they add a new dimension to Furmanovich's garden of delights. Her jewels are tropical and flamboyant, from hot orange carved chalcedony floral ear pendants to citrus-yellow pansy earrings. She believes that time rather than the materials is the real commodity in jewelry design. Gold, although rare, will circulate in society indefinitely, while the time it takes to learn and perfect a living craft, to pass it down through the generations, to manifest beauty with it as an ode to nature is where true value lies.

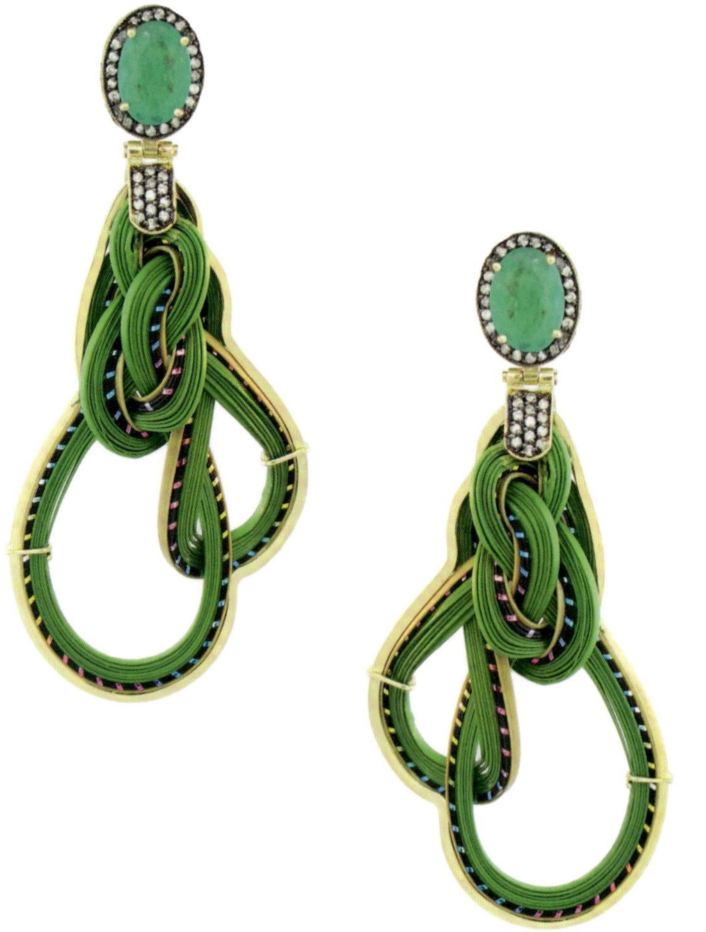

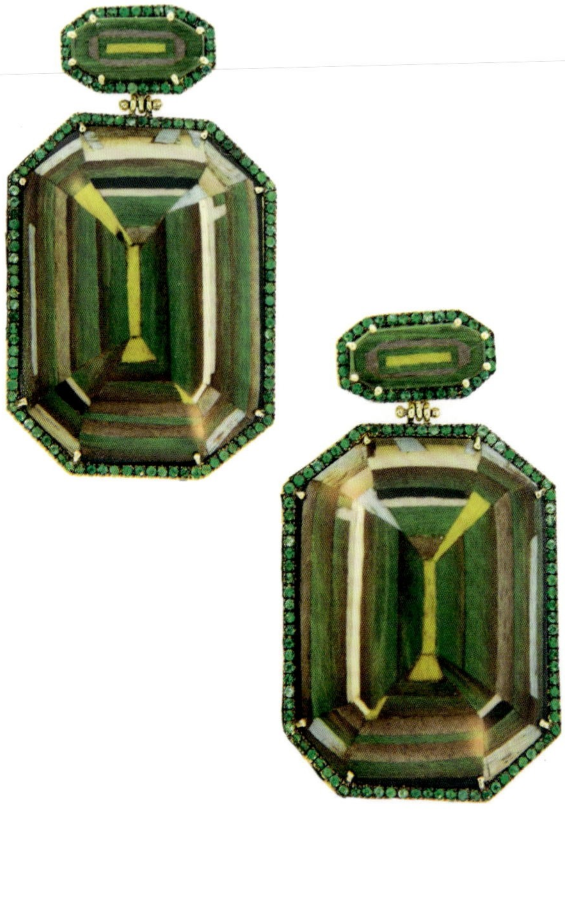

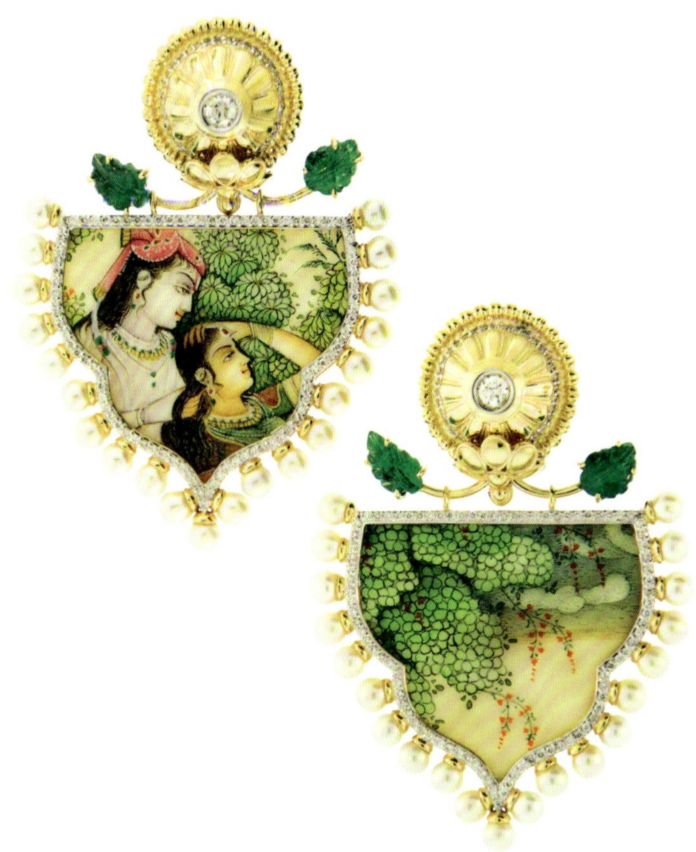

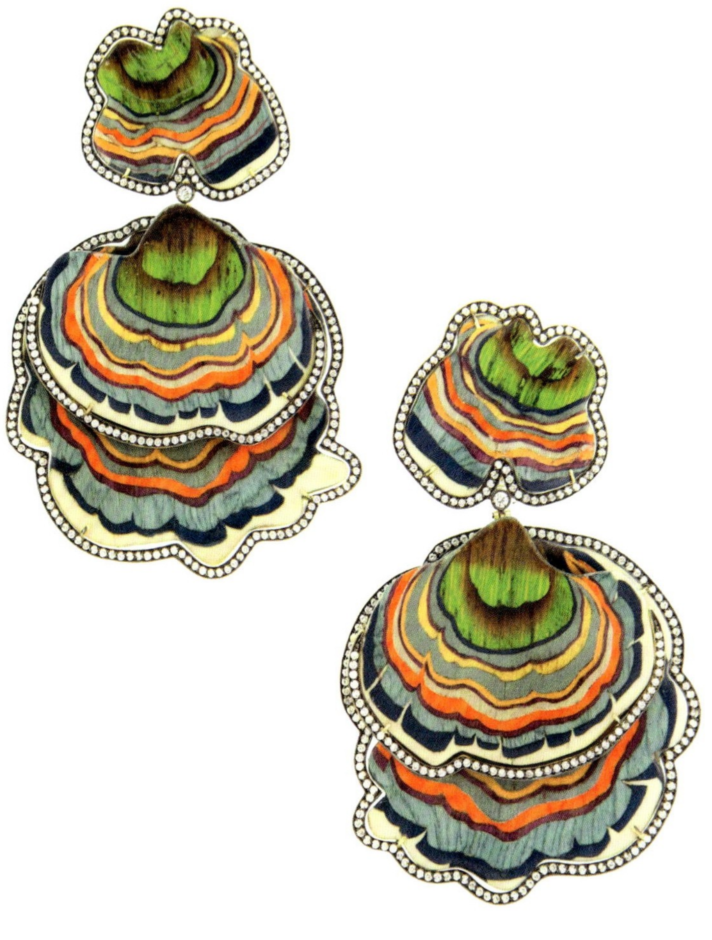

Bina Goenka
Tapestry Bangle, 2019
Mozambique rubies (489.63cts) in platinum and gold

Tapestry Cuff, 2019
Colombian emeralds (407.24cts) in gold

We need artists like Furmanovich who reinterpret long-forgotten art forms from even basic materials, such as wood and bone. As the world gets smaller with travel becoming commonplace, jewelry as an industry has become more competitive, requiring greater innovation in a crowded marketplace. Innovation can be creative as well as technical and Furmanovich constantly surprises us with a deft twist of hidden artistry. Her Bamboo collection resembles dried pasta bent into earrings (see p. 148), but she simply found a bamboo plantation in the north of Brazil and fashioned a lightweight material associated with the East into her own tropical jewels. No titanium or cleverly crafted man-made industrial materials, just a good old-fashioned natural plant.

It is easy to forget that gemstones are entirely natural, too. We may shape and polish them to our specifications, but they are as authentically part of the earth as anything botanical. Indian designer Bina Goenka has pushed the emerald to extremes and into a new realm of possibility. Taking the humble bangle—a jewel originating in India and of vital importance in Hinduism, where the bare female arm is considered inauspicious—and creating a unique garden on the wrist. While her designs tend to be abstract and thoroughly modern in their lack of visible gold, much of her design is inspired deeply by the natural world and celebrates its ceaseless wonder. In her Tapestry Emerald cuff she covers every available surface both inside and out in stones and in multiple dimensions using a myriad of cuts: marquise, square, round, baguette, and oval. The round Colombian outer emeralds symbolize a rain forest of trees in shades of green, while leaves curl on vines wrapping around the sides of the bangle, interspersed with square hedges.

This masterpiece of engineering took Goenka two years to construct and used 762 stones, all hand-carved and set into eighteen-carat gold. Its hot-blooded sister, a bangle of equal brilliance in red, is an explosion of fire on the arm, with even the invisible clasp carpeted in Mozambique rubies. Goenka drove her stone dealer to the brink in acquiring the color, quality, and quantity of gems she needed to fulfill her aspirations with both bracelets.

Goenka learned to take risks like these from her father-in-law, Krishna Murari Goenka, who left Pakistan for India when the countries divided in 1947. He set up a tea stall and slept underneath it to be sure he was the first to greet his customers each morning. His industriousness paid off: he became a hugely successful businessman, and he impressed upon her the importance of thinking differently. "To be successful is to reform the manner something is done," she says.

When Goenka started making jewelry in 1992, she was designing more refined, intricate jewels than most workshops could cope with; the lack of quality control when outsourcing production frustrated her, so in 1995 she started her own workshop, working mostly with topaz, citrines, and diamonds. Collaborating with Indian retailer Ravissant, she created a collection of electroform jewels that were thinner, bigger, and lighter, giving her the confidence to leave the commercial sector to start her own house. Gemfields, the colored-stone mining company, came calling in 2013, offering her top-quality emeralds, and she propelled herself beyond the domestic market, making from four to six pieces of high jewelry a year. Her flower necklace, with a single bloom fully engulfed in rubies, curves around the throat on vines of gold studded with emeralds. The execution and extremity of her stonework is as phenomenal as the scale of her jewelry, which is magnificent even for India. The traditional local jeweler who resets the family choker in buttery-soft twenty-two-carat yellow gold might still be the most prevalent force in Indian jewelry, but the future of design lies thankfully at the cutting edge.

For Robert Procop the power and beauty of rare natural stones is fundamental to his passion in what has been a personal treasure hunt since he set up his first store in 1983. To Procop, the stone is everything. He designs around large, unheated, untreated colored stones, intrigued by the science of each as a raw material around which he creates his art. In his Beverly Hills atelier, he can be seen waving a fluorescent light over his creations to demonstrate their purity. At fifteen years old he spent summers working at his father's engineering plant, learning

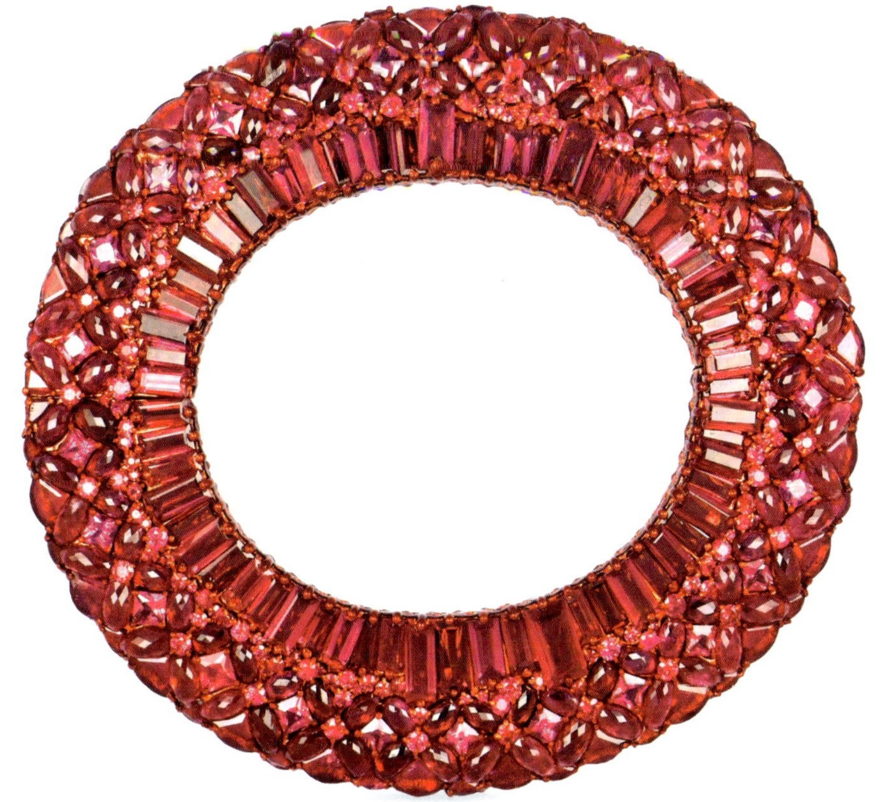

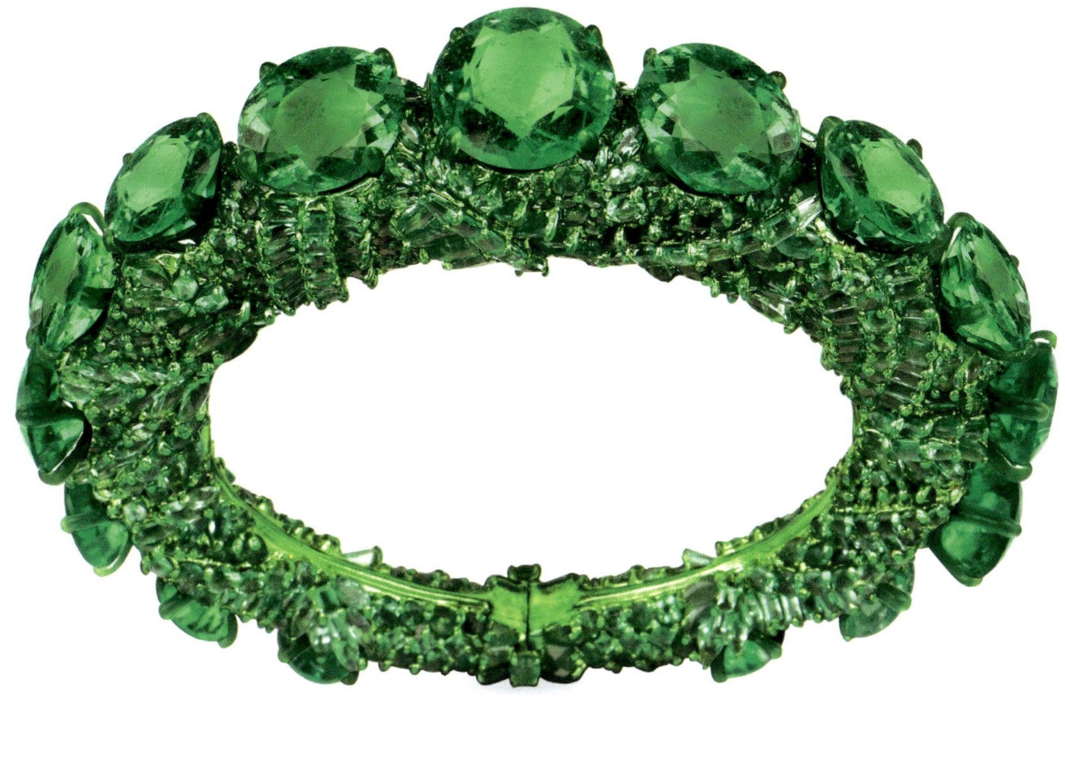

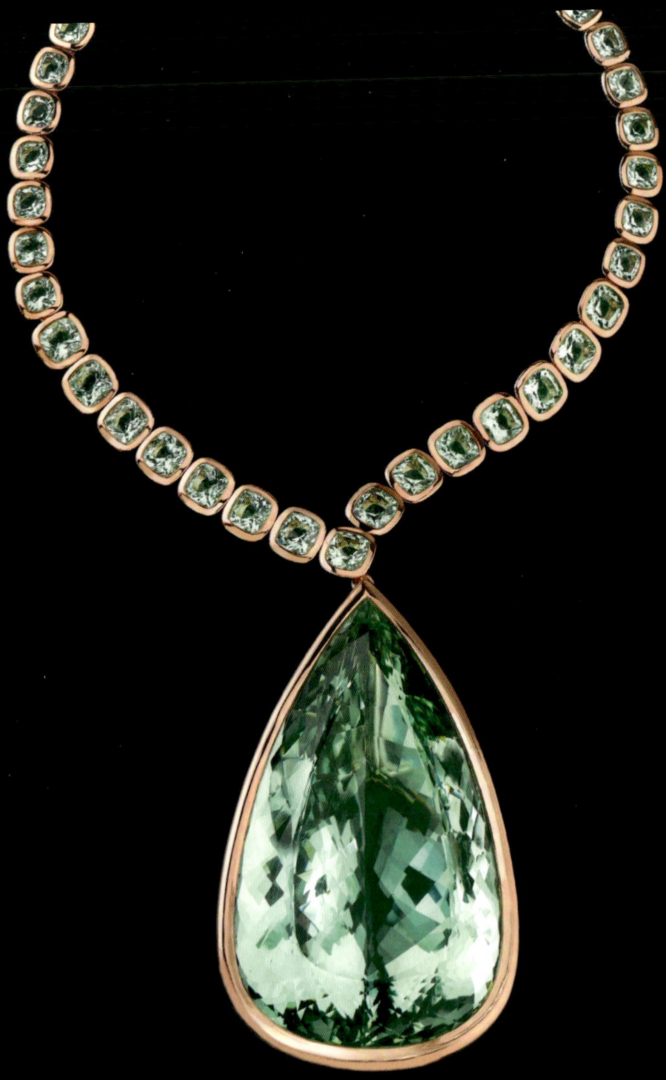

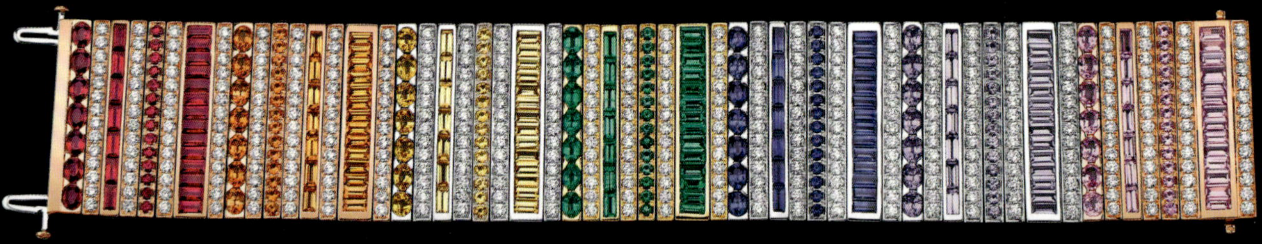

Robert Procop
Style of Jolie Necklace, 2012
Green beryl (353.40ct) and green quartz
in gold

Multicolor Masterpiece Bracelet
Diamonds, blue, orange and pink sapphires,
and emeralds in rose and yellow gold, and
platinum

about microprecision tooling, and at sixteen he hustled his way into a pawn shop to learn the finer points of the diamond trade. It was here that his enterprising spirit surfaced. While cleaning unloved jewelry, he noticed that a lot of gems were broken and he bought them all, working with a cutter he knew who taught him how to reshape them into entirely new stones. By the time he got to college, he was buying and selling diamonds in significant numbers and financed his way through his education, opening his first store, Diamonds on Rodeo, from the proceeds when he graduated. From there he began recutting and remounting stones to his own design for independent designers along the West Coast of the United States. His initiative paid off within the perfect storm of low rents, high appreciation of diamonds in the market, and a new thirst for "rarities" fueled by the hike in luxury spending of the 1980s. He was handling millions of dollars of gemstones mostly on consignment, and would resell them bolstered by a network of cutters and dealers who trusted his reputation for discretion. He was twenty-three years old.

    He met Ronald Reagan in 1984 when he was asked to make a selection of small circular gold pins for the headline-grabbing "Just Say No to Drugs" campaign. In 1999 Queen Elizabeth II asked him to clean and care for the British Crown Jewels, and he also took the opportunity to train with two master cutters—diamond specialist Gabi Tolkowsky and Colombian emerald specialist Adolfo Argotty—to extend his expertise. He was honing his skill on an international level, but at the foundation of all these experiences was his ability to reimagine the stone. It may represent investment to some, but Procop sees the gem as the starting point of his design. "We create a piece of art around the jewel," he says. Art and jewelry each have a different worth—one is intellectual and the other monetary—but he doesn't feel they cancel each other out. In 2012 he created an exquisitely simple collection with the actress Angelina Jolie, consisting of a natural green beryl and cushion-cut green quartz necklace and a big green beryl ring, the curvaceous lines of which were designed to illustrate the soft side of Jolie's personality in a sculptured, simple way using warm gold and minty green stones. Procop's design is often more complex and ornate than that, as demonstrated by his Rainbow bracelet, which uses an array of settings, stones, and cuts to dazzle the eye.

    The blend of styles cooked up between Procop and his collectors creates a new challenge each time, yet some of his oddest clients have trusted him to create entirely within his own taste and have changed his life in the process. In 1991, during a slow period in his business, a bank connected him with an investor who, although she didn't have a home or a car, deposited millions of dollars with them. Over the following two months, his business and fortunes were transformed. Despite looking virtually homeless, the woman bought some of the rarest pieces Procop has ever owned, including a forty-carat Kashmir sapphire, natural pearls, and Burmese rubies. Then one day, having cleared out her account to the last dollar, she disappeared, never to be seen again. Therein lies the magic of high jewelry. Rare natural stones coupled with admirable design triumph if the quality and personal vision of the designer are upheld when temptation and compromise seem inevitable.

    The American proclivity for size, fueled by the high-octane glamour of Hollywood, has tended to hamper the development of thoughtful, detailed, American-born design talent. The styles that dominated in the United States for much of the twentieth century—first the figurative flower work of Paulding Farnham for Tiffany (see pp. 58, 60–61), then later carved colored-stone medleys at Seaman Schepps and stylized animals from David Webb (see pp. 36–37)—have all but disappeared into a sea of identikit design produced for a market centered largely on commercialism. Great workshops are harder to come by, so there is a tendency to bluff with big stones instead of to showcase intricate design work. Until now. Nicholas Varney combines riotous color with painstaking craftsmanship in the oddly beautiful jewels he designs from his base in New York. He was eleven and on vacation in Switzerland with his family when his father took him to see a blue cabochon sapphire and diamond ring he was coveting as a Christmas present

Nicholas Varney
Onion Brooch, 2004
Baroque golden South Sea pearl, diamonds, moonstones, natural freshwater pearls, and tsavorite garnets in gold and platinum

Brook Trout Ear Clips, 2018
Agates, demantoid garnets, ebony, green and white diamonds, Montana blue sapphires, moonstones, and peach sapphires in gold

Japanese Chair Ring, 2019
Coquille d'oeuf mosaic, coral, orangy-brown diamonds, and pink tourmaline (44.68ct) in gold

for his mother. The duo went back and forth as Varney Senior conducted a slow-moving negotiation, all the while walking through Gstaad with its glamour, twinkling lights, and cafés covered in snow. The beauty and love that ring represented stayed with Varney and, from the moment his father presented it on Christmas morning to his mother, he knew that he would create.

His infatuation with nature came later, in Italy, when he was studying at the Gemological Institute of America in Vicenza. There, the Villa Rotonda, a Neoclassical villa designed by Andrea Palladio (1508–80), caught his eye. It was built for a wealthy priest who was retiring to the country, and that notion of the "gentleman farmer" has influenced Varney's entire life, from the materials he uses to the organic forms he leans toward. When allowed to design with no distractions, within the purity of his own thoughts, he describes a spiritual connection to the land. He takes eggshell from his farm in Pine Plains, New York, and applies it as mosaic to the base of rings. His pink tourmaline and coral Japanese Chair ring has a finish of *coquille d'oeuf* mosaic, which is crushed eggshell embedded in lacquer, an old Vietnamese technique. While the shape of the ring, one of his signature silhouettes, was inspired by a Japanese chair he stumbled across in a museum, nature is the thread that binds all his work, from his Brook Trout ear clips with their seamless pink and green pavé resembling light glinting on fish skin, to his Onion brooch, sprouting golden tentacles from a pearl bulb anchored to a moonstone-encrusted orchid. He is a maverick in a market where sales mean everything. "It's only art when you don't give a fuck if you sell it," he says evenly, and he enjoys the discomfort that brings.

The first jewel Varney ever made was a simple bracelet in gold and cork called Dogwood, fashioned after a birch tree he could see from his window; he wrestled with it for twenty years, perfecting it. Some of his best designs are his simplest. The swirl of his agate cuff, lined in gold and punched with diamonds, is pure ornament blessed with a reduction of artifice, making sure the art eclipses the materials, however luxurious. Varney is dragging American design into a better place.

The power of jewelry to transform, first the creator's soul and then the collector's reality, is crucial in understanding its meaning and place in the sphere of art. Beauty can be deceptive: look deeper and a jewel's many layers can talk of life, history, emotion, value, and power. Daniel Brush has spent the last fifty years creating art in a variety of media, including painting, sculpture, and jewelry, with his wife Olivia, also an artist. The multifaceted nature of his work represents a complex intelligence in which every stone, material, and component has meaning. The detail, sometimes expressed in thousands of flowing lines, is hand-carved into metal, whose chemical elements are each chosen for a specific purpose. He makes everything himself from his New York workshop, energized by the city around him. There is a historical context framing each technique, a link to philosophy or to what he describes as the "great dialogue" between art, culture, and the world.

Like Nicholas Varney, Brush apprehends jewelry's connection with nature in a more cerebral sense, his work informed by intense study of the elements, especially gold. He first turned to jewelry for relief from the intensity of painting: "Drinking and golf didn't work, so I started to study the gold working of the Etruscans," he says blithely. It brought him balance, but that obsession with gold, a metal so rich and warm and seductive that it has possessed humanity for millennia, took hold and compelled him to study its character for several years. Between 1983 and 1987 he made the largest granulated gold dome in history, using an ancient technique of great complexity, rarely exercised in the modern era. The gold granules were exquisitely small, of microscopic proportions, and fused with an intimate precision. Then he never made another granulated piece again.

He immerses himself completely when transfixed by a material, a subject, or a culture, soaking himself in its history, its truth, often until an object emerges: his role is to allow this to happen. His work is as varied as his interests. Over eleven years he created 117 large-scale drawings inspired by classical Japanese drama from the Noh theater; he has also produced sculptures such as *Scholar's Table #2*

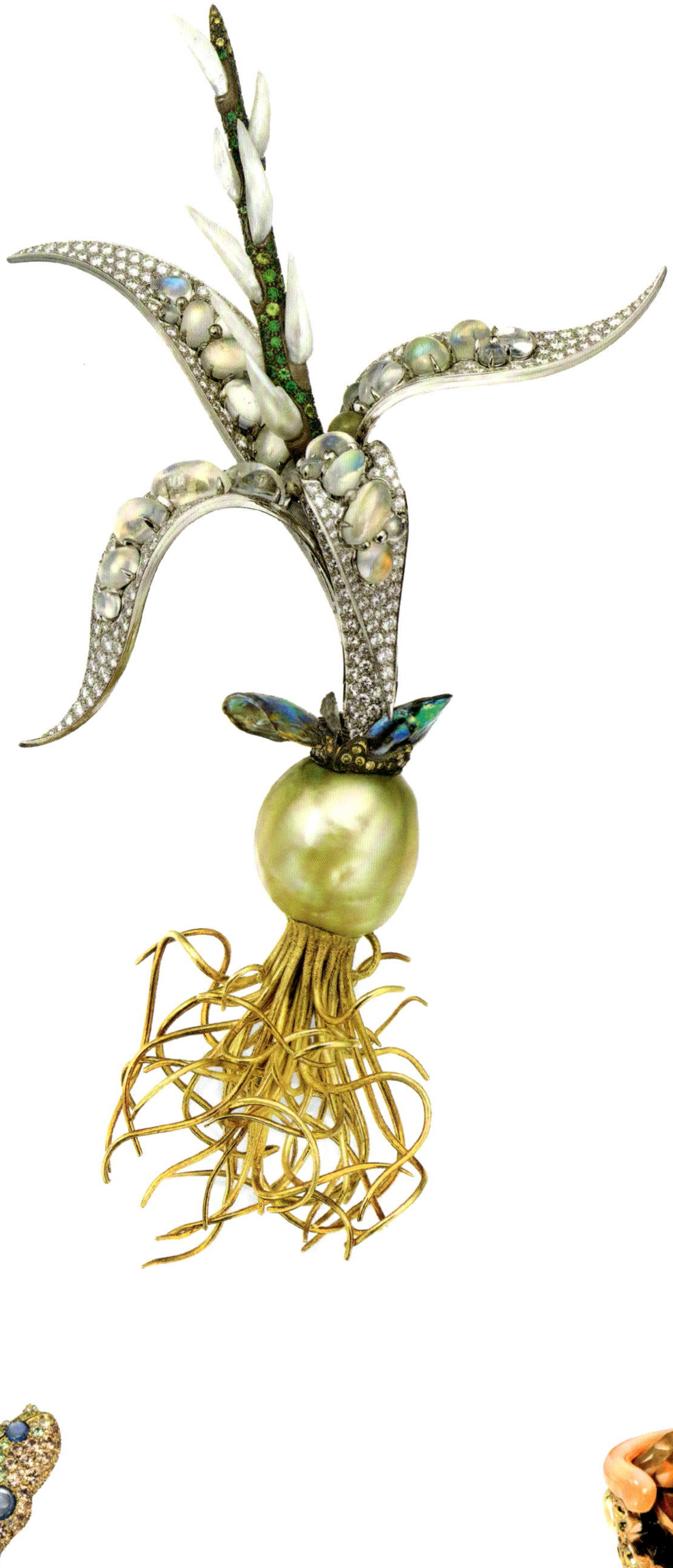

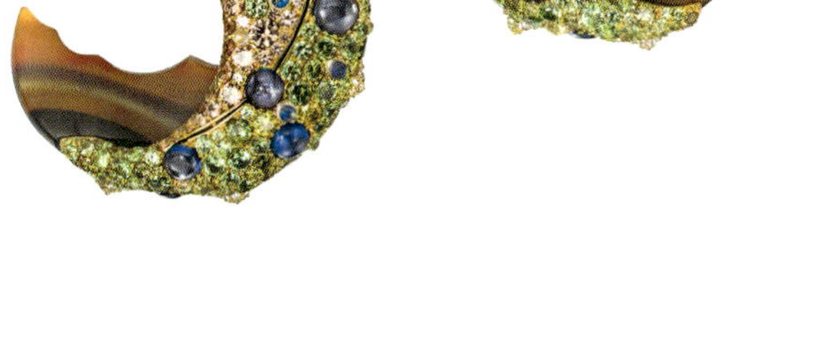

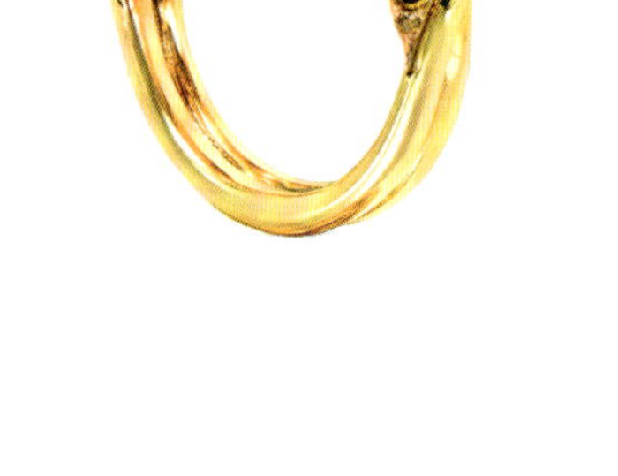

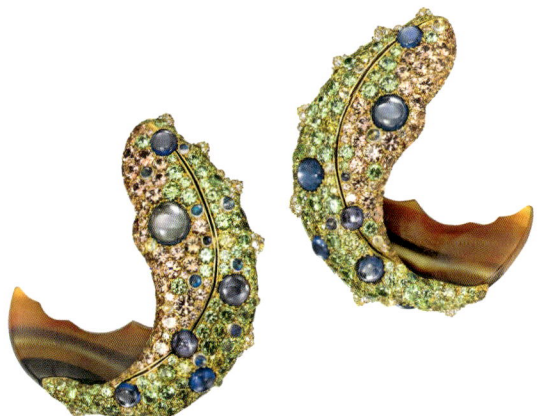

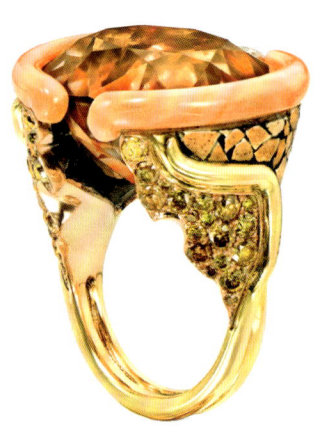

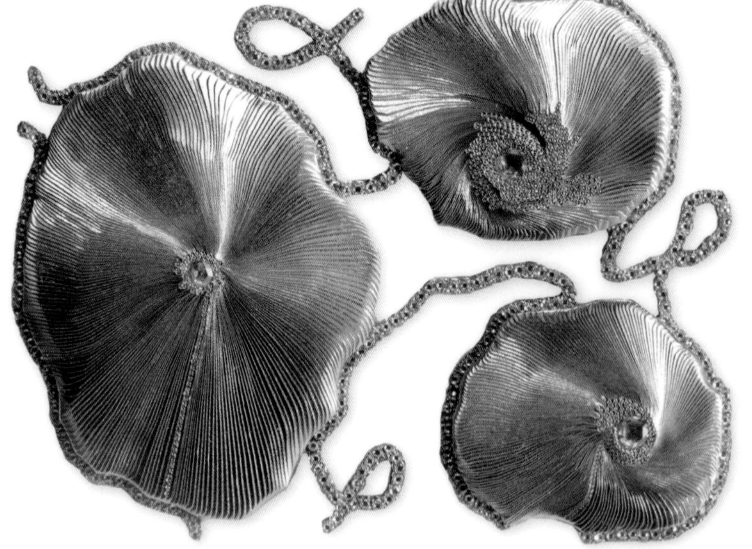

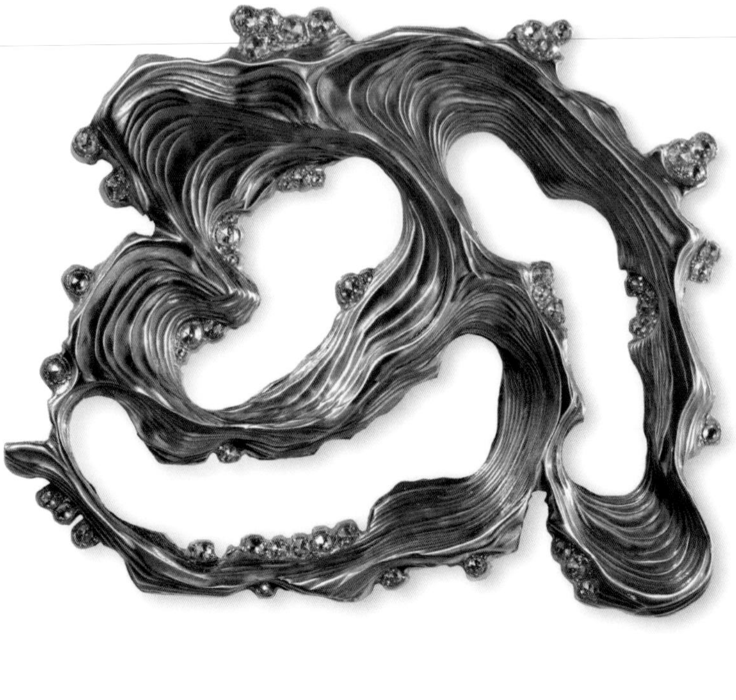

Daniel Brush
Poppies Wearable Sculpture, 2010
Diamonds in stainless steel
Private collection

Flowing Wearable Sculpture, 2010
Diamonds in stainless steel
Private collection

with steel on one side and pure gold on the other, as well as jewelry in steel and diamonds. The idea for his wearable sculpture Poppies came to him by accident when he was engraving one day. He witnessed an extraordinary play of light across the surface of the metal and set about researching the iridescence of flower petals and butterfly wings in a multitude of museums before creating it. His piece Flowing, also in steel and diamonds, resembles the shifting sands of Middle Eastern deserts and Jurassic rock formations in the north of England. Both Poppies and Flowing are carved by hand, from magnetic steel. They are pinned to clothing using a technique involving aerospace magnets that took him fifteen years to perfect so that he doesn't hurt the fabric of well-loved garments. His smaller jewelry sculptures often precede his bigger works on the wall.

His current obsession is with aluminum, which he describes as the most valuable metal on earth. In March 2019 he created one hundred sets of aluminum earrings entitled AL 13, after the element's symbol and atomic number. He sold these through long-time friend and collector Lee Siegelson at the annual TEFAF Maastricht art fair. "We are not in business," he asserts. Collectors such as Siegelson have always come to him. In 2018 Brush donated to the Metropolitan Museum of Art a torque made from the aluminum tubing used in airline refrigeration coils. He and Olivia had become transfixed by a great gold Scythian torque inscribed with animals and figures forty-eight years earlier when visiting Kiev, and the power of that piece inspired him. He took the humblest of materials and contorted it into a neck ring in the style once worn by ancient Persians and Romans as treasure, engraving the surface with geometric shapes and setting it with a subtle mix of colored diamonds.

Brush is a man capable of extreme intensity, reflection, and contemplation. He spent fifteen years in seclusion to consider the world more deeply, and thanks to this fluidity of thought his wearable sculpture defies the norm. He doesn't take commissions or sell pieces to fill a store window. When ideas struggle out of his subconscious, fighting to be born, they have no purpose other than to exist as art.

Daniel Brush destroys and reinvents the very concept of how a jewel should act, sit, and behave, refusing to take part in any of the accepted conventions associated with its creation. Other artists choose to destroy the material itself in order to dismantle the traditional notions that imprison it. Melanie Georgacopoulos has spent the last decade slicing, drilling, sanding, cutting, faceting, and in essence democratizing the cultured pearl. She cut her first freshwater pearl in half in 2007, because she wanted to truly understand the natural material—she was surprised to find rings fanning out at its center like the inside of a tree trunk.

For most people at that time the pearl represented conformity, its creative potential limited to an orb of lustrous perfection strung together in myriad configurations. Such was the history associated with the pearl's beauty that at first Georgacopoulos couldn't bear to tamper with it, but she knew she had to kill the monetary value to release anything bordering on original design. So she broke one in two, wrapped chains around it, smothered it in gold, carved it, imprisoned it in a cage, and finally stripped it bare of its outer shell, using the mother-of-pearl as the jewel itself. Her jewelry is now a fusion of sculpture, technique, and design, and she makes two collections a year with a selection of one-of-a-kind pieces. She abandoned the wholesale market in 2016 in favor of private clients, and her 2012 collaboration with Tasaki (see pp. 48–51), the Japanese pearl specialist, has given her more confidence and the financial stability she needs to take creative risks.

Her 2019 collection, entitled Nacre, is a modernist dream of mother-of-pearl-lined gold in sharp angular sculptures (see p. 158) with single pearls balanced on the tips of rings and bracelets to hold each piece in place. But here abstraction acts as the stage, on which the natural wonder of her materials is permitted to shine. When pearls touch the body, the oils released by the skin act as a lubricant, keeping the glow they emit alive. In Nacre, the silky-soft texture of pearl skin has a much bigger surface than the ½–¾-inch (15–20 mm) diameter of the average pearl, thereby giving Georgacopoulos's jewels a radiance of epic proportions and

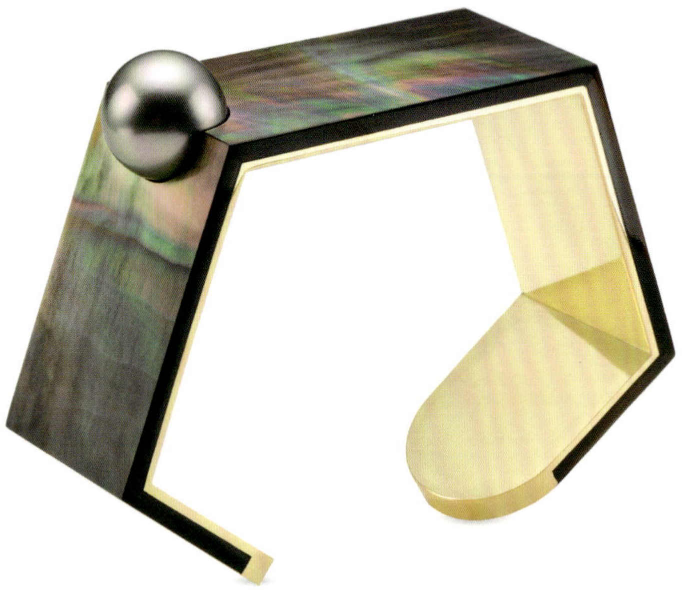

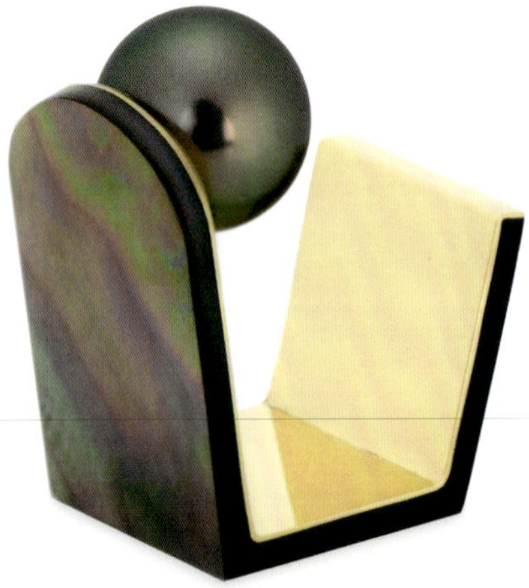

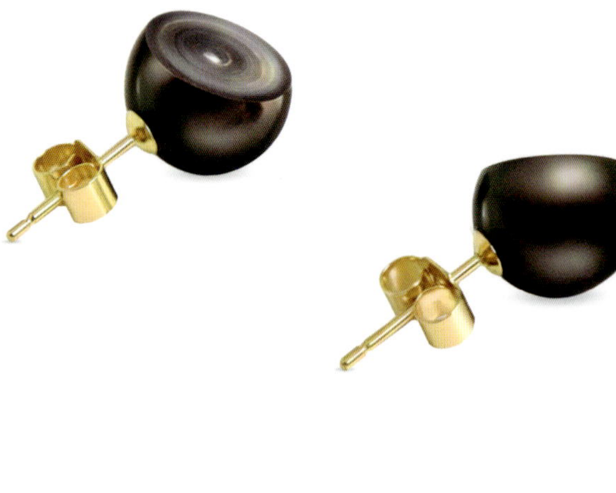

Melanie Georgacopoulos
Corner Nacre Bangle, 2019
Peacock mother-of-pearl and Tahitian
pearl in gold

Asymmetric Nacre Ring, 2019
Peacock mother-of-pearl and Tahitian
pearl in gold

Sliced Studs, 2012
Peacock freshwater pearls in gold

letting her experiment with form and value. Mother-of-pearl is of lower status than the pearl itself, but has been celebrated throughout history as inlay on functional objects such guns, knives, furniture, and ceiling tiles.

Georgacopoulos felt it was underused and underestimated. She wanted to push classic pearl jewelry beyond its preconceptions by creating pieces that were not immediately recognizable as jewelry. The client would have to work out how to wear them, how to apply them to the body, and in some way approach the ritual of putting on her jewels differently. Purists might call it sacrilege, but Georgacopoulos was confident her attempt to elevate this part of the pearl would benefit its design overall. "I think that if a piece is an honest expression of myself, someone will respond to that eventually," she says with a wry smile. She dreams of disrupting natural pearls or even diamonds next, breaking them apart to create a second life free from the constraints of expectation. Her curiosity is our gain.

The rarity and, therefore, cost of natural pearls prohibit most designers from tampering with them when synthetic and cultured pearls offer a bigger and less traumatic alternative. But Geneva-based Nadia Morgenthaler is an exception. She likes to suspend natural pearls along the borders of her jewelry as if they were floating along the banks of a pink and purple sea of spinels. She uses them as flourishes to edge her pastel palette of powder-pink and minty-green tourmalines, rock crystals, and moonstones, all enhanced by dramatically blackened gold to contrast with the softness of the stones.

Morgenthaler is as much an engineer as she is an artist, heading a workshop called Arts Fusion SA that has historically made jewelry for some of the most important houses in history: Cartier, Chopard, Piaget, Boghossian, Fabergé, and JAR. By 1998 she had been with the workshop for nearly a decade and was hungry for more creativity than her role there allowed, so she started making her own fine jewelry in her spare time and showing in Swiss galleries. Then her boss introduced her to JAR (see Introduction, p. 13) and she worked with him until 2009, before returning to take over as head of Arts Fusion but still producing her own work. She welcomes the inspiration JAR's work gave her. "It is obvious that my aesthetic has been influenced by the different projects I have worked on," she says, "just as I have influenced the aesthetics of those projects." Finding innovative solutions to technical problems provides a necessary challenge, and creating her own high jewelry satisfies her creative side. The tension between workshop and designer is ever present behind the scenes, however, in an industry where few high jewelers manufacture their own designs. Making the jewel takes real skill, but creating iconic design takes genius.

In the last twenty years a handful of craftsmen have emerged from the backbenches to create their own collections to a particularly high standard, having experienced the finer points of design through the work of others. Since the opening of his boutique on Place Vendôme in the 1970s, JAR has been as instrumental to the evolution of jewelry as a whole as he was to Morgenthaler's and, while the process of craftsmanship in high jewelry is hidden for the most part, Morgenthaler continues to revel in her technical prowess. The functional elements of her design have become decorative highlights: a tower of cultured pearls balances precariously on a diamond-studded blackened framework and a pear-green chrysoberyl ring stands to attention speared with natural pearls. The beauty and complexity hint at a technical perfection, the pursuit of which has consumed her since the beginning of her career. She sees natural pearls as a gift from nature, a uniquely powerful tool she uses to emphasize or punctuate her design. They are silky soft but have a strength of character that is deeply sensual. Earlier in her career, her jewels were more explicit representations of trees, flowers, and grains crafted from silver and copper, more obviously in tune with the Swiss countryside where she lives. But now her work makes much more subtle allusion to nature with forms that reference Art Nouveau and the romanticism of the Belle Epoque, while her lofty pearl stacks pay homage to Romanesque architecture and have become monochromatic and highly stylized.

Nadia Morgenthaler
Earrings, 2018
Diamonds, green-blue indigolites, light-green (29.48cts) and mint-green tourmalines, natural pearls, and violet spinels in blackened silver underlined by red gold

Earrings, 2018
Blue long agate drops (86.08cts), diamonds, opals, purple kunzites (44.06cts), and white natural pearls in platinum and silver

Whether directly representing nature or discovering unique ways to express more abstract interpretations of it, independent jewelers are still judged on each and every piece they create. Building a collector base for life entails striving for perfection despite market forces. The artistic intention of the creator defines the jewel, placing it in either a collectors' art market or a more commercial investors' index of intrinsic value. The reality of both mean that independent designers have to choose their path early on, often before the full implications of that decision become apparent and while they are under pressure financially. It can be tempting for designers to adjust the price, follow trends, or rush the creation of a jewel to accommodate a client or the market, but that rarely ends well. Patrons and collectors play a key role in forming collaborations, providing vital income while protecting creativity, pushing the jeweler into taking risks they can ill afford alone. "I see jewelry as a lifetime investment like art," says collector of both Valeria Napoleone. "Collecting is not about branded pieces. One should have a vision to go beyond the brand and find new talents with real integrity." Designers such as Ilgiz Fazulzyanov resurrect techniques that become a language to collectors, the more obscure and quirky the better. Daniel Brush sits between worlds, defying any kind of explanation of what jewelry is or can be.

In whatever shape it finds, jewelry that holds within it and communicates such deep reverence of nature offers genuine expression of independent thought, immortalizing the world around us and ensuring accessibility to all. The snail, the worm, the hen, or the monkey poke fun at the serious business of investment and bring humor to an industry that can sometimes take itself all too seriously. Burying a thirty-carat opal deep into a crab's back as Daniela Villegas does certainly brings risk into the sales equation, but then art is all about freedom. How these creators interpret nature is affected as much by a leaf, a flower, or a shaft of light as it is by the major art movements and by their own individual connection as human beings. The ecosystem that gives us diamonds and gold, materials that sometimes don't feel natural at all, eventually yields jewelry as an art that mirrors life in all the glorious forms in which we choose to live it. Independent designers, unhampered by the need to impress shareholders, are simply freer to express life's diversity, with the result that creativity reigns. The bravery of independent design often lies in its strangeness and humor, forgoing cuteness for an eccentricity that shapes the group consciousness of jewelry as a whole, whether that is behind the scenes, when they anonymously design collections for bigger brands, or when balancing an orchid on an onion in spectacular fashion à la Nicholas Varney. These designers operate at the sharp end and, while the artistic and financial battles claim many casualties, those who survive give us magic.

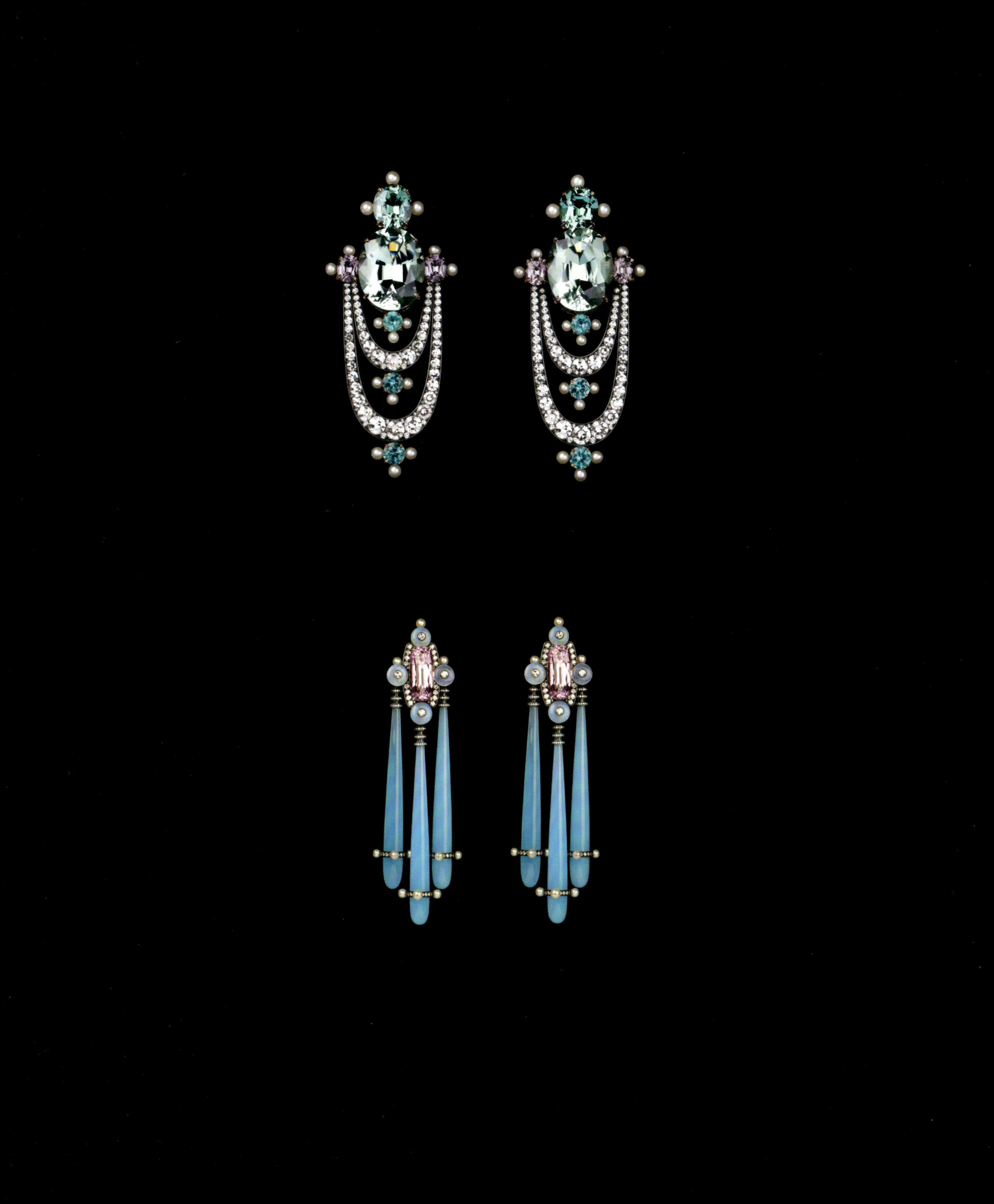

FIVE

THE FEMALE AGE: REBELS, GODDESSES, AND ALTER EGOS

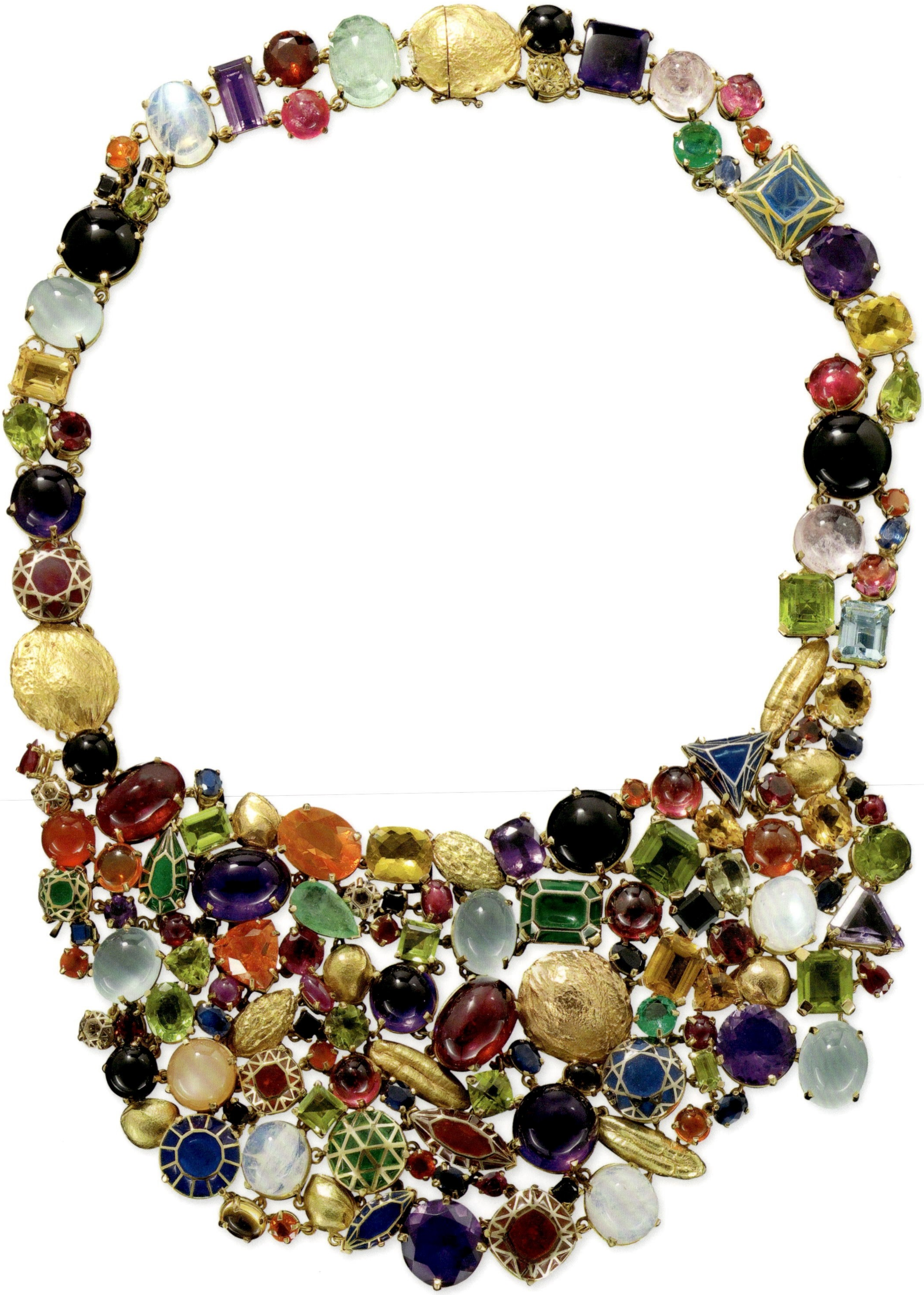

Solange Azagury-Partridge
Stoned Necklace, 2009
Amethysts, aquamarines, citrines, emeralds, fire opals, moonstones, onyx, peridot, rose quartz, rubies, sapphires, yellow beryls, and *plique-à-jour* enamel in yellow gold

Power, for most of documented history, has been male. From gods to kings to presidents, it has passed down the male line, taking with it land, money, religious doctrine, and the accepted notion that men rule. Women have in the main been assigned a variety of supporting roles, most important of which being wife and mother, with the general understanding that those rebellious enough to overstep this boundary are met with violence and intimidation. In terms of jewelry, the old-fashioned idea has always been that respectable women don't wear much of it, as if to do so were a declaration of vacuousness and overt femininity. It goes hand in hand with the view that intelligence is inherently plain, austere, and probably masculine.

Because male authority was so entrenched, women had to be both strategic and creative in order to rule. One of the most powerful women of her age, Queen Elizabeth I (1533–1603) came to the throne of England in 1558, ushering in a period of relative peace and prosperity and laying the foundations for future imperial dominance. As important as the protection of any armor, the Virgin Queen's jewel-encrusted robes asserted her power and dominance as a divinely appointed monarch. She used jewelry to create a spectacle, layering elaborate strings of baroque pearls and weaving them into her hair. An inventory of her collection revealed 628 items, many of them given to her by suitors, courtiers, and ambassadors attempting to win her favor. Two huge pendants, one featuring a yellow gold phoenix and another a white gold pelican, were immortalized in portraits of the queen by court painter Nicholas Hilliard. The phoenix symbolized rebirth and chastity, the pelican self-sacrifice.

For a long time after Elizabeth, influential women exerted much of their power behind the scenes as the consorts and regents of their husbands and sons. By the end of the eighteenth century, however, a new movement was forming, an ideology that wanted to see women acknowledged as equal to men in society, deserving of privileges and opportunities beyond the realm of motherhood. It would later be called feminism and it became one of the deepest struggles of modern times. In England two centuries ago, a woman could be divorced but could not initiate proceedings herself, and she could be beaten, sexually assaulted, and denied access to her own property and financial assets. If she committed adultery, she was often barred from ever seeing her children again; by marrying she was in effect being passed from father to husband in a deal sanctioned by the state. The Matrimonial Causes Act (1857) and the Married Woman's Property Act (1882) helped to protect women from legalized abuse, but it wasn't until 1918 that a first wave of rebellion achieved the vote for any British women. In the United States, voting rights were granted by individual states and weren't finally ratified in the Constitution until 1920.

The only women who were free from the strict moral codes of Victorian England in the nineteenth century were courtesans who lived a kind of double life as professional mistresses to powerful men. They were excluded from society but were desired by men for their beauty and wildness, as well as envied by women for their independence and freedom at a time when chastity was the ultimate female virtue. Cora Pearl (1836–86) was one such seductress; born in England but living most of her life in France, she became famous for her couture crinolines, her priceless pearls, and her erotically charged daily jaunts along the Champs Elysées. She wore enormous diamonds; her jewels were rumored to be worth a million francs (around €9 million or $10 million today); and she had pearls sewn into her clothes to accentuate her voluptuous charms. Wearing jewelry and little else during

THE FEMALE AGE

CHANEL High Jewelry
"Franges Necklace" (worn as a tiara), 1932
Created by Mademoiselle Chanel in 1932
for her one and only "Bijoux de Diamants"
High Jewelry Collection

SARAFANE Headpiece Necklace
Necklace transformable into a
headpiece, 2019
Cultured pearls and diamonds
in white gold
"Le Paris Russe de Chanel" High
Jewelry Collection

the parties she threw was a brazen act of rebellion, and this notion of vanity and recklessness has never truly left jewelry. Some women, however, have found a way to combine a tomboy elegance with an abundance of jewels to dramatic effect, breaking all the rules of what traditional beauty looks like in the process.

In an era when all women were expected to marry and have children, Gabrielle "Coco" Chanel (1883–1971) did neither; instead she created a fashion empire, taking a series of high-profile, well-connected, and often aristocratic lovers who helped introduce her to a life of luxury beyond the humble existence she was born into. Her mother died when Chanel was twelve and she was sent to live in Aubazine Abbey, a convent for orphans in the Limousin region of France, run by a strict order of nuns. Here she learned to sew and, when she left, she used her wages as a seamstress alongside her earnings as a cabaret singer to scratch a living—until she began a relationship with Etienne Balsan, a textile heir who moved her into his chateau. Next came a love affair with Arthur "Boy" Capel and in a very civilized agreement, Balsan and Capel agreed to share the cost of setting up her new hat business. By 1918 she opened her maison at 31 Rue Cambon, a fashionable street in central Paris, where she created a new modern silhouette, releasing women from the suffocating confines of the corset and using soft lines in slouchy fabrics, such as jersey.

Side by side, with the development of her fashion business, came a growing interest in jewelry, resulting in her first and only high jewelry collection. It was fueled by lavish gifts from the extremely wealthy Duke of Westminster: a deluge of priceless jewels complete with huge emeralds, rubies, and sapphires. Deep in the depression of the early 1930s, struggling diamond dealers looking for new ways to spark interest turned to the daring couturier and presented her with a selection of phenomenal white diamonds. Chanel set them in platinum, creating a collection called Bijoux de Diamants, the only high jewelry collection she produced in her lifetime. Although the cost of making the collection ran to many millions of francs—perhaps as much as $50 million in today's terms—Chanel kept the designs simple. Stars littered her work, inspired by her time at Aubazine Abbey, which had constellations etched into its stone floors. It was important to her that the pieces could be worn in a variety of ways, so that a brooch could also be a pendant and that a clasp could be mastered without assistance. She wanted her collectors to experience absolute freedom, even a sense of escape, when wearing her creations. For years before the depression took hold, she had made and promoted the glass and plated metal of costume jewelry as a reaction against the vast wealth of some sectors of society. Now, as the world struggled financially, she swung the other way, embracing high-quality diamonds with her customary relish.

She displayed the fifty pieces of the 1932 Bijoux de Diamants collection on wax mannequins created to look like real women with hair, lipstick, and alabaster skin. This was a huge departure from the usual high-caliber jewels on velvet cushions presented by somber men in the hushed salons of the Place Vendôme. Chanel's mannequins were placed around her home at 29 rue du Faubourg Saint-Honoré, perched like friends peering out from the corners of her living room. The intimacy and informality shocked the other jewelers of the Place Vendôme, who used their influence to force the breaking up of her designs and return of the stones as punishment for such a flagrant break with tradition. Ever the rebel, however, she later took a handful of special orders and, while most of the jewels of the collection have been lost, the Comète brooch with its five-pointed star of multilayered white diamonds remains in the Chanel archives as a treasured reminder.

The pieces Chanel created were modernist, simple but extravagant. She combined opposites—tradition and revolution, sophistication and primitivism, sensuality and formality—with platinum fringes bristling with diamonds designed to fall across the forehead, sparkling feathers that clung sensuously to the bosom, bows arching on the collarbone, and a bow tie as choker that clung to the neck. The Fontaine necklace with its double fringe cascaded toward the navel, encapsulating Chanel's style perfectly. Unorthodox, spirited, and stylish,

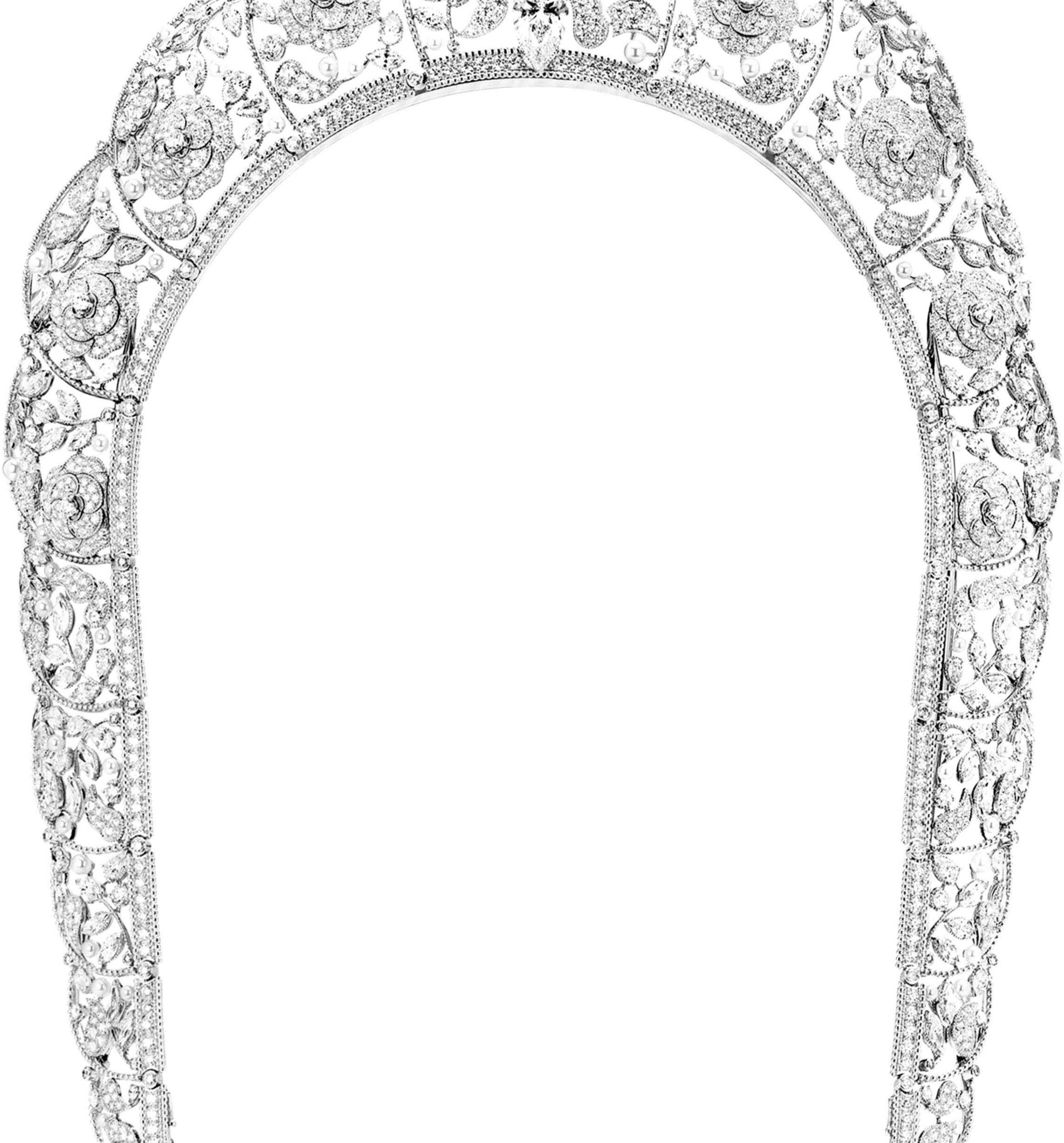

Chopard
Peacock Bracelet, 2010
Black, brown, gray, and white diamonds, emeralds, lazulites and lapis lazuli, Paraíba tourmalines, sapphires, and tsavorites in white gold

(Following pages)
Chopard
Earrings, 2019
Diamonds, opals (9.7cts), pink sapphires, and tsavorites in titanium

Earrings, 2019
Amethysts, tsavorites, white opals (2cts), and yellow diamonds in titanium

Necklace, 2017
Rubies in white gold and aluminum

she turned her personal brand of femininity into a lifestyle that other powerful women were drawn to. Her legacy, beyond the design codes that endure, is one of female empowerment. She designed for herself. She made her own path to be independent, to be free, and everything she designed fed those needs.

Women like Chanel, who prioritize their own pleasures, have traditionally been treated with suspicion. But one arena where high jewelry is celebrated without apology is on the red carpet, an extension of the Hollywood studio system where the fantasy of the silver screen spills out into the real world. Elizabeth Taylor (1932–2011), reputed to be the first actress to be paid a million dollars for a single movie—*Cleopatra* in 1963—was also perhaps the most notoriously bejeweled movie star in living memory, encouraging her seven husbands to give generously as well as buying jewels for herself. High jewelry was a part of her personal brand, an added layer of her magnetic beauty.

In more recent times, Chopard, a maker of precision watches and jewelry based in Geneva, has championed the jewel for the red carpet. Their first collection for the Cannes Film Festival in 2007 featured sixty unique creations by Caroline Scheufele, copresident and artistic director. In homage to the ritualistic "mounting of the steps," briolettes—elongated pear-shaped stones—featured heavily: 170 of them, in necklaces designed to curve around the collarbone, in a rainbow swirl of color and light. Long, narrow ear pendants with bunches of diamond briolettes at the tips grazed the shoulders and red rubies flashed within titanium earrings. Scheufele has also made jewels for the French Césars, the BAFTAs, and the Academy Awards, agreeing that jewelry can and should express female empowerment. "It is a nice feeling not to have to wait for a loved one to offer you a piece of jewelry," she says thoughtfully. "I believe [consumption] could be linked to the rise and power of women in today's society." And who better to sum up this newfound female authority than the A-list actress being paid millions of dollars a movie.

Scheufele asserts that the most important aspect of high jewelry is how women feel when they wear it, and these award ceremonies brim with emotion on the most famous faces of our time. A flurry of bejeweled flowers encrusted with opals, pink sapphires, tsavorites and diamonds cascade to the shoulder as part of her Red Carpet collection (see p. 170), with smaller amethyst buds in purple set ablaze with color. The fiery red of her haute joaillerie necklace (see p. 171) with its ruby tassels knotted around the throat is pure theatre. The spiral splendor of an elaborate jewel, such as Chopard's Peacock bracelet, as it swirls around the arm, feathers glinting for the cameras, encapsulates a shift in power from the monarchy to the media during the last century. Worried by accusations of extravagance, today's royals have been forced to play down their jewelry, but a captivated audience can still luxuriate in the gloriously expensive jewels that are an intrinsic part of the spectacle of Hollywood and Cannes.

Another arena that has no qualms about extravagance is the fashion catwalk. But even there, the strengthening of women's rights, and of gay and black liberation, has shifted the perception of what is socially acceptable. Bibi van der Velden, a designer and sculptor based in Amsterdam, found herself on the wrong side of that line in 2009 when she conceived a fashion show called Afrozonian Affluence, in which black models wore her oversize jewelry. The backlash that followed centered on the fact her models were bare-breasted, except for her jewels and some strategically placed feathers. The freethinking, liberal environment van der Velden enjoyed in the Netherlands had not prepared her for the hostility of the British press. They condemned as objectification something that she had seen as a celebration of black women, and she was horrified. As an artist she was used to being provocative, but intentionally so.

Despite the negative reaction, she continued to develop her style, moving from the fashion world to the miniature treasures of precious jewelry. Her fashion-week days were about sculpture as performance, with birds flying over the catwalk, but now her theater is more concentrated, with scarab-wing earrings (see p. 172)

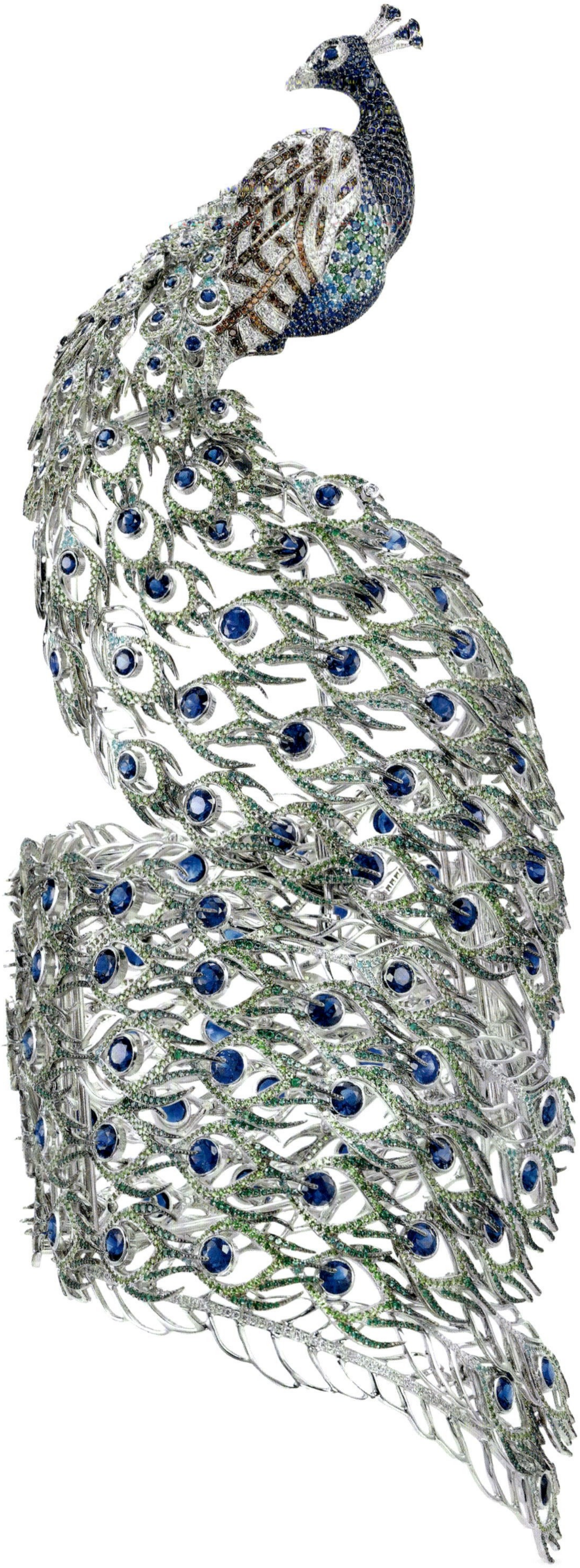

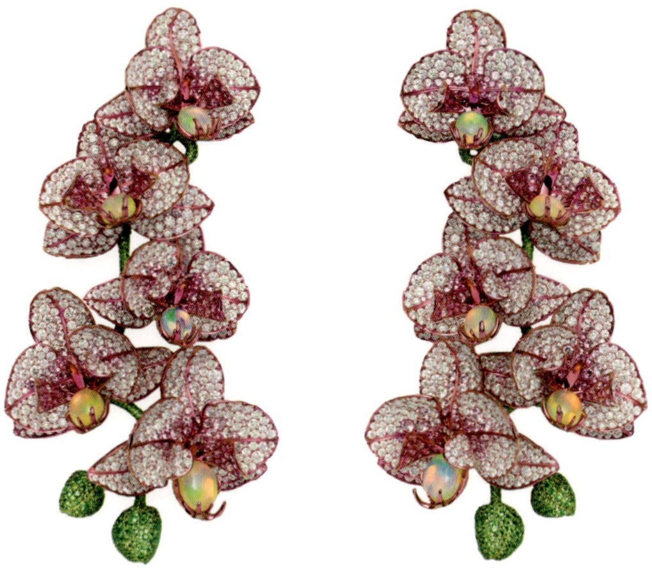

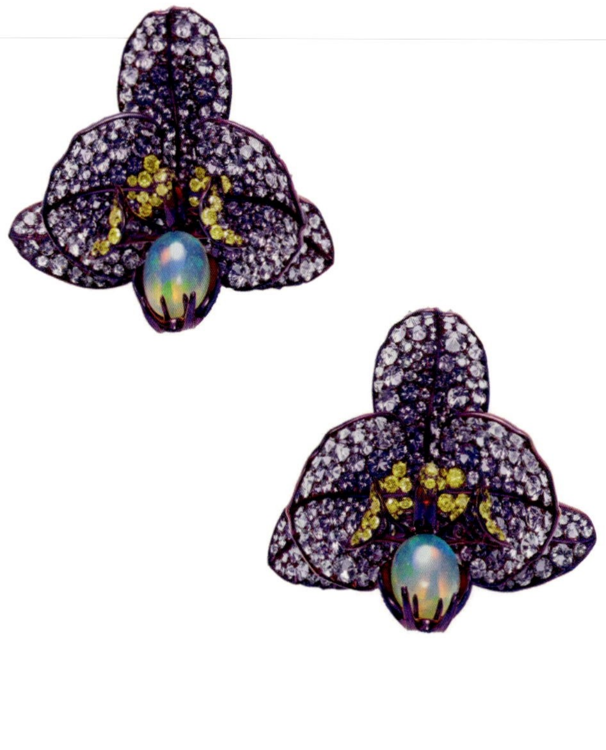

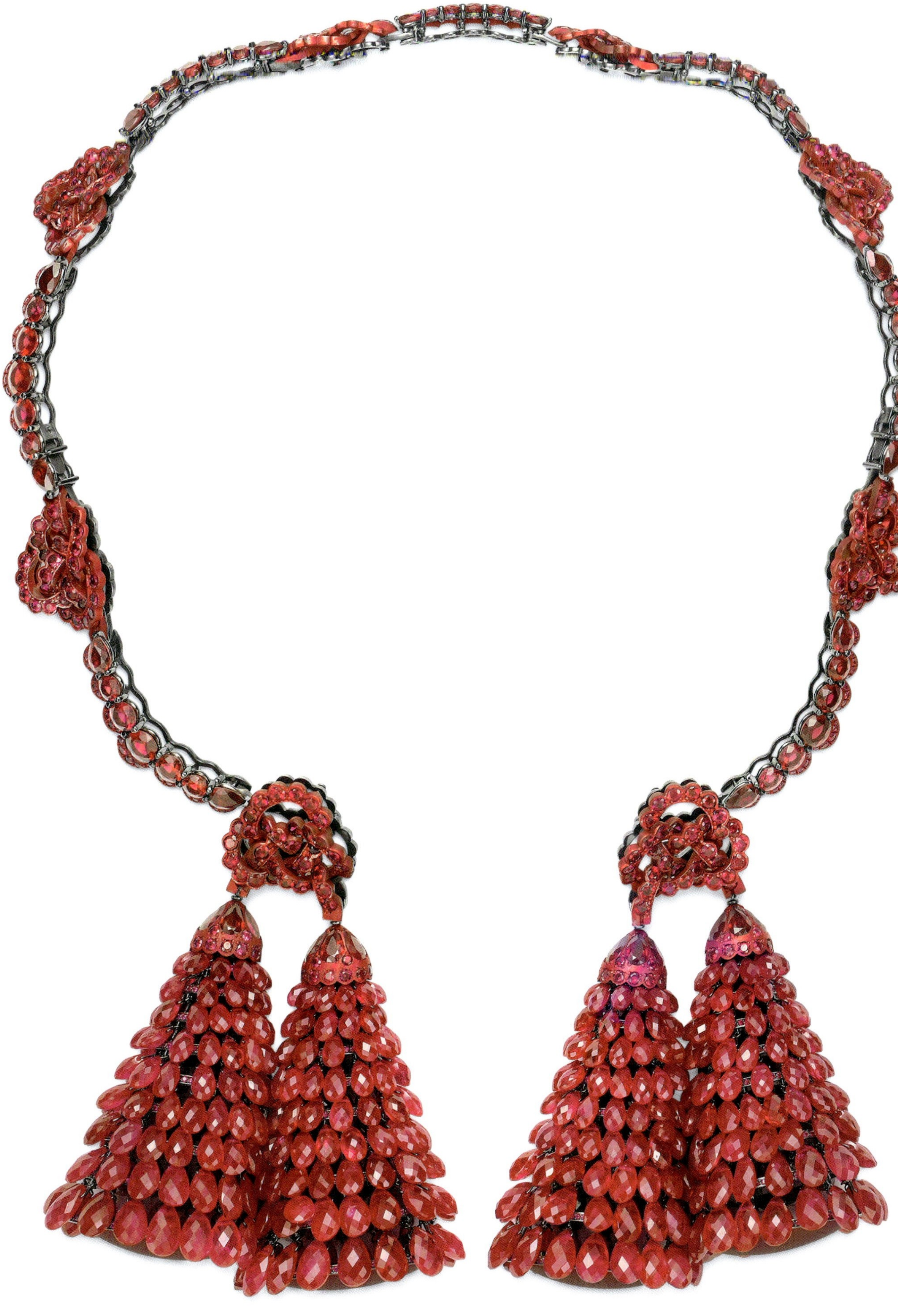

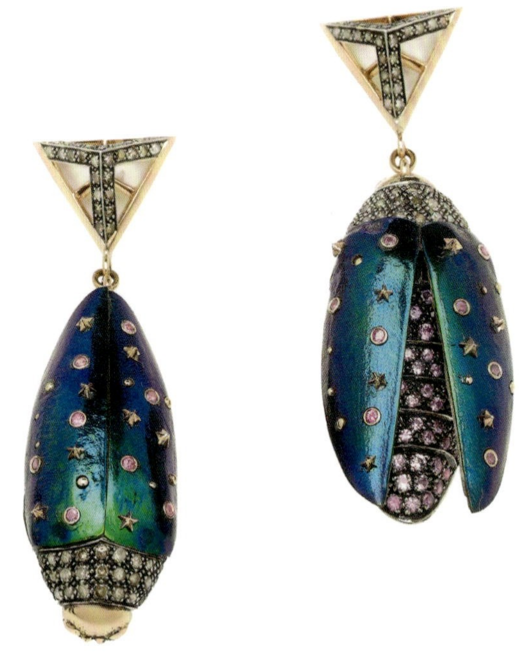

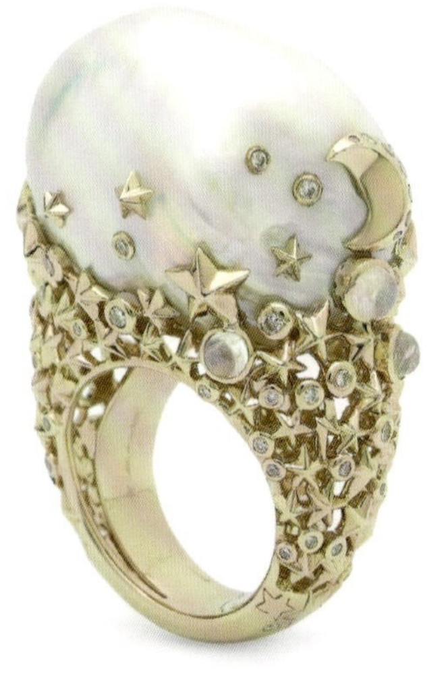

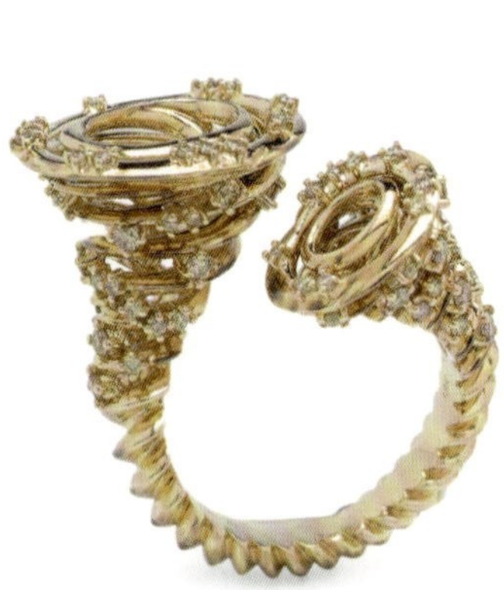

Bibi Van der Velden
Scarab Upside Down Earrings, 2018
Amethysts, brown diamonds, pink
sapphires, and scarab wings in sterling
silver and rose gold

Starry Night Ring, 2018
Baroque pearl, moonstones, and white
diamonds in white gold

Tornado Ring, 2019
Light brown and white diamonds
in white gold

THE FEMALE AGE

in silver and gold studded with sapphires, tsavorites, diamonds, and amethysts. Each earring opens and closes or detaches and morphs into alternative designs, expressing her personal need to reinvent and push her technical limits.

Van der Velden's 2018 Forces of Nature collection kept its political edge firmly in the area of environmental sustainability—both in terms of themes and choice of materials—with a series of tornado-inspired jewels immortalized in twisted gold and diamonds. "We were getting feedback from people in the States saying that this is a very sensitive subject, because they have devastating tornados," she says, but she maintains that it is important to discuss difficult ideas openly, and that jewelry can be used to express human struggles. Her focus on unorthodox materials, such as the scarab wings or the sixty-thousand-year-old mammoth tusk she carves into the form of dragons, crocodiles, snails, and unicorns, comes from a childhood steeped in creativity and surrounded by strong women. Her parents divorced when she was eight and she moved from Great Britain to the Netherlands with her mother, who began working as a stonemason, using heavy machinery, and also as a sculptor in clay and stone. She remembers her mother forging a new identity for herself through her work and waiting for her to come home in overalls covered in dust. Her grandmother was a celebrated psychiatrist who also raised five children, and it is that tenacity van der Velden intends to pass down to her daughter. "Women having their own careers, their own identities, and materializing their own dreams should really be a part of a child's upbringing. It's been an inspiration for me."

Everything van der Velden makes is first hand-carved in wax so that each form can reveal itself in its own time. She enjoys the sculpting process of shaping gold and gemstones, an echo of a time when as a child she would work on clay or soft stone and help to polish her mother's sculptures in a studio at the bottom of their garden. She feels that the rhythm and rigor of work let women be more relaxed in experimenting with new identities and that in time this will undermine inequality as clichés of gender roles shift naturally.

In terms of identity, gender fluidity is perhaps the newest challenge to the status quo, with traditional concepts changing on an almost weekly basis. Grayson Perry, a British artist who works in ceramics, embroidery, photography, and jewelry, is also a transvestite with an alter ego, Claire, and embodies this new duality. He describes his Essex upbringing in the south of England as acultural, with no art or books and not much music, except for the television and the "easy listening" of BBC Radio 2. Art saved him and he became intrigued by the ability of "lower status" art forms, such as ceramics and jewelry, to disrupt the art world, which has a class system and gender bias just like the outside world. When in 2003 he became the first ceramic artist to win the Turner Prize, art critics struggled. "I've always enjoyed using these mediums in their classical forms," says Perry, who has peppered his work with jewelry over the years. "I don't make art versions of anything and if I make a piece of jewelry, it's not some sort of art gallery-based installation piece of jewelry. It's a real piece of jewelry you could wear out if you wanted to . . . if your neck was strong enough."

For the solid brass charm necklace *I Am a Man* (see p. 174), which he created in 2014, he strung charms, including a dog, hammer, rocket, guitar, and phallus, around a simple band, playing with the idea of what masculinity looks like in jeweled form. He also made *Doll Pendant* (2009) out of silver and fabric, which is less challenging to wear but just as beautiful. Jewelry for Perry is part of a lexicon of female adornment, that fascinates him. He describes it as "little advertising hoardings we carry around with us," sharing where we fit into society like a badge with a political slogan. "A lot of men dress to be invisible, because they like to think of themselves as the subject and women as the object," he says. They steer clear of bright colors and he feels their avoidance of jewelry is part of that. Restrictive gender orthodoxies limit many men to the nondescript suit but give them social freedom while allowing women unlimited choice in terms of outfit but restraining them in terms of power. In his 2016 book *The Descent of Man,* Perry argues that

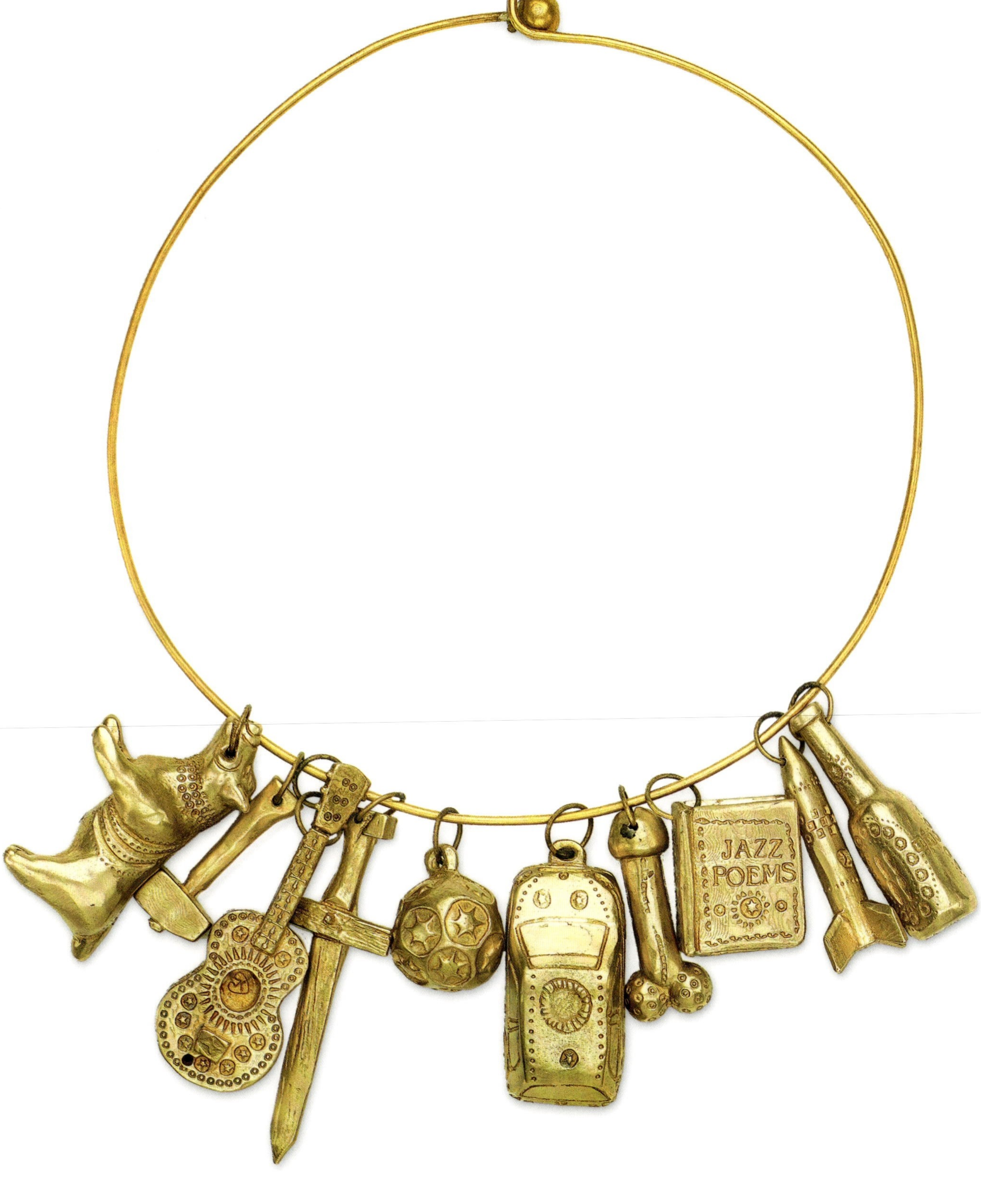
JAZZ
POEMS

Grayson Perry
I am a Man Necklace, 2014
Solid brass
Developed with Kit Grover for the
National Portrait Gallery, London

rigid masculinity destroys society and so feminism is a valuable balance, fighting the unyielding roles we are given in childhood.

For Perry, Claire acts as a kind of shorthand, symbolizing his femininity, while his masculinity is represented by a teddy bear called Alan Measles, another recurring theme in his work. Claire holds less meaning for him as he gets older, however, because all sides of his personality are now just Grayson. He thinks of her as a feminist but, he concedes, "There is no one more sexist than a transvestite," because they are dependent on the rigid gender roles that forbid a man from wearing a dress or heels. If we all become postgender tomorrow, that dangerous, adrenaline-fueled walk down the street in a pink satin catsuit will not hold the same allure.

Solange Azagury-Partridge, a London-based designer of jewels and art pieces, feels that unlike "unwearable jewels," such as rugs, tables, chandeliers, and clocks, jewelry has the power both to change and to protect us. Early on in her career, she worked for the antiques dealer Gordon Watson and she remembers a woman coming into the store looking scruffy and disheveled but wearing a fabulous Cartier ring that transformed her, turning perceptions of her upside down. Azagury-Partridge's grandmother wore an armful of bangles every day and they affected the young Solange subconsciously, so that jewelry seemed part of the person instead of a separate object. It was that ritual of bedecking oneself to leave the house, for protection from the many forces that conspire against women in their daily lives, that stayed with her.

Azagury-Partridge opened her first store in West London in 1995. Back then, Westbourne Grove was full of old launderettes and dusty antique shops, but she saw an opportunity and business followed. Rents were low and jewelry was split between costume and traditional gem-led design churned out by the big brands. As a self-taught designer, Azagury-Partridge saw a niche for her adventurous, quirky style and decided to experiment to see where her own brand might take her. She had been fascinated by art as a child, but it wasn't until she was forced to design her own engagement ring (see p. 177) as an alternative to the plodding diamond solitaire that it really took hold. She jammed a heft of uncut diamond into a gold dome in a design that still looks as if it was made yesterday. When she started, she had barely enough jewelry to stock her store, so she put a single piece in the window under a magnifying glass. "I felt like an outsider for a long time. Imposter syndrome is the phrase," she says. Women take time to feel they deserve a place among the still male-dominated upper echelons of the industry.

As a student of linguistics at university, Azagury-Partridge found a deeper meaning in words that inspired her, and that became another creative starting point, mixing her love of language and irreverent view of life. Scribbles, a collection she launched in 2018, immortalized her doodles in ceramic and lacquer set with stones in mouthwatering colors (see p. 176). All her thirty collections are explosions of color on the body, and all possess a streak of impudent fun. One necklace in her Stoned collection (see p. 164) is a mad jumble of gems cascading down the chest like a bib in rainbow colors—purple, orange, green, red, blue, pink, gold, black, and white stones all in different cuts, some edged in *plique-a-jour* enamel and yellow gold. The enamel apes the color and consistency of a significant stone, so that in some pieces, such as the Rectangle Real Fake ring, what looks like a large emerald is, in fact, enamel. An ironic play on the value and importance of the stone itself.

In addition to designing her own jewels, Azagury-Partridge worked as creative director at Boucheron from 2001 to 2004, which gave her a deeper understanding of how much effort goes into building a global brand. She left more confident in her abilities, but having her jewels made exactly as she would like them remains a challenge: there is still resistance to women being unequivocal in their requirements. She never accepts no from a manufacturer, because, as she says, if we can send a man to the moon, "we can make a bloody diamond ring." It is this kind of attitude that brings other women at the top of their game in fields such as

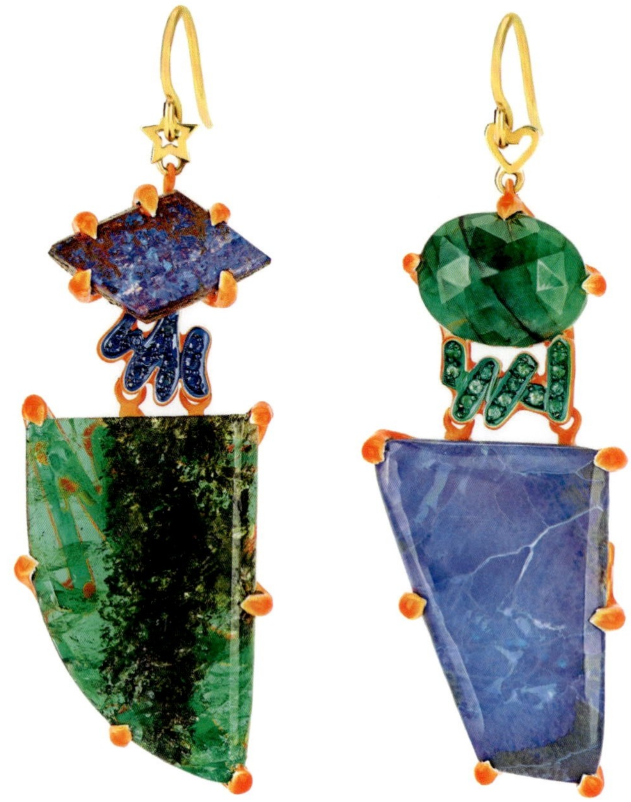

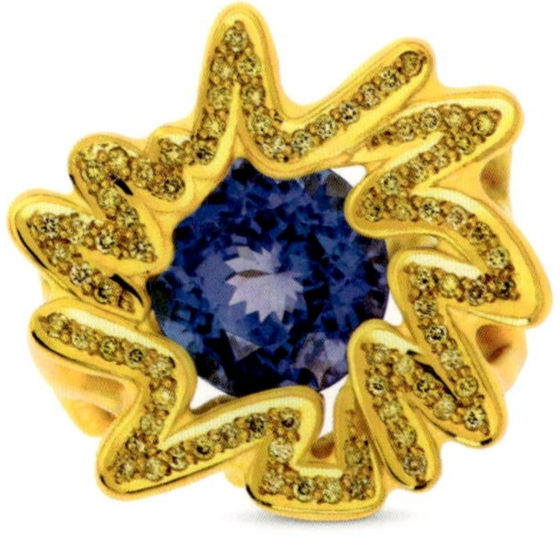

Solange Azagury-Partridge
Scribbles Blue Green & Orange
Earrings, 2018
Blue opals, emeralds, lacquer, and
sapphires in ceramic plate and gold

Scribbles Blue & Yellow Ring, 2018
Lacquer, tanzanite (5.19ct), and yellow
diamonds in ceramic plate and gold

Solange's Engagement Ring, 1987
Rough diamond in gold

(Following pages)
Leyla Abdollahi
Lust & Lure Wing Ring, 2014
Diamonds and emeralds in white gold

Lust & Lure Mismatch Wings Earrings,
2014
Diamonds, emeralds, and onyx
in white gold

Sharon Khazzam
Atteba Necklace, 2015
Black diamonds, emerald (44.20ct),
and Paraiba tourmalines in platinum

THE FEMALE AGE

law, art, and entertainment into her ateliers in London and New York. Jewelry, like the women who now make it, has become tougher, more insistent, with collections, such as Scribbles, that look like plastic but in reality are reassuringly expensive. Her clients aren't trying to prove anything. They have real power, and it shows. "They [the jewels] are slightly fuck off, aren't they, slightly fuck you?" Azagury-Partridge says gleefully.

Iranian-British designer Leyla Abdollahi may not express it in quite those terms, but her key collections are also aimed at bold, self-assured women. In 2014 she produced her second collection, Lust & Lure—a triumph of onyx, emeralds, and diamonds in winged configurations reflecting her love of Art Deco and the bold style of the 1920s. From oversize ear cuffs to knuckle-grazing rings (see p. 178), her attraction to Gothic drama is evident in all she does. Her mission is to reposition jewelry for a younger, more eclectic crowd, and in Lust & Lure she strips the emerald of its unattainable mystique. She carved the onyx and blackened some of the gold, but admits that she might not have made it at all had she considered the cost of production more thoroughly, and the fact that risk-averse retailers would be worried about selling it. Ironically, it sold out at launch, but she realized that retailers were showcasing her work to lure customers in to buy the archetypal pearl stud. This was partly because sales assistants were reluctant to get her more substantial jewels out of the case—a key component of jewelry being that it must be seen on the body to fulfill its true potential. Also, customers felt too intimidated to ask to look at it more closely, because its preciousness scared them. A $10,000 handbag was much easier to grab off the shelf than a $3,000 ring, which could feel "untouchable."

The retail environment with its security guards and nervous sales assistants gave Abdollahi a wider platform but was also acting like a barrier, which is why many designers prefer to sell one on one. "Women are fearless when it comes to jewelry," she says emphatically. "Fearless because they understand it." She had a client whose husband made an appointment to buy his wife a present. Abdollahi presented him with a selection of pieces and he couldn't tell the difference between the earrings and a bracelet. Earrings to him were the kind of safe studs his mother used to wear, not the Gothic chandeliers with hanging chains and triangular-cut gemstones of Abdollahi's Trinity collection. Abdollahi and her customer were both bemused, but in that moment she had shown him how magnificent jewelry could be. Now he buys from her all the time—for himself as well as for his wife.

Some jewelers have had a much better experience with retail. In 1999 Barneys, the luxury New York department store (now closed), approached designer Sharon Khazzam because they were expanding their jewelry offering and they wanted to carry a collection with her name on it. American customer service is proverbially some of the best in the world and the stylish but edgy Barneys philosophy really appealed to Khazzam. She wanted to create jewelry her grandmother wouldn't wear, but her first collection, Stitches, was a cautious attempt held back by the vast personal investment she had to make in terms of materials. It was at least unisex, which was a bold move, even if the design was, as she puts it, "meek." Judy Collinson, her contact at Barneys, told her to take risks and that they would support her. Unlike many retailers, who were moving to a sale-or-return model, Barneys was willing to pay for the jewelry upfront, and from this tentative start grew a twenty-year collaboration.

For Khazzam, the shift in female power became noticeable around the beginning of the twenty-first century and was symbolized by a soon-to-be-client who was buying some shoes in Barneys Chicago. The woman looked up, saw a costly bracelet, bought that too, and has subsequently bought many, many more jewels. She did not run the idea past a husband, but did it on a whim, and now 90 percent of Khazzam's collectors are self-purchasing women just like her. "We all sit around over lunch and work together on a piece. No man anywhere in the equation—there is just something really exciting about it," Khazzam says.

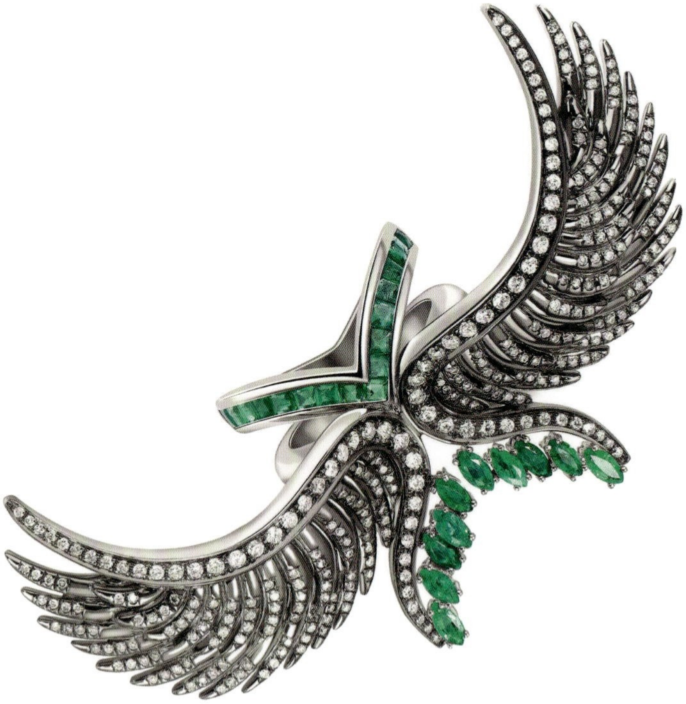

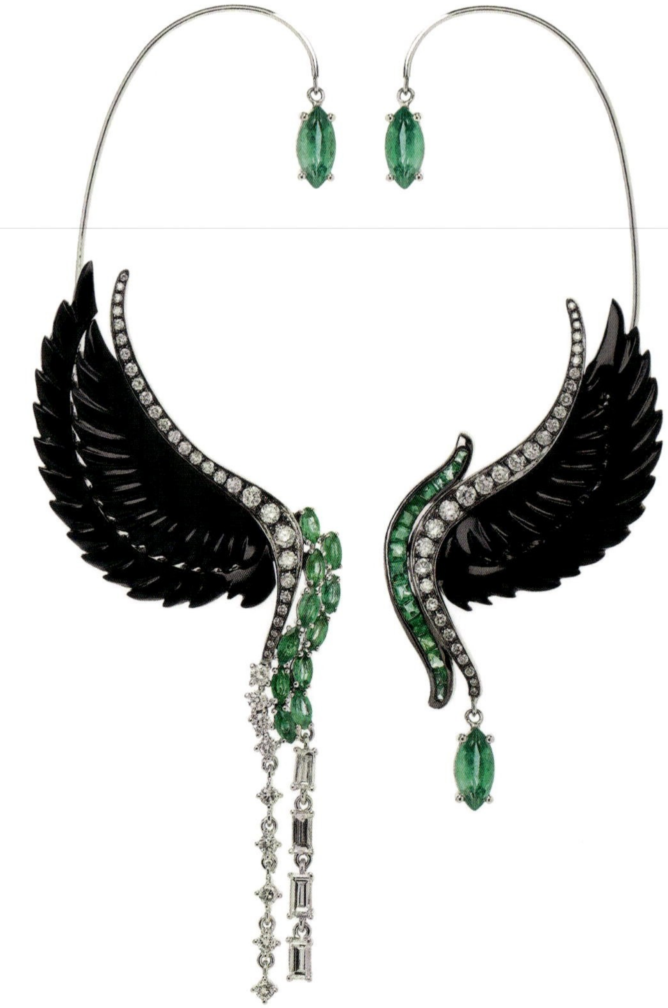

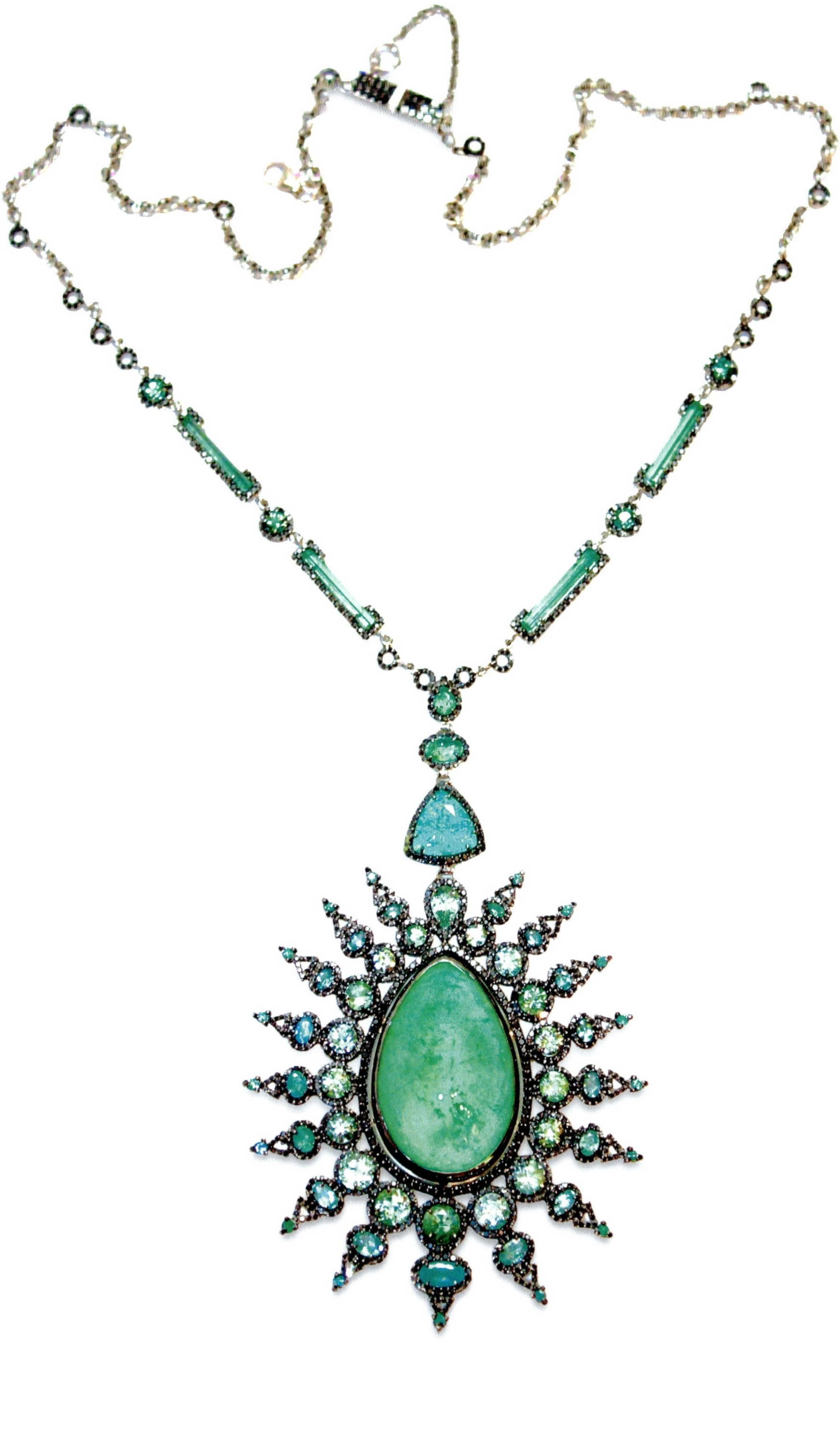

HStern
Feathers Bracelet, 2004
Gold

"Like I'm living a kind of woman's dream." Her Atteba necklace (see p. 179) is a striking example of the boisterous design that appeals to her clients in Chicago, Boston, New York, and California. It has a forty-four-carat emerald cabochon stone at its heart and was inspired by the eyes of a stranger. While trying to figure out what to do with such a huge emerald, Khazzam was visiting an office for an appointment. She noticed a woman with the most hypnotic green eyes lined in black kohl and in homage made the emerald into a necklace edged with 1,200 black diamonds. It was a poignant tribute to the freer world she knew as a child in Iran, which was changed forever by the Islamic Revolution in 1979, after which eyeliner became a dangerous transgression. Overnight, women who had worn miniskirts, shorts, and makeup were told to cover themselves in public in an agonizing reversal of women's rights. Khazzam was thirteen when she left and knows firsthand that the freedom women have in the West can be taken away at any moment.

The transition to a world of greater female power hasn't always been easy, especially in parts of the world where machismo has traditionally reigned. In Brazil, famed for its colored stones and flamboyant style, it is hampered by regular recessions—five since the year 2000—and persistent crime, which compels women to find ingenious ways to wear their jewelry. Regardless, this hasn't stopped HStern, a design house based in Rio de Janeiro, from creating bold, extravagant jewels with a modernist bent. In 1939 a seventeen-year-old Jewish boy called Hans Stern (1922–2007) fled Essen in Nazi Germany for Brazil, where he quickly learned Portuguese while working for an exporter of crystals who dazzled him with stones. Brazil had at first supported Germany and Italy but switched sides as the war progressed, so that in 1945 boatloads of American tourists felt it was safe to descend on Rio. Stern was there to greet them with his first small store on the docks. He offered more than a chance to buy: he offered an education, taking visitors on whirlwind tours of his workshops and explaining the origins of indigenous stones, such as tourmalines and topaz.

Stern was a stone lover at heart and his fascination with minerals never left him. He opened a gemstone laboratory in 1958 and some years later invented a new gold alloy the company referred to as noble gold: softer, browner, and less garish than the traditional yellow. A cuff followed in noble gold, with diamonds emblazoned in the form of a star at its center, fanning outward, splaying around the wrist. The combination of these elements would define the unique sophistication of the Stern style and stand them in good stead when the market turned in the 1990s and women became more important as buyers. In 2004 Stern—which translates as "star" in German—created its own asymmetrical diamond cut called the Stern Star, with twenty internal facets resembling the points of a star creating a dazzling kaleidoscope.

Stern's eldest son Roberto had by this time taken over as president and creative director and gave the house a design-led philosophy, collaborating with other creative heavyweights, such as the fashion designer Diane von Fürstenberg. Roberto was attracted to the duality of von Fürstenberg, a self-made businesswoman who showed that independence, strength, and a soft femininity need not be mutually exclusive. The modern woman could be all three. The rock-crystal and eighteen-carat-gold Power ring that, as von Fürstenberg put it, literally had the ability to knock men out, was one of the results of their eleven-year collaboration. It was bold and sculptural, tough yet sleek—a daring move in a market known for its appreciation of color. "Daring costs a lot," says Roberto. "It is much easier to replenish an existing collection than to risk something new. You only know what will become a classic years later." His focus on design has paid off with stone-free creations, such as the Feathers bracelet, a triumph of engineering with a thousand metal feathers on tiny links that flash and chime as they move. Made in homage to the Native American tradition of weaving feathers into the clothes and hair as a mark of respect to the spirit world, this mystic plumage from an ancient culture is brought to life as a colossal gold showstopper in the Stern style providing women with the art through which to express the liberty they now enjoy.

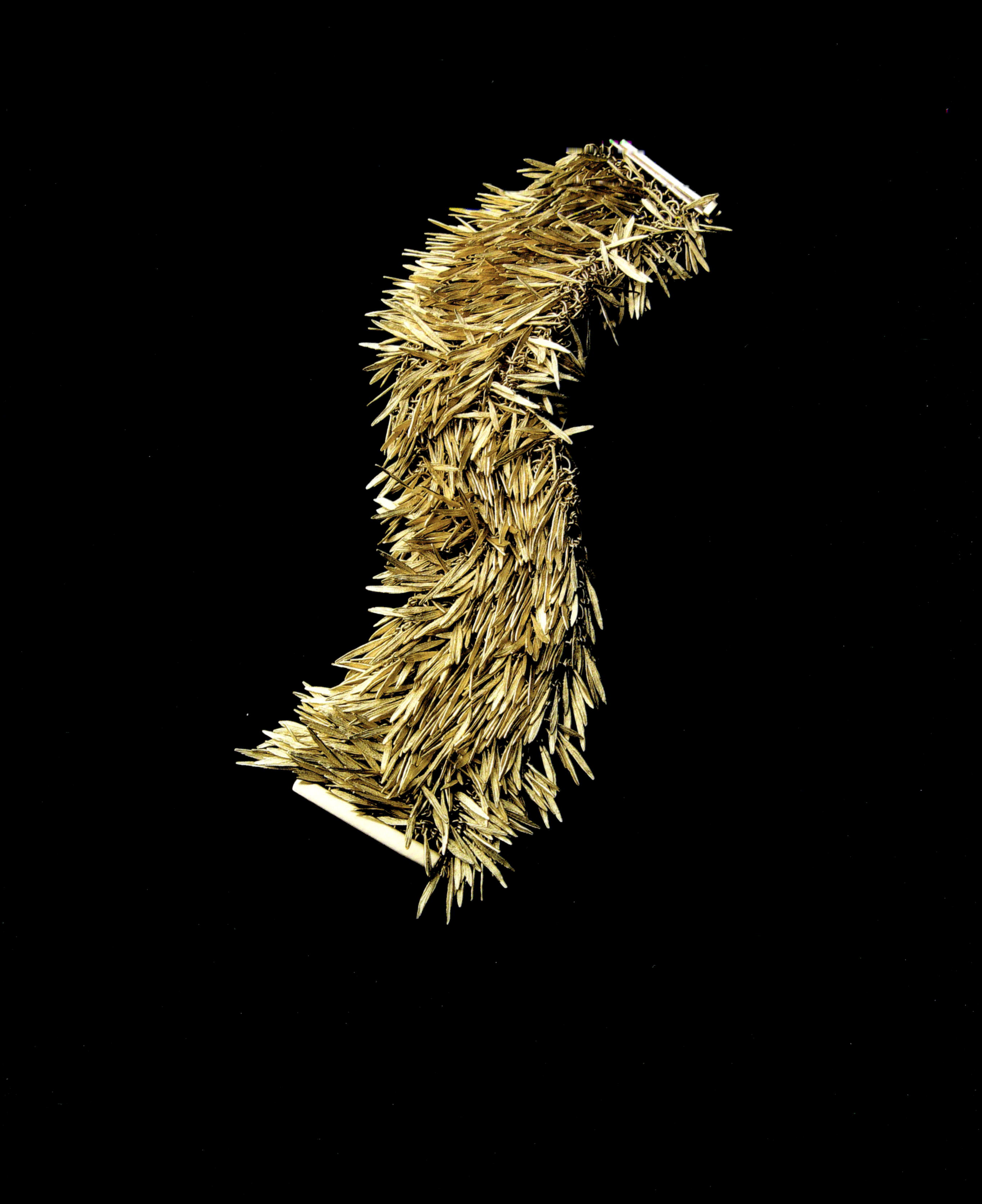

Mellerio dits Meller
Rose brooch, 1864
Diamonds in gold and silver

Just as the young immigrant Hans Stern built a business from nothing in his new country, so did the founders of Mellerio dits Meller, a venerable French design house going back fifteen generations. They arrived in France at the beginning of the sixteenth century after the Great Italian Wars forced them out of their home village in Piedmont. They were traders, peddlers, and chimney sweeps, and legend has it that one of them overheard a plot to assassinate King Louis XIII of France (1601–43) while sweeping a flue at the Louvre Palace. So grateful was the king's mother Marie de' Medici (1575–1642) that she granted the family special dispensation to trade in Paris, unhampered by the usual bureaucracy. This prompted a close and lasting relationship between the Mellerios and the French aristocracy despite the French Revolution, leading eventually to them opening a store on Rue de la Paix, off Place Vendôme, in 1815, where they served up one-of-a-kind pieces inspired by classical Naturalism and the garland style that had been popularized by Napoleon a decade earlier.

Not so long ago high jewelry in Europe was reserved for the nobility, gold for the wealthy middle classes, and base metals for those lower down the chain. Sumptuary laws, which limited an individual's expenditure and regulated their conduct, tied jewelry and clothing to social rank in many countries, so that an obvious hierarchy could be maintained. Laure-Isabelle Mellerio, president of the house and its first female artistic director, recognizes that times have changed. "Now all women wear jewels no matter what their social background," she observes. So it is no surprise that class barriers are slowly breaking down as the empowerment of women (and their jewelry) gains traction. The delicate beauty of a Mellerio rose brooch glistening with diamonds or the arch of a floral corsage is now open to all.

When Laure-Isabelle assumed control in 2015, Paris was protesting about the cost of living, with mass demonstrations the result of government tax reforms. The mood turned against conspicuous consumption. Mellerio, however, continued to glide serenely onward, safe in the knowledge that the hunger for fabulous jewels can never be truly satisfied. The United States, Japan, and China beckon, fascinated by the allure of French culture, and while Millennials and Generation Z the world over claim to be more interested in experiences than in extravagant possessions, the brand knows from its extensive history that jewelry tends to have the last laugh.

Members of Generation X, those born between approximately 1965 and 1984, experienced rapid social change as children. A rise in divorce rates coupled with more mothers in full-time work afforded them less parental supervision than previous generations. This freedom enabled an immersion in music and art, often with entrepreneurial results. Jessica McCormack, a jewelry designer of this generation, grew up in New Zealand, where her father was an antiques dealer and auctioneer and she was surrounded by art, from Maori carvings to Georgian jewels. He taught her the value of storytelling, passing on his knowledge of history and culture so that when she began working in the Sotheby's jewelry department at the age of twenty-five, she had a deeply entrenched respect for creativity in all its many forms. A few years later she went into partnership with diamond expert Michael Rosenfeld and Rachel Slack, granddaughter of Harry Oppenheimer, the former chairman of De Beers, and started her own design house.

Today she works from an elegant nineteenth-century townhouse crammed full of artworks in London's Mayfair, where she instructs her on-site workshop in the finer points of the Georgian techniques that she combines with big glossy white diamonds. The Georgian cut-down setting involves metal surrounding the center stone being castellated to accentuate the contrasting elements of the jewel. The technique is most evident in McCormack's Superdelic collection, a delight of simplicity inspired by 1960s Pop and psychedelic art and complete with fluffy clouds, rainbows, and teardrops. Earrings feature brilliant white diamonds outlined with blackened gold (see p. 184), cementing traditional techniques with modern design.

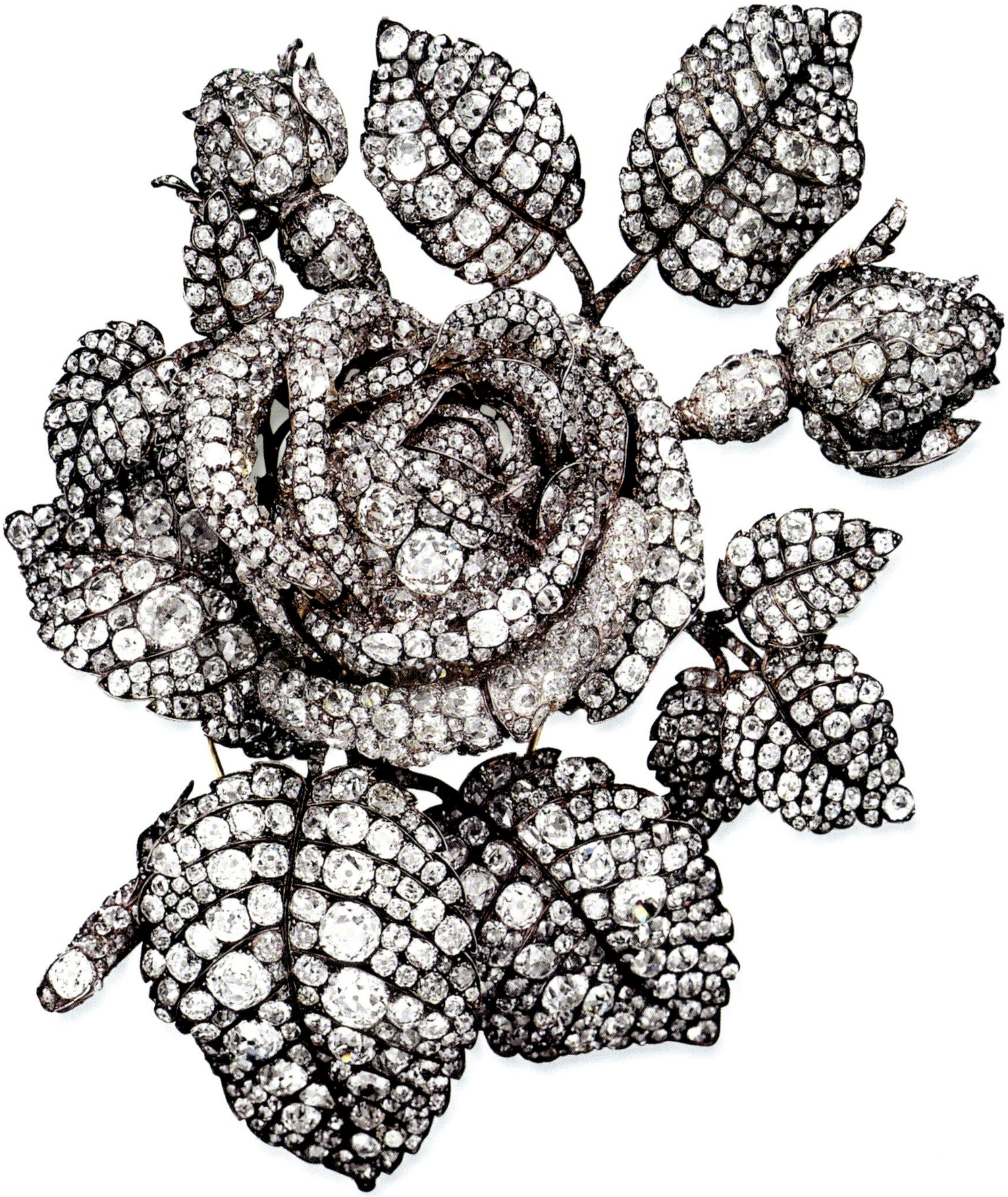

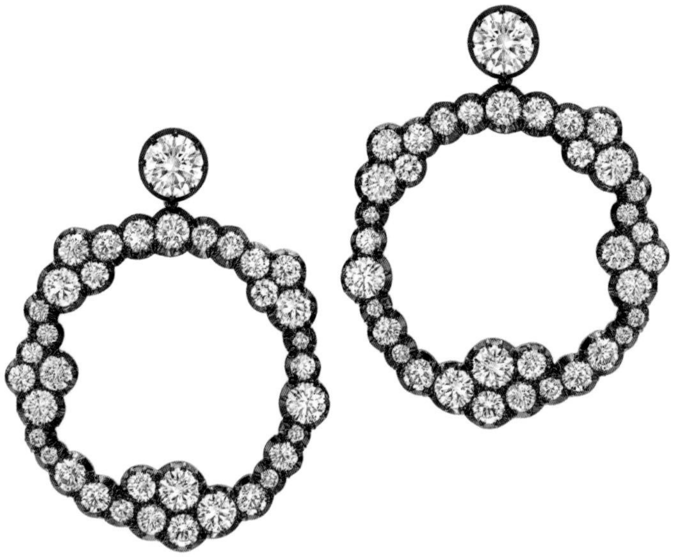

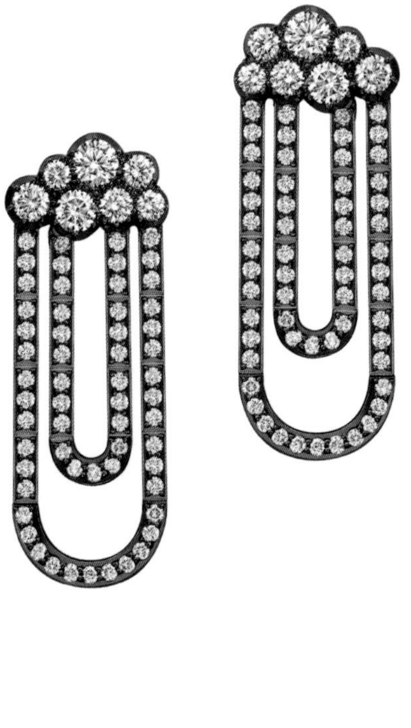

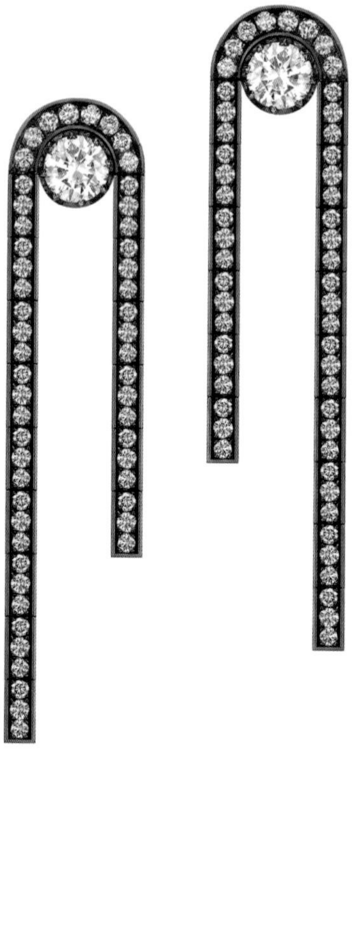

Jess McCormack
Superdelic Cloud Diamond Hoop
Earrings, 2019
Diamonds in blackened white gold and
yellow gold

Superdelic Rainbow and Cloud Diamond
Earrings, 2019
Diamonds in blackened white gold and
yellow gold

Superdelic Rainbow Diamond
Earrings, 2019
Diamonds in blackened white gold and
yellow gold

Art is still an overwhelming influence for McCormack, from the black-and-white conceptual photography of African-American feminist Lorna Simpson to Bauhaus Modernism and Mid-century Modern American architecture, while Maori culture especially seeped into her consciousness. Her Tattoo collection in blackened gold and diamonds references the ancient tradition of *Ta Moko*, a Polynesian ritual of tattooing the body and face with swirling patterns that denote social status and power within the clan. Aside from art, McCormack has been spurred on by female mavericks in jewelry design, such as Coco Chanel, Suzanne Belperron (see pp. 31–33), Juliette Moutard of René Boivin (see p. 131), and Jeanne Toussaint (see p. 131), who was artistic director of high jewelry at Cartier from 1933 to 1970 and created the iconic Cartier Panthère collection. Like them, McCormack had to earn the respect of her peers. "Persevering and remaining true to one's DNA are critical in order to be taken seriously," she says. "It's about results." And those results are obvious. The bareness of her style is masterful and while she has been the darling of glossy magazines for some years, her work would arguably have received more critical acclaim if a man had created it.

McCormack's biggest contribution to the feminist cause in terms of design has been the improbable-sounding Party Jacket, her way of reinvigorating an unworn or unwanted ring while preserving the essence of the original jewel. This entails building an outer shell that clips shut around the existing ring, showing just the stone. It is a way for a woman to reinvent an engagement ring that may have been given with the best of intentions but that she knows in her soul she cannot wear for life. Many men still insist on choosing a ring for their partner alone, in the belief they have the ability to select a style, cut, fit, tone, and design she can love forever. But a ring of this magnitude must claim the woman when she tries it on, not the other way around. In McCormack's hands a metamorphosis is possible, avoiding embarrassment for all and bringing joy to women who might otherwise have to resign themselves to frightful jewelry.

While McCormack brings joy to the bride to be, Canadian designer Nick Koss used his talent to create a unique divorce present. Named after the mythological Norse metalsmith Völund, who created replica after replica of his bride's gold wedding ring to console himself when she vanished, Koss set up his design house Volund in 2015 when Canada, a country with huge natural resources, was hit by rock-bottom oil prices. Luckily for him, his newly acquired clients continued to buy. The divorce gift, commissioned by one such new patron for herself, was a statuesque eighteen-carat white gold and platinum ring in the shape of a thistle (see p. 186), with protruding spikes set with baguette and round white diamonds. Koss describes it as fragile on the inside but sharp like a weapon on the outside, representing a new brand of confidence felt by women, which enables them to be tough while sharing their vulnerabilities. "We're seeing a resurgence of classical multifaceted femininity and I think it is beautiful," he says.

Not so long ago Koss was working in finance for the Canadian government, but he felt lost and unfulfilled. As children, he and his sister had been dragged around countless museums by their father, who pointed out cultural highlights. While young Nick was bored witless, he later came to the realization that entire cultures could and did disappear from history; even languages could be extinguished, leaving just the art. It was a kind of immortality that he sought to represent, but he didn't know how. The answer came when he deciphered a mysterious historical manuscript that led him to the Nevada desert to carry out a complex ritual during the solar eclipse. The financier in him struggled with that idea but he couldn't resist the mystery of it all, so off he went. While he was there, he stumbled across a small can of gold nuggets, just 1 ounce (30g) in weight, which he saw as a sign to pursue jewelry as a career, and this discovery changed the course of his life.

While Koss also looks to history and mysticism for his understanding of jewelry, he cites Catherine de' Medici (1519–89) as a figure who has affected his idea of female empowerment. As regent of France in the sixteenth century—the same time that Queen Elizabeth I was on the throne in England—she ruled over men

THE FEMALE AGE

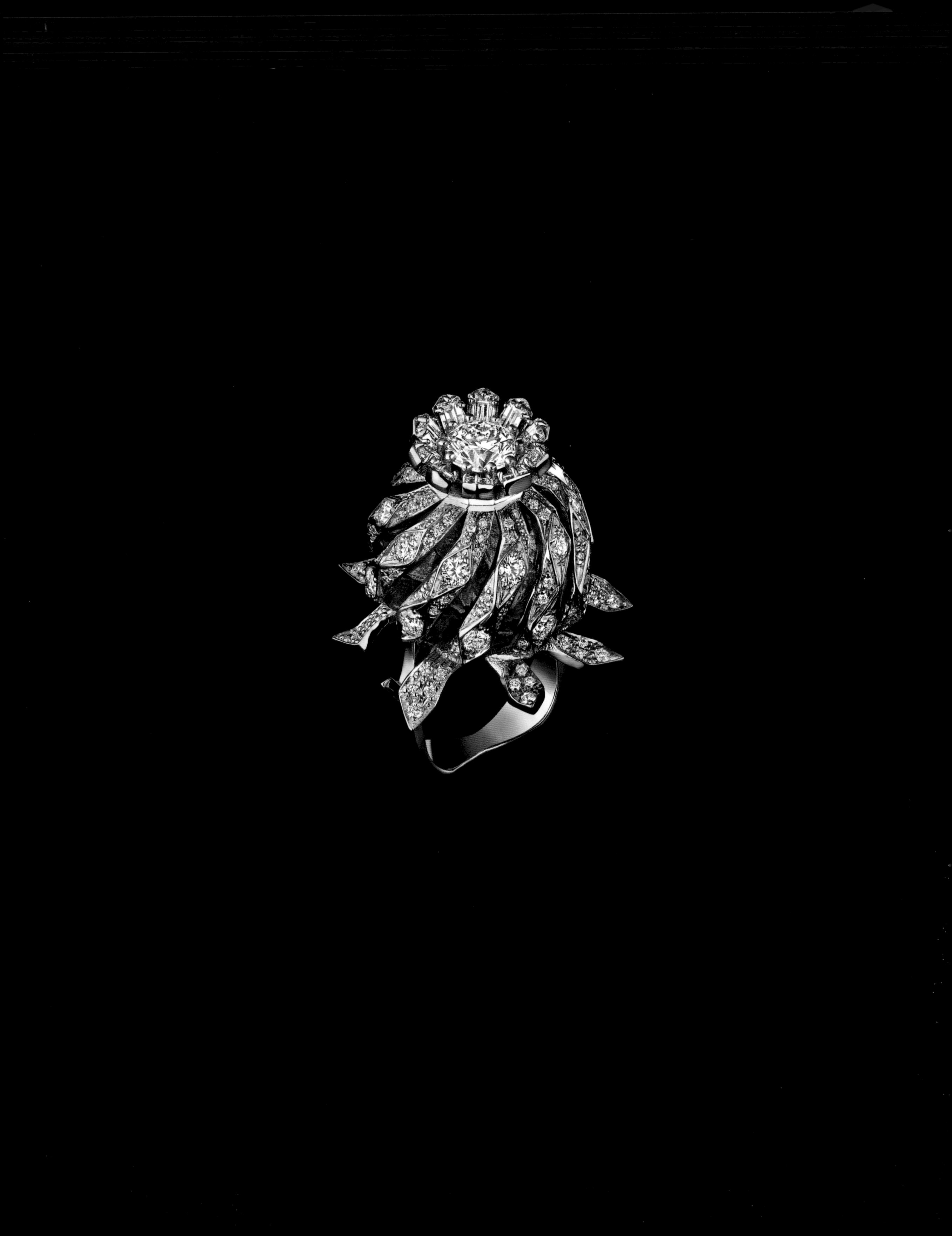

Volund
Thistle Ring, 2018
Diamonds in platinum and white gold

Thistle Ring Gouache, 2018
Gouache on heavy stock paper

who considered power to be "unfeminine." Yet she unleashed the full force of her ruthless strategic mind onto the world around her, becoming one of the most influential women of her day. She used jewelry as a talisman, with depictions of Jupiter showing respect for authority and Venus symbolizing love and power, but also had devilish symbols representing lust etched into pieces she owned. Koss imbues his creations with that complexity, using symbolic meaning in his design. He is fond of the lion as a symbol of universal strength and power, encapsulating its ferocity in a ring with gem-encrusted mane and penetrating green, gem-set eyes. For earrings, two golden lions balance atop crescents of diamonds and pearls, ready to pounce on some distant prey.

While Koss embraces multifaceted femininity in North America, the increasing impact of female style in Great Britain was captured perfectly by fashion designer Alexander McQueen (1969–2010). The jewelry he commissioned to send down the catwalk as an extension of his Gothic yet romantic style was created by his friend, the goldsmith Shaun Leane. Whereas the 1960s and 1970s gave us Women's Lib and the 1980s saw women fight their way through the corporate jungle, the 1990s were all about freedom of identity. Boundaries were shifting. In jewelry, women's growing courage saw grunge-inspired spikes, claws, and chains take hold and designers such as Leane, who had been conditioned to create classic diamond-drop earrings in London's Hatton Garden jewelry quarter, had a decision to make: either submit to the traditional aesthetic or rebel. Leane chose the latter, opting for subversive spears that arched from the lips, and a crown and cape of thorns. McQueen unleashed something in Leane that was waiting to be set free, a dark, fragile, sensual rawness that saw him produce large-scale body pieces in aluminum, brass, and silver, fusing metal into tough tribal silhouettes.

In 1999 Leane launched his own jewelry collection, evolving some of his catwalk creations into smaller gem-set jewels. His Tusk earrings from McQueen's 1995 show Hunger became silver hooks, an offshoot of which are his newer Sabre earrings with swordlike curves of white gold sweeping past the jawline. His Fuchsia brooch (see p. 189) with its enameled articulated flowers was made for a man and felt as if it might have grown from a macabre botanical garden deep within Victorian history. It is a combination of decaying, gnarled branches and curved, vibrant buds, referencing the transient nature of life and new beginnings. Leane's work is beyond gender, designed for anyone who can see its beauty. He feels there is more room for expression through jewelry for both sexes. The psychological connection between the client's vision of themselves and how they wear that vision is an ongoing conversation recorded artistically by designers such as Leane. "People said to me when I started, you're crazy, no one is going to buy this jewelry, it's sharp and it's dangerous," he laughs. Self-purchasing women now represent 90 percent of his client base. When he works with Bergdorf Goodman in New York, there is a $10,000 sweet spot below which his clientele buy on a whim without question. He argues that there is nothing left for men to buy women, because independence now means if a woman really wants something, she buys it herself. Avant-garde jewelry—especially the chic, romantic warrior jewels Leane creates—still confounds some men, yet if he had his way more men would wear it, too.

Women may be experiencing a new kind of economic freedom, but many still find themselves waiting for a man to "put a ring on it" with a formal proposal. London-based designer Hannah Martin feels the big diamond engagement ring is more about male possession or "a price tag on one's life" than it is about artistic expression. Yet if that rock were moved to a different finger it would symbolize an entirely different form of achievement. The female body continues to be political even down to its extremities. The rigorous judgment and surveillance of women's bodies also extends to female designers, who walk a tightrope when they begin interacting with the media. On the one hand, physical good looks get more press attention; but, on the other, it can be harder for young and beautiful women to be taken seriously in their chosen field. Humanity may be hardwired to seek out symmetrical youth and beauty but, as Martin can attest, the ramifications

Shaun Leane
Fuchsia brooch, 2048
Diamonds, enamel, and tsavorites in silver
Private collection

include well-meaning older men patronizing her, which she has found enormously frustrating throughout her career.

She launched her design house in 2005 just after graduating from Central St Martins with a first-class honors degree in jewelry design, but the infatuation with jewelry had entered Martin's life much earlier when as a young teenager in the late 1980s she became transfixed by the American horror movie *The Lost Boys*. The plot centers around two brothers who fight a gang of vampires, and she took to wearing a single dangly earring adopted from Kiefer Sutherland's vampire character David. From there she fell in love with music by such singers as Courtney Love, Kim Gordon, and Patti Smith, and their darkly sensuous style has influenced her work ever since.

The rebellion of rock and roll and of punk attracted her, because it pushed against the boundaries of what society considered acceptable. While the gentle heart or flower replayed over and over again within traditional codes of jewelry, it held little allure for Martin. "I felt I had something new to say and I wanted to say it as loudly as I could," she smiles. "I could never understand why beautiful, sensual jewelry did not really exist for me." This type of femininity was tough and dark, raw and edgy, representing a side of her that felt instinctively dangerous. Her first collection was called The Forgotten Treasure of the Infamous Aguila Dorada and included a shackle bracelet that alluded to sexual restraint but also to freedom. Her Spur ring (see p. 190), with its curves and sharp edges, was a meeting of masculine and feminine, hard and soft, a duality that lies at the core of all her work.

Her latest collection, A New Act of Rebellion, is inspired by the idea of an imaginary army marching forward into an unknown world armed with a manifesto for change. She actually constructed a manifesto for the collection, detailing a call to action for a new reality filled with "unsanitized" liberation and a way of living where wildness rules. The resulting jewelry is her battle dress, and it is fiercely utilitarian. Gold bands are pierced with safety pins, bolts punch through earlobes and wrap oversize around knuckles (see p. 190). Wood in the form of ebony makes its first appearance in her design, and malachite, an opaque green stone, is pierced like flesh welded to chunks of yellow gold. The collection is defiantly diamond-free, which is perhaps her ultimate act of rebellion. Her show of strength is the creative act itself and its lack of adornment. She quotes the musician Nick Cave, who describes creativity as an act of war against inner demons, and A New Act of Rebellion is her ode to freedom after a turbulent few years during which she parted company with her husband and then with her business partner. "I was caged," she says, and this collection is part of her escape.

A large part of jewelry's appeal comes down to escapism, but not just of the emotional kind. In India a woman's jewelry is an indication of wealth, that increasingly symbolizes her independence, instead of just the status of her father or husband. It represents a personal power with a hybrid identity, set apart from fashion, which is more formulaic, according to Alice Cicolini, a London-based designer whose jewelry is inspired by the Indian subcontinent. The hybrid character of jewelry lured her, following a decade spent curating exhibitions on fashion and contemporary design as director of arts and culture for the British Council in India. It compelled her to complete an MA in jewelry design at Central St Martins and to seek out talented craftspeople in Jaipur who could bring her vision to life. Her mother, an enthusiastic collector of jewelry, first introduced her to the idea of patronizing the work of a single autonomous designer, with her taste for Philip Lowery, a silversmith popular in the 1960s and 1970s. Alice realized she could be one such designer.

When she graduated in 2009, the Lehman Brothers bank had recently collapsed and she was freelancing as a jeweler within a fragile economy rocked by the global financial crisis. The enormity of what she was trying to achieve scared her, but she realized that dull, safe, traditional design was not an option if she wanted to survive. So she surrendered to the magnificence of Indian style, creating

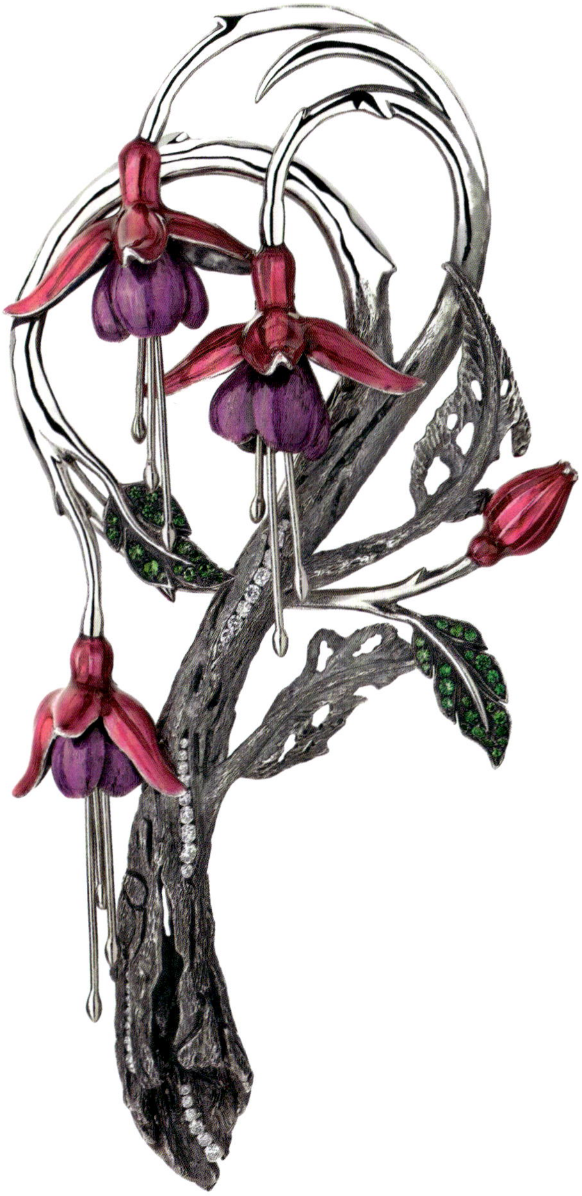

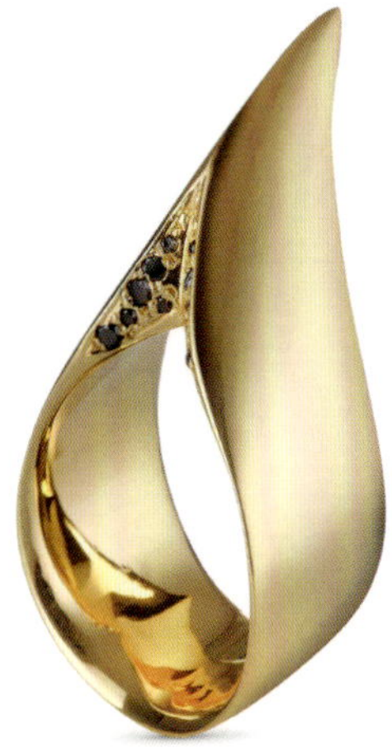

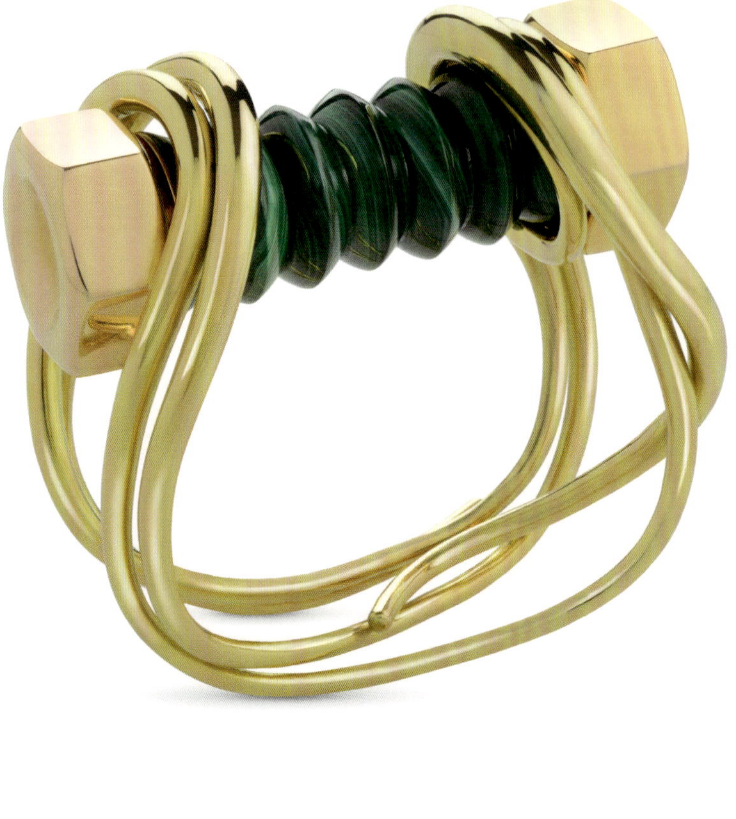

Hannah Martin
Spur Yellow Gold Ring, 2006
Black diamonds in gold

New Rebel Bolt Bangle, 2020
Malachite in rose and yellow gold

flamboyant, twenty-two-carat gold jewelry in sumptuous colors, populated by such stones as sapphires, peridots, tourmalines, garnets, and opals. Her Memphis Jaipur Bougainvillea Muzo earrings (see p. 192) sport large hexagonal emeralds at the front, with a jungle of pink foliage and gold geometry at the back. These are jewels that must be appreciated from every angle. She champions the ancient art of Meenakari, the painting of metal with enamel, commissioning artisan Kamal Kumar Meenakar to hand-paint many of her jewels.

In Indian culture, jewelry goes beyond decoration in a place where decoration is everything. It is tied to custom, religion, wealth, eroticism, and spirituality. When Cicolini stumbled across a simple jewelry box during a visit to the Mehrangir Fort Museum in Jodhpur, she gained valuable insight into the power of Indian jewelry and the significance of how it is applied. Inside the box were all the elements needed for the *solah shringar*, an adornment ritual that is carried out by married women in sixteen stages, nine of which involve jewelry. The ceremony begins with a scented bath that includes sandalwood, turmeric, and milk, and goes on by adding jewels to the hair, winding them around the ears, and using them as a nose ring, a necklace, bangles for protection, thumb rings, an anklet, sometimes with bells, and a bejeweled waistband.

Some of this adornment originated as flowers, but as wealth increased it morphed into gold, diamonds, and pearls. This was a daily ritual that the fifteenth-century poet Vallabhadeva argued would help women become attuned to Hindu mythology, but in modern life it is more fully explored in weddings. Sound is a key part of sensual movement in India, with jewelry being used to reveal a woman's presence as part of an alluring combination of perfume, the rustling of silks, and the chiming of bangles. The mystique and allure of femininity has jewelry at its core, in a culture where beauty is a multilayered process. Just as Indian gods and goddesses are bedecked, so each woman wears stones believed to hold magical powers. Cicolini calls it a "mental elevation," where women present themselves to the world completely confident in their powers. "I find this the ancient equivalent of self-love," she says. "Beauty is embraced and you are occupying your own space with confidence." This is not about the attractiveness you are born with but instead the beauty you apply. In her design, Cicolini is spreading that joy to others.

Weddings are still the biggest jewelry opportunity in India, with parents paying but their adult children guiding consumption. Among the young, jewelry may be worn more casually but, according to Sameer Lilani, commercial director of Indian jeweler Amrapali for Europe, the Middle East, and Africa, for the industrial elite what used to be a blue topaz or aquamarine on a simple chain is now a blue diamond. Women are in "the club," spending millions on rare colored stones instead of simply aspiring to own them. This discreet but powerful acceleration in extreme wealth is also a part of "bonus season" on Wall Street and the City of London's Square Mile, where jewelry and watches are being moved to key stores as more women are in jobs that attract lavish bonuses. Yet according to Amanda Triossi, a jewelry historian, lecturer, and consultant, the big money is still spent by men, who remain transfixed by the power of large, rare gemstones. She argues that the jewel itself is still seen as self-indulgent when women acquire it, although they can afford to do so. Until it is socially acceptable in the West for men from all walks of life to wear jewelry as they do in India and, to some extent, China, it will be considered a frippery. As most of the people in workshops, design studios, and working as stone dealers and auctioneers are men, so the preoccupation with hefty and expensive stones in high jewelry continues. Yet the new wave of innovative materials is more in tune with the female gaze, with design prized over investment potential. The emergence of serious female designers selling in the million-dollar-plus category is another sign that taste is following a more female line, but ultimately it will all become unisex. "Jewelry is irresistible because it is transcultural, trans-social, and transgender," says Triossi. It is inherently human, completely unnecessary, and utterly spellbinding, tied to the ongoing evolution of humanity in complex and glorious ways.

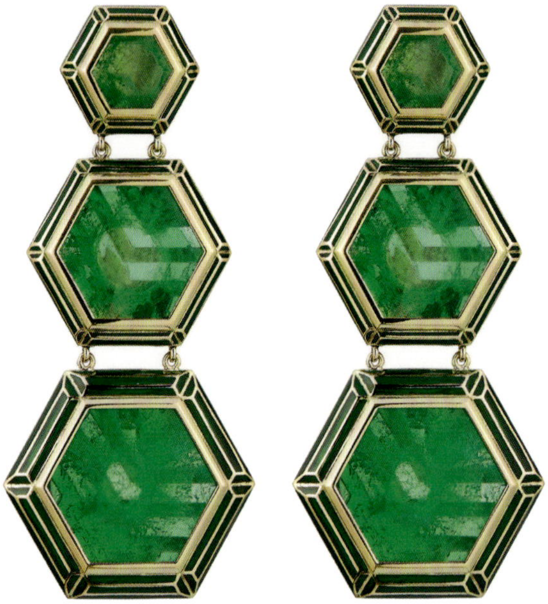

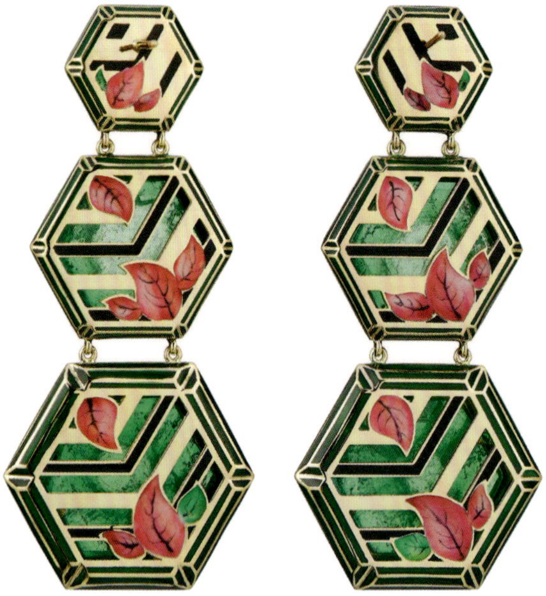

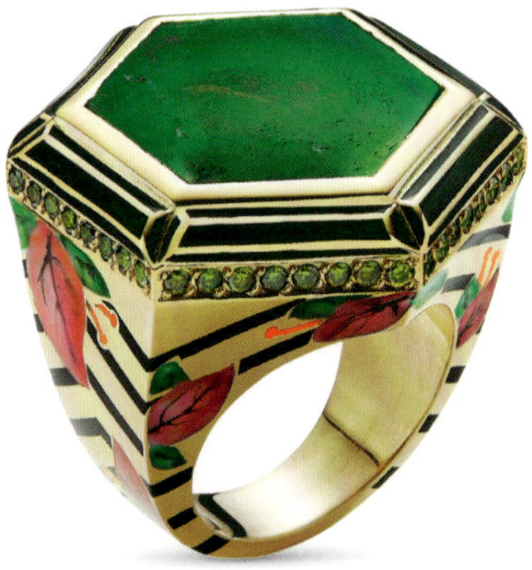

Alice Cicolini
Memphis Jaipur Bougainvillea Muzo
Chandelier Earrings (front and back),
2019
Lacquer, Muzo trapiche emeralds, and
plique-à-jour enamel in gold

Memphis Jaipur Bougainvillea Muzo
Ring, 2019
Green diamonds, lacquer, Muzo trapiche
emerald (16ct), and *plique-à-jour* enamel
in gold

Like Cora Pearl, Queen Elizabeth I wore jewelry as armor, harnessing its power to overwhelm her detractors in what amounted to a dangerously free life. In 1603, the coronation ring she wore during the entirety of her forty-five-year rule was removed on the advice of her physician as it had eaten into her flesh. She died one week later.

Our relationship with the jewel is much deeper than the touch of metal on skin or simply of the value of the materials that comprise it. And it is deeper still, when the artistry of an object transcends that of the everyday alternatives; elevated above the standard offerings and repetition of fine or costume jewelry. Before feminism firmly staked the claim for women's equality with men in all spheres, before female jewelers rose to equal prominence with their male counterparts and before women as consumers of jewelry became the taste-making, gloriously opinionated and unshackled core of the market, the art within jewelry was less boisterous. Its purpose was to create allure and mystery, to captivate. But now as the position of women in society evolves, the art has accelerated, mirroring the freedom many women now enjoy. New and unusual materials have diffused value and increased the poetry of the jewel. Novel, previously overlooked or historical techniques of stone-setting, enamelling and engraving are sought out and combined. And female jewelers now create unashamedly large, attention-grabbing pieces that refuse emphatically to hide in the shadows. These are jewels that command attention, that refuse to be ignored and that press even more insistently at the openings for women's advancement, widening the way for those to come.

High jewelry has always adorned those with ultimate power and, where once that meant royalty, in modern times it is increasingly self-purchasing women who are challenging its creators to break new ground. While museums and auction houses have fully grasped its artistic merits, there is still a reluctance, particularly among female designers, to call themselves artists, to break this final barrier, and, in turn, to urge members of the art world to admit that anything can be art if the intention is to create instead of to sell. The future of jewelry lies in the art of jewelry. While gold and diamonds will always seduce, without genius, they are meaningless.

GLOSSARY

The 4Cs

Robert M. Shipley established the Gemological Institute of America in 1931 to regulate the jewelry industry in the United States. Part of his mission as a retail jeweler was to provide an index or universal standard of value for the diamond market. In 1940 he collaborated with De Beers on an advertising campaign promoting the 4Cs, and by the 1960s it was the accepted standard for defining diamond quality.

- Carat: The weight of a diamond is measured in milligrams. A metric carat is 200mg and each carat has 100 points, therefore a 1.79ct stone is 279mg in weight. The bigger the stone, the more valuable, but quality and rarity often trump size, and to secure the highest prices, it must be colorless if white or intense if colored, flawless, and with good fire.
- Clarity: A lack of internal imperfections or "inclusions" visible to a grader at 10x magnification is considered "flawless." Inclusions develop when small crystals are trapped inside the stone as it is forming deep inside the earth. There are eleven grades of clarity in total.
- Color: White diamonds start at "D," which is colorless but looks white, and is considered to be the most valuable, through to "Z," which is light yellow. Colored diamonds are valued for their intensity with "fancy vivid" and "fancy deep" the most coveted.
- Cut: More than simply shape, the cut is a measure of how well a diamond transmits light. Graders look for an even proportion of light and dark in the stone for maximum value, scoring from "Excellent" to "Poor." This is the hardest category to judge, with qualities of "brightness," "fire," and "sparkle" key to a grader's decision.

Artisan

A person skilled in the applied arts, typically making high-quality items in small numbers by hand using traditional methods. Within jewelry, this includes bead, metal, and enamel work, as well as stone cutting. The very existence of these skills is in danger because younger workers are seeking more lucrative fields. Some designers consider this one of the biggest threats to the production of high jewelry.

Atelier

The workshop or studio of an artist or designer. For designers with a store, workshops usually occupy the same building or are located nearby, so that timely alterations can be made. Master polisher Benjamin Ray is part of David Webb's (see pp. 36–37) New York workshop and has been at the company since 1965. In Munich, Hemmerle (see pp. 6, 20–22) have more than twenty artisans with different skills, each working on pieces from design to completion. Most workshops are run by a master jeweler who oversees quality control.

Castellated

When the metal surrounding the center stone, known as a collet, is serrated with deep grooves. In the Georgian era (1714–c.1830), stones were placed in a "cut-down" setting, where thin sheets of metal were attached tightly to the stone with tiny prongs like turrets of a castle. The metal held fast to the stone to stop air and moisture getting to the foil placed behind clear stones to intensify the color in closed-back settings.

Ceramic

Jewelry-grade ceramic is usually made from titanium carbide with a hard-wearing high luster. Just like enamel, it enables jewelers to apply intense color in the absence of stones, The use of ceramics is enjoying a revival in jewelry circles, with James de Givenchy (see pp. 28, 30–31), Boucheron (see pp. 84, 86–89), Bvlgari (see pp. 11, 61–63), and Fernando Jorge (see pp. 46–47) all using it in their work.

- Faience: A material, mostly sand or crushed quartz, applied to stoneware, earthenware, and jewelry for a colorful saturated finish. In ancient Egypt blue green was the most popular color and its smoothness against the skin made it a perfect alternative to turquoise, which was harder to obtain.
- Porcelain: A strong, delicate, translucent, and usually white ceramic that originated in China during the Tang dynasty (AD 618–907): Also known as fine or bone China. Marco Polo called it "Porcellana" when he returned to Europe from his travels in the East and European potters quickly tried to copy it. In jewelry, it became popular in the nineteenth century, painted and glazed with elaborate portraits, but its use is unusual in high jewelry today.

Cut/Polished

The proportion, symmetry, and type of shape given to an unpolished stone or "rough" before setting it into jewelry. Lapidary, or stone cutting, takes years of training and even then, the character, imperfections, and brittleness of the stone must be taken into consideration. Diamond cutting sits apart, as a specialized field and now often involves computer mapping and analysis to chart the best cutting combinations (see Graff, pp. 95–98). While some designers create their own custom cuts, the most common shapes in high jewelry are designed to keep waste or discarded stone to a minimum:

- Baguette: Thin rectangles or fan shapes if tapered. Popular since the Art Deco period.
- Brilliant: Often round with many facets to let maximum light enter the stone and achieve "brilliance." Still the most desirable cut for engagement rings.
- Briolette: An elongated pear that is often used for beads or for drop earrings, especially in the nineteenth century.
- Bullet: A rectangle stone that is flat at one end and V shape at the other, often used as the "shoulders" of a ring, supporting a larger center stone.
- Cabochon: Dome shape with a flat underside but not faceted. One of the oldest cuts, typically applied to opaque gemstones before faceting was invented.
- Emerald: Rectangular or square, it has step facets that run parallel to the

girdle of the stone and cropped corners. Considered a bold cut for the clearest of stones. Applied to emeralds but works equally well on diamonds.
- Sugarloaf: Similar to a cabochon but resembling a smooth four-sided pyramid. It is designed to express the color of a stone more intensely. Named for the tall pointed cone shape of refined dark molasses that arrived in Europe from the Caribbean and Brazil until the late nineteenth century.
- Trillion: Triangular with rounded edges, this cut is unusual and difficult to set due to the delicate corners of the stone. It tends to be used on stones supporting a larger center stone.
- Uncut (Rough): An uncut stone looks dull and "rough" in its unpolished state, almost like common glass. However, buying rough can be less expensive and some designers use them to add texture to their designs. (see De Beers pp. 96, 99–100)

Electroform
Growing metal like a skin onto a conductive surface in an electrolytic bath (electrodeposition) to form an object. This can take hours or days, depending on how thick the shell of the jewel is designed to be. Typical metals used are gold, silver, or copper.

Enamel
Powdered glass that is heated and poured onto metal, setting into a glossy, semi-opaque colorful finish. Enameling enables a jeweler to paint directly onto an object, combining fine art with jewelry and metallurgy. As a technology it flourished in the Byzantine Empire (AD 330–1453), as artisans in Constantinople (now Istanbul) experimented with cloisonné enamel. Earlier, Celtic tribes of Gaul had developed the techniques of champlevé and basse-taille.
- Basse-taille: Translucent enamel applied over an engraved, stamped, or carved design in gold or silver, allowing for the picture beneath to show through. Fabergé's famous eggs (see pp. 108–9, 111) used this technique.
- Champlevé: The artist carves channels, lines, or grooves into the metal and fills them with enamel, often to illustrate a figurative scene. The technique travelled with migrating Celtic tribes across Europe, becoming known in ancient Greece and eventually Russia.
- Meenakari: From the Persian Minakari, referring to the color of heaven and invented in Iran during the Sasanian period (AD 224–651) it was carried by the Mongols to India where today specialized craftspeople continue to practice the tradition. In Jaipur, Kamal Kumar Meenakar uses 23.5 carat gold for its softness, which brings out greater detail. He applies his art on the reverse of the jewel as a secret dialogue with the collector (see Alice Cicolini pp. 188, 191–92).

Engraving
Carving or etching a design into a precious metal by hand or mechanical means, nowadays including the use of high-power laser beams.
- Guilloché: A method of mechanical engraving using symmetrical architectural patterns often looped or interwoven into each other and often covered by a translucent enamel.

Filigree
Delicate ornamental open metalwork, usually constructed in soldered gold or silver wire, that is thought to resemble lace. Arab migrants brought the concept to Europe via Portugal in the eighth century AD, where it was perfected and became a distinct part of Portuguese and Spanish design culture. Filigree jewelry is still particularly popular in India.

Gem quality
There is no universally accepted grading system for gemstones other than diamonds. In order to separate a pebble from a ruby, gemologists, stone dealers, and designers must decide which stones are precious enough to be used in jewelry. Most mined diamonds are used for industrial purposes, but gem-quality stones are saved and sold at a higher price. In high jewelry some designers are now purposefully combining stones of lower value with expensive precious stones to demonstrate their art.

Gold
Natural pure gold is yellow, dense, and soft. It can be found in rocks, streams, and rivers as grains or nuggets, and is humanity's earliest recorded metal, used throughout history as money or as a store of wealth. Its purity is measured in karats (US) carats (British), with 24kt/24ct being the purest form on the market.
- Granulated gold: A minutely textured gold surface created by fusing or soldering tiny granules of gold together on a gold base.
- Noble gold: A new metal created by Brazilian designer HStern in 2003 (see pp. 180–82) using a secret mix of alloys to create something warmer than white gold but subtler than yellow gold and to suit any skin tone.
- Virgin gold: Suzanne Belperron (see pp. 31–33) refers to the 22kt yellow gold she uses in her work as "virgin" or "raw" gold, labeled as such for its buttery warmth which is the basis of her sculptural designs.

Hero Stone/Noble Stone
An exceptional gemstone. The Argyle mine in Western Australia offers a handful of "hero" stones during its annual diamond tender that are superior in size, color, and quality to the other diamonds it produces.

Honeycomb
A type of hexagonal setting cut into metal to ape the natural formations found in a honey beehive: Nicholas Varney (see pp. 153–55) applies this in yellow gold to a selection of his rings.

Imperfection

Imperfections are "inclusions" or fissures inside a stone making it less valuable than a flawless example. They are sometimes called "birthmarks," because every stone has an individual inner structure, much like a fingerprint. Imperfections on the surface of the stone are called "blemishes." The number and extent of a stone's imperfections affect its "clarity" (see the 4Cs). While imperfections decrease the value of most precious stones, emeralds are the exception. The character of an emerald is considered enhanced by the "garden" of imperfections inside it, which appear like vines snaking through the stone. Rutilated quartz is a clear gemstone with visible inclusions like needles piercing its center, often in gold, silver, red, or black tones—these inclusions are actually a mineral called rutile. Such stones are believed to bring physical and mental balance.

Intrinsic Value

The fundamental value of an object regardless of the current market price. Bank notes have no intrinsic value because they are worthless outside of their country of origin, but gold coins are desirable because of the underlying value of the gold itself. Jewelry retains an undiminished value, because its component materials are durable, hard to fake, rare, and beautiful.

Lab-Grown (stones)

Otherwise known as a synthetic or cultured diamonds, lab-grown stones are created within controlled conditions instead of being mined from the earth. In 2018, the Federal Trade Commission in the United States altered its definition of a diamond to include synthetic stones. They are currently approximately 30 percent cheaper, in some cases even less, but impossible to distinguish from the real thing with the naked eye.

Lacquer

A tough, scratch-resistant varnish with a high-gloss, high-color finish, used by designers such as Victoire de Castellane (see pp. 131–33) for a dramatic departure from the usual gold or platinum.

- Coquille d'oeuf (lit. "crushed eggshell"): An old Vietnamese lacquer technique where pieces of shell are pieced together and embedded into lacquer for a mosaic-style finish.

Lost Wax Technique

Jewelry formed or cast when hot metal is poured into a mold and left to cool into a particular shape. The mold is originally made of wax, which is easy for the designer to manipulate, then surrounded by plaster and baked in an oven. The wax melts and is "lost" before molten gold is poured in and cools to form the final design.

Luster

A term for the soft glow, sheen, or radiance of pearls.

Manufacturer

The production of high jewelry is often contracted out to small, highly skilled private workshops that specialize in casting, goldsmithing, stone setting, polishing, engraving, and enamelling, with the designer approving the final outcome.

Marquetry

Delicate slivers of wood, metal, bone, or mother-of-pearl attached as a veneer on a surface to form a highly complex design. Commonly used in antique European furniture and decorative ornaments but now used in miniature for jewelry by designers such as Silvia Furmanovich (see pp. 147–50).

Metal treatments

To enhance the texture of a metal or to increase the contrast between metal and stone, some designers add treatments.

- Anodized: An electrochemical process that coats metal, such as titanium or aluminum with an oxide layer, resulting in a bright colorful finish.
- Blackened/Oxidized: The application of sulfides to silver or gold to create a stylized patina that apes the natural aging process. This darkening or blackening of the metal affects only the surface and can wear off with use.
- Electroplated/Rhodium-plated: A thin layer of metal added to an object that elevates it in some way. A brass ring may be plated with 24k gold to amplify its charm, or rhodium plating may be added to white gold to tone it down.

Parure

A matching set or "suite" of jewels. A full parure for royalty, for example, can contain up to sixteen jewels, including necklace, earrings, ring, brooch, and tiara, but a demi-parure begins with just two pieces.

Pavé

Many tiny stones (often diamonds) set into a jewel so close together that the piece looks paved or carpeted. JAR (see Introduction, p. 13) sometimes covers the entire surface of an oversize flower or butterfly with pavé in a radical departure from the industry norm, which is to sprinkle a little here and there to maximize sparkle on a budget.

Pearl

Large natural pearls were once the most valuable jewel in the world, yet diamonds now supersede them in high jewelry. Today there are many types to choose from:

- Akoya: A species of marine oyster originally farmed in Japan by Kokichi Mikimoto in 1893. The cultured versions are well-known as the classic string of white pearls, but natural Akoya pearls also come in silver, gold, and shades of blue.
- Cultured: Natural or wild pearls are so rare that pearl farms were created where tiny fragments of shell ("Mother-of-Pearl") are inserted into the oyster to create pearls to order.
- Freshwater: The most common cultured pearls, available in a huge variety of shapes, sizes, and colors, from lavender to stick shape. Now overwhelmingly sourced from China.

- Mabe: Grown on the wall of the oyster shell instead of in the body of the mollusk, it is flat on one side and known as a half or blister pearl.
- Natural: Pearls found in the wild. The Persian Gulf historically had some of the richest deposits and free divers would go perilously deep to find them. One of the most elusive is the Orange Melo, made by sea snails off the coast of Vietnam.

Prototype

A three-dimensional model of a custom-made design. Traditionally made in silver, brass, or bronze, it is now increasingly made using CAD and 3D printing techniques.

Pyritized

The iron sulfide known as "fools gold" is also called Pyrite. In the right conditions it can grow over prehistoric animal bone to form fossils with a metallic, granular exterior.

Retail

Independent jewelers can sell direct to their collectors from an atelier or own brand store, but some entrust their work to a network of retailers, usually department stores, to reach new clients. The jeweler usually has little say over how their jewelry is presented and sold, and many retailers operate on a sale-or-return basis. If successful the designer can be pressed to produce many new designs quickly while bearing the full cost of materials. Despite this challenge, retail can be a valuable sales channel.

Satellite stone

Just as a satellite orbits a star or planet, a satellite stone comes from or is related to a much larger and more important center stone. When an enormous rough, such as Graff's Lesedi La Rona (see pp. 95–96) is discovered, it may yield a polished marvel of epic proportions, but dozens of lesser-known satellite stones are also cut from the same flawless rough in order to create as many jewels as possible.

Semi-Precious (Stones)

Traditionally semiprecious stones were considered less valuable than precious stones in an informal gemstone hierarchy, but the boundaries between the two have blurred in modern times, just like the class hierarchies in society. In Medieval Europe, jewelry acknowledged rank, with the nobility owning the best and most precious stones, such as pearls, diamonds, rubies, and emeralds, and those lower down wearing semiprecious rock crystal, jet, coral, amber, and quartz. Today, coral is rare and some diamonds are common, so the term is no longer as relevant.

Set/Setting

The metal structure holding gemstones in place. Each setting has a purpose and some are part of a designer's signature style. The Tiffany setting, for example, is designed to hold a solitaire diamond at an elevated position above the band or shank of the ring, using six prongs, increasing the amount of light going through the stone. It was created in 1886 and is mostly used for engagement rings.
- Inlay: A stone-setting technique in which channels are carved into precious metals with stones slotted and locked into each one, often at an angle to prevent movement. Stones and metal sit flush with each other forming a type of puzzle. Boghossian (see pp. 114–16) has perfected a technique of inlaying stones within other stones. This is a modern take on a tradition developed in ancient Persia and favored across Asia since the ninth century AD.

Sustainable/Sustainably Sourced

Ethical jewelry, fair trade and sustainable sourcing are all part of a modern movement to protect both environment and society from the devastation of mining and manufacturing jewelry. It can include using recycled materials and conflict-free stones, limiting waste, providing workers with decent conditions and fair contracts, and protecting biodiversity. Sustainability is one of the most important issues currently facing the jewelry industry.

Treated/Untreated Stones

The heating, dyeing, oiling, or irradiating of a gemstone is done to amplify its natural beauty and make it more desirable in the market. Cutting and polishing does not qualify as treatment in this sense so an untreated stone is still allowed to be faceted, but if the color or clarity is artificially enhanced, this should be disclosed to the buyer.

Wholesale

Wholesale distributors buy jewelry in bulk from a designer who wants to reach more customers before selling it on for a profit to a third party. The wholesale price paid by the distributor is much lower than the retail price eventually paid by the consumer. The designer has to make sure they can afford to sell at a low enough price to secure a wholesale deal but still ensure the retail price is affordable. Many artist jewelers are withdrawing from the wholesale market and are now using social media to sell directly to a larger audience.

BIBLIOGRAPHY

Adamson, John and Prior, Katherine. *Maharajas' Jewels*. London: Vendome Press, 2000.

Anand, Anita and Dalrymple, William. *Koh-I-Noor: The History of the World's Most Infamous Diamond*. London: Bloomsbury, 2017.

Andrews, Maggie and Talbot, Mary M., eds. *All the World and Her Husband: Women in Twentieth-Century Consumer Culture*. London: Continuum, 2000.

Astfalck, Jivan, Broadhead, Caroline, Derrez, Paul and Grant, Catherine. *New Directions in Jewellery*. London: Black Dog Publishing, 2005.

Becker, Vivienne, Geoffroy-Schneiter, Bérénice, Hardy, Joanna and Talley, André Leon. *Cartier Panthère*. New York: Assouline, 2015.

Bliss, Simon. *Jewellery in the Age of Modernism 1918–1940: Adornment and Beyond*. London: Bloomsbury, 2018.

Broude, Norma and Garrard, Mary D. *Feminism And Art History: Questioning The Litany*, Reprint ed. Abingdon: Routledge, 2018.

Cailles, Francoise. *Rene Boivin: Jeweller*. London: Quartet Books, 1995.

Carpenter, Bruce W. and Richter, Anne. *Gold Jewellery of the Indonesian Archipelago*. Singapore: Editions Didier Millet, 2012.

Chapman, Martin, Hall, Michael, Rainero, Pierre Young-Sanchez, Maragaret, and Zapata, Janet. *Cartier in the 20th Century*. London: Vendome Press, 2014.

Coffin, Sarah D. and Menkes, Suzy. *Set in Style: The Jewelry of Van Cleef & Arpels*. London: Thames & Hudson, 2011.

Corbett, Patricia, Landrigan, Nico, and Landrigan, Ward. *Jewellery by Suzanne Belperron*. London: Thames & Hudson, 2015.

Corbett, Patricia. *Verdura: The Life and Work of a Master Jeweller*. London: Thames & Hudson, 2008.

Costa, Guido, Golding, Nancy, Greer, Germaine, Juncosa, Enrique, and McQuiston, Liz. *Suffragettes to She-Devils: Women's Liberation and Beyond*. London: Phaidon, 1997.

den Besten, Liesbeth. *On Jewellery: A Compendium of International Contemporary Art Jewellery*. Stuttgart: Arnoldsche Art Publishers, 2011.

Wallace Chan: The Path to Enlightenment – Art and Zen. Exhibition catalog. Biennale des Antiquaires, Paris, 2012

Falino, Jeannine, and Scanian, Jennifer, eds. *Crafting Modernism: Midcentury American Art and Design*. New York: Abrams Books, 2011.

Frankopan, Peter. *The Silk Roads: A New History of the World*, Reprint ed. London: Bloomsbury, 2015.

Gregorietti, Guido. *Jewelry: History and Technique from the Egyptians to the Present*. Secaucus, NJ: Chartwell, 1979.

Guinness, Louisa. *Art as Jewellery: From Calder to Kapoor*. New York: ACC Art Books, 2017

Herridge, Elizabeth with Wood, Frances. *Bringing Heaven to Earth: Silver Jewellery and Ornament in the Late Qing Dynasty*. London: Ianthe Press in collaboration with Paul Holberton Publishing, 2016.

Hickman, Katie. *Courtesans*, New ed. Harper Perennial, 2011.

Jaffer, Amin. *Treasures of the Mughals and the Maharajas: The Al Thani Collection*. Skira, 2017.

JAR: Paris, 2 Vols. London: Phaidon, 2013
LaCava, Stephanie and Taffin De Givenchy, James. *Taffin: The Jewelry of James Taffin De Givenchy*. New York: Rizzoli, 2016.

Lindermann, Wilhelm. *Thinking Jewellery: On the Way Towards a Theory of Jewellery*. Stuttgart: Arnoldsche Art Publishers, 2011.

Loring, John. *Paulding Farnham: Tiffany's Lost Genius*. New York: Abrams Books, 2000.

Phillips, Clare. *Jewels & Jewellery*, 2nd ed. London: Thames & Hudson, 2019.

Picardie, Justine. *Coco Chanel the Legend and The Life*, New Ed. New York: Harper Collins, 2017.

Possémé, Evelyne. *Van Cleef & Arpels: The Art of High Jewelry*. Paris: Les Arts Decoratifs, 2012.

Raden, Aja. *Stoned: Jewelry, Obsession, and How Desire Shapes the World*, Reprint ed. New York: Ecco Press, 2017.

INDEX

A

Abdollahi, Leyla 177
   Lust & Lure Mismatch Wing earrings *178*
   Lust & Lure Wing ring 177, *178*
abstract design 16–51
Academy Awards 168
Adonis 86
African diamonds 95
Albert, Prince 95
Albert II, Prince 125
Alexander, Vaughan 77
Alexander III, Czar 108
Alexandra, Queen 56
Alexis Bittar 77
aluminium 13, 20
Amrapali 191
andalusite 125
Aphrodite 86
Apollo 70
Argotty, Adolfo 153
Armstrong, Nak 125
   Encrusted Ruched Roman Helmet ring 125, *126*
   Parrot earrings 125, *126*
Armstrong, Scott, Vertiges tiara for Chaumet *71*, 72
Arnault, Bernard 132
Arp, Jean 96
Arsalans 142
Art Deco 19–20, 31, 49, 56, 64, 106, 122, 127, 177
Art Nouveau 8, 43, 49, 58, 127, 132, 159
Arts Fusion SA 159
Asia 55, 56, 74
Assimon, Céline 112, 116
Assumption Cathedral, Moscow 135
Astor, Caroline 58
Astor, Vincent 28
Astor family 8, 58, 61
Aubazine Abbey 166
avant-garde jewelry 187
Azagury-Partridge, Solange 175, 177
   Scribbles Blue Green & Orange earrings 175, *176*
   Scribbles Blue & Yellow ring 175, *176*
   Scribbles collection 175, *176*, 177
   Solange's Engagement ring 175, *177*
   Stoned necklace *164*, 175

B

Bacon, Francis 96
BAFTAs 168
Ballet Russes 56
Balsan, Etienne 166
Barneys 125, 177
Baroque 84
Basquiat, Jean-Michel 96
Bauhaus 20, 185
Bäumer, Lorenz 122–5
   Diamond tiara "Ecume de mer" *124*
   Scarabee d'Automne brooch 122, *123*
   Scarabee d'Ete brooch *123*
Beethoven, Ludwig van 78
Belle Epoque 159
Belperron 127
   pair of paisley spiral brooches *32*
   paisley "Serti Couteau" ear clips *33*
   Toi et Moi ring 31, *33*
Belperron, Suzanne 28, 31–2, 77, 139, 185
Bennett, David 127
Bergdorf Goodman 125, 187
Bergson, Henri 19
Bhagat, an important natural pearl and diamond necklace *65*
Bhagat, Viren 61, 64, 78, 86
Biennale des Antiquaires, Paris 66
Black Orlov 112
Bodino, Giampiero 106
   Teodora cuff (chrysoprase, diamonds and purple sapphires in white gold) 106, *107*
   Teodora cuff (pink opals and pink sapphires in pink gold) 106, *107*
Boghossian 116, 159
   Flawless No Oil Emerald and Diamonds necklace *115*
   Merveilles Icicle Diamond long earrings *114*, 119
   Palmette necklace *114*
Boghossian, Albert 116
Bohan, Marc 132
Boivin 31, 32
Boivin, Jeanne 131
Boivin, René 131, 185
Bos, Nicolas 72, 74
Botswana 95
Boucheron 72, 84, 175
   Cape de Lumière (Cape of Light) *87*
   drawing of necklace for the Maharajah of Patiala *86*
   Feuilles D'Acanthe necklace *88*
   Grosgrain necklace *89*
Boucheron, Frédéric 84
Boussac Group 132
British Council, India 188
British Crown Jewels 95, 153
bronze 20
Brunei, Sultan of 68
Brush, Daniel 154, 157, 160
   Flowing wearable sculpture *156*, 157
   Poppies wearable sculpture *156*, 157
   Scholar's Table #2 154, 157
Brush, Olivia 154, 157
Buccellati 84, 86
   Anemone necklace 86, *91*
Buccellati, Andrea 84, 86
Buccellati, Gianmaria 86
Buccellati, Mario 84, 86
Buddha 64
Buddhism 64, 66, 112, 142
Bukhara 68
Bulgari, Gianni 64, 106
Burmese rubies 13, 78
Bvlgari 8, 22, 61, 64, 106
   Cinemagia high jewellery necklace 61, *62*
   Heritage necklace *63*
   Heritage Necklace (with convertible sautoir-brooch) *11*

C

Camurati, Angela 26
Cannes Film Festival 168
Capel, Arthur "Boy" 166
carbon fiber 13, 22
Cartier 22, 55, 56, 68, 72, 74, 86, 106, 131
   Art Deco 8
   design of a ceremonial necklace *58*
   Duchess of Windsor 127
   Elizabeth Gage and 136
   English Art Works 100
   Jeanne Toussaint at 131, 185
   Nadia Morgenthaler 159
   necklace *59*
   Panthère collection 131, 185
   Ranjitsinhji 58
   Tutti Frutti 56, 58
Cartier, Jacques 56, 58

Cartier, Louis-François 56
Cartier, Pierre 56, 102
Castellane, Victoire de 131, 132
   Acidae Lili Pervertus bracelet *133*
   Cana Bisextem Now bracelet 132, *133*
   Diorissimo necklace for Dior Joaillerie 132, *133*
Catherine the Great, Empress 135
the catwalk 168, 187
Cave, Nick 188
Central Saint Martins, London 46, 72, 188
Césars 168
chalcedony 55
champakali 64
Chan, Wallace 64, 66, 68, 80, 86
   Butterfly Nebula brooches *67*, 68
   Forever Dancing – Qingping Brooch *2*
   Hera brooch and ring *54*
   the Unknown World earrings *67*
   "Wallace Cut" 64, *66*
Chanel 13, 28, 74, 166
   Franges necklace *166*
   SARAFANE Necklace *167*
Chanel, Gabrielle "Coco" 26, 28, 49, 166–8, 185
Chao, Cindy 13, 86, 119
   Peony (Black Label Masterpiece XVIII) brooch *117*
   Royal Butterfly (Black Label Masterpiece I) brooch *94*
Chaumet 15, 70, 72
   Scott Armstrong Vertiges tiara *71*, 72
Chaumet, Joseph, study for a leaf tiara *70*
Chin, Edmond 78
China 55, 61, 64, 66, 68, 72, 74, 80, 84
Choisne, Claire 84
Chopard 159, 168
   earrings (amethysts, tsavorites, white opals and yellow diamonds in titanium) *170*
   earrings (diamonds, opals, pink sapphire and tsavorites in titanium) *170*
   necklace 168, *171*
   Peacock bracelet 168, *169*
Christie's 28, 78, 80, 100, 102, 112
chrysoprase 106
Cicolini, Alice 188, 191
   Memphis Jaipur Bougainvillea Muzo Chandelier earrings 191, *192*
   Memphis Jaipur Bougainvillea Muzo ring *192*
Cipriani, Elisabetta 38
   Wearable Art 38, *40*

la cire perdue 119
Codognato, Attilio 90
Colbert, Claudette 131
Colbert, Jean-Baptiste 7, 72
Collinson, Judy 177
color 26, 119
Columbus, Christopher 55
costume pearls 49
Courbet, Gustave 19
Courteille, Lydia 139
   Chicken ring 139, *140*
   Dragon cuff *140*
   Marie Antoinette Dark Side collection 139, *140*
   Monkey earrings *140*
   Pendant Skull 139, *141*
   Spiderweb tiara *141*
courtesans 165
Cron, Vanessa 127
Crown of Charlemagne 70
Crown Jewels
   "alternative Crown Jewels" 127
   British 95, 153
   French 8, 58, 70
Curiel, François 102

D
Dalí, Salvador 8, 80, 139
Dani, Neha 77–8, 86
   Nurah "Bright Moon" ring *79*
   Vaneesha "Queen of the Universe" necklace *79*
Danish Museum of Decorative Arts 43
De Beers Jewellers 58, 96, 100, 182
   Portraits of Nature, Knysna Chameleon necklace *99*
   Portraits of Nature, Knysna Chameleon earrings *99*
de Grisogono 61, 112, 116
   Melody of Colours earrings (amethysts and turquoises in pink gold) *113*
   Melody of Colours earrings (emeralds and turquoises in platinum) *113*
   Melody of Colours ring (amethysts and turquoises in pink gold) *113*
   Melody of Colours ring (peridot, tsavorites, and turquoises in white gold) *113*
del Verrocchio, Andrea 7
Delage, François 96
Denmark 136

Di Roberto, Mauro 61
di Verdura, Duke Fulco, 26, 28,
   Medusa brooch *29*
Diaghilev, Sergei 56
diamonds 7, 13, 55, 92–127
   4C grading system 96
   black diamonds 112
   Black Orlov 112
   Hope Diamond 102
   Koh-i-Noor (Mountain of Light) 95
   Lesedi La Rona 95–6
   Lesotho diamond 102
   Millennium Star 100
   Stern Star 180
   "will of the diamond" 95–6
dinosaur bone 22, *25*
Dior, Christian 49
   floral design 131–2
   New Look 131
Dior Jewelry (Dior Joaillerie) 13, 74, 132
   Victoire de Castellane Diorissimo necklace 132, *133*
   dragon motifs 55
Duleep Singh, Maharaja of Punjab 95

E
East India Company 95
Edward VII 56
Edward VIII 127
Egypt 20, 56
ehl-I hiref 43
Eiffel Tower, Paris 44
Elizabeth I 7, 165, 185, 193
Elizabeth II 95, 153
Emanuel, Mark 36
emeralds 119
English Art Works 100
Ernst, Max 131, 139
Eugénie, Empress 58
Exposition Internationale des Arts et Techniques dans la Vie Moderne de Paris 72
Exposition Universelle 84
Eye of Horus 20

F
Fabergé 111, 159
   Clover ring *109*, 111
   Hibiscus Gold and Silver Flower cuff bracelet *109*, 111

Potato 108, 111, 135
Fabergé, Peter Carl 108, 111, 135
Fabergé, Sarah 111
Fabergé Heritage Council 111
Farnham, George Paulding 58, 153
fashion catwalks 168, 187
Fazulzyanov, Ilgiz 132–5, 160
   Artichoke ring *134*, 135
   Carp ring *134*, 135
   Doves ring *134*
feminism 165
Feng J 74, 77
   Cloud Atlas brooch *76*
   Yellow Ginkgo Leaf brooch 74, *76*
Field, Patricia 77
figurative jewelry 26, 32
"flappers" 19–20
fossils 22
French Crown Jewels 8, 58, 70, 102
Frieze 90
Furmanovich, Silvia 147–50
   Bamboo earrings *148*, 150
   Geometric Trompe L'Oeil Marquetry earrings *148*
   India earrings 147, *149*
   Mushroom earrings 147, *149*
Fürstenberg, Diane von 180

G

Gage, Elizabeth 135–6
   Caribou brooch 136, *137*
Gaj Singh II, Maharaja of Jodhpur 84
Galli, Maurice 80
Gansu Gangtai Holdings 86
Garrard 95
Gates, Bill 68
Gaudí, Antoni 119
Geffroy, Anne-Eva 96
Gemfields 111, 150
Gemological Institute of America (GIA) 28, 78, 80, 96, 154
Generation X 182
Georgacopoulos, Melanie 157–9
   Asymmetric Nacre ring 157, *158*
   Corner Nacre bangle 157, *158*
   Nacre collection 157, *158*
   Sliced Studs *158*
George IV 102
George V 56

Gilded Age 58
Givenchy, Hubert de 28
Givenchy, James de 28, 31, 51
   brooch *30*
   light brown and yellow diamonds in blue, green and yellow ceramic ring 28, *30*
   natural blue emerald and natural Ceylon sapphire ring 28, *30*
Goenka, Bina 150
   Tapestry bangle 150, *151*
   Tapestry cuff 150, *151*
Goenka, Krishna Murari 150
Golconda diamonds 13
gold 13, 19, 20, 38, 43, 78
Golden Horde 135
Goldman Sachs 26
Gordon, Kim 188
Gothic style 177, 187
Gothic Surrealism 139
Graff 96
   Graff inspired by Twombly necklace 96, *97*
   the Graff Lesedi La Rona *96*
   Threads necklace *98*
Graff, Laurence 95, 96
Graham, Martha 36
grandidierite 125
Grima 36
   "Bird's Nest" ring 32, *34*
   diamonds and South Sea pearl ring 32, *35*, 36
   diamonds and tourmaline ring 32, *34*
   Lightening earrings 32, *35*
   turquoise brooch *34*
Grima, Andrew 32
Grima, Francesca 32, 36
Grima, Jojo 32
Gripoix 13
Gruosi, Fawaz 61, 112, 116
Guillaume, Ania 38

H

Hadid, Zaha 43
   Twin Cuff 623A for Georg Jensen *41*, 43
   Twin Ring 623D for Georg Jensen *41*, 43
Hambling, Maggi 8
   Eye brooch 8, *12*
Harry Winston, Inc. 8, 104
Hatton Garden, London 187
Hayek, Nayla 104
Hemingway, Ernest 19

Hemmerle 20, 22, 51
   bangle 6, 20
   earrings *21*
   ring *21*
Hemmerle, Anton 20
Hemmerle, Christian 20, 22
Hemmerle, Joseph 20
Hemmerle, Stefan 20
Hemmerle, Sylveli 20
Hemmerle, Yasmin 20
Hermitage, St. Petersburg 108
Herz, Bernard 31
Herz, Jean 31
Herz-Belperron 32
Hilliard, Nicholas 165
Hinduism 64, 150, 191
Hiramatsu, Yasuki 19, 77
   necklace *18*, 19
hollowware 19
Hollywood 102, 153, 168
Hope, Henry Philip 102
Hope Diamond 102, *102*
HStern 180
   Feathers bracelet 180, *181*
Hu, Anna 78, 80, 86
   Enchanted Orchid bangle *82*
   Rainbow Chryscolla Butterfly brooch/pendant *81*
   Red Magpie brooch II *83*

I

India 13, 55, 56, 61, 90
   Black Orlov 112
   diamonds 95, 100
   gem traders 68
   importance of jewelry 191
   Koh-i-Noor (Mountain of Light) 95
   weddings 191
inlay technique 116
Inupiat tribes 22
iron 20
Italian design 84
Italian Renaissance 84

J

jade 55, 61, 66, 78
Jam Sahib, Maharaja, design of a ceremonial necklace 58
Japan 19, 49, 56, 70, 72, 90

INDEX 203

JAR 13, 159
jasper 55
Jazz Age 19–20
Jensen, Georg 43, 51
   Zaha Hadid Twin Cuff 623A *41*, 43
   Zaha Hadid Twin Ring 623D *41*, 43
Jolie, Angelina 153
Jorge, Fernando 46
   Satellite earrings 46, *47*
   Stream cuff 46, *47*
Josephine, Empress 70
Joyce, James 19
Jupiter 187

K
Kandinsky, Wassily 56
Kazan 135
Kennedy, Jacqueline 102
Kent Institute of Art & Design 44
Khazzam, Sharon 177, 180, 181
   Atteba necklace *179*, 180
Klimt, Gustav, The Kiss 8
Koh-i-Noor (Mountain of Light) 95
Kōkichi, Mikimoto 46
Kollur mines, Golconda, India 13, 102
Koppel, Henning 43
Koss, Nick 185, 187
Koulis, Nikos 120–2
   Feelings earrings *121*, 122
   Oui earrings *121*, 122
Krakoff, Reed 58
   bracelet for Tiffany *60*
   brooch for Tiffany *9*
   pendant for Tiffany 58, *60*, 61
Krasnoyarsk State Fine Art Institute 142
Kublai Khan 55

L
labradorites 125
Lagerfeld, Karl 139
Lalique, René 8, 131
Landrigan, Nico 28, 32, 49
Landrigan, Ward 32
Lane, Kenneth Jay 13
lapis lazuli 55
Leane, Shaun 187
   Fuchsia brooch 187, *189*
Lee, Tuan 120

Lehman Brothers 188
Leonardo da Vinci 7
Lesedi La Rona 95–6
Lesotho diamond 102
Lilani, Sameer 191
Lincoln, President Abraham 58
The Lost Boys 188
Louis XIII 182
Louis XIV 7, 72, 80, 102
Louis XVI 70, 102
louis d'or 80
Love, Courtney 188
Lowery, Philip 188
Lucaire, Laurin 44
Lucara Karowe 95
LVMH 132
Lynggaard, Charlotte 139
   Wild Rose brooch for OLE LYNGGAARD COPENHAGEN 15, *138*, 139
   Wild Rose tiara for OLE LYNGGAARD COPENHAGEN *138*, 139
Lynggaard, Ole 136–9

M
McCormack, Jessica 182, 185
   Superdelic Cloud Diamond Hoop earrings 182, *184*
   Superdelic collection 182, *184*
   Superdelic Rainbow and Cloud Diamond earrings 182, *184*
   Superdelic Rainbow Diamond earrings 182, *184*
Macklowe Gallery, New York 78
McLean, Evalyn Walsh 102
McQueen, Alexander 187
Magritte, René 8, 139
Mansvelt, Jean-Marc 72
Manville, Nicholas 43
Maori culture 185
Maria Feodorovna 108
Marie Antoinette 70
Markasky, Evelyn 36, 38
   Dangerous Vagina ring 36, *39*
   Primitive Organic Armor Neckpiece 36, *39*
marquetry 147
Martin, Hannah 187–8
   New Rebel Bolt bangle *190*
   Spur Yellow Gold ring 188, *190*

Matisse, Henri 31
Medici, Catherine de' 185, 187
Medici, Marie de' 182
Meenakar, Kamal Kumar 191
Meenakari 191
Mehmed II 43
Mehrangir Fort Museum, Jodhpur 191
Mellerio, Laure-Isabelle 182
Mellerio dits Meller 72, 182
   Rose brooch *183*
Metropolitan Museum of Art, New York 13, 15, 147, 157
Michelangelo 119
Mid-century Modernism 185
Middle East 68, 119
Millennium Star 100
Modernism 19, 20, 26, 32, 49, 58, 127, 185
Moore, Edward C. 58
Moore, John 120
   Verto necklace *118*, 120
Mor, Alexandra 111–12
   diamond and smoky topaz in Areng ebony, gold, and tagua seed ring *110*
   diamonds and emerald in white and yellow gold ring *110*
   rich orange garnet in gold and tagua seed ring *110*
   Subang hoop earrings *110*
morganite 58
Morgenthaler, Nadia 159–60
   earrings (blue long agate drops, diamonds, opals, purple kunzites) *161*
   earrings (diamonds, green blue indigolites, light green tourmalines) *161*
Morris, Robert Lee 49
Motonobu, Kano 49
Mountbatten, Countess of 58
Moussaieff 68, 70
   high jewelry earrings *69*
   high jewelry flower earrings *69*
Moussaieff, Alisa 68
Moussaieff, Rehavia 68
Moutard, Juliette 131, 185
Mughal design 64
Musée des Arts Décoratifs, Paris 74
Museum of Cairo 139
Museum of Contemporary Art, Rome 38

N

Namdakov, Balzhin 142
Namdakov, Dashi 142
   Arsalan pendant 142, *143*
   Beetle Deer 142, *143*
   Lemur ring 142, *143*
Napoléon Bonaparte 70, 108, 182
Napoleon III 58
Napoleone, Valeria 160
Native Americans 147, 180
Naturalistic design 130–61, 182
Nawanagar, Maharaja of 58
Neanderthals 7
Nguyen, Nghi 77
Nitot, François-Regnault, wheat-ear tiara 70, *71*, 72
Nitot, Marie-Étienne 70
noble gold 180
Nouri, Chabi 80

O

obsidian 22
OLE LYNGGAARD COPENHAGEN
   Charlote Lynggaard Wild Rose brooch *138*, 139
   Charlote Lynggaard Wild Rose tiara 15, *138*, 139
Onassis, Aristotle 102
Ong, Michelle 13, 104–6
   Mezmerizing Lily brooch *14*, 104
   Sapphire Swim brooch 104, *105*
Oppenheimer, Harry 182
Orientalist style 58

P

Paley, Dorothy 31
Palladio, Andrea 154
Palmyra 116
Pan-Russian Exhibition, Moscow 108
Paris, Place Vendôme 8, 72, 74, 84, 132, 159, 166
parures 32, 127
Patiala, Maharajah of 58
   Boucheron necklace for 84, *86*
Péan, Monique 22, 26
   diamond and pyritized dinosaur bone ring 22, *24*
   diamonds and Sikhote-Alin meteorite ring 22, *24*
   necklace 22, *25*

Pearl, Cora 165–6, 193
pearls 32, 46, 49
Perry, Grayson 173–5
   Claire 173, 175
   I Am a Man necklace 173, *174*
Persia, gem traders 68
Petochi 22
photography 20
Piaget 72, 80, 84, 159
   Golden Dali pendant *84*
   Limelight Manchette Story cuff *85*
   Limelight Mediterranean Garden cuff *85*
Piaget, Georges-Édouard 80
Picasso, Pablo 8, 56, 96
Place Vendôme, Paris 8, 72, 74, 84, 132, 159, 166
platinum 55
pointillism 74
Polo, Marco 55, 56, 70
porcelain 66
Porter, Cole 26, 28
Procop, Robert 150, 153
   Multicolor Masterpiece bracelet *152*
   Style of Jolie necklace *152*, 153

Q

Qatar 68

R

Rabun, Jacqueline 43
Rainero, Pierre 56, 58
Rapa Nui people 22
Ravissant 150
Ray, Man 8
Reagan, Ronald 153
the red carpet 112, 168
Renaissance 7, 127
Richemont 86, 106
Rockefeller family 8, 58
Rococo art 84
Rodriguez de Rivas, Silvia, Countess of Castilleja de Guzmán 131
Rogers, Millicent 131
Romanesque architecture 159
Rosenfeld, Michael 182
Rosenthal, Joel Arthur 13, 15
Roule, Christopher 44
Roule & Co 44, 46
   Starburst Halo bangle 44, *45*
Royal Collection 56

rubber 13
rubies 13, 78
Rupert, Johann 106
Russian gem traders 68

S

Sabbadini, Pierandrea 106, 108
Saint Laurent, Yves 132, 139
sakura cherry blossom 49
Salimah Aga Khan, Begum 116
Salini, Fabio 22, 49
   bracelets *23*
   earrings *23*
San Yu 74
Sanraku, Kano 49
sapphires 13, 64
Schepps, Seaman 153
Scheufele, Caroline 168
   haute joaillerie necklace 168, *171*
   Red Carpet collection 168, *170*
Schlumberger, Jean 28
Schlumberger, São 131
serti poinçon 100
settings, Georgian cut-down 182
Siegelson, Lee 157
Sikhote-Alin meteorite 22, *24*
Silk Road 55, 68, 116
silver 38, 43, 136
Simpson, Lorna 185
Singh, Duleep 95
Siu Man Cheuk 104
Slack, Rachel 182
Smith, Patti 188
Smithsonian Institute, Washington 96, 119
solah shringar 191
Sotheby's 13, 32, 78, 108, 127, 182
Spiro, Glenn 100, 102
   necklace 100, *101*
steel 13, 20
Stein, Lea 13
Stella, Frank 38, 44
   Ring for Elisabetta Cipriani – Wearable Art 38, *40*
Stella-Sawicka, Jo 90
Stern, Hans 180, 182
Stern, Roberto 180
Suciyan, Arman 43–4
   Gliding Goddess and Gliding Spirits United Stacking ring *42*, 44

INDEX

Goddess Wing Drop earrings *42*
sumptuary laws 182
Surrealism 8, 49, 80, 139
Sutherland, Kiefer 188

T
Ta Moko 185
Taffin
   James de Givenchy brooch *30*
   James de Givenchy rings 28, *30*
tagua seeds 111
Tajima, Toshikazu 49
tanzanite 58
TASAKI 49, 157
   Pyramid Pearls Ring *48*
   SHELL Ring *48*, 49
   Surge necklace *50*
Tate Gallery 8
Taylor, Elizabeth 127, 168
TEFAF Maastricht art fair 66, 157
Theory of Five Elements 61, 66
Tho Duong, Sam 136
   Frozen necklace *130*, 136
Tiffany & Co 55, 58, 153
   Reed Krakoff bracelet *60*
   Reed Krakoff brooch *9*
   Reed Krakoff pendant 58, *60*, 61
Tiffany, Charles Lewis 8, 58
titanium 13, 20, 66
Tolkowsky, Gabi 153
Toros, Misak 43
Toussaint, Jeanne 131, 185
Tower of London, Jewel House 95
Traglio, Carlo 26
Traglio, Maurizio 26
Triossi, Amanda 191
Tupinamba people 46
Turner Prize 173
Tutankhamun 20
Twombly, Cy 96, *97*

U
University of Creative Arts 44

V
Van Cleef & Arpels 72–4, 80, 86, 106
   Art Deco 8
   Duchess of Windsor 72, 127
   Pylones clips, 74, *75*

Vagues Mystérieuses clip 74, *75*
Zip Antique Transformable Necklace 72, *73*
Vanderbilt family 8, 58
Varney, Nicholas 153–4, 160
   Brook Trout ear clips 154, *155*
   Japanese Chair ring 154, *155*
   Onion brooch 154, *155*
Vasiliev, Gennady 142
vegetable ivory 111
Velden, Bibi van der 168, 173
   Scarab Upside Down earrings 168, *172*
   Starry Night ring *172*
   Tornado ring *172*
Venus 187
Verdura 8
   Kaleidoscope ring *29*
   Theodora Byzantine pendant *29*
Verdura, Duke of 26, 28
   Medusa brooch *29*
Vhernier 26
   Eclisse ring 26, *27*, 49
   Serpente brooch *27*
Victoria, Queen 56, 95
Victoria and Albert Museum, London 136
Vienna Secession 8
Vigna, Giorgio 38
   Vento ring for Elisabetta Cipriani –
     Wearable Art 38, *40*
Vikings 51
Villa Mozart 106
Villegas, Daniela 142, 145, 160
   Grannus ring *144*, 145
   Sunset Chameleon necklace *144*, 145
   Victoria earrings 142, *144*, 145
Vitellius, Aulus 46
Vogue 56
Volund 185
   Thistle ring 185, *186*
   Thistle ring gouache *187*
Voulgaris, Costantino 61
Voulgaris, Giorgio 61
Voulgaris, Sotirio 61

W
wabi-sabi 77
Wangjing Soho, Beijing 43
War of Liberation (1813) 20, 51
Warhol, Andy 96
Watson, Gordon 175

Webb, David 36, 153
   Archival Totem pendant rendering *36*
   Chevron ring *37*
   Mega Cubist ring *37*
   Shoulder cuff *37*
wedding jewelry, Middle Eastern 68
Westminster, Duke of 166
wheat 70, 72
Windsor, Duchess 13, 36, 72
   "alternative Crown Jewels" 127
   Sotheby's auction 13, 127
   Toussaint Panther brooch 131
   Zip necklace 72
Winston, Harry 8, 80, 102, 104
   clustering technique 104
   Hope Diamond *102*
   Secret Combination Diamond necklace *10*
   Winston Cluster Diamond earrings *103*
   Winston Cluster Diamond Wreath
     necklace *103*
Wittstock, Charlene 125
World War I (1914–1918) 19
World War II (1939–1945) 28, 31, 43, 77

X
Xerente people 145

Y
Yih Shun Lin 64
Yoko 145
Yokoo, Tadanori 49
Yue, Wendy 145
   Dangling Bats ear cuffs *146*
   Opalised Snail earrings *146*
   Serpent Wrap ring *146*
Yupik tribes 22

Z
Zao Wou-Ki 74
Zen Buddhism 64, 66
zodiac themes 55

PICTURE CREDITS

All images are courtesy the brands and designers, with additional credits as follows:

Archives Cartier London © Cartier: p. 58; Photograph: Mehmet ARDA: p. 42; BHAGAT Images: p. 65; Photograph: Isabelle Bonjean: p. 87; © Photography of Robert BRESSON, Collection "Bijoux de Diamants," CHANEL, 1932: p. 166; © Daniel Brush. Photography © 2012 Takaaki Matsumoto: p. 156; © Carnet Jewellery: pp. 14, 105; © CHANEL, High Jewelry Collection "Le Paris Russe de Chanel," 2019: p. 167; © Christies Images Limited: p. 183; © Collections Chaumet: p. 70; Photograph: Colin Crisford: pp. 12, 190; Courtesy Victoire de Castellane. Courtesy Dior Joaillerie: pp. 132, 133; Photo © Clay Grier: p. 126; Photo: Laziz Hamani: p. 107; © Nils Herrmann – Chaumet: p. 71; Nils Herrmann, Collection Cartier © Cartier: pp. 57, 59; Photograph: Petra Jaschke: p. 130; © Grayson Perry. Courtesy the artist, Kit Grover and Victoria Miro: p. 174; © C. Roule: p. 45; Schmuckmuseum Pforzheim. Photograph Rüdiger Flöter: p. 18; Photography by Russell Starr at Starr Digital. Property of Alexandra Mor ©: p. 110; Photo: Enrico Suà Ummarino: p. 27

In captions throughout, all gold is 18–24k yellow gold, unless otherwise stated, and carat weight is listed for main or hero stones only.

Title page:
Wallace Chan
Forever Dancing – Qingping Brooch, 2012
Butterfly specimen, crystal, demantoid garnet, diamonds and fancy colored diamonds, jadeite, and mother-of-pearl in titanium

ACKNOWLEDGMENTS

My heartfelt thanks go to Maudi, my mother who taught me as a child that my wildest dreams were possible and that I could achieve anything. Her encouragement meant the world to me. To my father Roy, for his selfless generosity and brilliant friendship, and to my brother Alex, for inspiring me to work harder—I dedicate this book to you.

To my best friends Sofire Walker and Christiana Savvides, for listening to the endless updates for three years with such good humor, and to my mentor Mark Hearn, without whom none of this would have actually happened. To the talented writers and editors at *The Economist* who nurtured me from the beginning: Rosie Blau, Fiammetta Rocco, Emma Duncan, Tim de Lisle, Isabel Lloyd, Maggie Fergusson, and Ingrid Esling. To Phaidon's publisher Deb Aaronson, and the wider team there for coaxing this first tome out of me—Victoria Clarke, Caroline Taggart, Tom Furness, Sarah Kramer, Hans Stofregen, Julia Hasting, Inca Waddell, and Siobhan Bent. Also to Hyperkit, for their brilliant design and my agent Chris Wellbelove for his sage advice.

To the marketing specialists and personal assistants, the unsung heroes of the jewelry world who have doggedly set up interviews and delivered mountains of information: Emma Beckett PR, LM Communications, This is Mission, Joan Rolls, Sarah Corke, Emily Goad, Ghislaine Cardon, Natalia Filatova, Julie Valentin, Cherry Rao, Hugh Monk, Tefkros Iordanis Sophocleous Christou, Katie Mandelson, Marianna Laboccetta, Violet Fraser, David Xu, Leanna Thomas, Caroline Packer and the in-house teams at Chanel, Cartier, Tiffany, and Harry Winston. To historians Vanessa Cron and Amanda Triossi, for their insight and wisdom, also the National Art Library at the Victoria and Albert Museum and the British Library for letting me camp out for what turned out to be years.

I started writing about jewelry by chance when Silvia Steffen-Ehl from Cartier invited me to cover an exhibition in Paris. I left the Grand Palais profoundly changed and every jewelry artist since has taken me to new heights. Wallace Chan, Joel Arthur Rosenthal, James de Givenchy, Viren Bhagat, Hemmerle, Nicholas Varney, Michelle Ong, Fabio Salini, Nicolas Bos, Bina Goenka, Claire Choisne, and Daniel Brush deserve a special mention for their tireless creativity, but really everyone in this book has changed the world in their own way. Jewelry would be meaningless without you.

Melanie Grant

Melanie Grant is a journalist who works at the *Economist*. She has also worked at the BBC, *The Financial Times*, *The Times,* and *The Independent*, among others. She is Luxury Editor of the *Economist's* sister publication *1843*, for which she writes, styles, and commissions, editing an annual jewelry supplement. Grant speaks regularly on watches and jewelry at events and venues including London Craft Week, Phillips auction house, the Science Museum, and The Royal Academy.

Phaidon Press Limited
2 Cooperage Yard
London E15 2QR

Phaidon Press Inc.
65 Bleecker Street
New York, NY 10012

phaidon.com

First published 2020
© 2020 Phaidon Press Limited

ISBN 978 1 83866 149 6

A CIP catalogue record for this book is available from the British Library and the Library of Congress.

All rights reserved. No part of this publication may be reproduced, stored in a retrieval system or transmitted, in any form or by any means, electronic, mechanical, photocopying, recording or otherwise, without the prior permission of Phaidon Press Limited.

Commissioning Editor: Victoria Clarke
Project Editor: Tom Furness
Production Controller: Sarah Kramer
Cover Design: Julia Hasting
Interior Design: Hyperkit

Printed in Italy